TEAMWORK MEANS YOU CAN'T PICK THE SIDE THAT'S RIGHT

Other DILBERT® books from Andrews McMeel Publishing

How's That Underling Thing Working Out for You?
ISBN: 978-1-4494-0819-0

Your Accomplishments Are Suspiciously Hard to Verify
ISBN: 978-1-4494-0102-3

Problem Identified and You're Probably Not Part of the Solution
ISBN: 978-0-7407-8534-4

I'm Tempted to Stop Acting Randomly
ISBN: 978-0-7407-7806-3

14 Years of Loyal Service in a Fabric-Covered Box
ISBN: 978-0-7407-7365-5

Freedom's Just Another Word for People Finding Out You're Useless
ISBN: 978-0-7407-7815-5

Dilbert 2.0: 20 Years of Dilbert
ISBN: 978-0-7407-7735-6

This Is the Part Where You Pretend to Add Value
ISBN: 978-0-7407-7227-6

Cubes and Punishment
ISBN: 978-0-7407-6837-8

Positive Attitude
ISBN: 978-0-7407-6379-3

Try Rebooting Yourself
ISBN: 978-0-7407-6190-4

What Would Wally Do?
ISBN: 978-0-7407-5769-3

Thriving on Vague Objectives
ISBN: 978-0-7407-5533-0

The Fluorescent Light Glistens Off Your Head
ISBN: 978-0-7407-5113-4

It's Not Funny If I Have to Explain It
ISBN: 978-0-7407-4658-1

Don't Stand Where the Comet Is Assumed to Strike Oil
ISBN: 978-0-7407-4539-3

Words You Don't Want to Hear During Your Annual Performance Review
ISBN: 978-0-7407-3805-0

When Body Language Goes Bad
ISBN: 978-0-7407-3298-0

What Do You Call a Sociopath in a Cubicle? Answer: A Coworker
ISBN: 978-0-7407-2663-7

Another Day in Cubicle Paradise
ISBN: 978-0-7407-2194-6

When Did Ignorance Become a Point of View?
ISBN: 978-0-7407-1839-7

Excuse Me While I Wag
ISBN: 978-0-7407-1390-3

Dilbert—A Treasury of Sunday Strips: Version 00
ISBN: 978-0-7407-0531-1

Random Acts of Management
ISBN: 978-0-7407-0453-6

Dilbert Gives You the Business
ISBN: 978-0-7407-0003-3

Don't Step in the Leadership
ISBN: 978-0-8362-7844-6

Journey to Cubeville
ISBN: 978-0-8362-6745-7

I'm Not Anti-Business, I'm Anti-Idiot
ISBN: 978-0-8362-5182-1

Seven Years of Highly Defective People
ISBN: 978-0-8362-3668-2

Casual Day Has Gone Too Far
ISBN: 978-0-8362-2899-1

Fugitive from the Cubicle Police
ISBN: 978-0-8362-2119-0

It's Obvious You Won't Survive by Your Wits Alone
ISBN: 978-0-8362-0415-5

Still Pumped from Using the Mouse
ISBN: 978-0-8362-1026-2

Bring Me the Head of Willy the Mailboy!
ISBN: 978-0-8362-1779-7

Shave the Whales
ISBN: 978-0-8362-1740-7

Dogbert's Clues for the Clueless
ISBN: 978-0-8362-1737-7

Always Postpone Meetings with Time-Wasting Morons
ISBN: 978-0-8362-1758-2

Build a Better Life by Stealing Office Supplies
ISBN: 978-0-8362-1757-5

TEAMWORK
MEANS YOU CAN'T
PICK THE SIDE
THAT'S RIGHT

A DILBERT™ BOOK
BY SCOTT ADAMS

**Andrews McMeel
Publishing, LLC**

Kansas City • Sydney • London

Andrews McMeel Publishing, LLC
an Andrews McMeel Universal company
1130 Walnut Street, Kansas City, Missouri 64106
www.andrewsmcmeel.com

12 13 14 15 16 RR2 10 9 8 7 6 5 4 3 2 1

ISBN: 978-1-4494-1018-6

Library of Congress Control Number: 2011932659

www.dilbert.com

—— **ATTENTION: SCHOOLS AND BUSINESSES** ——

For Shelly

Introduction

In the past hundred years, the word *committee* has morphed from a description of a group of people attempting to accomplish something useful into what we now generally perceive as an insult. In modern times, people view committee decisions the same way they might view, for example, Satan falling in love with a donkey and producing a child. Even the donkey wouldn't love that child.

Meanwhile, long ago, the people who did real work, such as raising barns, or passing buckets of water to extinguish fires, were taking full advantage of something called *teamwork*. It was a wonderful thing, and it propelled civilization forward. Teamwork earned an excellent reputation, while at the same time the world started to view committees as plagues on humanity.

Decades later, white-collar managers wisely borrowed the word *teamwork* to refer to the committee-like activities within their departments, and by that I mean the complaining, backstabbing, lying with PowerPoint slides, swilling coffee, shirking responsibility, and focusing on the wrong priorities. Managers hoped the word *teamwork,* with its decades of accrued goodwill, would inspire employees to act in selfless and coordinated ways toward common goals. That didn't work out.

While managers like to use the word *teamwork* for group projects, employees prefer more honest labels such as *weaselfest, skunk dance,* and a colorful term involving the word *cluster.* If you work in an office, it's a safe bet that the only time you use the world *teamwork* is when you're trying to manipulate a co-worker into doing his own work plus some of yours. If you can pull that off, you probably have management potential.

In today's modern workplace, teamwork has become a form of punishment. If you're not talented enough to work independently, your boss will make you pay dearly by putting you on a team full of people who are just like you. It won't be long before managers squeeze all of the goodwill out of the word *teamwork* and start looking for a fresh word to spoil. When that happens, I will happily mock the situation for your entertainment. Remember, you and I are on the same team. But I don't recommend bragging about it.

WE HAVE TO LEARN TO DO MORE WITH LESS.
LESS MEETINGS?
NO. WE'LL NEED **MORE** MEETINGS TO FIGURE OUT HOW TO DO MORE WITH LESS.
LESS MICRO-MANAGEMENT?
NO, I'LL HAVE TO WATCH YOU MORE CLOSELY THAN EVER TO MAKE SURE YOU'RE DOING MORE WITH LESS.
I'M TALKING ABOUT USING LESS MONEY.
OH, LIKE A DEATH SPIRAL. WHY DIDN'T YOU JUST SAY THAT IN THE FIRST PLACE?
IT'S AS IF YOU'RE TALKING MORE TO SAY LESS.
SHOULD WE BE MORE LIKE YOU OR LESS?
©2011 Scott Adams, Inc.\Dist. by Univeral Uclick
2-13-11

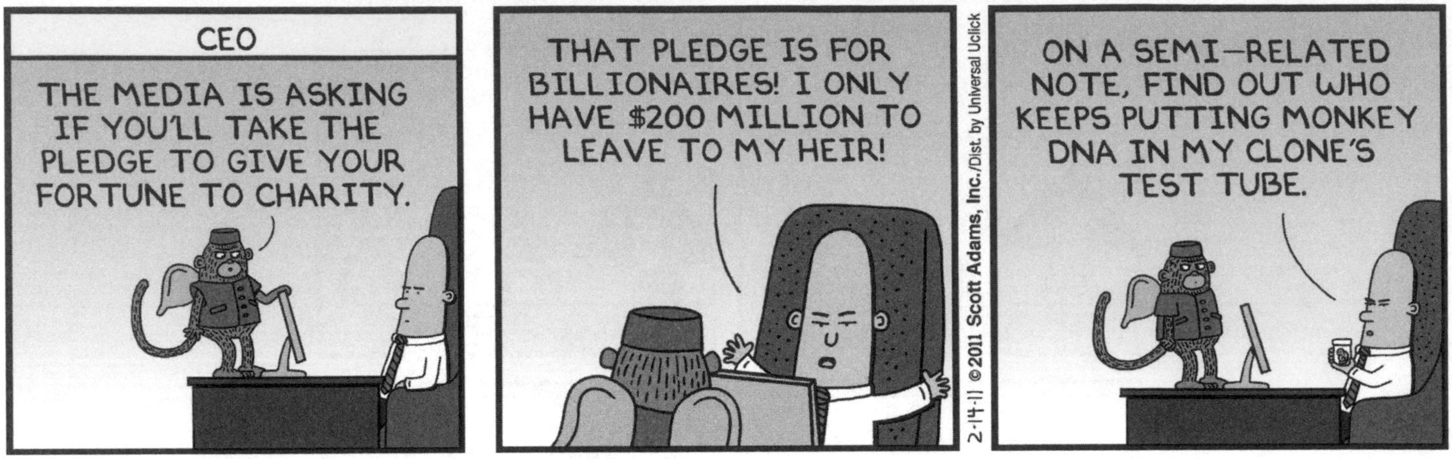
CEO
THE MEDIA IS ASKING IF YOU'LL TAKE THE PLEDGE TO GIVE YOUR FORTUNE TO CHARITY.
THAT PLEDGE IS FOR BILLIONAIRES! I ONLY HAVE $200 MILLION TO LEAVE TO MY HEIR!
2-14-11 ©2011 Scott Adams, Inc./Dist. by Universal Uclick
ON A SEMI—RELATED NOTE, FIND OUT WHO KEEPS PUTTING MONKEY DNA IN MY CLONE'S TEST TUBE.

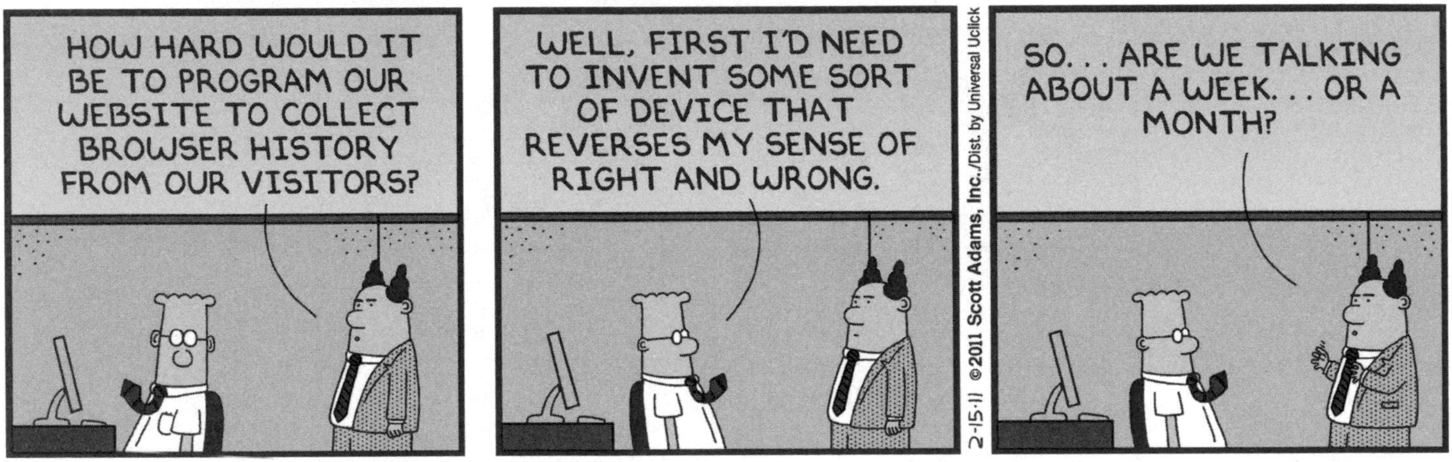
HOW HARD WOULD IT BE TO PROGRAM OUR WEBSITE TO COLLECT BROWSER HISTORY FROM OUR VISITORS?
WELL, FIRST I'D NEED TO INVENT SOME SORT OF DEVICE THAT REVERSES MY SENSE OF RIGHT AND WRONG.
2-15-11 ©2011 Scott Adams, Inc./Dist. by Universal Uclick
SO. . . ARE WE TALKING ABOUT A WEEK. . . OR A MONTH?

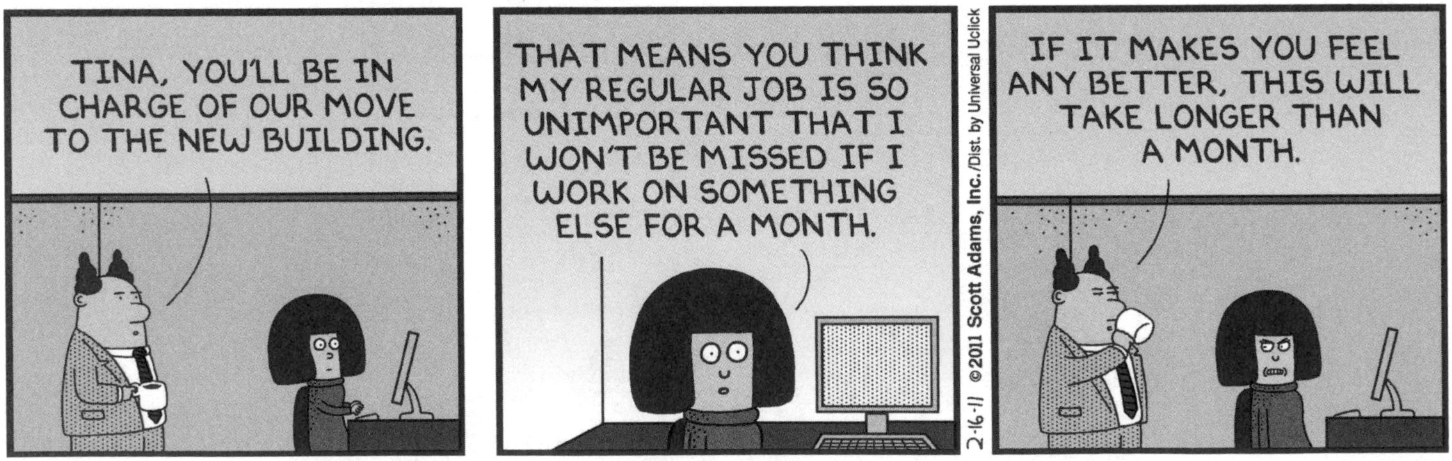
TINA, YOU'LL BE IN CHARGE OF OUR MOVE TO THE NEW BUILDING.
THAT MEANS YOU THINK MY REGULAR JOB IS SO UNIMPORTANT THAT I WON'T BE MISSED IF I WORK ON SOMETHING ELSE FOR A MONTH.
2-16-11 ©2011 Scott Adams, Inc./Dist. by Universal Uclick
IF IT MAKES YOU FEEL ANY BETTER, THIS WILL TAKE LONGER THAN A MONTH.

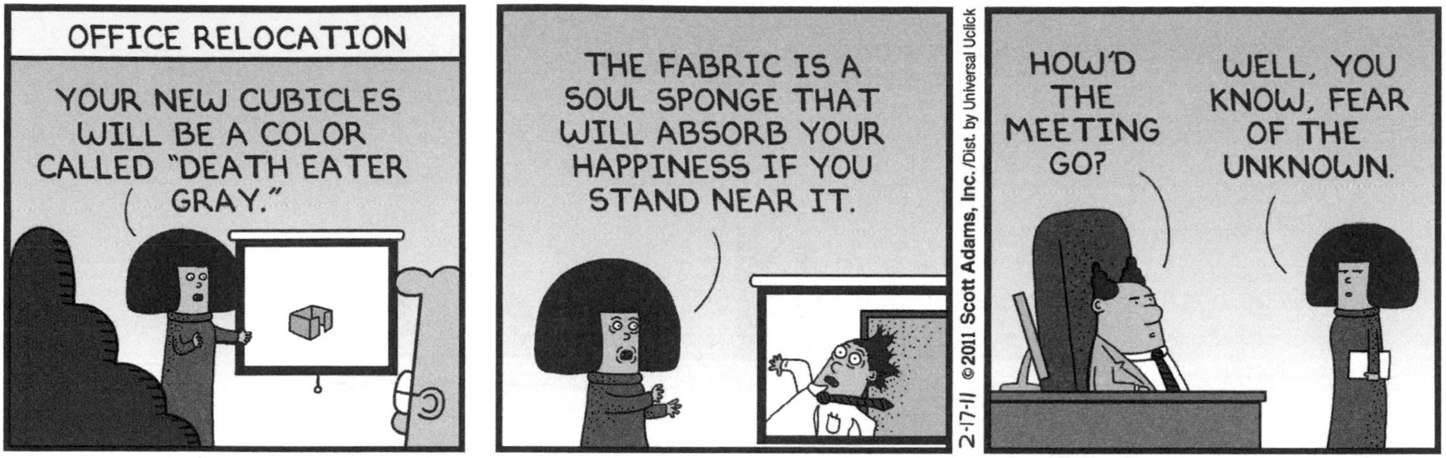
OFFICE RELOCATION
YOUR NEW CUBICLES WILL BE A COLOR CALLED "DEATH EATER GRAY."
THE FABRIC IS A SOUL SPONGE THAT WILL ABSORB YOUR HAPPINESS IF YOU STAND NEAR IT.
2-17-11 ©2011 Scott Adams, Inc./Dist. by Universal Uclick
HOW'D THE MEETING GO?
WELL, YOU KNOW, FEAR OF THE UNKNOWN.

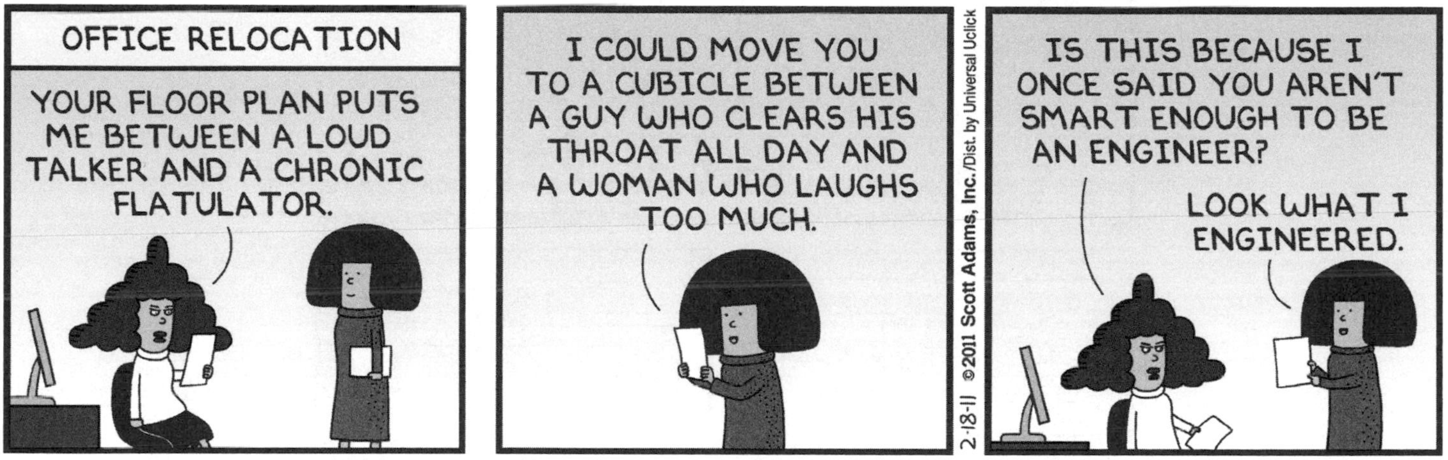
OFFICE RELOCATION
YOUR FLOOR PLAN PUTS ME BETWEEN A LOUD TALKER AND A CHRONIC FLATULATOR.
I COULD MOVE YOU TO A CUBICLE BETWEEN A GUY WHO CLEARS HIS THROAT ALL DAY AND A WOMAN WHO LAUGHS TOO MUCH.
2-18-11 ©2011 Scott Adams, Inc./Dist. by Universal Uclick
IS THIS BECAUSE I ONCE SAID YOU AREN'T SMART ENOUGH TO BE AN ENGINEER?
LOOK WHAT I ENGINEERED.

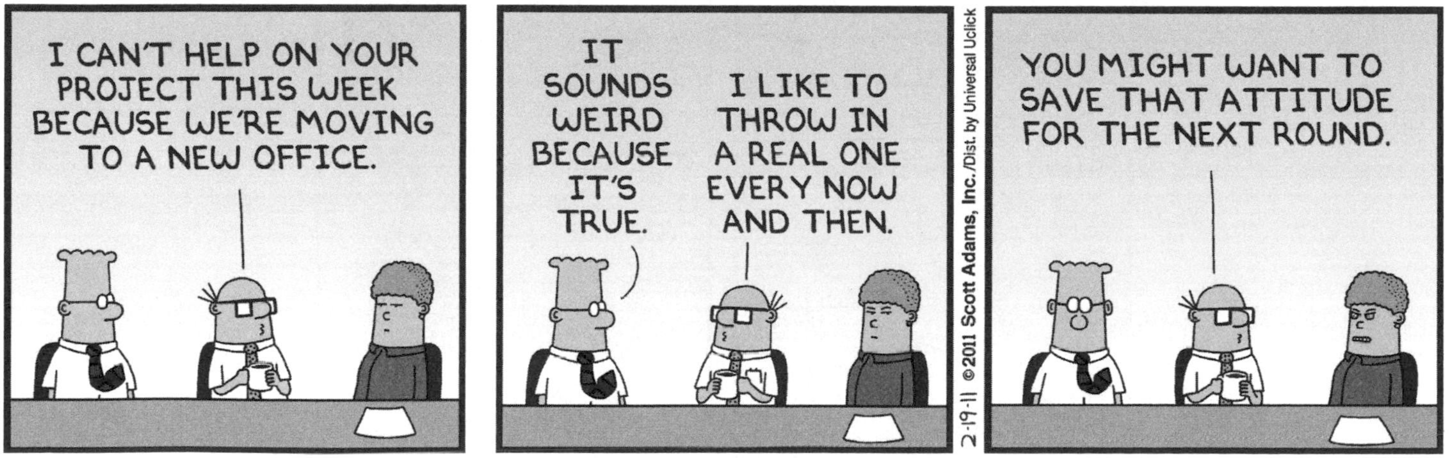
I CAN'T HELP ON YOUR PROJECT THIS WEEK BECAUSE WE'RE MOVING TO A NEW OFFICE.
IT SOUNDS WEIRD BECAUSE IT'S TRUE.
I LIKE TO THROW IN A REAL ONE EVERY NOW AND THEN.
2-19-11 ©2011 Scott Adams, Inc./Dist. by Universal Uclick
YOU MIGHT WANT TO SAVE THAT ATTITUDE FOR THE NEXT ROUND.

I HAVE A BUDGET MEETING TOMORROW WITH OUR CFO.
I'LL BE COMPETING AGAINST ALL OF THE OTHER DEPARTMENTS FOR PRECIOUS BUDGET DOLLARS.
THIS WON'T BE EASY BECAUSE ALL OF THE OTHER DEPART-MENTS ARE STAFFED WITH PROFESSIONAL LIARS.
THAT'S A BIT OF AN EXAGGERATION, DON'T YOU THINK?
WHAT DO YOU CALL MARKET-ING?
OKAY, I'LL GIVE YOU THAT ONE.
SALES?
RIGHT, BUT. . .
P.R.?
WELL, YES. . .
FINANCE?
I FORGOT ABOUT THAT ONE.
LEGAL?
WOW.
DO THE NEXT ONE YOURSELF.
HOW ABOUT HUMAN RESOUR. . .
YOU WIN.
©2011 Scott Adams, Inc.\Dist. by Univeral Uclick
2-20-11

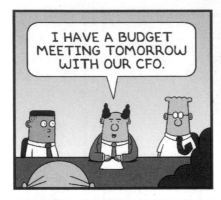

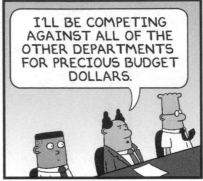

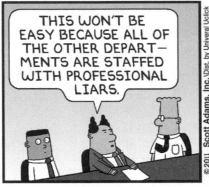

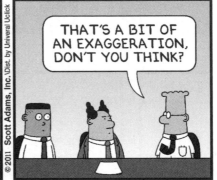

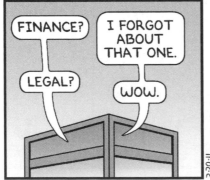

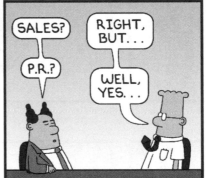

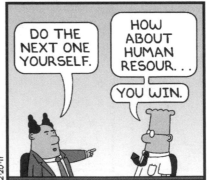

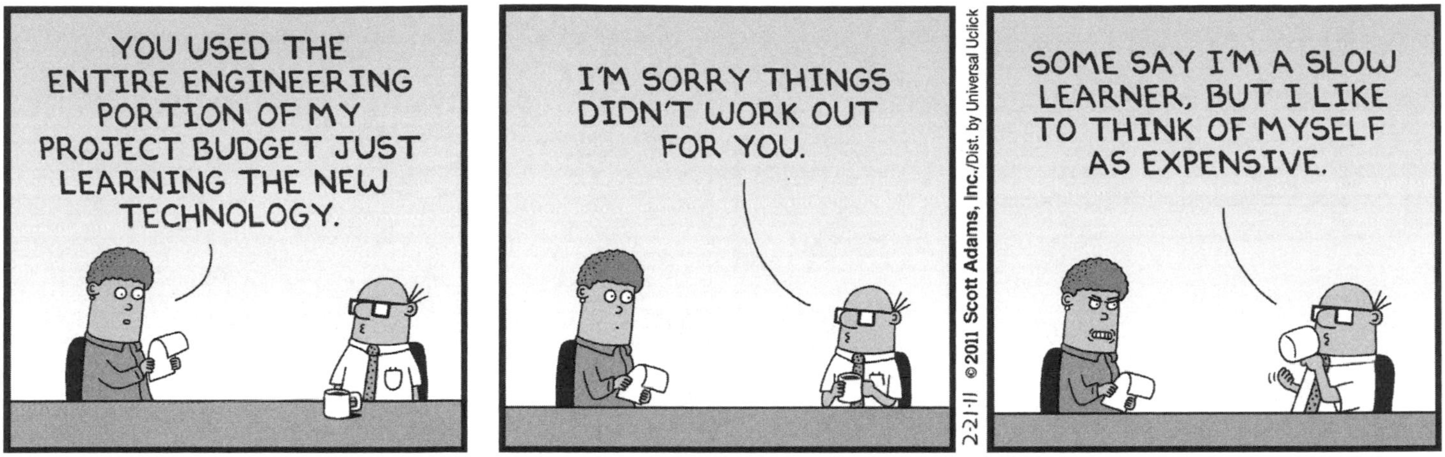
YOU USED THE ENTIRE ENGINEERING PORTION OF MY PROJECT BUDGET JUST LEARNING THE NEW TECHNOLOGY.
I'M SORRY THINGS DIDN'T WORK OUT FOR YOU.
2·21·11 ©2011 Scott Adams, Inc./Dist. by Universal Uclick
SOME SAY I'M A SLOW LEARNER, BUT I LIKE TO THINK OF MYSELF AS EXPENSIVE.

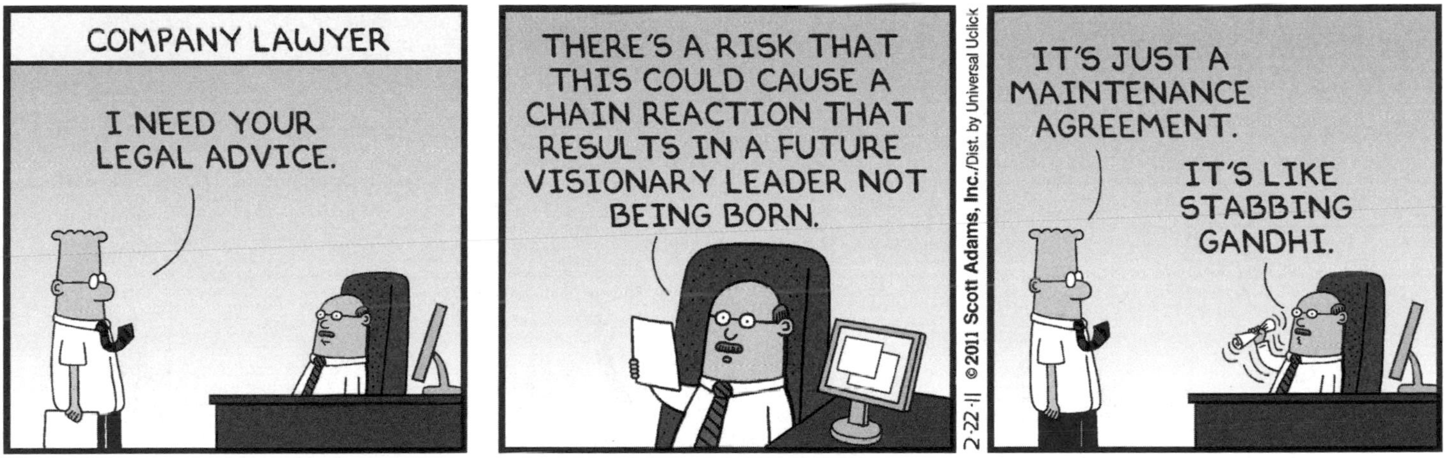
COMPANY LAWYER
I NEED YOUR LEGAL ADVICE.
THERE'S A RISK THAT THIS COULD CAUSE A CHAIN REACTION THAT RESULTS IN A FUTURE VISIONARY LEADER NOT BEING BORN.
2·22·11 ©2011 Scott Adams, Inc./Dist. by Universal Uclick
IT'S JUST A MAINTENANCE AGREEMENT.
IT'S LIKE STABBING GANDHI.

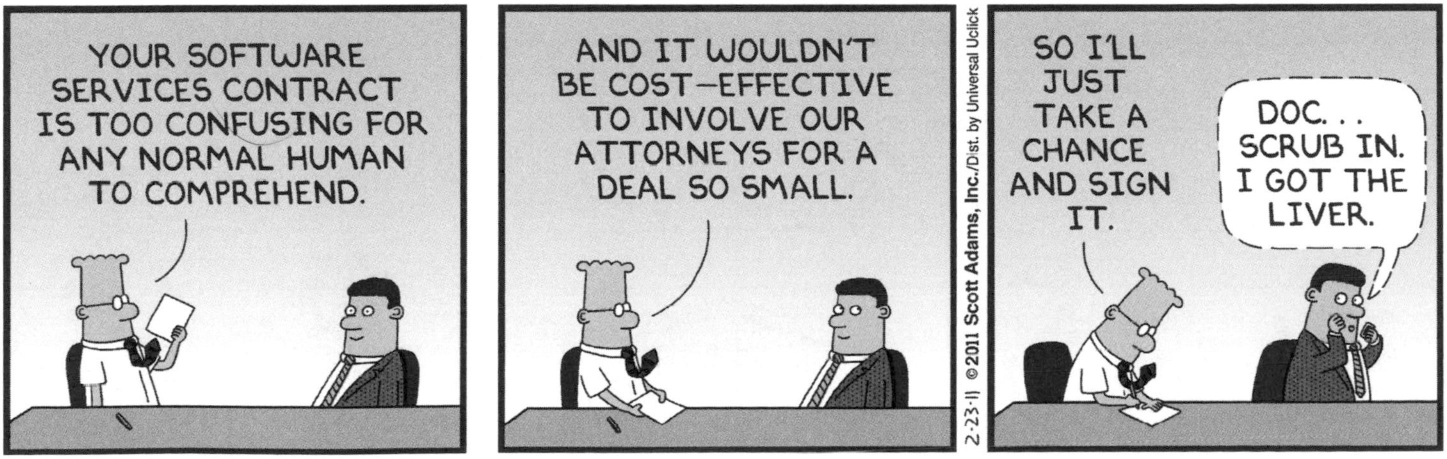
YOUR SOFTWARE SERVICES CONTRACT IS TOO CONFUSING FOR ANY NORMAL HUMAN TO COMPREHEND.
AND IT WOULDN'T BE COST-EFFECTIVE TO INVOLVE OUR ATTORNEYS FOR A DEAL SO SMALL.
2·23·11 ©2011 Scott Adams, Inc./Dist. by Universal Uclick
SO I'LL JUST TAKE A CHANCE AND SIGN IT.
DOC. . . SCRUB IN. I GOT THE LIVER.

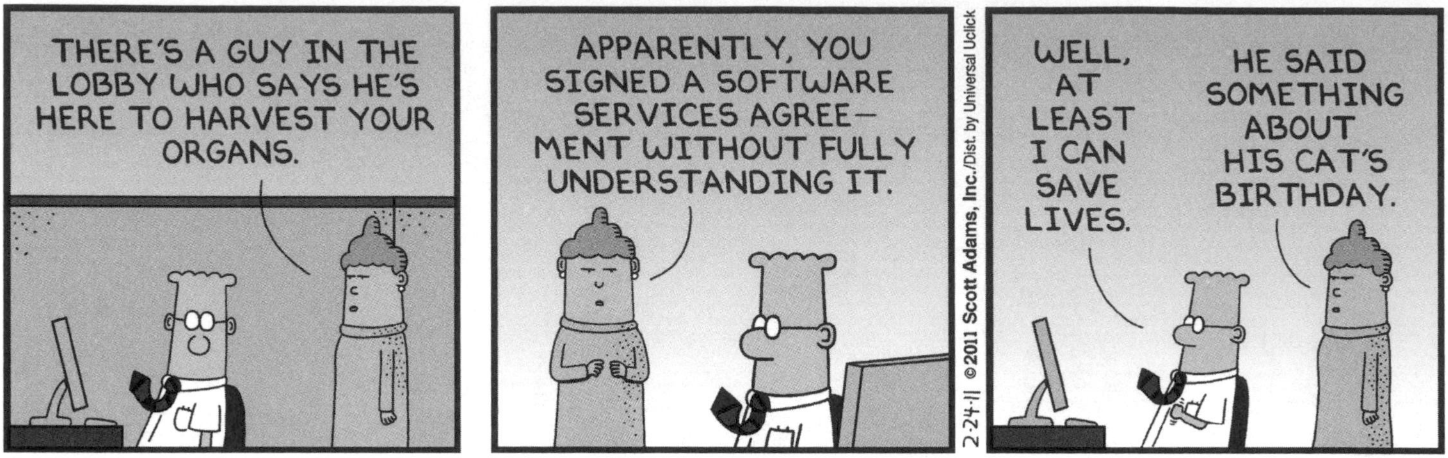
THERE'S A GUY IN THE LOBBY WHO SAYS HE'S HERE TO HARVEST YOUR ORGANS.
APPARENTLY, YOU SIGNED A SOFTWARE SERVICES AGREE— MENT WITHOUT FULLY UNDERSTANDING IT.
2·24·11 ©2011 Scott Adams, Inc./Dist. by Universal Uclick
WELL, AT LEAST I CAN SAVE LIVES.
HE SAID SOMETHING ABOUT HIS CAT'S BIRTHDAY.

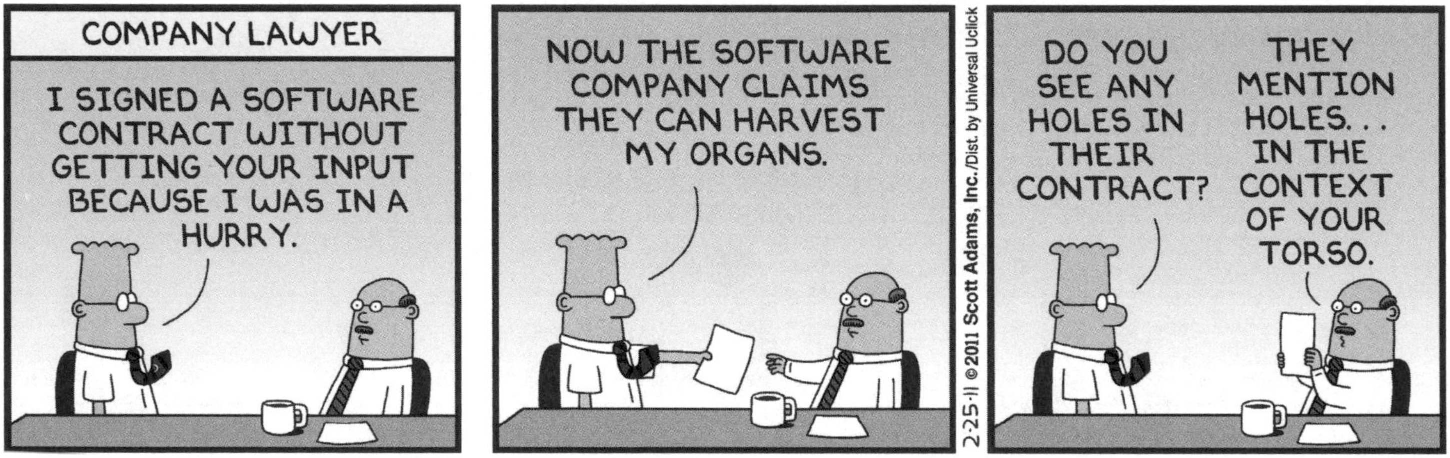
COMPANY LAWYER
I SIGNED A SOFTWARE CONTRACT WITHOUT GETTING YOUR INPUT BECAUSE I WAS IN A HURRY.
NOW THE SOFTWARE COMPANY CLAIMS THEY CAN HARVEST MY ORGANS.
2·25·11 ©2011 Scott Adams, Inc./Dist. by Universal Uclick
DO YOU SEE ANY HOLES IN THEIR CONTRACT?
THEY MENTION HOLES. . . IN THE CONTEXT OF YOUR TORSO.

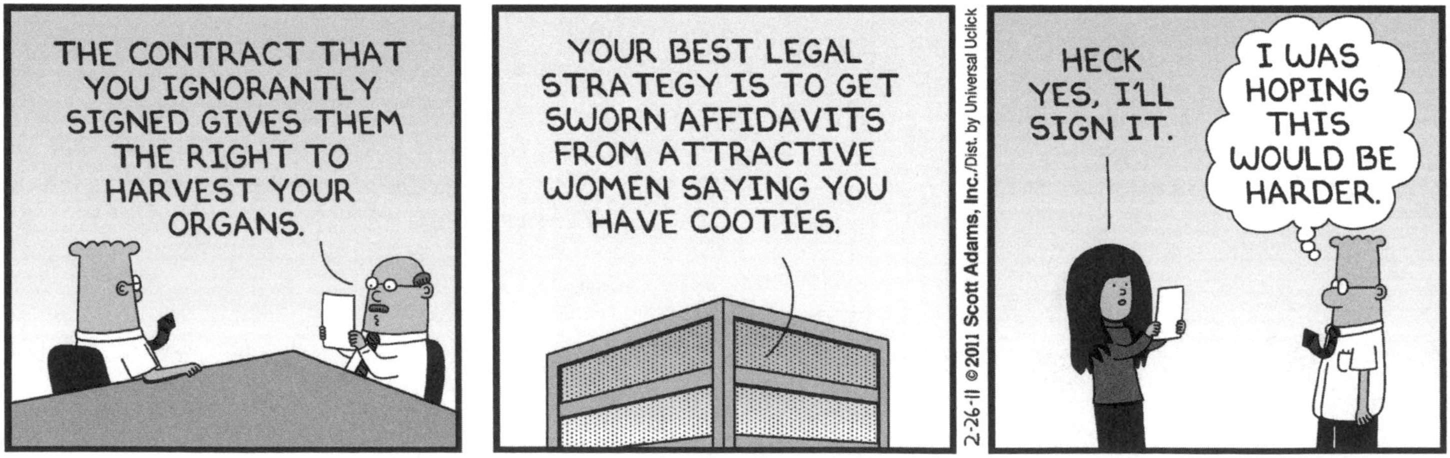
THE CONTRACT THAT YOU IGNORANTLY SIGNED GIVES THEM THE RIGHT TO HARVEST YOUR ORGANS.
YOUR BEST LEGAL STRATEGY IS TO GET SWORN AFFIDAVITS FROM ATTRACTIVE WOMEN SAYING YOU HAVE COOTIES.
2·26·11 ©2011 Scott Adams, Inc./Dist. by Universal Uclick
HECK YES, I'LL SIGN IT.
I WAS HOPING THIS WOULD BE HARDER.

BUILD A NEW SERVER TO REPLACE THE ONE WITH THE CORRUPT OPERATING SYSTEM.
THAT'S WHAT I'M DOING RIGHT NOW.
RECOVER THE DATA FROM THE BAD SERVER AND PUT IT ON THE NEW ONE.
THAT'S THE WHOLE POINT.
THEN SEE IF YOU CAN REINSTALL THE OPERATING SYSTEM ON THE OLD ONE AND REDEPLOY IT.
DO YOU HAVE ANY INSTRUCTIONS THAT ARE NOT BLINDINGLY OBVIOUS?
THIS IS CALLED MANAGING.
THE ALTERNATIVE IS CHAOS.
HOW DID YOU JUST MAKE CHAOS SOUND LIKE A GOOD THING?
YOU SHOULD TEST THE NEW SERVER.
SERIOUSLY, CAN WE TRY THE CHAOS THING?
©2011 Scott Adams, Inc. /Dist. by Univeral Uclick
2-27-11

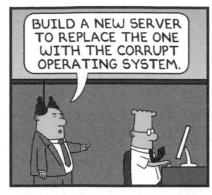

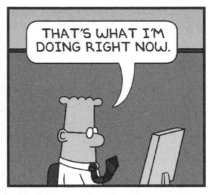

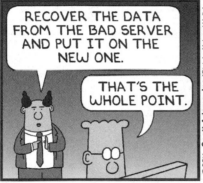

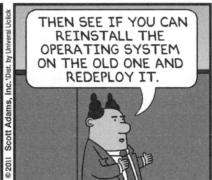

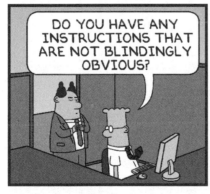

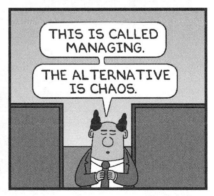

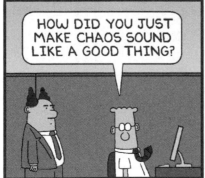

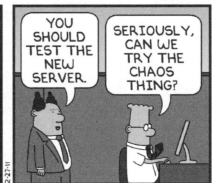

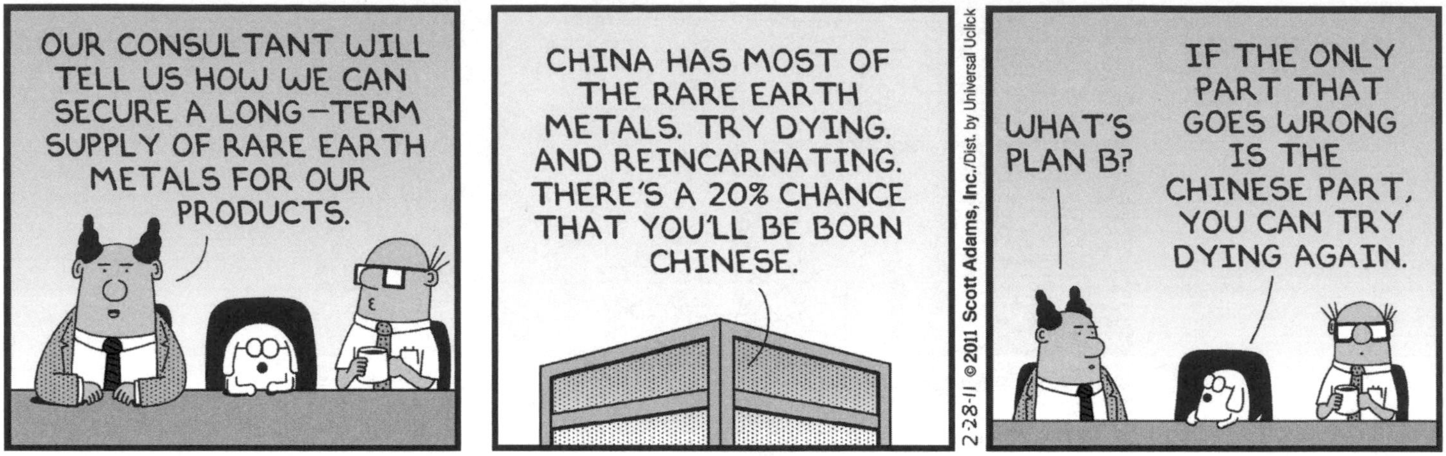
OUR CONSULTANT WILL TELL US HOW WE CAN SECURE A LONG-TERM SUPPLY OF RARE EARTH METALS FOR OUR PRODUCTS.
CHINA HAS MOST OF THE RARE EARTH METALS. TRY DYING. AND REINCARNATING. THERE'S A 20% CHANCE THAT YOU'LL BE BORN CHINESE.
2-28-11 ©2011 Scott Adams, Inc./Dist. by Universal Uclick
WHAT'S PLAN B?
IF THE ONLY PART THAT GOES WRONG IS THE CHINESE PART, YOU CAN TRY DYING AGAIN.

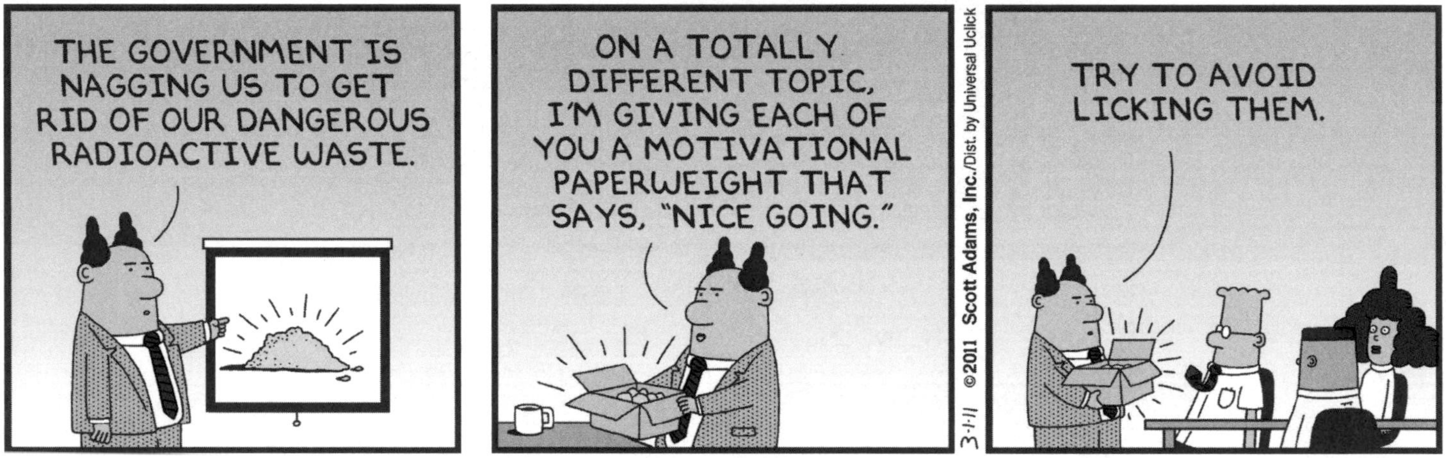
THE GOVERNMENT IS NAGGING US TO GET RID OF OUR DANGEROUS RADIOACTIVE WASTE.
ON A TOTALLY DIFFERENT TOPIC, I'M GIVING EACH OF YOU A MOTIVATIONAL PAPERWEIGHT THAT SAYS, "NICE GOING."
3-1-11 ©2011 Scott Adams, Inc./Dist. by Universal Uclick
TRY TO AVOID LICKING THEM.

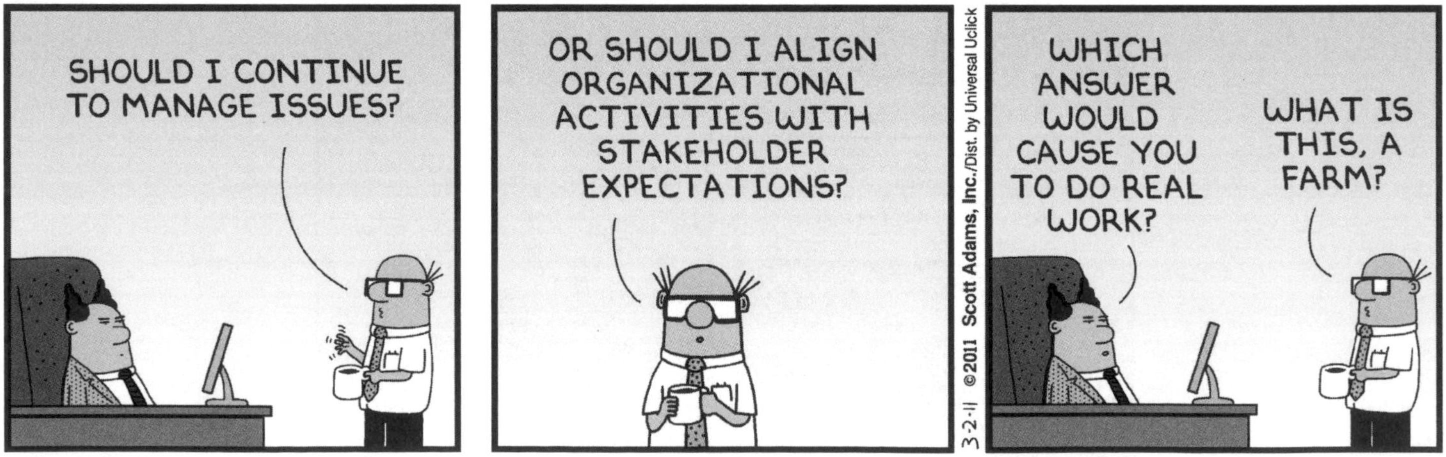
SHOULD I CONTINUE TO MANAGE ISSUES?
OR SHOULD I ALIGN ORGANIZATIONAL ACTIVITIES WITH STAKEHOLDER EXPECTATIONS?
3-2-11 ©2011 Scott Adams, Inc./Dist. by Universal Uclick
WHICH ANSWER WOULD CAUSE YOU TO DO REAL WORK?
WHAT IS THIS, A FARM?

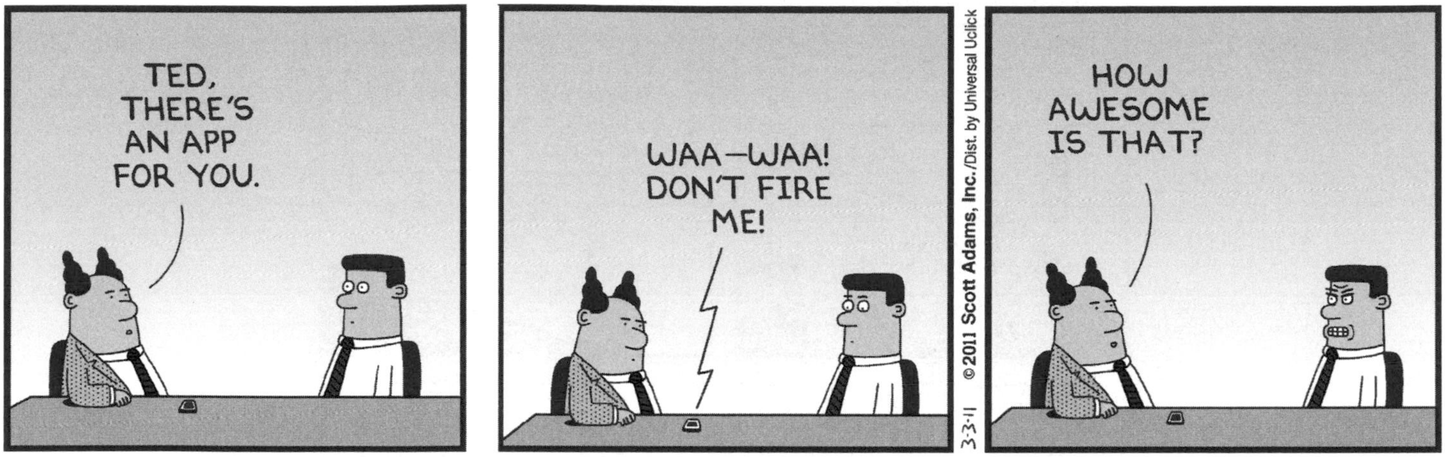
TED, THERE'S AN APP FOR YOU.
WAA—WAA! DON'T FIRE ME!
HOW AWESOME IS THAT?
3-3-11 ©2011 Scott Adams, Inc./Dist. by Universal Uclick

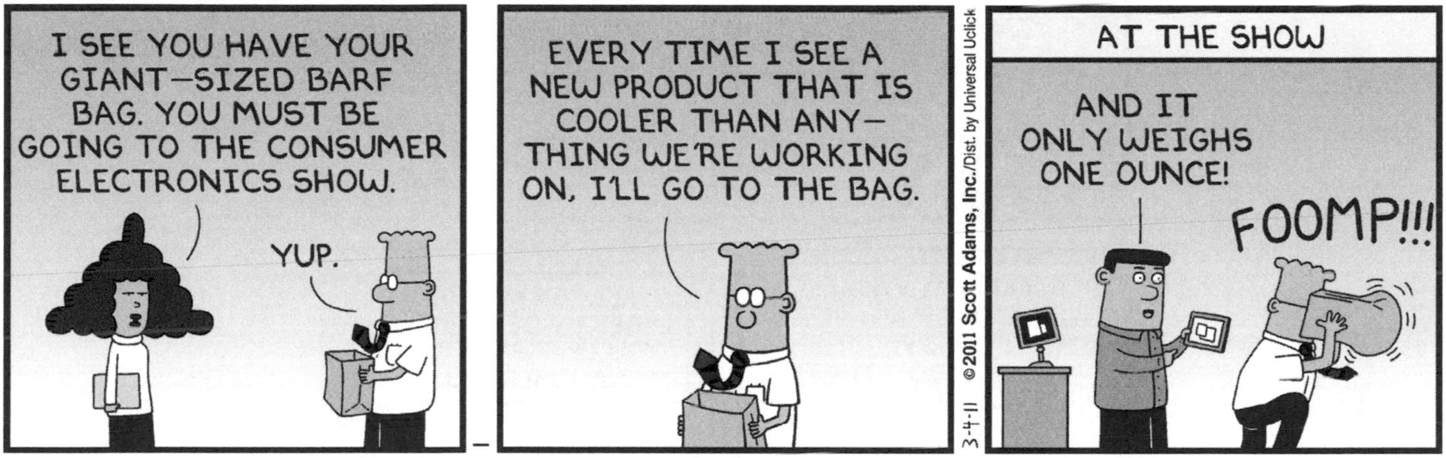
I SEE YOU HAVE YOUR GIANT—SIZED BARF BAG. YOU MUST BE GOING TO THE CONSUMER ELECTRONICS SHOW.
YUP.
EVERY TIME I SEE A NEW PRODUCT THAT IS COOLER THAN ANY—THING WE'RE WORKING ON, I'LL GO TO THE BAG.
AT THE SHOW
AND IT ONLY WEIGHS ONE OUNCE!
FOOMP!!!
3-4-11 ©2011 Scott Adams, Inc./Dist. by Universal Uclick

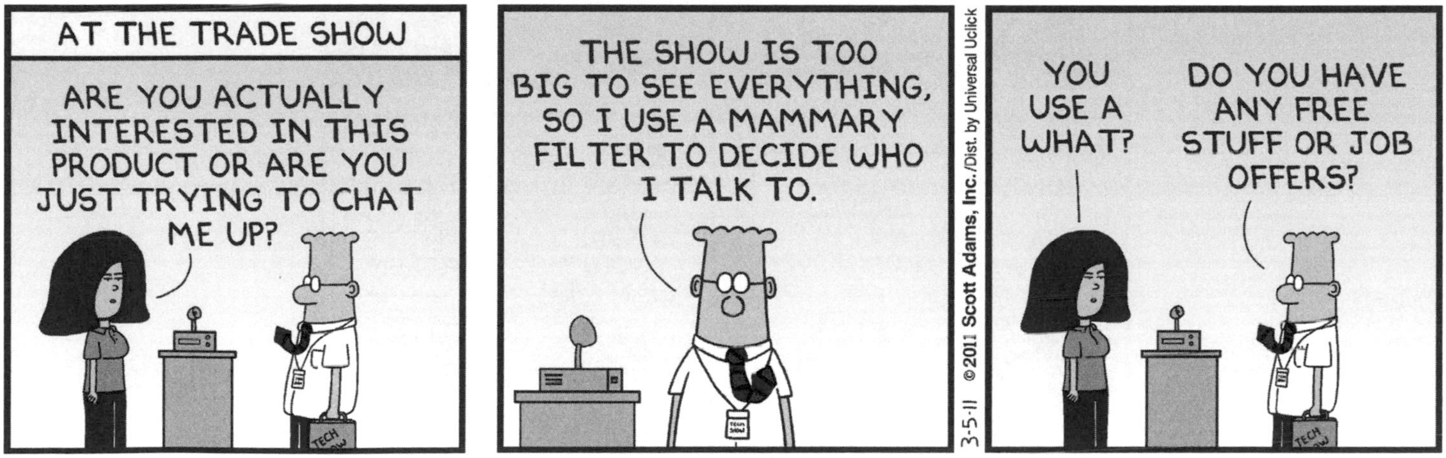
AT THE TRADE SHOW
ARE YOU ACTUALLY INTERESTED IN THIS PRODUCT OR ARE YOU JUST TRYING TO CHAT ME UP?
THE SHOW IS TOO BIG TO SEE EVERYTHING, SO I USE A MAMMARY FILTER TO DECIDE WHO I TALK TO.
YOU USE A WHAT?
DO YOU HAVE ANY FREE STUFF OR JOB OFFERS?
3-5-11 ©2011 Scott Adams, Inc./Dist. by Universal Uclick

YOU NEED TO BE MORE PROACTIVE.
I CAN ONLY APPEAR TO BE PROACTIVE IF YOU STOP TELLING ME TO DO THINGS I'VE ALREADY PLANNED.
HOW AM I SUPPOSED TO KNOW WHAT YOU PLAN TO DO EVERY MINUTE?
I COULD SEND YOU AN E-MAIL EVERY TIME I HAVE A THOUGHT.
I DON'T HAVE TIME FOR THAT!
APPARENTLY YOUR BAD TIME MANAGE-MENT IS CREATING THE ILLUSION THAT I'M NOT PROACTIVE.
I'LL TAKE THE LIBERTY OF SIGNING YOU UP FOR A TIME MANAGEMENT CLASS.
SO. . . I SHOULD NOT BE PROACTIVE?
DON'T DO THAT!
JUST DO WHAT I WANT BEFORE I KNOW I WANT IT.
I HOPE THE NEXT THING YOU WANT IS SARCASM.
©2011 Scott Adams, Inc. \Dist. by Univeral Uclick
3-6-11

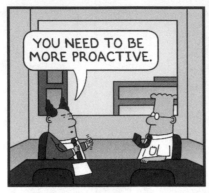

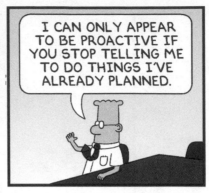

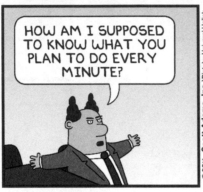

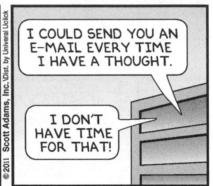

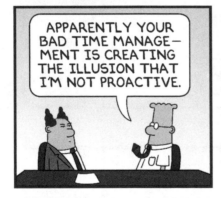

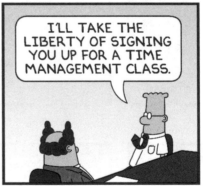

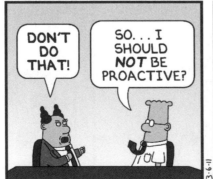

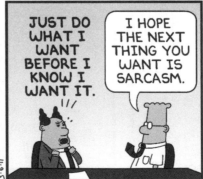

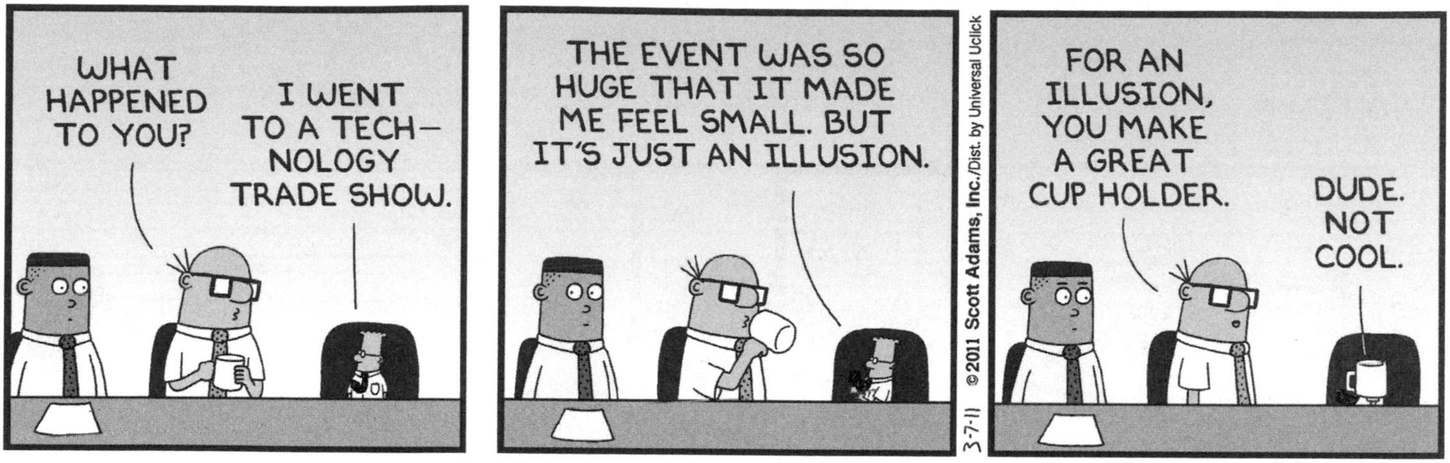
WHAT HAPPENED TO YOU?
I WENT TO A TECH-NOLOGY TRADE SHOW.
THE EVENT WAS SO HUGE THAT IT MADE ME FEEL SMALL. BUT IT'S JUST AN ILLUSION.
3-7-11 ©2011 Scott Adams, Inc./Dist. by Universal Uclick
FOR AN ILLUSION, YOU MAKE A GREAT CUP HOLDER.
DUDE. NOT COOL.

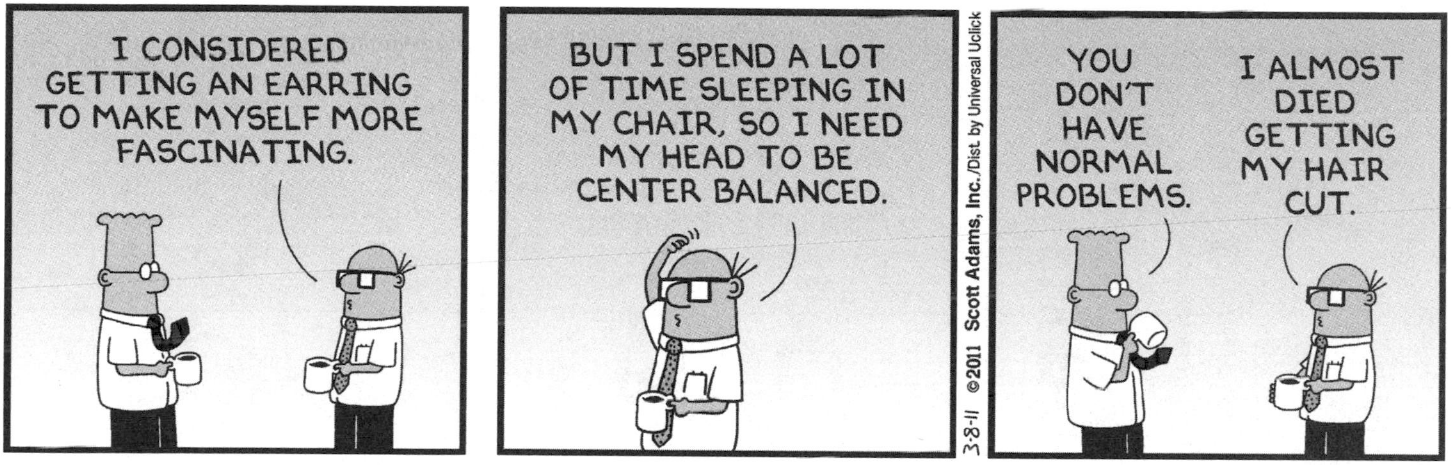
I CONSIDERED GETTING AN EARRING TO MAKE MYSELF MORE FASCINATING.
BUT I SPEND A LOT OF TIME SLEEPING IN MY CHAIR, SO I NEED MY HEAD TO BE CENTER BALANCED.
3-8-11 ©2011 Scott Adams, Inc./Dist by Universal Uclick
YOU DON'T HAVE NORMAL PROBLEMS.
I ALMOST DIED GETTING MY HAIR CUT.

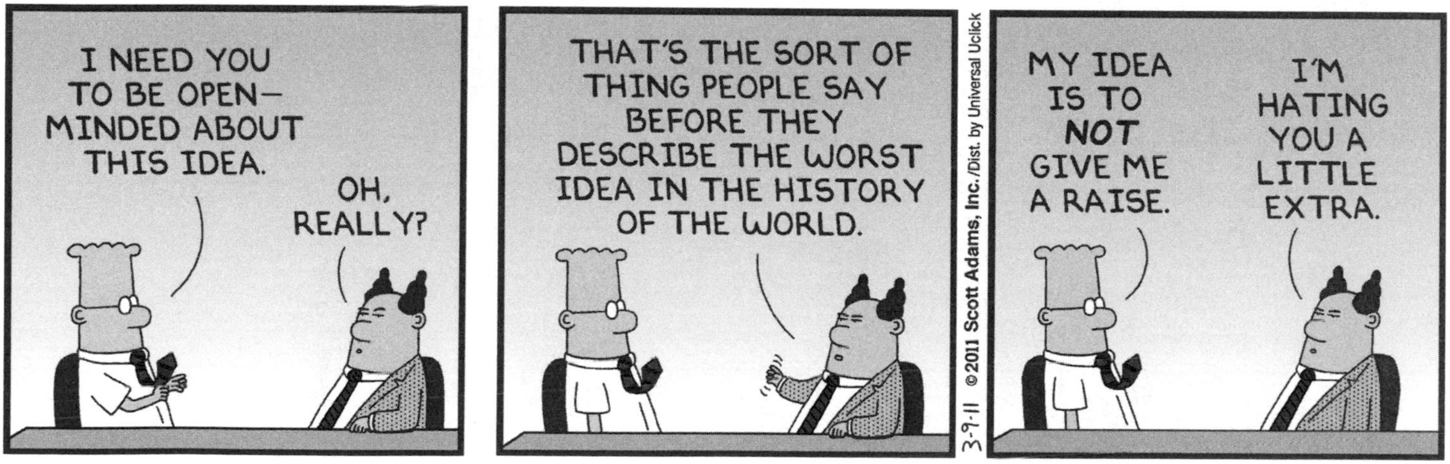
I NEED YOU TO BE OPEN-MINDED ABOUT THIS IDEA.
OH, REALLY?
THAT'S THE SORT OF THING PEOPLE SAY BEFORE THEY DESCRIBE THE WORST IDEA IN THE HISTORY OF THE WORLD.
3-9-11 ©2011 Scott Adams, Inc./Dist. by Universal Uclick
MY IDEA IS TO NOT GIVE ME A RAISE.
I'M HATING YOU A LITTLE EXTRA.

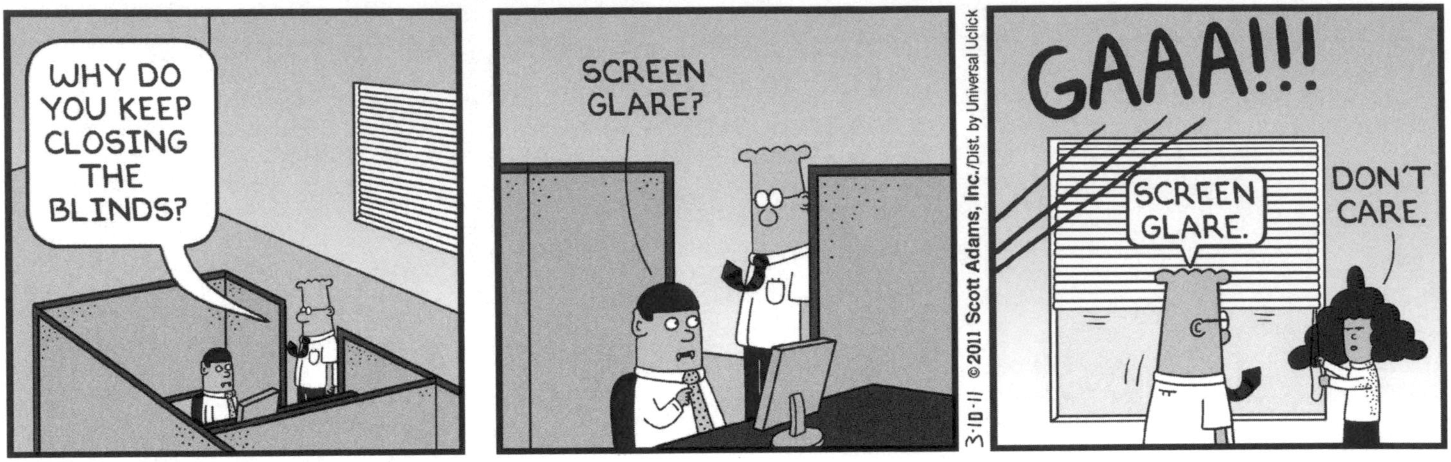
WHY DO YOU KEEP CLOSING THE BLINDS?
SCREEN GLARE?
3·10·11 ©2011 Scott Adams, Inc./Dist. by Universal Uclick
GAAA!!!
SCREEN GLARE.
DON'T CARE.

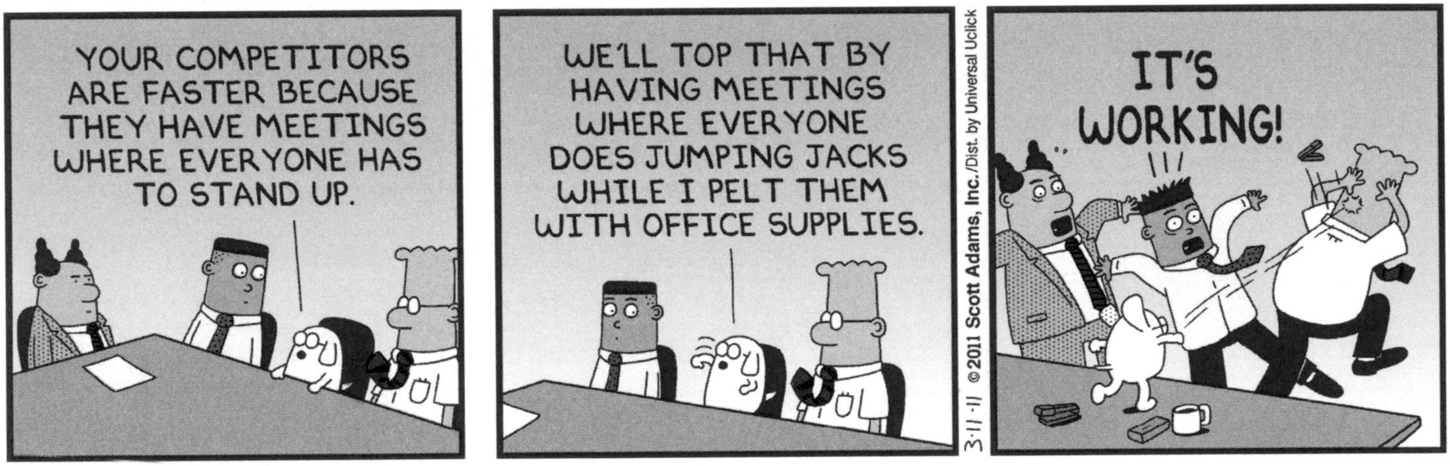
YOUR COMPETITORS ARE FASTER BECAUSE THEY HAVE MEETINGS WHERE EVERYONE HAS TO STAND UP.
WE'LL TOP THAT BY HAVING MEETINGS WHERE EVERYONE DOES JUMPING JACKS WHILE I PELT THEM WITH OFFICE SUPPLIES.
3·11·11 ©2011 Scott Adams, Inc./Dist. by Universal Uclick
IT'S WORKING!

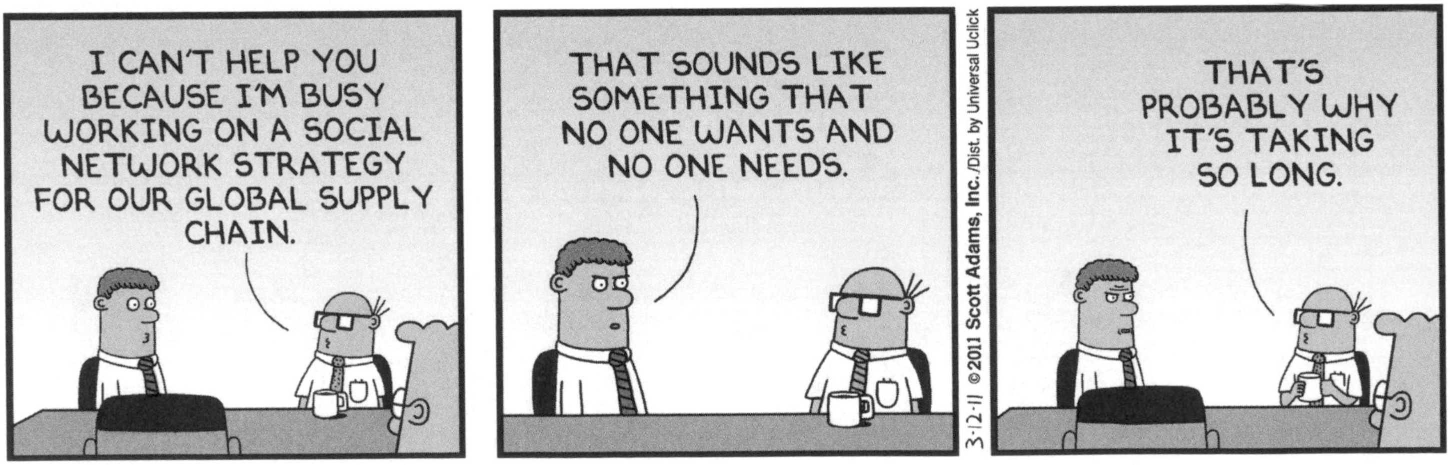
I CAN'T HELP YOU BECAUSE I'M BUSY WORKING ON A SOCIAL NETWORK STRATEGY FOR OUR GLOBAL SUPPLY CHAIN.
THAT SOUNDS LIKE SOMETHING THAT NO ONE WANTS AND NO ONE NEEDS.
3·12·11 ©2011 Scott Adams, Inc./Dist. by Universal Uclick
THAT'S PROBABLY WHY IT'S TAKING SO LONG.

I CAN'T SIGN OFF ON THIS PLAN. IT'S TOO EXPENSIVE.
YOU HEARD ME SAY THAT DOING NOTHING WILL END UP COSTING YOU TWICE AS MUCH, RIGHT?
YES.
AND YOU UNDERSTAND THAT THIS IS YOUR ONLY ALTERNATIVE?
©2011 Scott Adams, Inc.\Dist. by Univeral Uclick
I HAVE ANOTHER MEETING. MAYBE DILBERT CAN EXPLAIN IT TO YOU.
UM. . . OKAY. I'LL TRY.
MY BOSS DOESN'T UNDERSTAND THAT COSTS SHOULD BE COMPARED TO ALTERNATIVES.
OH.
3-13-11
TEAMWORK MEANS YOU CAN'T PICK THE SIDE THAT'S RIGHT.

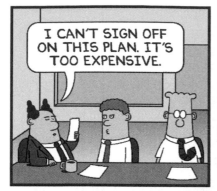

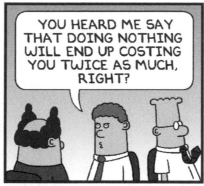

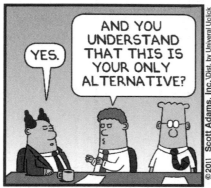

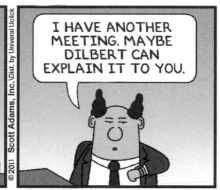

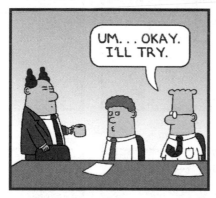

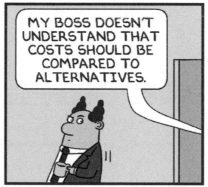

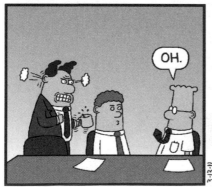

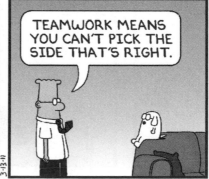

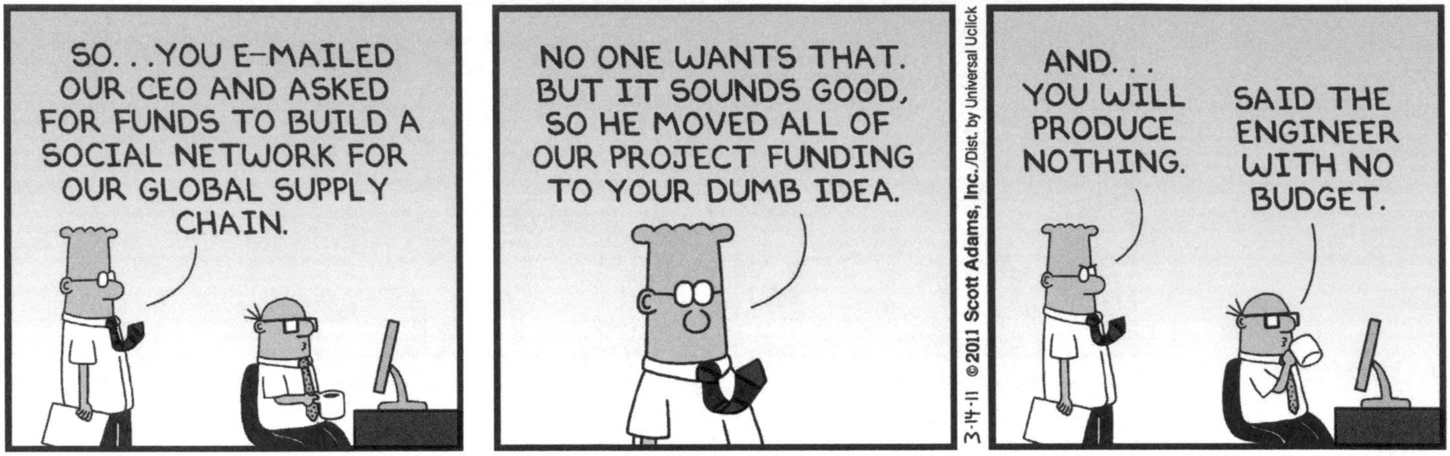
SO. . .YOU E-MAILED OUR CEO AND ASKED FOR FUNDS TO BUILD A SOCIAL NETWORK FOR OUR GLOBAL SUPPLY CHAIN.
NO ONE WANTS THAT. BUT IT SOUNDS GOOD, SO HE MOVED ALL OF OUR PROJECT FUNDING TO YOUR DUMB IDEA.
3-14-11 ©2011 Scott Adams, Inc./Dist. by Universal Uclick
AND. . . YOU WILL PRODUCE NOTHING.
SAID THE ENGINEER WITH NO BUDGET.

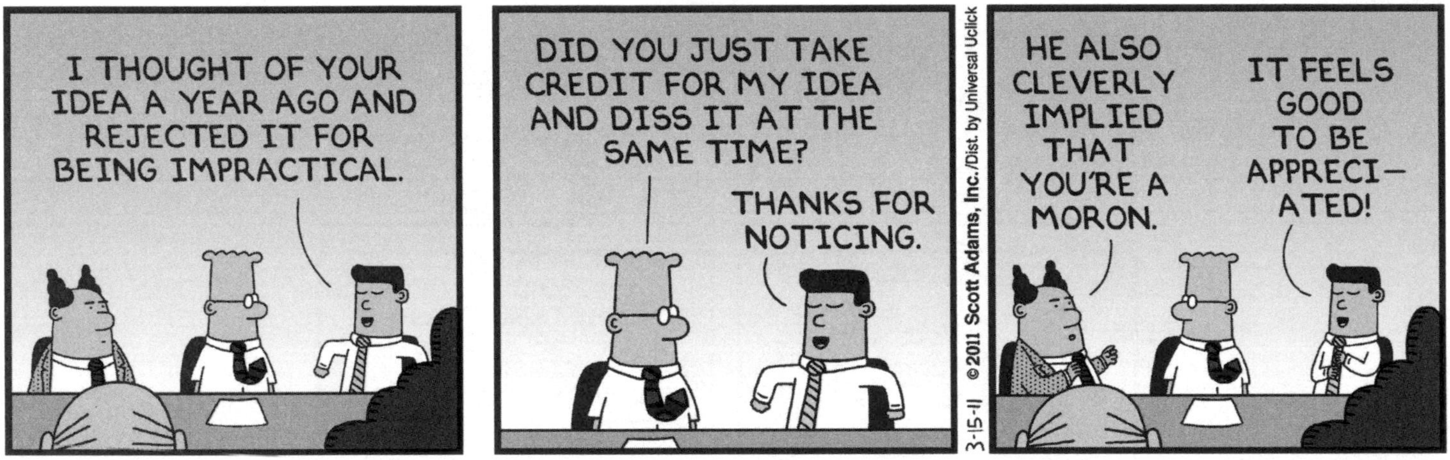
I THOUGHT OF YOUR IDEA A YEAR AGO AND REJECTED IT FOR BEING IMPRACTICAL.
DID YOU JUST TAKE CREDIT FOR MY IDEA AND DISS IT AT THE SAME TIME?
THANKS FOR NOTICING.
3-15-11 ©2011 Scott Adams, Inc./Dist. by Universal Uclick
HE ALSO CLEVERLY IMPLIED THAT YOU'RE A MORON.
IT FEELS GOOD TO BE APPRECI-ATED!

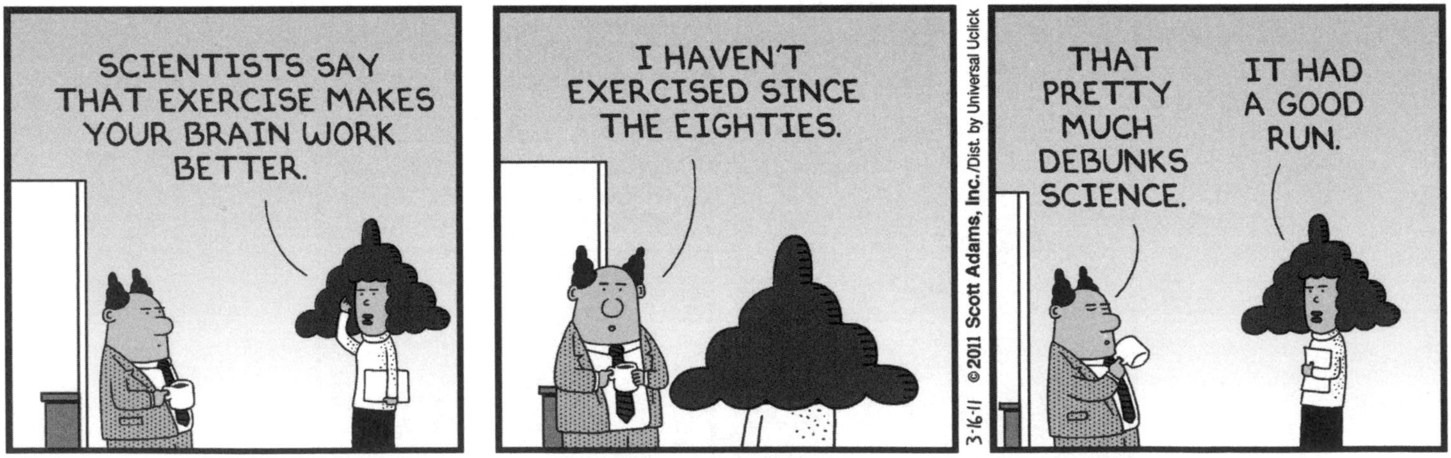
SCIENTISTS SAY THAT EXERCISE MAKES YOUR BRAIN WORK BETTER.
I HAVEN'T EXERCISED SINCE THE EIGHTIES.
3-16-11 ©2011 Scott Adams, Inc./Dist. by Universal Uclick
THAT PRETTY MUCH DEBUNKS SCIENCE.
IT HAD A GOOD RUN.

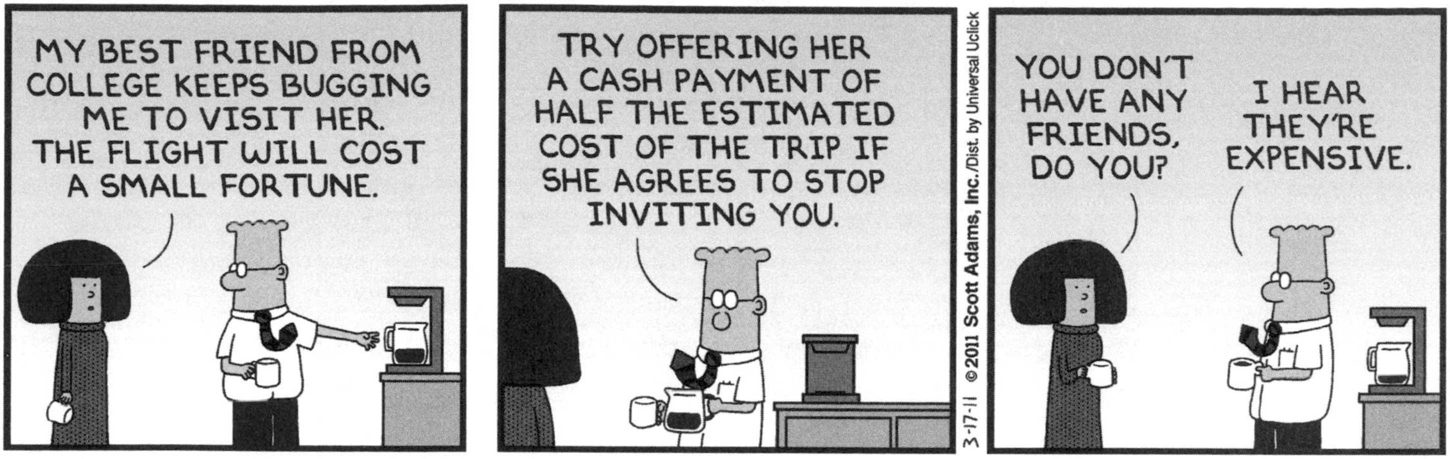
MY BEST FRIEND FROM COLLEGE KEEPS BUGGING ME TO VISIT HER. THE FLIGHT WILL COST A SMALL FORTUNE.
TRY OFFERING HER A CASH PAYMENT OF HALF THE ESTIMATED COST OF THE TRIP IF SHE AGREES TO STOP INVITING YOU.
3-17-11 © 2011 Scott Adams, Inc./Dist. by Universal Uclick
YOU DON'T HAVE ANY FRIENDS, DO YOU?
I HEAR THEY'RE EXPENSIVE.

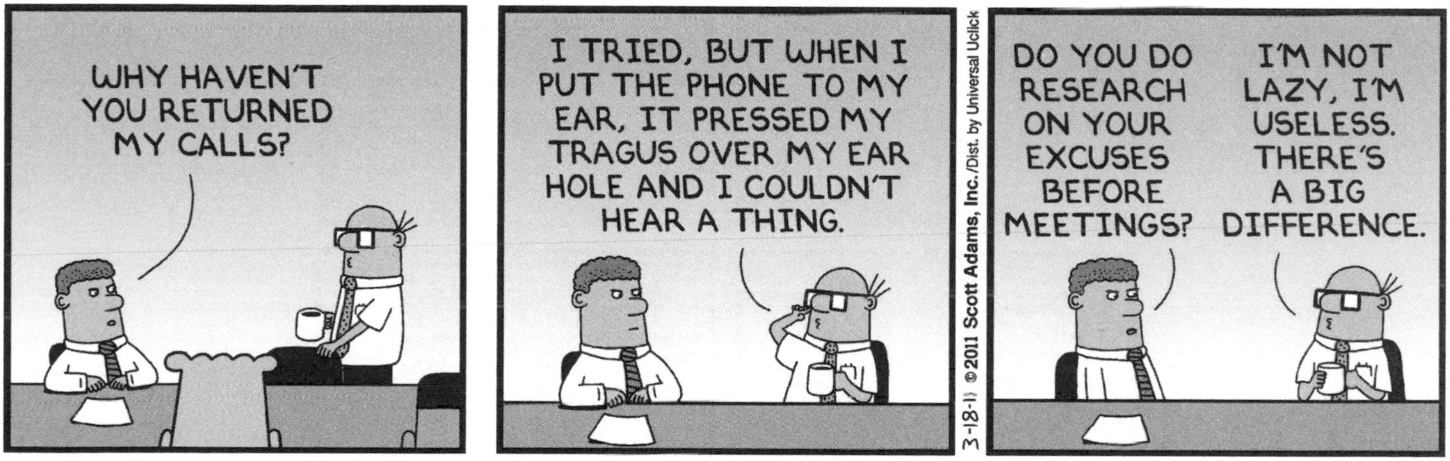
WHY HAVEN'T YOU RETURNED MY CALLS?
I TRIED, BUT WHEN I PUT THE PHONE TO MY EAR, IT PRESSED MY TRAGUS OVER MY EAR HOLE AND I COULDN'T HEAR A THING.
3-18-11 © 2011 Scott Adams, Inc./Dist. by Universal Uclick
DO YOU DO RESEARCH ON YOUR EXCUSES BEFORE MEETINGS?
I'M NOT LAZY, I'M USELESS. THERE'S A BIG DIFFERENCE.

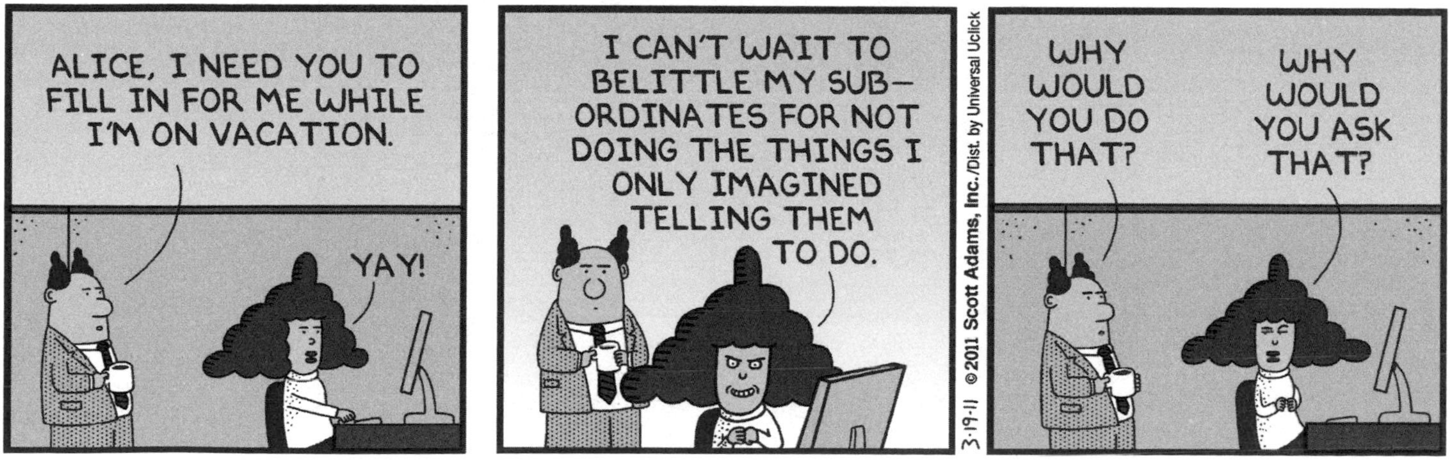
ALICE, I NEED YOU TO FILL IN FOR ME WHILE I'M ON VACATION.
YAY!
I CAN'T WAIT TO BELITTLE MY SUB-ORDINATES FOR NOT DOING THE THINGS I ONLY IMAGINED TELLING THEM TO DO.
3-19-11 © 2011 Scott Adams, Inc./Dist. by Universal Uclick
WHY WOULD YOU DO THAT?
WHY WOULD YOU ASK THAT?

ASOK, GET ME THE RELIABILITY STATS FOR OUR PREVIOUS MODEL.
I AM FAIRLY CERTAIN THE DATA DOES NOT EXIST.
WALLY CAN SHOW YOU HOW TO GET IT.
COME WITH ME.
YOU START BY TYPING RANDOM NUMBERS INTO A SPREADSHEET.
THEN WHAT?
THEN YOU'RE DONE.
ALL BUSINESS DATA IS INTENTIONALLY MISLEADING. I JUST TAKE IT TO THE NEXT LEVEL.
A DEEP UNDERSTAND–ING OF REALITY IS EXACTLY THE SAME THING AS LAZINESS.
CLICK CLICK CLICK CLICK CLICK
THAT CAN'T BE RIGHT.
HAVE YOU EVER SEEN A STATUE OF BUDDHA JOGGING?
©2011 Scott Adams, Inc.\Dist. by Univeral Uclick
3-20-11

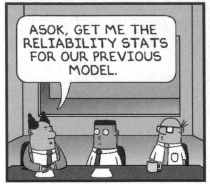

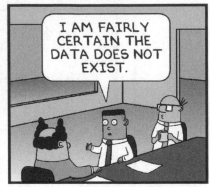

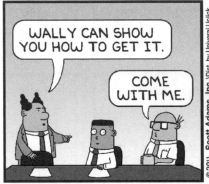

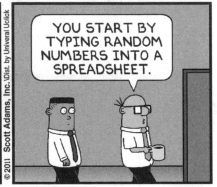

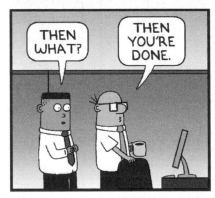

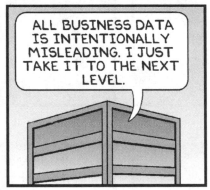

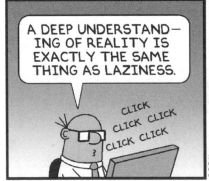

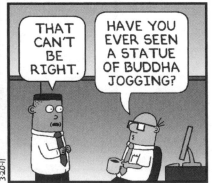

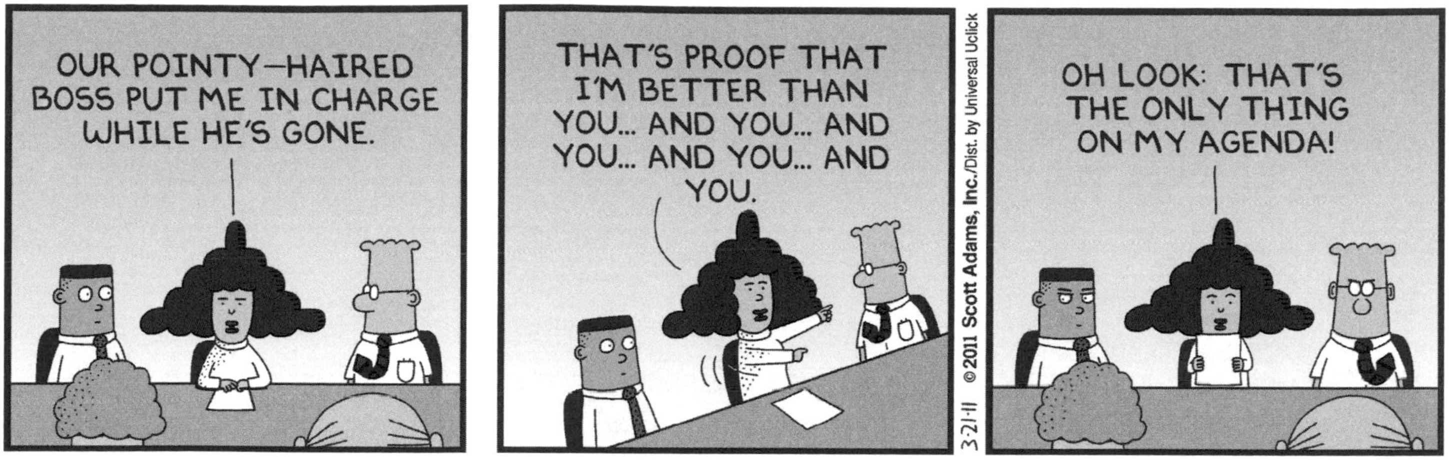
OUR POINTY—HAIRED BOSS PUT ME IN CHARGE WHILE HE'S GONE.
THAT'S PROOF THAT I'M BETTER THAN YOU... AND YOU... AND YOU... AND YOU... AND YOU.
3-21-11 ©2011 Scott Adams, Inc./Dist. by Universal Uclick
OH LOOK: THAT'S THE ONLY THING ON MY AGENDA!

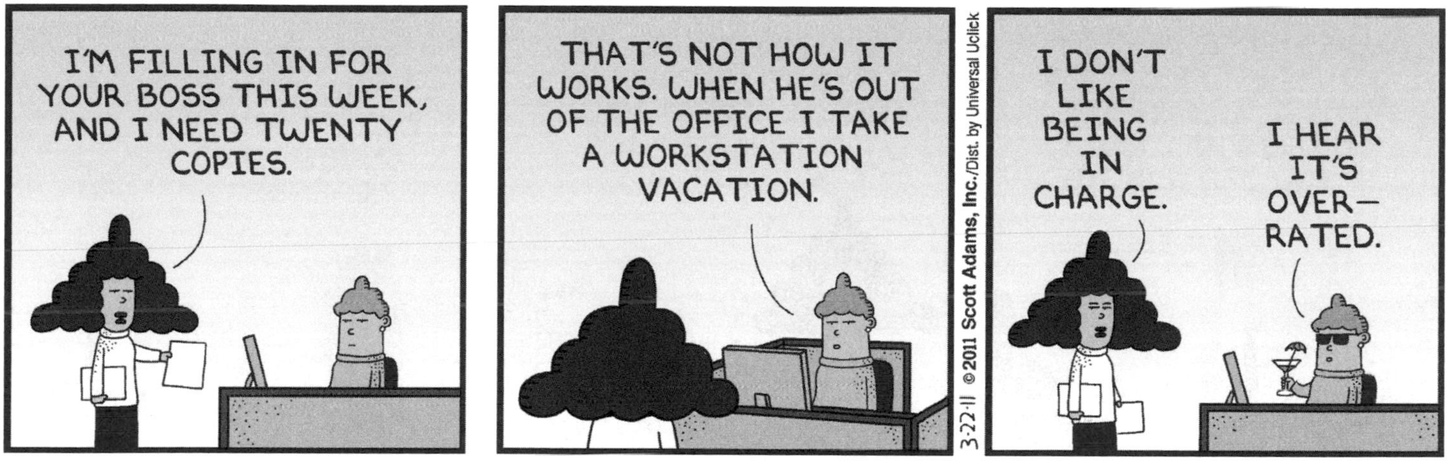
I'M FILLING IN FOR YOUR BOSS THIS WEEK, AND I NEED TWENTY COPIES.
THAT'S NOT HOW IT WORKS. WHEN HE'S OUT OF THE OFFICE I TAKE A WORKSTATION VACATION.
3-22-11 ©2011 Scott Adams, Inc./Dist. by Universal Uclick
I DON'T LIKE BEING IN CHARGE.
I HEAR IT'S OVER—RATED.

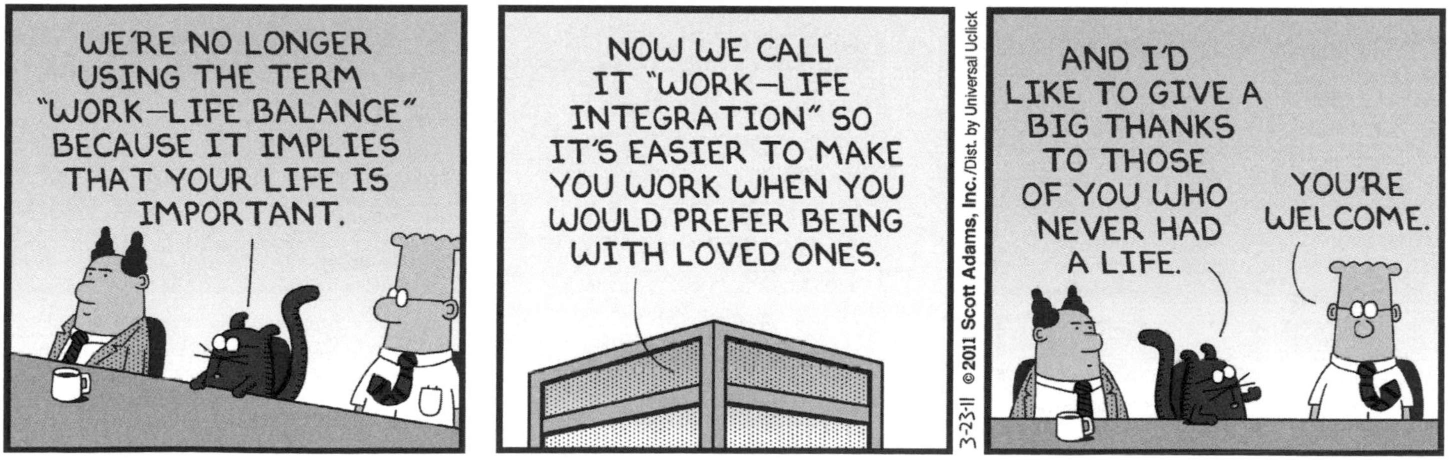
WE'RE NO LONGER USING THE TERM "WORK—LIFE BALANCE" BECAUSE IT IMPLIES THAT YOUR LIFE IS IMPORTANT.
NOW WE CALL IT "WORK—LIFE INTEGRATION" SO IT'S EASIER TO MAKE YOU WORK WHEN YOU WOULD PREFER BEING WITH LOVED ONES.
3-23-11 ©2011 Scott Adams, Inc./Dist. by Universal Uclick
AND I'D LIKE TO GIVE A BIG THANKS TO THOSE OF YOU WHO NEVER HAD A LIFE.
YOU'RE WELCOME.

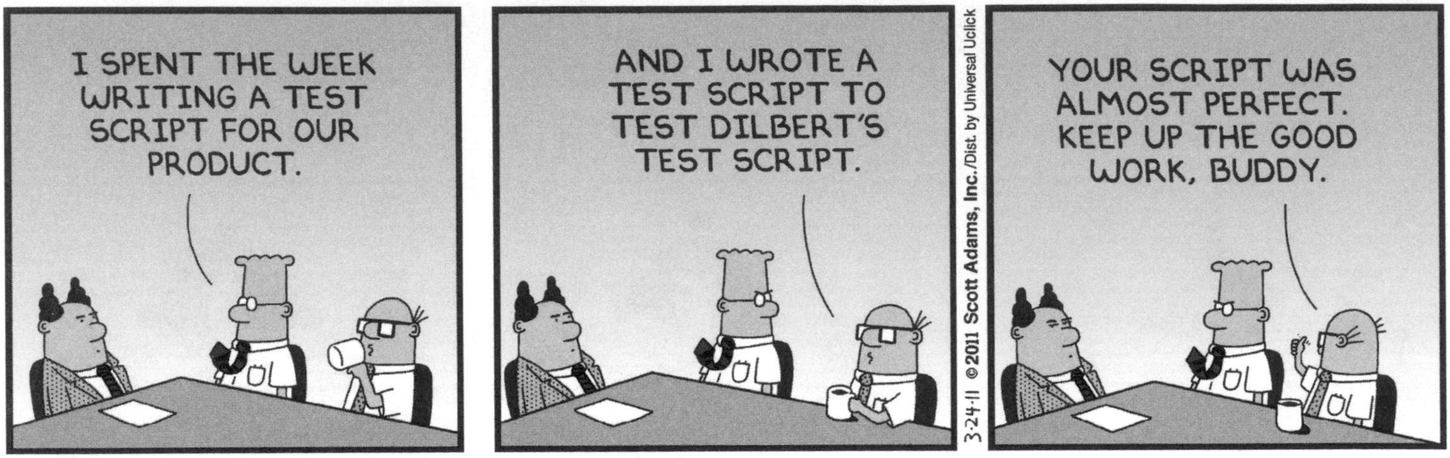
I SPENT THE WEEK WRITING A TEST SCRIPT FOR OUR PRODUCT.
AND I WROTE A TEST SCRIPT TO TEST DILBERT'S TEST SCRIPT.
3·24·11 ©2011 Scott Adams, Inc./Dist. by Universal Uclick
YOUR SCRIPT WAS ALMOST PERFECT. KEEP UP THE GOOD WORK, BUDDY.

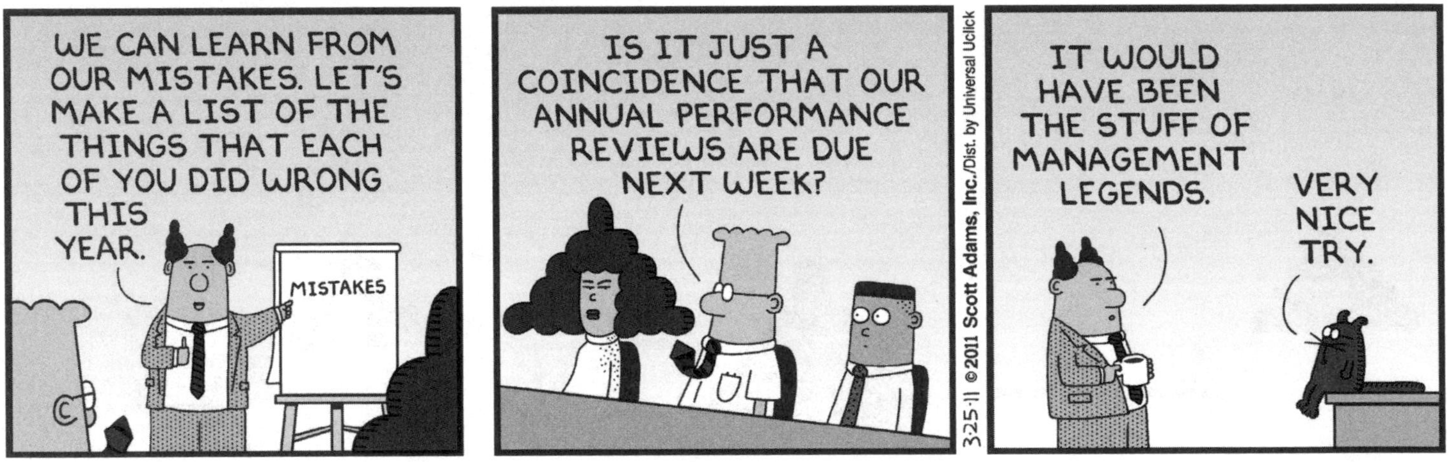
WE CAN LEARN FROM OUR MISTAKES. LET'S MAKE A LIST OF THE THINGS THAT EACH OF YOU DID WRONG THIS YEAR.
MISTAKES
IS IT JUST A COINCIDENCE THAT OUR ANNUAL PERFORMANCE REVIEWS ARE DUE NEXT WEEK?
3·25·11 ©2011 Scott Adams, Inc./Dist. by Universal Uclick
IT WOULD HAVE BEEN THE STUFF OF MANAGEMENT LEGENDS.
VERY NICE TRY.

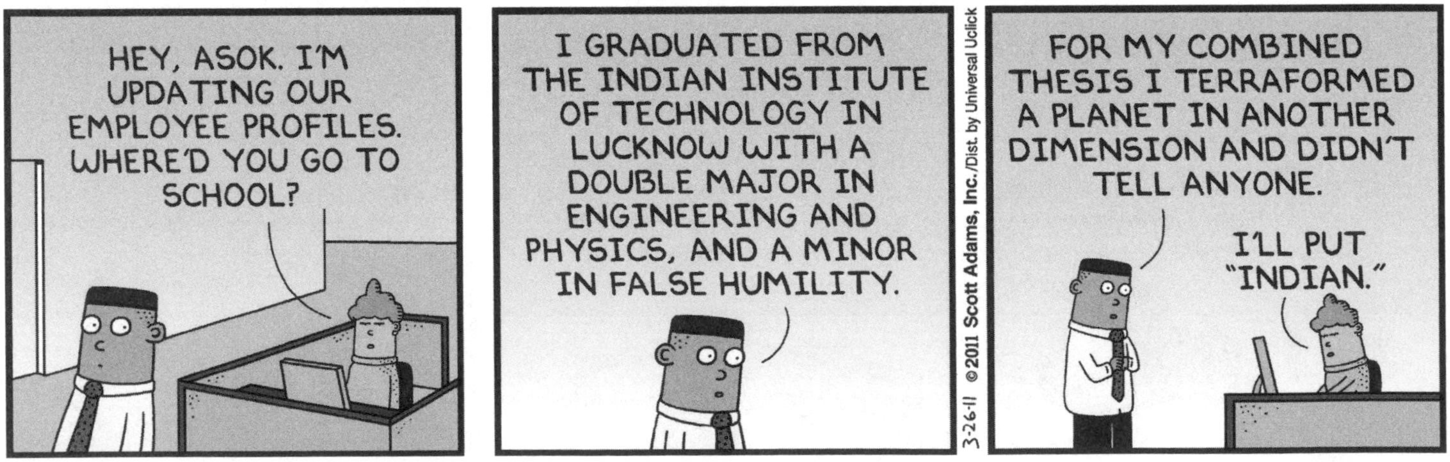
HEY, ASOK. I'M UPDATING OUR EMPLOYEE PROFILES. WHERE'D YOU GO TO SCHOOL?
I GRADUATED FROM THE INDIAN INSTITUTE OF TECHNOLOGY IN LUCKNOW WITH A DOUBLE MAJOR IN ENGINEERING AND PHYSICS, AND A MINOR IN FALSE HUMILITY.
3·26·11 ©2011 Scott Adams, Inc./Dist. by Universal Uclick
FOR MY COMBINED THESIS I TERRAFORMED A PLANET IN ANOTHER DIMENSION AND DIDN'T TELL ANYONE.
I'LL PUT "INDIAN."

WALLY, CAN YOU REVIEW THIS FOR ANY ENGINEERING ISSUES?
WHAT ISSUES DO YOU THINK IT HAS?
I DON'T KNOW. I'M NOT AN ENGINEER.
YOUR REQUEST IS TOO VAGUE. YOU NEED TO TELL ME WHAT ISSUES I'M LOOKING FOR!
DID YOU JUST ASK ME TO DO WHAT I JUST ASKED YOU TO DO?
I DON'T KNOW. I'M AN ENGINEER, NOT A LINGUIST.
I'VE SUDDENLY LOST ALL FAITH IN HUMANITY!
ON THE PLUS SIDE, YOU FOUND AN ISSUE.
© 2011 Scott Adams, Inc. /Dist. by Univeral Uclick
3-27-11

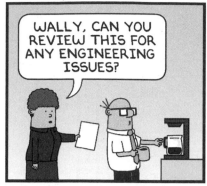

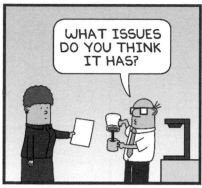

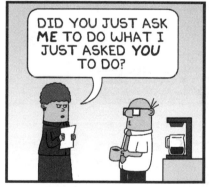

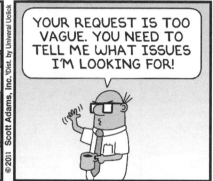

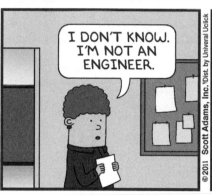

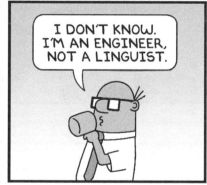

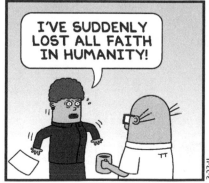

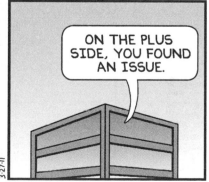

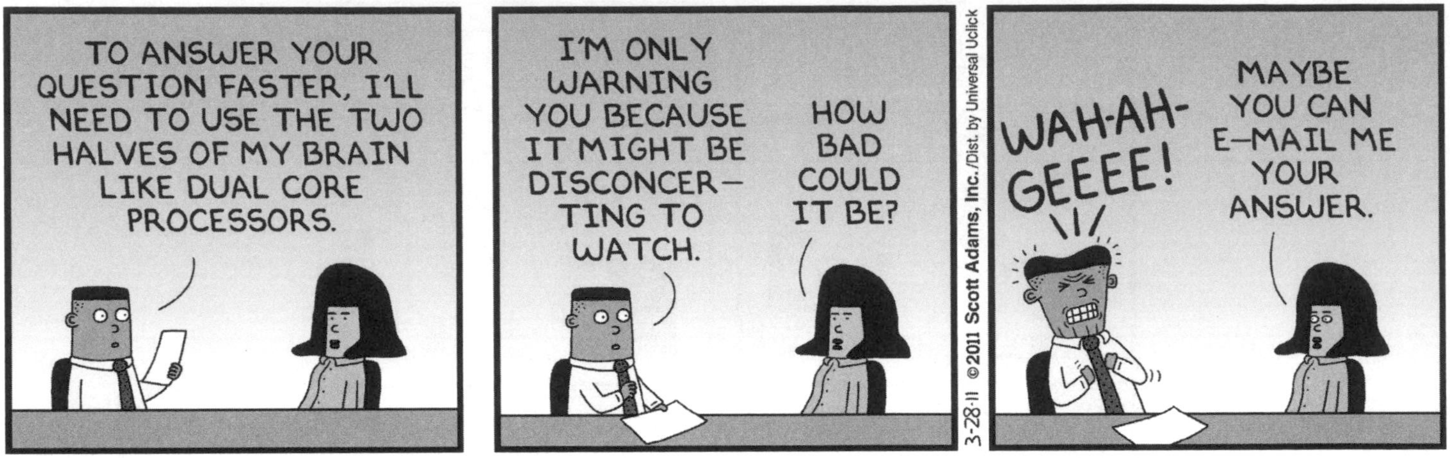
TO ANSWER YOUR QUESTION FASTER, I'LL NEED TO USE THE TWO HALVES OF MY BRAIN LIKE DUAL CORE PROCESSORS.
I'M ONLY WARNING YOU BECAUSE IT MIGHT BE DISCONCER– TING TO WATCH.
HOW BAD COULD IT BE?
3-28-11 ©2011 Scott Adams, Inc./Dist. by Universal Uclick
WAH-AH-GEEEE!
MAYBE YOU CAN E–MAIL ME YOUR ANSWER.

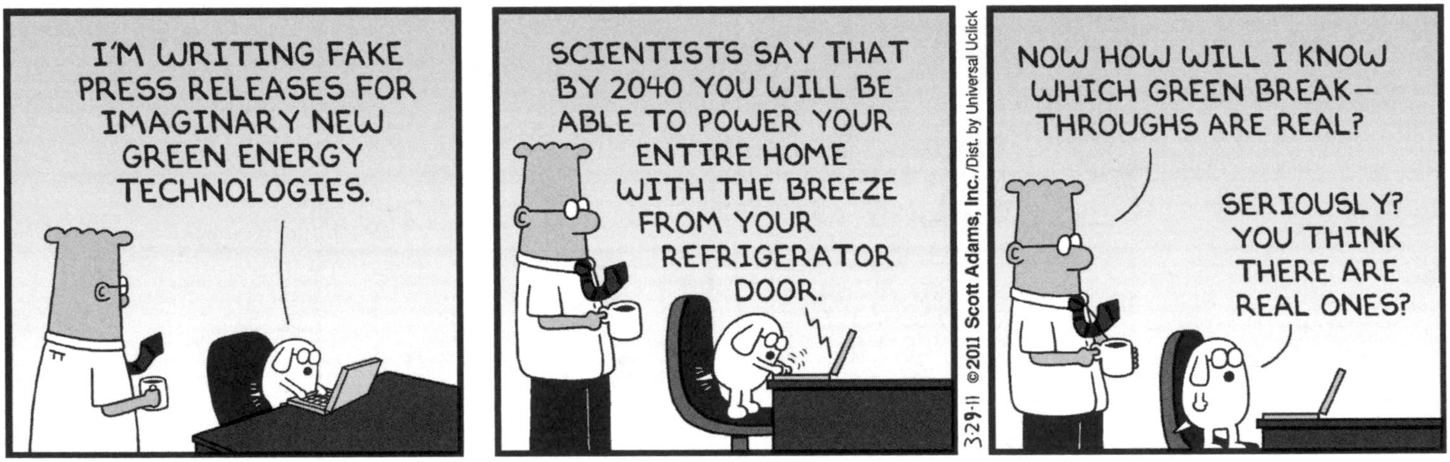
I'M WRITING FAKE PRESS RELEASES FOR IMAGINARY NEW GREEN ENERGY TECHNOLOGIES.
SCIENTISTS SAY THAT BY 2040 YOU WILL BE ABLE TO POWER YOUR ENTIRE HOME WITH THE BREEZE FROM YOUR REFRIGERATOR DOOR.
3-29-11 ©2011 Scott Adams, Inc./Dist. by Universal Uclick
NOW HOW WILL I KNOW WHICH GREEN BREAK– THROUGHS ARE REAL?
SERIOUSLY? YOU THINK THERE ARE REAL ONES?

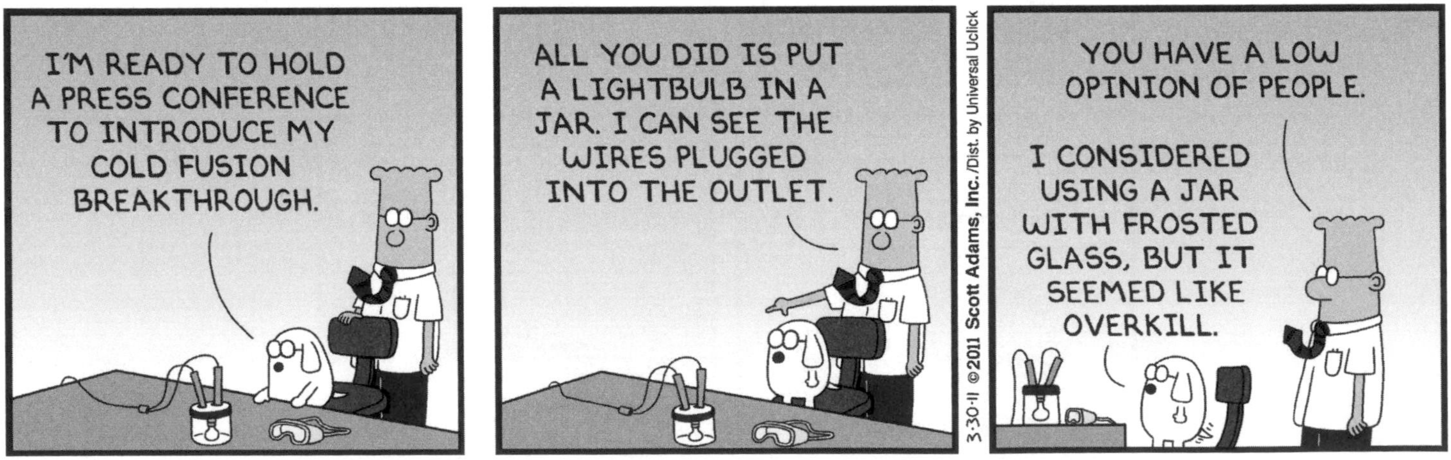
I'M READY TO HOLD A PRESS CONFERENCE TO INTRODUCE MY COLD FUSION BREAKTHROUGH.
ALL YOU DID IS PUT A LIGHTBULB IN A JAR. I CAN SEE THE WIRES PLUGGED INTO THE OUTLET.
3-30-11 ©2011 Scott Adams, Inc./Dist. by Universal Uclick
YOU HAVE A LOW OPINION OF PEOPLE.
I CONSIDERED USING A JAR WITH FROSTED GLASS, BUT IT SEEMED LIKE OVERKILL.

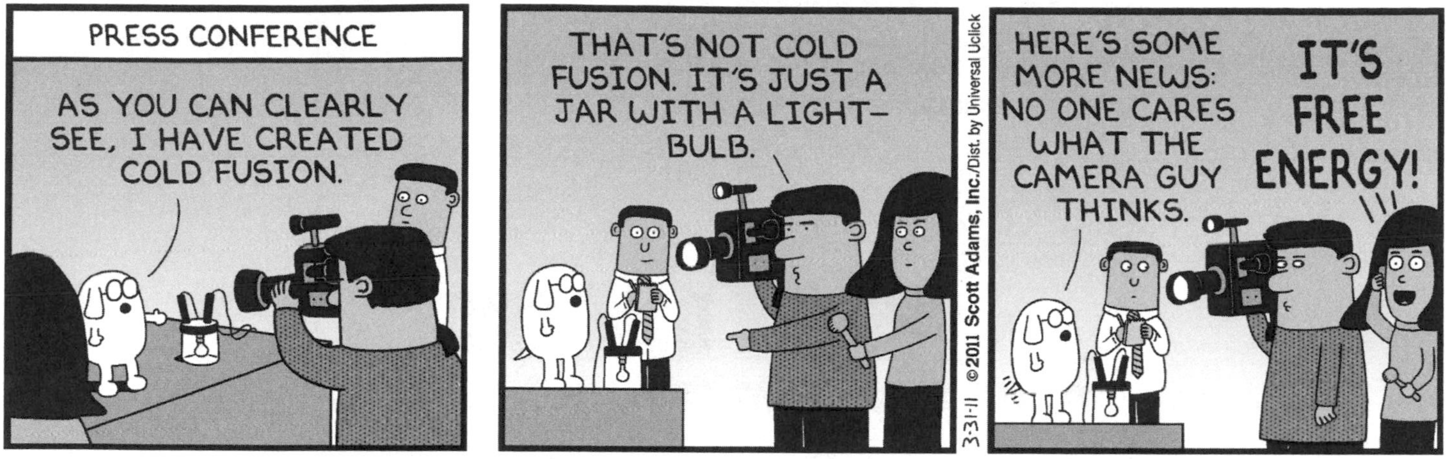
PRESS CONFERENCE
AS YOU CAN CLEARLY SEE, I HAVE CREATED COLD FUSION.
THAT'S NOT COLD FUSION. IT'S JUST A JAR WITH A LIGHT-BULB.
3·31·11 ©2011 Scott Adams, Inc./Dist. by Universal Uclick
HERE'S SOME MORE NEWS: NO ONE CARES WHAT THE CAMERA GUY THINKS.
IT'S FREE ENERGY!

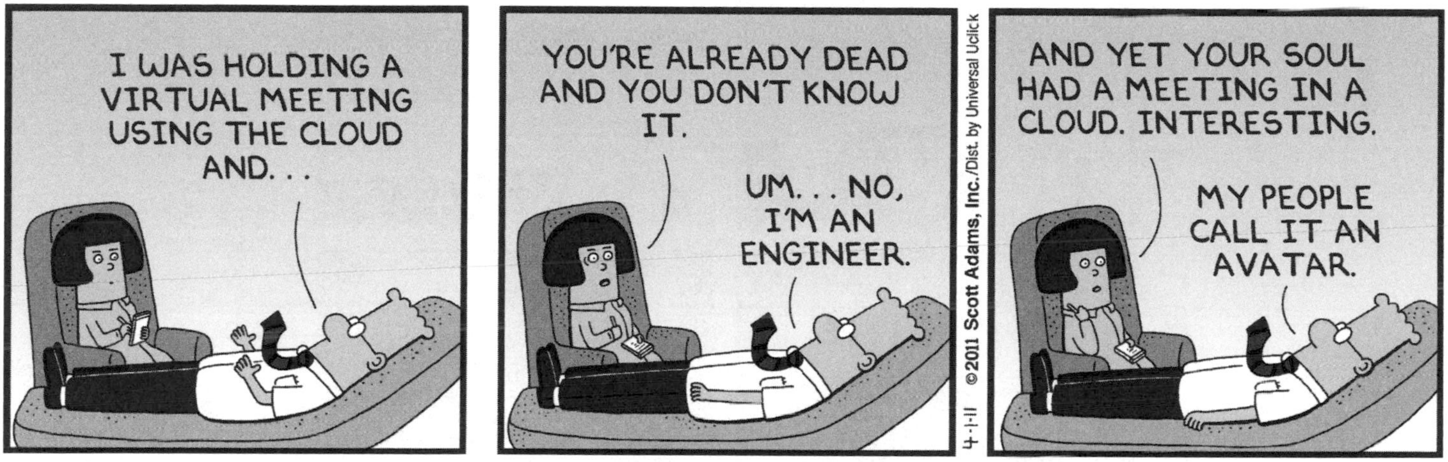
I WAS HOLDING A VIRTUAL MEETING USING THE CLOUD AND. . .
YOU'RE ALREADY DEAD AND YOU DON'T KNOW IT.
UM. . . NO, I'M AN ENGINEER.
4·1·11 ©2011 Scott Adams, Inc./Dist. by Universal Uclick
AND YET YOUR SOUL HAD A MEETING IN A CLOUD. INTERESTING.
MY PEOPLE CALL IT AN AVATAR.

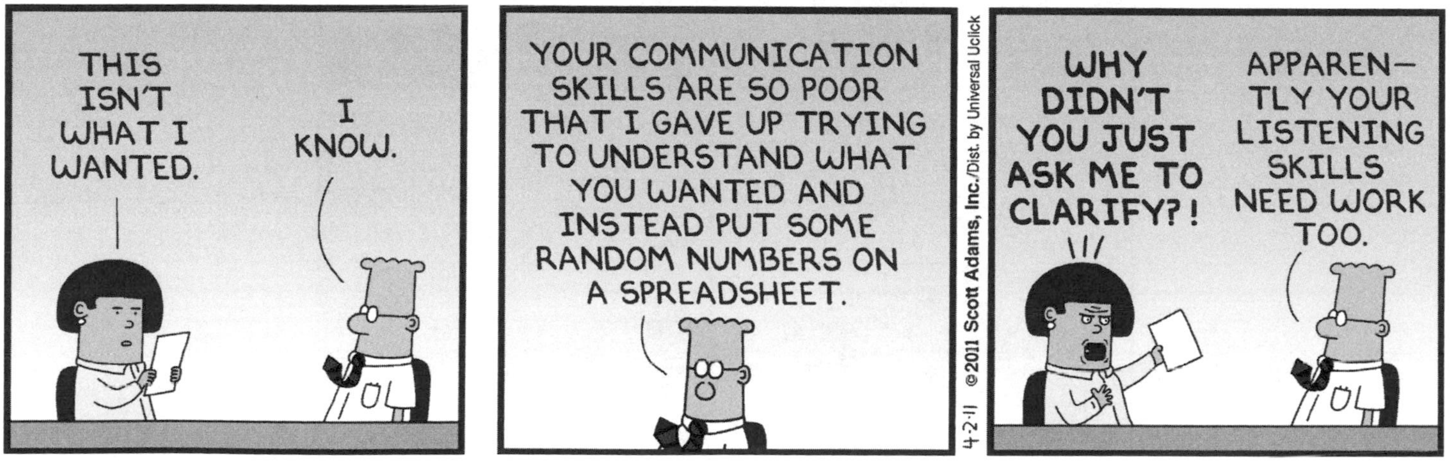
THIS ISN'T WHAT I WANTED.
I KNOW.
YOUR COMMUNICATION SKILLS ARE SO POOR THAT I GAVE UP TRYING TO UNDERSTAND WHAT YOU WANTED AND INSTEAD PUT SOME RANDOM NUMBERS ON A SPREADSHEET.
4·2·11 ©2011 Scott Adams, Inc./Dist. by Universal Uclick
WHY DIDN'T YOU JUST ASK ME TO CLARIFY?!
APPAREN-TLY YOUR LISTENING SKILLS NEED WORK TOO.

DOGBERT'S CEO INTERVIEW SERIES
I DON'T LIKE PEOPLE.
WHAT MAKES YOUR COMPANY SO PROFITABLE?
4/3
I GIVE ALL OF THE CREDIT TO OUR FINE EMPLOYEES.
©2011 Scott Adams, Inc. Dist. by Universal Uclick
IS THAT ANOTHER WAY OF SAYING YOU'RE OVERPAID AND USELESS?
UM. . . NO. I'M THEIR LEADER. I SET THE DIRECTION.
BECAUSE THE EMPLOYEES ARE TOO DUMB TO SET THEIR OWN DIRECTION?
NO! THEY'RE SMART!
BUT NOT AS SMART AS YOU?
WHO'S GOING TO SEE THIS?
NO ONE, ASSUMING YOU'RE THE HIGHEST BIDDER.

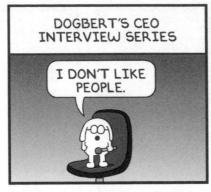

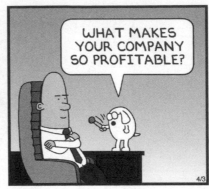

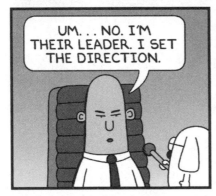

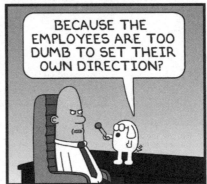

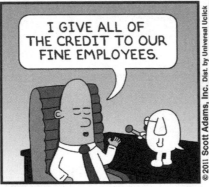

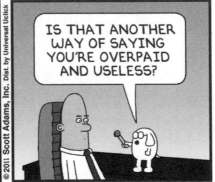

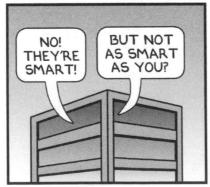

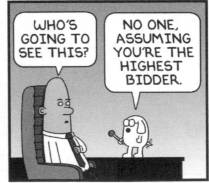

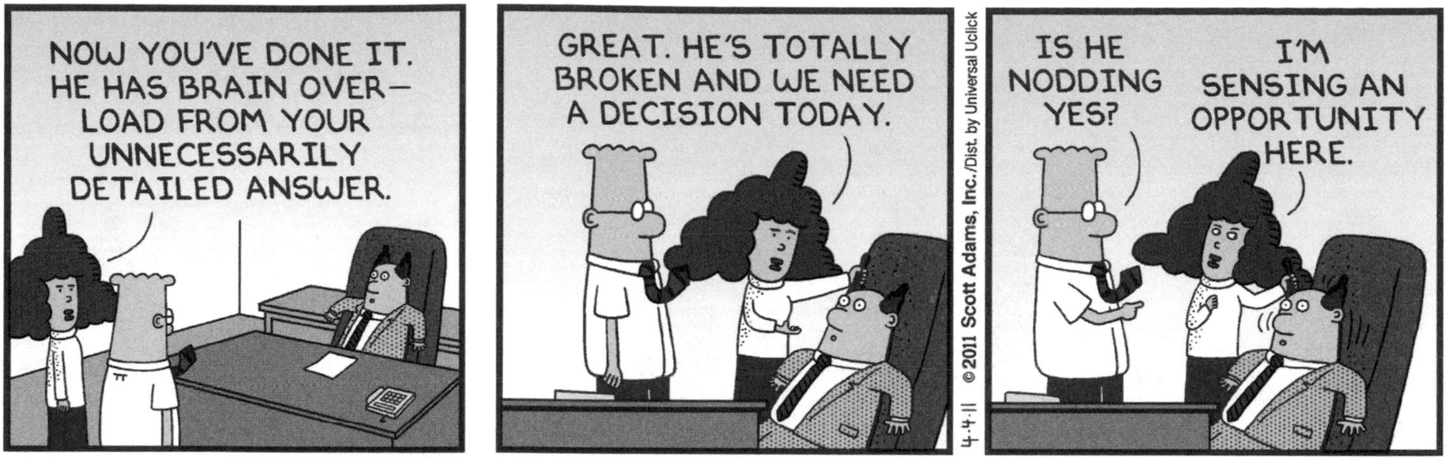
NOW YOU'VE DONE IT. HE HAS BRAIN OVER-LOAD FROM YOUR UNNECESSARILY DETAILED ANSWER.
GREAT. HE'S TOTALLY BROKEN AND WE NEED A DECISION TODAY.
IS HE NODDING YES?
I'M SENSING AN OPPORTUNITY HERE.
4-4-11 ©2011 Scott Adams, Inc./Dist. by Universal Uclick

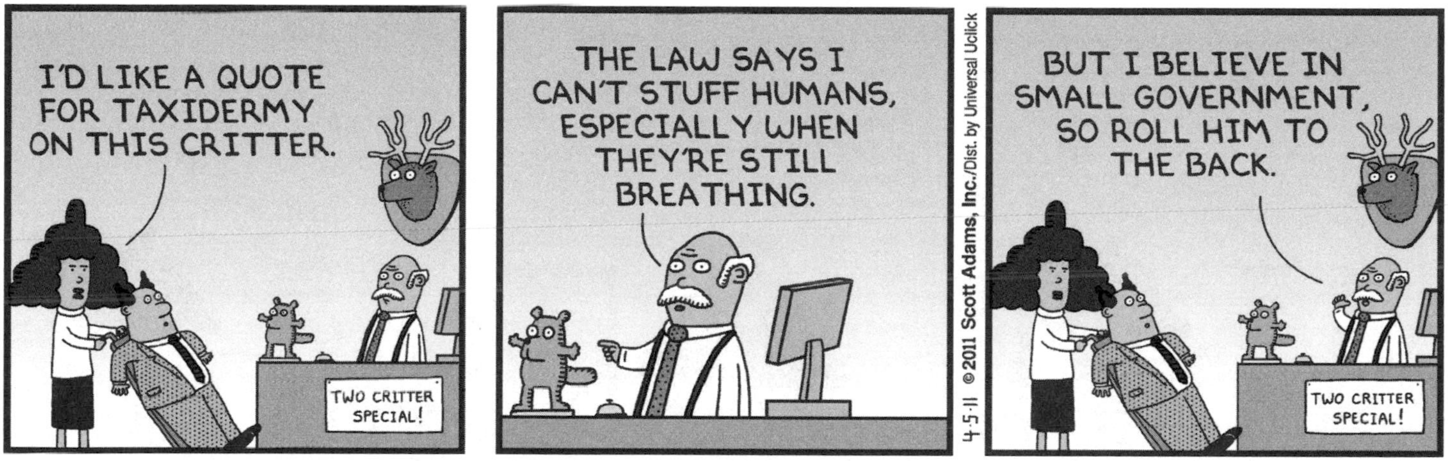
I'D LIKE A QUOTE FOR TAXIDERMY ON THIS CRITTER.
TWO CRITTER SPECIAL!
THE LAW SAYS I CAN'T STUFF HUMANS, ESPECIALLY WHEN THEY'RE STILL BREATHING.
BUT I BELIEVE IN SMALL GOVERNMENT, SO ROLL HIM TO THE BACK.
TWO CRITTER SPECIAL!
4-5-11 ©2011 Scott Adams, Inc./Dist. by Universal Uclick

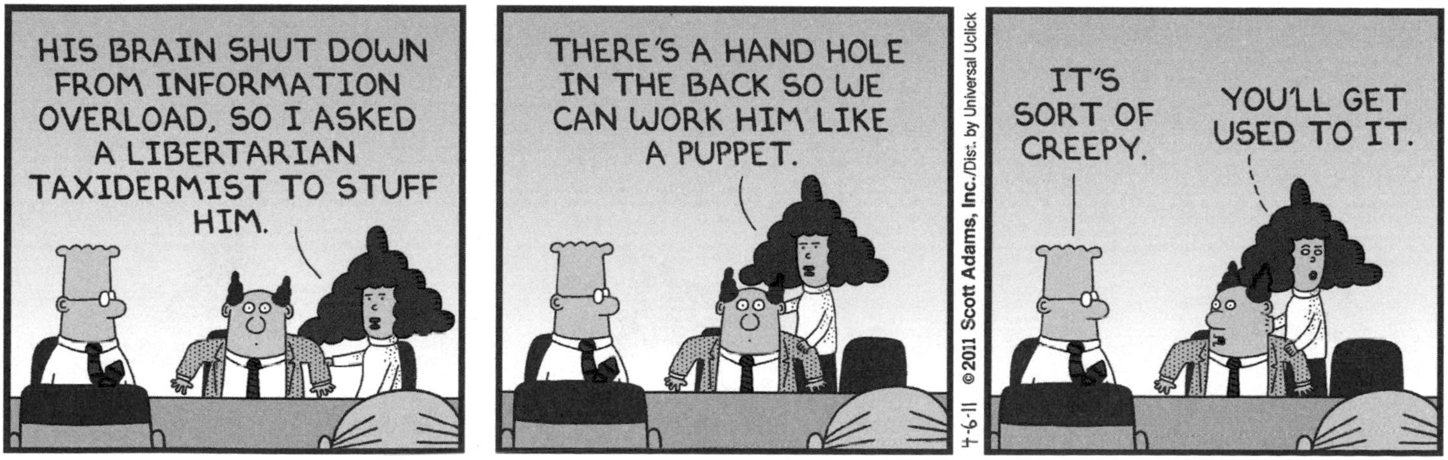
HIS BRAIN SHUT DOWN FROM INFORMATION OVERLOAD, SO I ASKED A LIBERTARIAN TAXIDERMIST TO STUFF HIM.
THERE'S A HAND HOLE IN THE BACK SO WE CAN WORK HIM LIKE A PUPPET.
IT'S SORT OF CREEPY.
YOU'LL GET USED TO IT.
4-6-11 ©2011 Scott Adams, Inc./Dist. by Universal Uclick

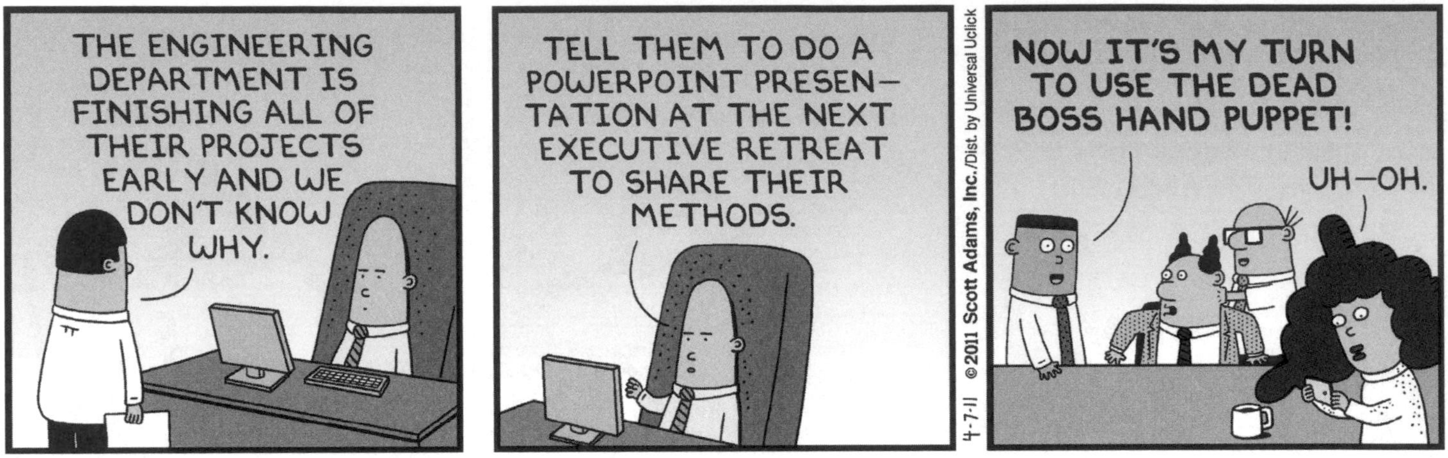
THE ENGINEERING DEPARTMENT IS FINISHING ALL OF THEIR PROJECTS EARLY AND WE DON'T KNOW WHY.
TELL THEM TO DO A POWERPOINT PRESEN–TATION AT THE NEXT EXECUTIVE RETREAT TO SHARE THEIR METHODS.
4-7-11 ©2011 Scott Adams, Inc./Dist. by Universal Uclick
NOW IT'S MY TURN TO USE THE DEAD BOSS HAND PUPPET!
UH–OH.

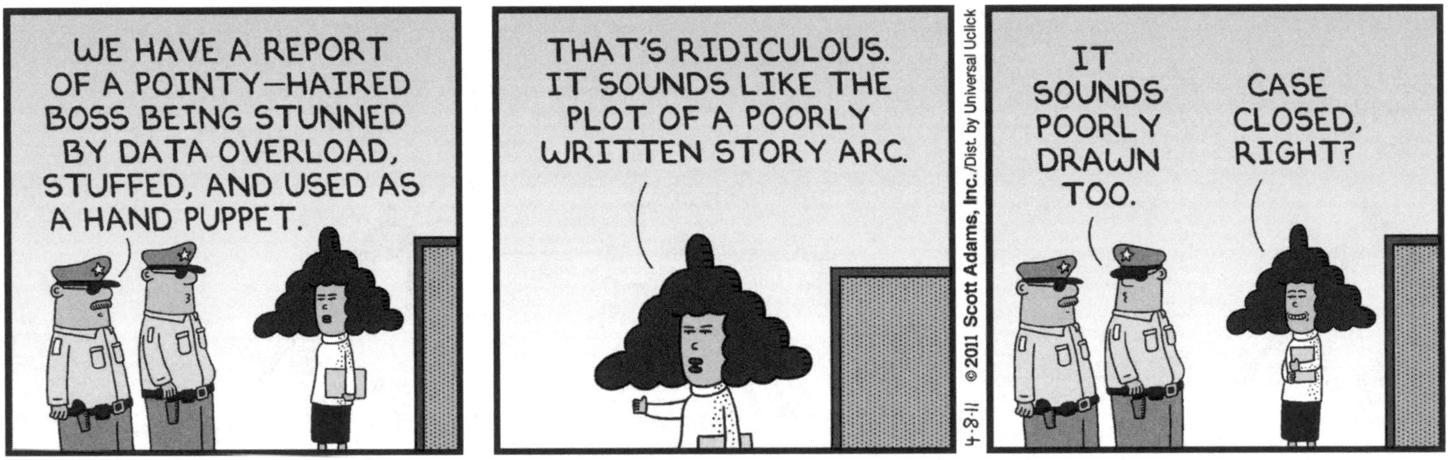
WE HAVE A REPORT OF A POINTY–HAIRED BOSS BEING STUNNED BY DATA OVERLOAD, STUFFED, AND USED AS A HAND PUPPET.
THAT'S RIDICULOUS. IT SOUNDS LIKE THE PLOT OF A POORLY WRITTEN STORY ARC.
4-8-11 ©2011 Scott Adams, Inc./Dist. by Universal Uclick
IT SOUNDS POORLY DRAWN TOO.
CASE CLOSED, RIGHT?

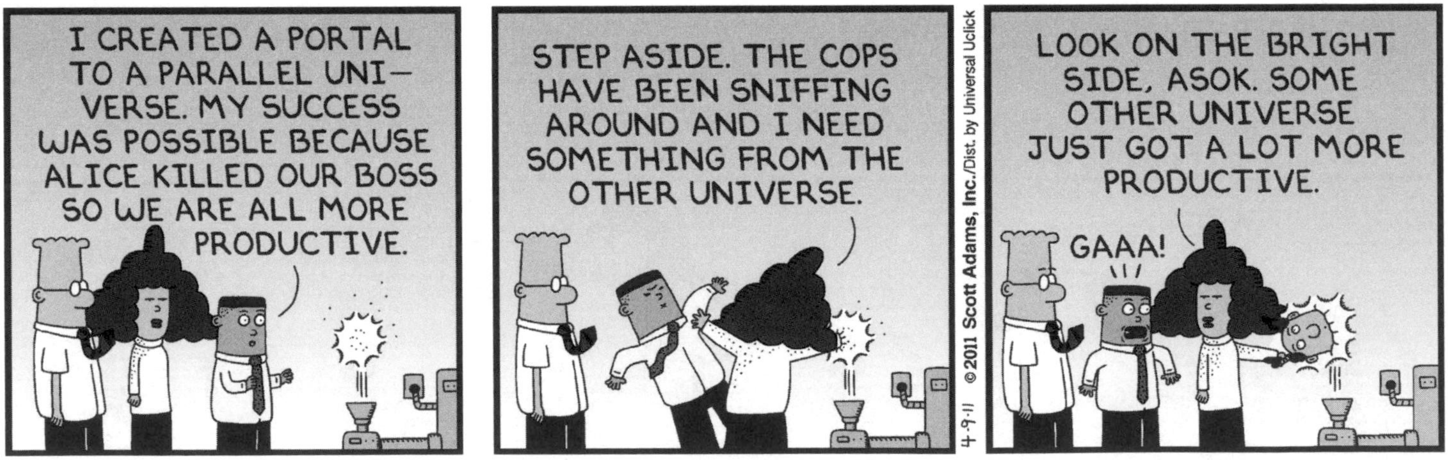
I CREATED A PORTAL TO A PARALLEL UNI–VERSE. MY SUCCESS WAS POSSIBLE BECAUSE ALICE KILLED OUR BOSS SO WE ARE ALL MORE PRODUCTIVE.
STEP ASIDE. THE COPS HAVE BEEN SNIFFING AROUND AND I NEED SOMETHING FROM THE OTHER UNIVERSE.
4-9-11 ©2011 Scott Adams, Inc./Dist. by Universal Uclick
LOOK ON THE BRIGHT SIDE, ASOK. SOME OTHER UNIVERSE JUST GOT A LOT MORE PRODUCTIVE.
GAAA!

MELTDOWN IN CUBICLE 459540!
THAT'S TED. HE MUST HAVE REACHED HIS T.W.L.
HIS WHAT?
THEORETICAL WORKLOAD LIMIT
IN LAYMAN'S TERMS, HIS BRAIN IS FULL.
©2011 Scott Adams, Inc. Dist. by Universal Uclick
IT STARTS WHEN JUST ONE OF YOUR PROJECTS BECOMES OVERDUE.
YOU END UP SPENDING ALL OF YOUR TIME EXPLAINING WHY YOU DIDN'T GET IT DONE.
THAT MAKES ALL OF YOUR OTHER PROJECTS OVERDUE. WHEN EVERY TASK BECOMES URGENT, YOUR BRAIN CAN'T DECIDE WHAT TO DO NEXT.
BRAINS MAKE A FUNNY NOISE WHEN THEY SHUT DOWN.
POINK
4-10-11
UH-OH. I JUST MISSED A DEAD-LINE.
AND SO IT BEGINS.

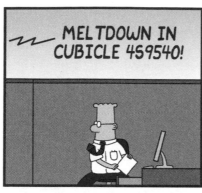

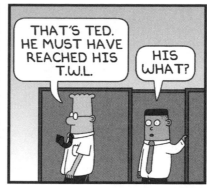

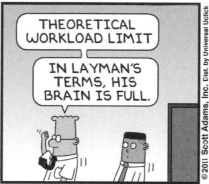

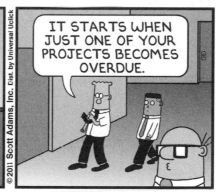

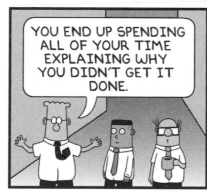

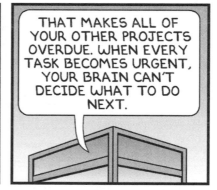

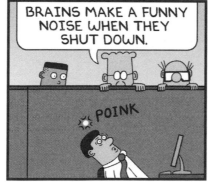

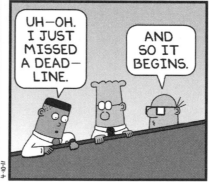

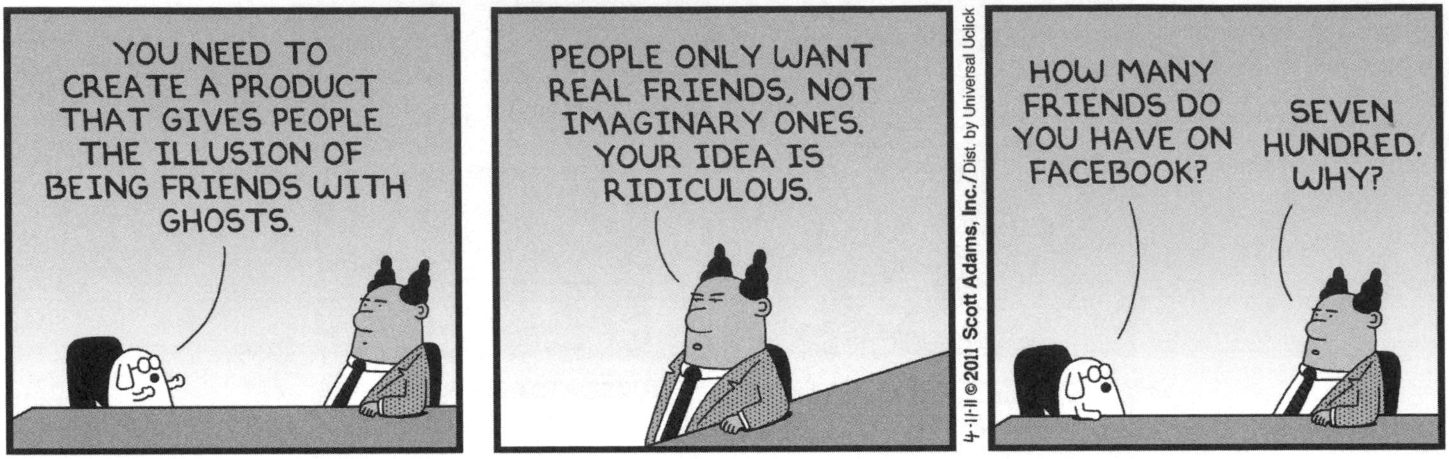
YOU NEED TO CREATE A PRODUCT THAT GIVES PEOPLE THE ILLUSION OF BEING FRIENDS WITH GHOSTS.
PEOPLE ONLY WANT REAL FRIENDS, NOT IMAGINARY ONES. YOUR IDEA IS RIDICULOUS.
4-11-11 © 2011 Scott Adams, Inc./Dist. by Universal Uclick
HOW MANY FRIENDS DO YOU HAVE ON FACEBOOK?
SEVEN HUNDRED. WHY?

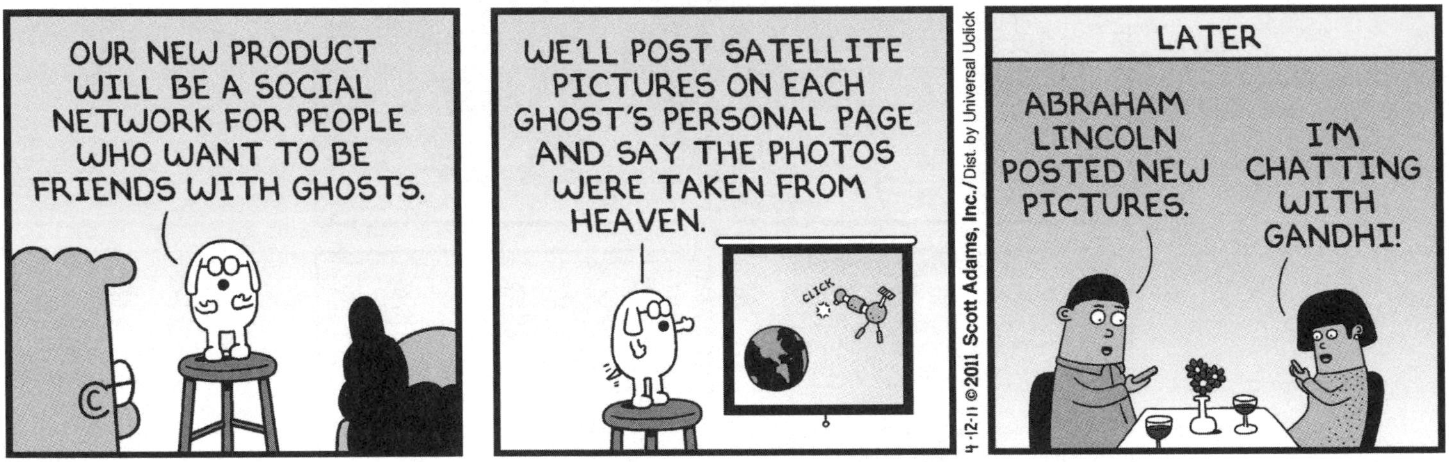
OUR NEW PRODUCT WILL BE A SOCIAL NETWORK FOR PEOPLE WHO WANT TO BE FRIENDS WITH GHOSTS.
WE'LL POST SATELLITE PICTURES ON EACH GHOST'S PERSONAL PAGE AND SAY THE PHOTOS WERE TAKEN FROM HEAVEN.
CLICK
4-12-11 © 2011 Scott Adams, Inc./Dist. by Universal Uclick
LATER
ABRAHAM LINCOLN POSTED NEW PICTURES.
I'M CHATTING WITH GANDHI!

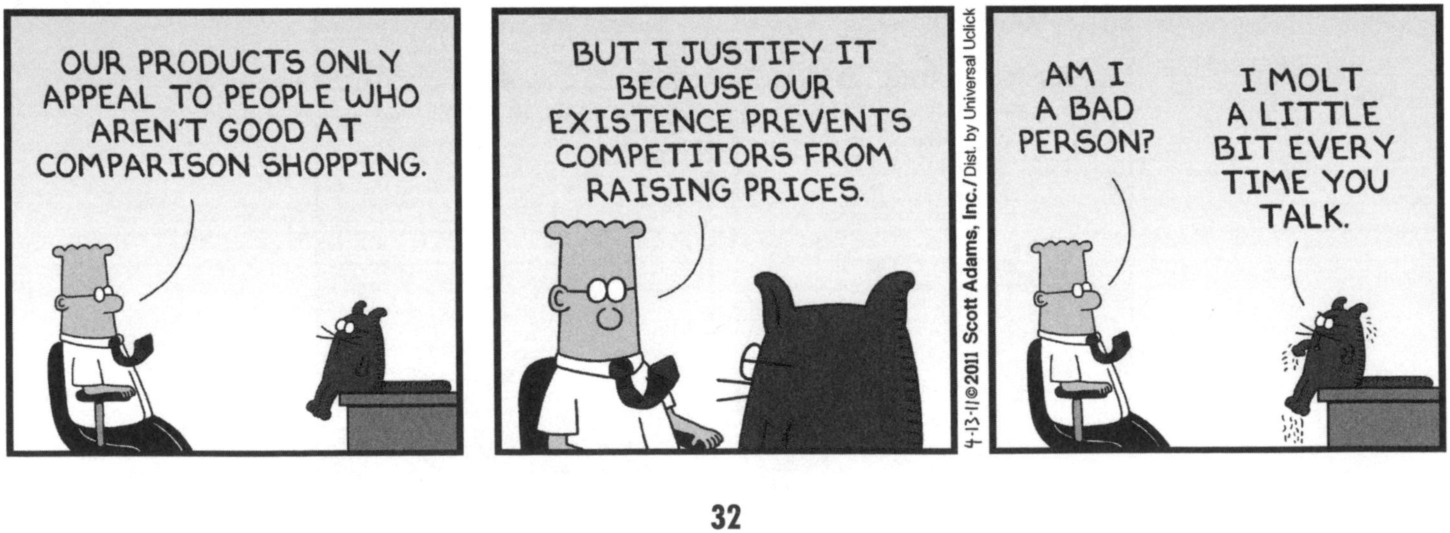
OUR PRODUCTS ONLY APPEAL TO PEOPLE WHO AREN'T GOOD AT COMPARISON SHOPPING.
BUT I JUSTIFY IT BECAUSE OUR EXISTENCE PREVENTS COMPETITORS FROM RAISING PRICES.
4-13-11 © 2011 Scott Adams, Inc./Dist. by Universal Uclick
AM I A BAD PERSON?
I MOLT A LITTLE BIT EVERY TIME YOU TALK.

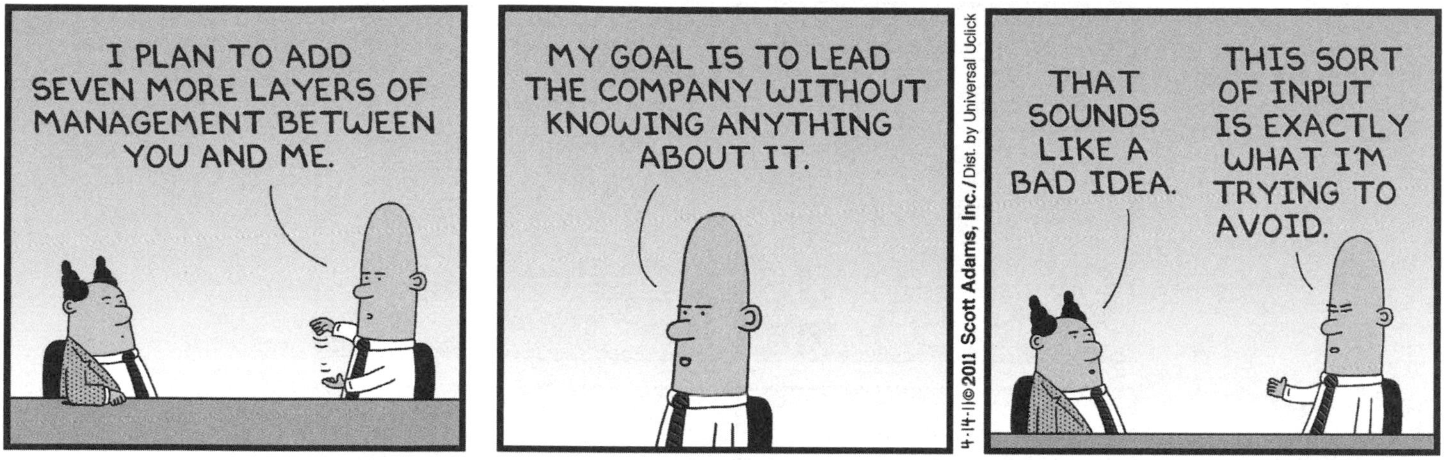
I PLAN TO ADD SEVEN MORE LAYERS OF MANAGEMENT BETWEEN YOU AND ME.
MY GOAL IS TO LEAD THE COMPANY WITHOUT KNOWING ANYTHING ABOUT IT.
4-14-11 ©2011 Scott Adams, Inc./Dist. by Universal Uclick
THAT SOUNDS LIKE A BAD IDEA.
THIS SORT OF INPUT IS EXACTLY WHAT I'M TRYING TO AVOID.

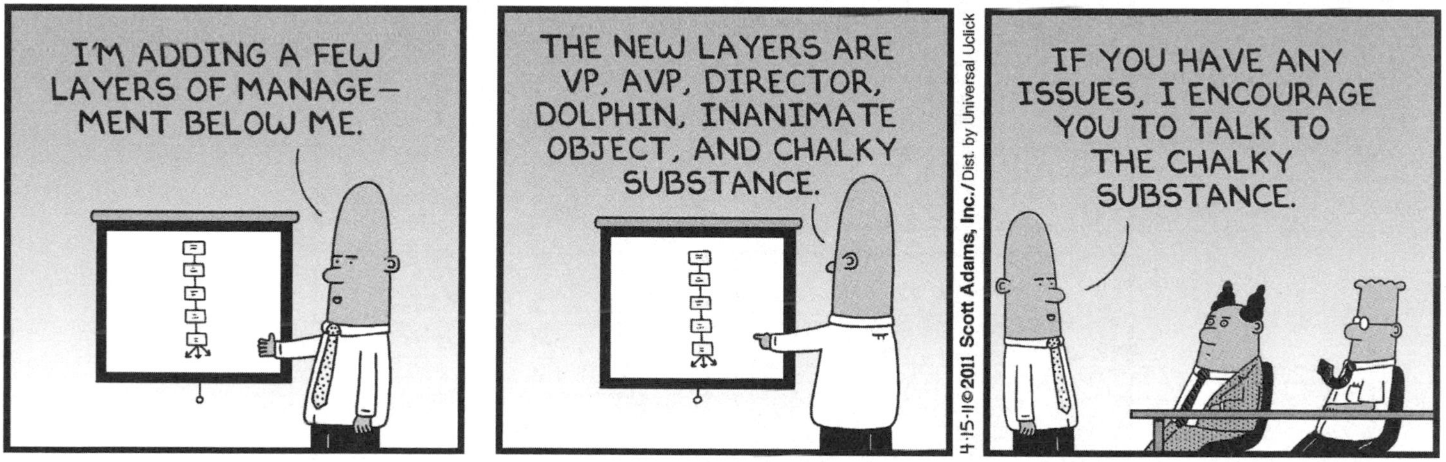
I'M ADDING A FEW LAYERS OF MANAGE-MENT BELOW ME.
THE NEW LAYERS ARE VP, AVP, DIRECTOR, DOLPHIN, INANIMATE OBJECT, AND CHALKY SUBSTANCE.
4-15-11 ©2011 Scott Adams, Inc./Dist. by Universal Uclick
IF YOU HAVE ANY ISSUES, I ENCOURAGE YOU TO TALK TO THE CHALKY SUBSTANCE.

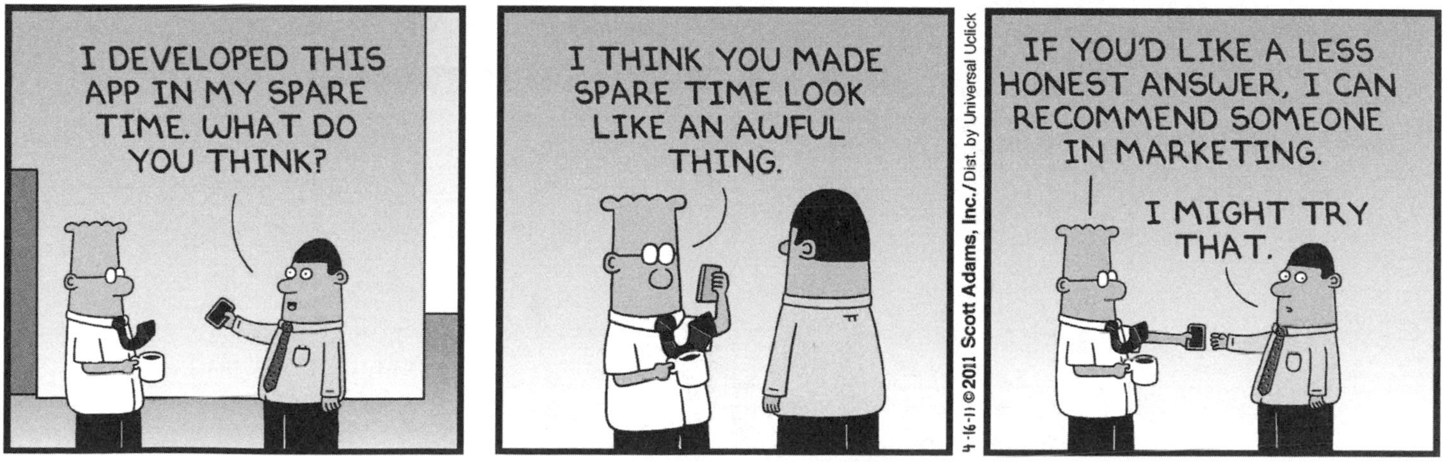
I DEVELOPED THIS APP IN MY SPARE TIME. WHAT DO YOU THINK?
I THINK YOU MADE SPARE TIME LOOK LIKE AN AWFUL THING.
4-16-11 ©2011 Scott Adams, Inc./Dist. by Universal Uclick
IF YOU'D LIKE A LESS HONEST ANSWER, I CAN RECOMMEND SOMEONE IN MARKETING.
I MIGHT TRY THAT.

AND WE PLAN TO BESTSHORE THE PRODUCTION.
WHAT?
WE SAY BESTSHORE NOW INSTEAD OF OFFSHORE.
IS THAT BECAUSE WE NEVER TRIED TO PICK THE BEST SHORE UNTIL NOW?
OF COURSE WE TRIED TO PICK THE BEST SHORE!
BUT WE NEVER SUCCEEDED BECAUSE WE'RE INCOMPETENT?
ALL I'M SAYING IS THAT SOME COUNTRIES ARE BETTER THAN OTHERS!
WE'RE RACISTS?
© 2011 Scott Adams, Inc. Dist. by Universal Uclick
4-17-11

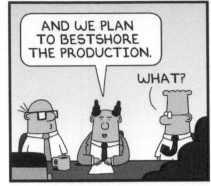

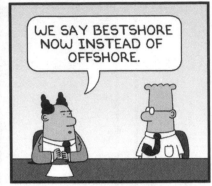

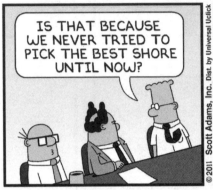

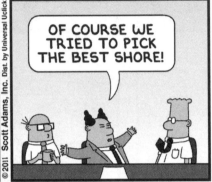

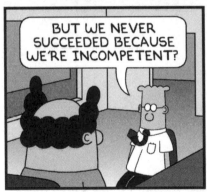

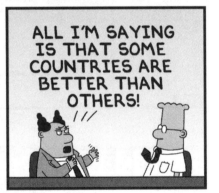

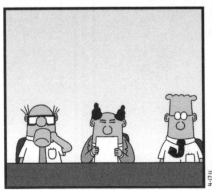

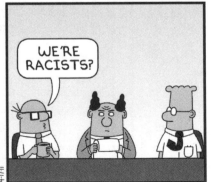

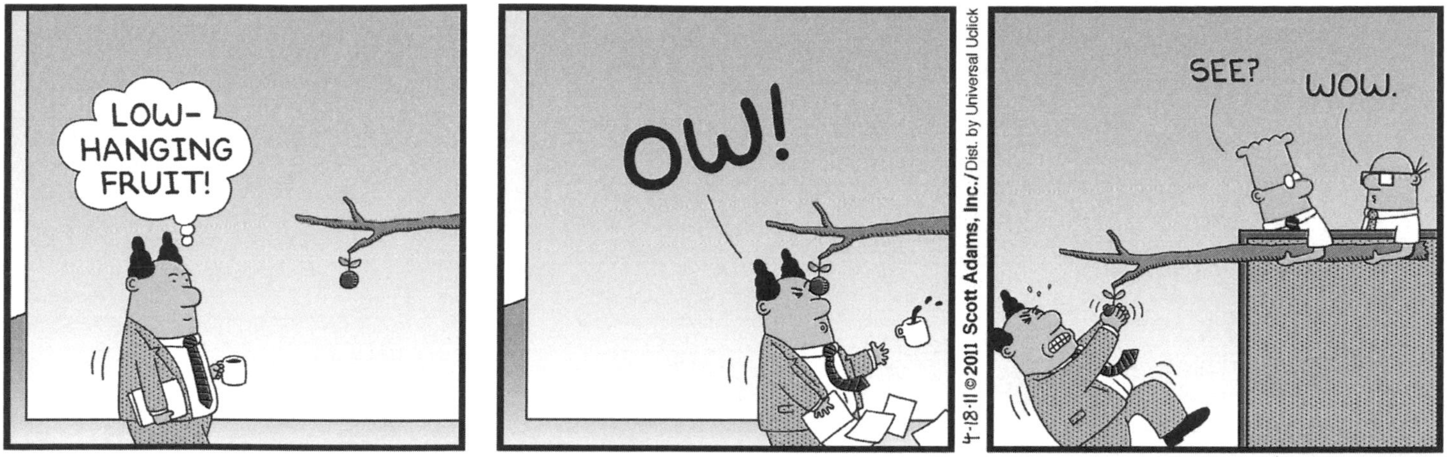
LOW-HANGING FRUIT!
OW!
4-18-11 © 2011 Scott Adams, Inc./Dist. by Universal Uclick
SEE?
WOW.

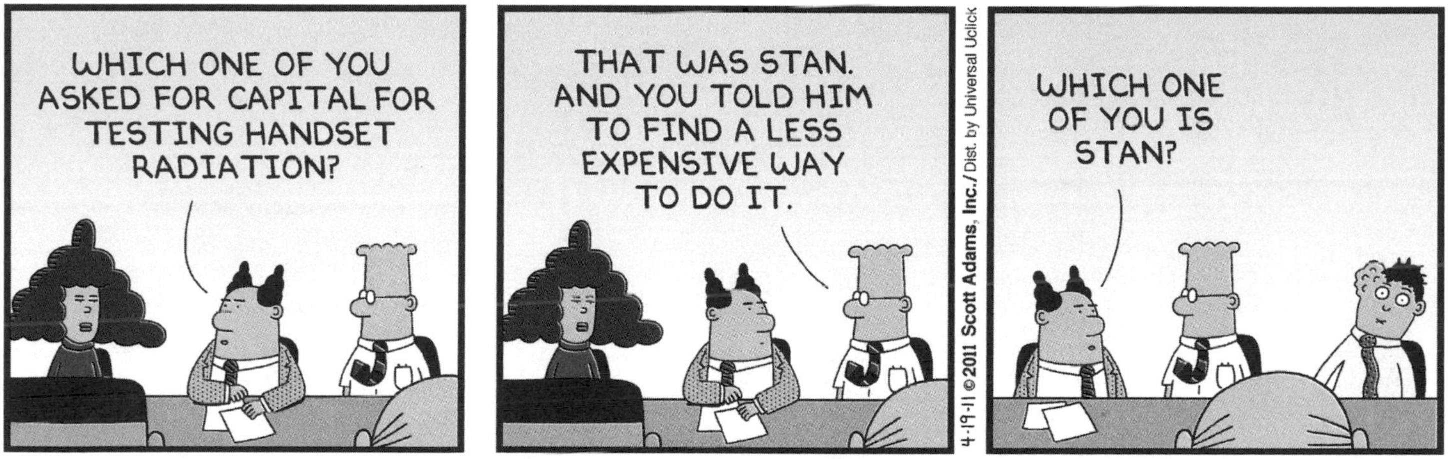
WHICH ONE OF YOU ASKED FOR CAPITAL FOR TESTING HANDSET RADIATION?
THAT WAS STAN. AND YOU TOLD HIM TO FIND A LESS EXPENSIVE WAY TO DO IT.
4-19-11 © 2011 Scott Adams, Inc./Dist. by Universal Uclick
WHICH ONE OF YOU IS STAN?

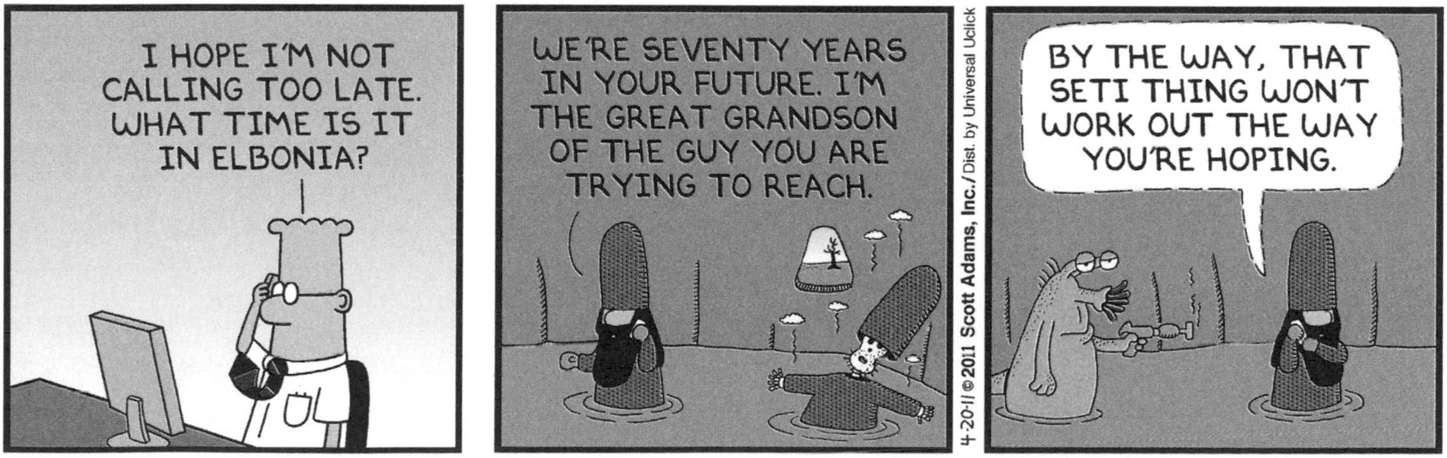
I HOPE I'M NOT CALLING TOO LATE. WHAT TIME IS IT IN ELBONIA?
WE'RE SEVENTY YEARS IN YOUR FUTURE. I'M THE GREAT GRANDSON OF THE GUY YOU ARE TRYING TO REACH.
4-20-11 © 2011 Scott Adams, Inc./Dist. by Universal Uclick
BY THE WAY, THAT SETI THING WON'T WORK OUT THE WAY YOU'RE HOPING.

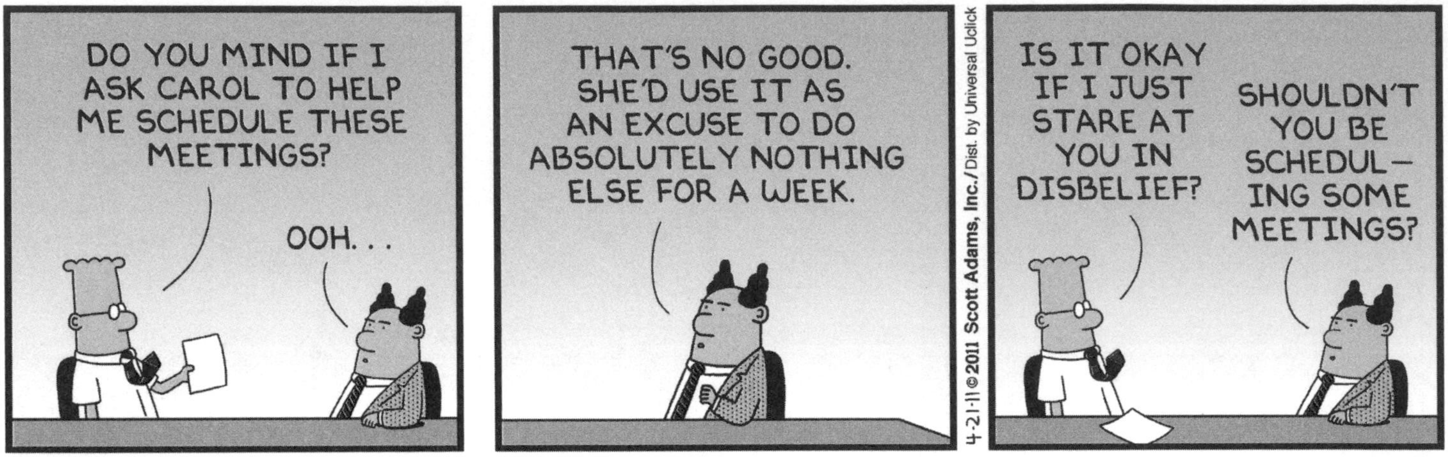
DO YOU MIND IF I ASK CAROL TO HELP ME SCHEDULE THESE MEETINGS?
OOH. . .
THAT'S NO GOOD. SHE'D USE IT AS AN EXCUSE TO DO ABSOLUTELY NOTHING ELSE FOR A WEEK.
4·21·11 ©2011 Scott Adams, Inc./Dist. by Universal Uclick
IS IT OKAY IF I JUST STARE AT YOU IN DISBELIEF?
SHOULDN'T YOU BE SCHEDUL-ING SOME MEETINGS?

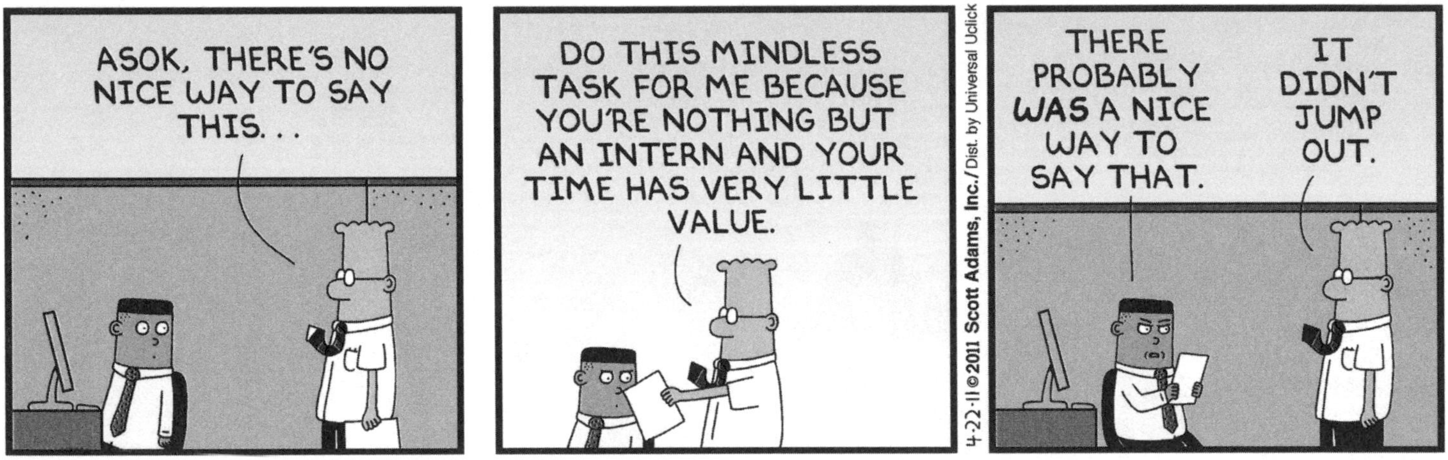
ASOK, THERE'S NO NICE WAY TO SAY THIS. . .
DO THIS MINDLESS TASK FOR ME BECAUSE YOU'RE NOTHING BUT AN INTERN AND YOUR TIME HAS VERY LITTLE VALUE.
4·22·11 ©2011 Scott Adams, Inc./Dist. by Universal Uclick
THERE PROBABLY WAS A NICE WAY TO SAY THAT.
IT DIDN'T JUMP OUT.

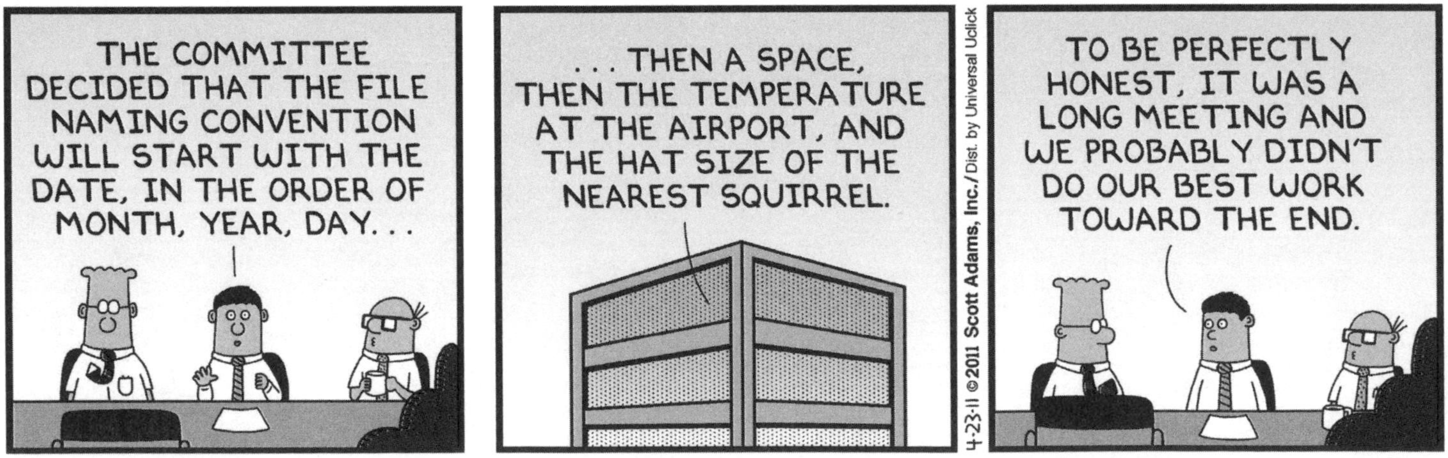
THE COMMITTEE DECIDED THAT THE FILE NAMING CONVENTION WILL START WITH THE DATE, IN THE ORDER OF MONTH, YEAR, DAY. . .
. . . THEN A SPACE, THEN THE TEMPERATURE AT THE AIRPORT, AND THE HAT SIZE OF THE NEAREST SQUIRREL.
4·23·11 ©2011 Scott Adams, Inc./Dist. by Universal Uclick
TO BE PERFECTLY HONEST, IT WAS A LONG MEETING AND WE PROBABLY DIDN'T DO OUR BEST WORK TOWARD THE END.

THE FIRST THING ON THE AGENDA. . .
HOLD ON. I DON'T KNOW ANYTHING ABOUT THIS GUY.
WHAT'S THE DIFFERENCE?
I NEED TO KNOW HOW IMPORTANT HE IS.
SHOULD I PRETEND TO LIKE HIS JOKES? SHOULD I NOD IN AGREEMENT NO MATTER WHAT HE SAYS?
YOU CAN CALL ME ANYTHING. JUST DON'T CALL ME LATE FOR DINNER.
HA HA HA HA HA HA HA HA HA HA!!!
I HOPE I DIDN'T WASTE THAT.
©2011 Scott Adams, Inc. Dist. by Universal Uclick
4-24-11

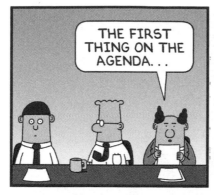

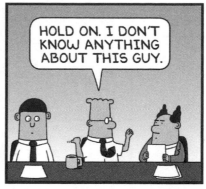

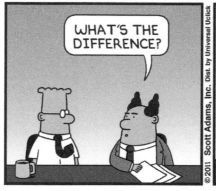

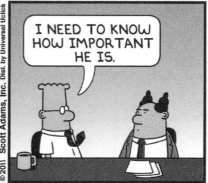

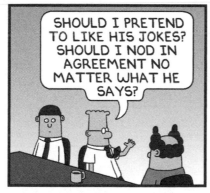

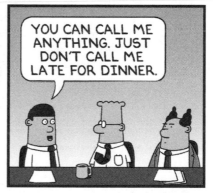

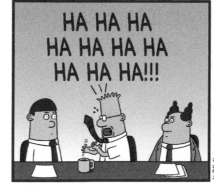

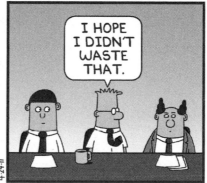

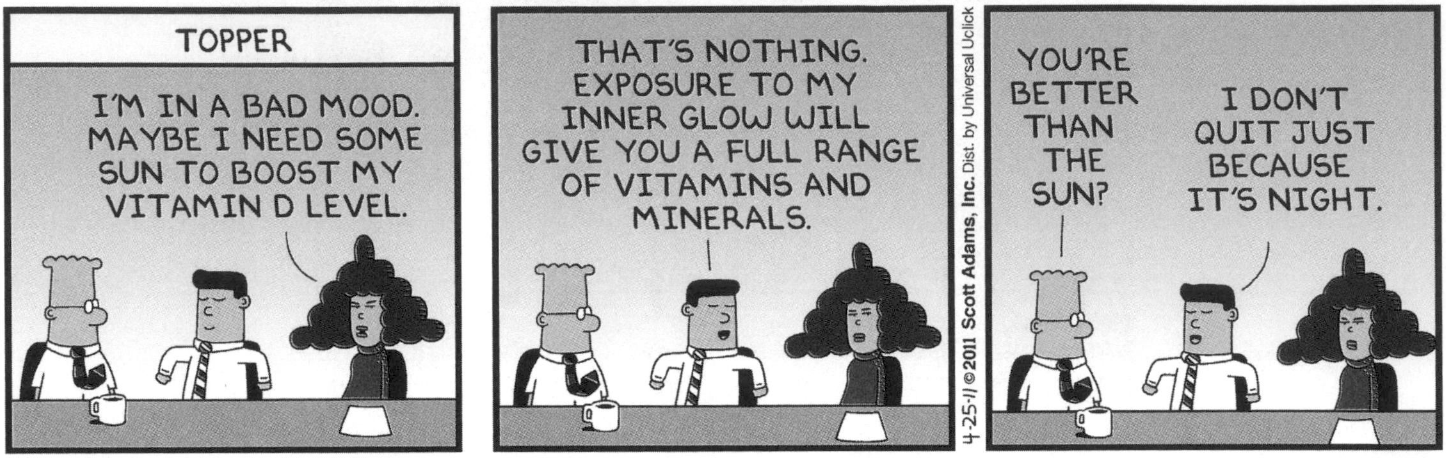
TOPPER
I'M IN A BAD MOOD. MAYBE I NEED SOME SUN TO BOOST MY VITAMIN D LEVEL.
THAT'S NOTHING. EXPOSURE TO MY INNER GLOW WILL GIVE YOU A FULL RANGE OF VITAMINS AND MINERALS.
4-25-11 ©2011 Scott Adams, Inc. Dist. by Universal Uclick
YOU'RE BETTER THAN THE SUN?
I DON'T QUIT JUST BECAUSE IT'S NIGHT.

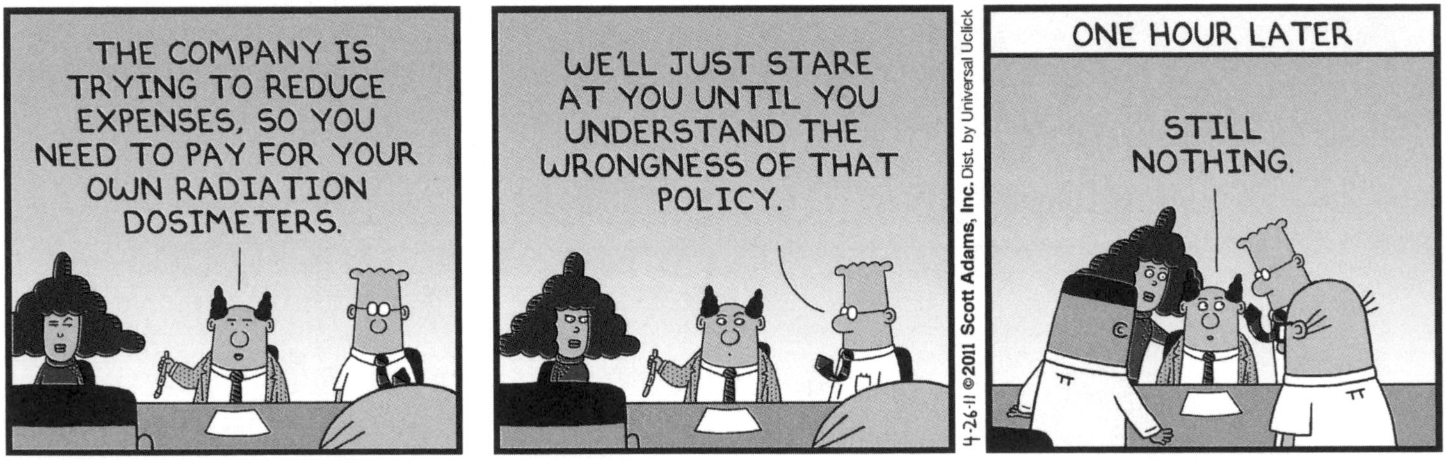
THE COMPANY IS TRYING TO REDUCE EXPENSES, SO YOU NEED TO PAY FOR YOUR OWN RADIATION DOSIMETERS.
WE'LL JUST STARE AT YOU UNTIL YOU UNDERSTAND THE WRONGNESS OF THAT POLICY.
4-26-11 ©2011 Scott Adams, Inc. Dist. by Universal Uclick
ONE HOUR LATER
STILL NOTHING.

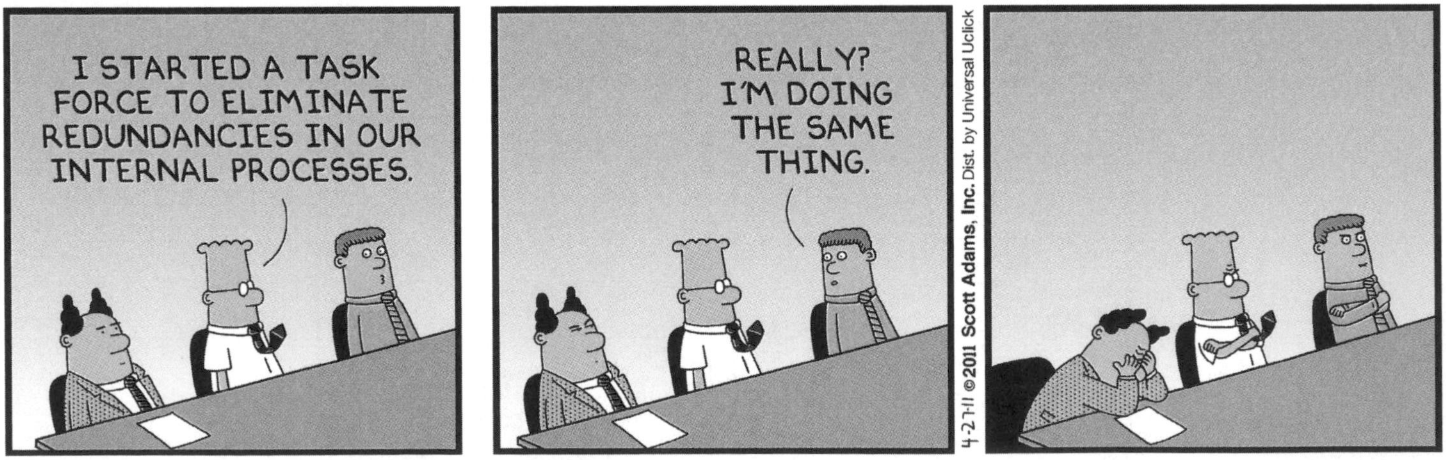
I STARTED A TASK FORCE TO ELIMINATE REDUNDANCIES IN OUR INTERNAL PROCESSES.
REALLY? I'M DOING THE SAME THING.
4-27-11 ©2011 Scott Adams, Inc. Dist. by Universal Uclick

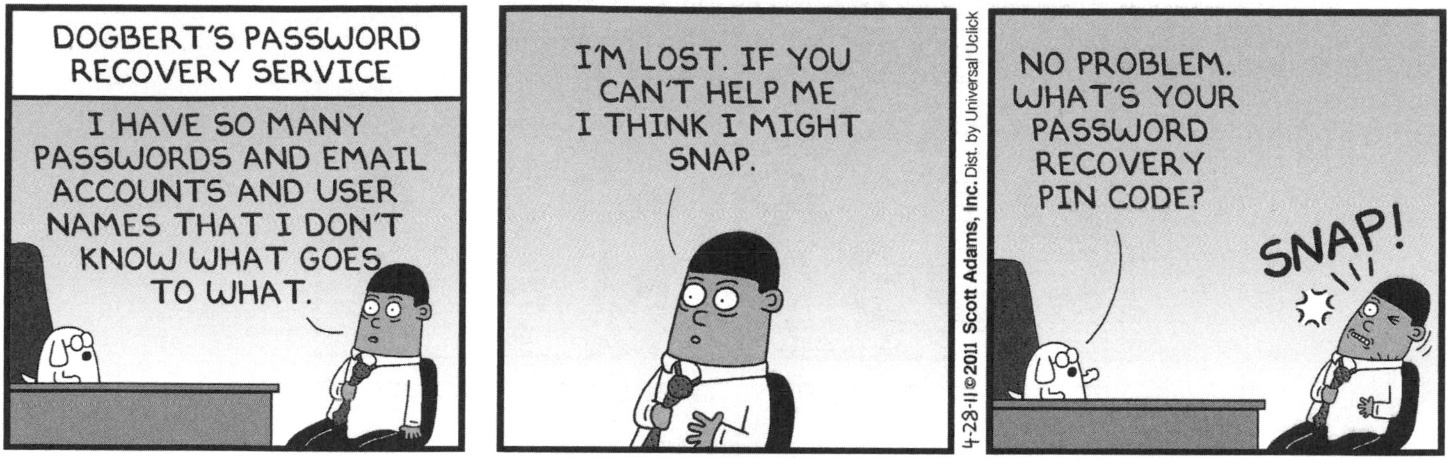
DOGBERT'S PASSWORD RECOVERY SERVICE
I HAVE SO MANY PASSWORDS AND EMAIL ACCOUNTS AND USER NAMES THAT I DON'T KNOW WHAT GOES TO WHAT.
I'M LOST. IF YOU CAN'T HELP ME I THINK I MIGHT SNAP.
4-28-11 ©2011 Scott Adams, Inc. Dist. by Universal Uclick
NO PROBLEM. WHAT'S YOUR PASSWORD RECOVERY PIN CODE?
SNAP!

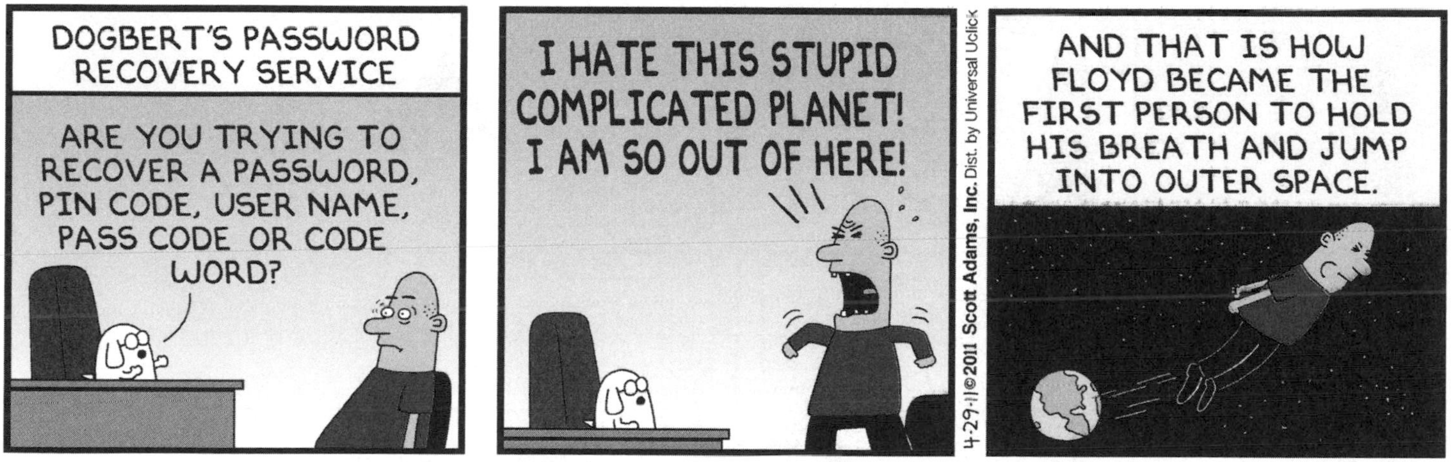
DOGBERT'S PASSWORD RECOVERY SERVICE
ARE YOU TRYING TO RECOVER A PASSWORD, PIN CODE, USER NAME, PASS CODE OR CODE WORD?
I HATE THIS STUPID COMPLICATED PLANET! I AM SO OUT OF HERE!
4-29-11 ©2011 Scott Adams, Inc. Dist. by Universal Uclick
AND THAT IS HOW FLOYD BECAME THE FIRST PERSON TO HOLD HIS BREATH AND JUMP INTO OUTER SPACE.

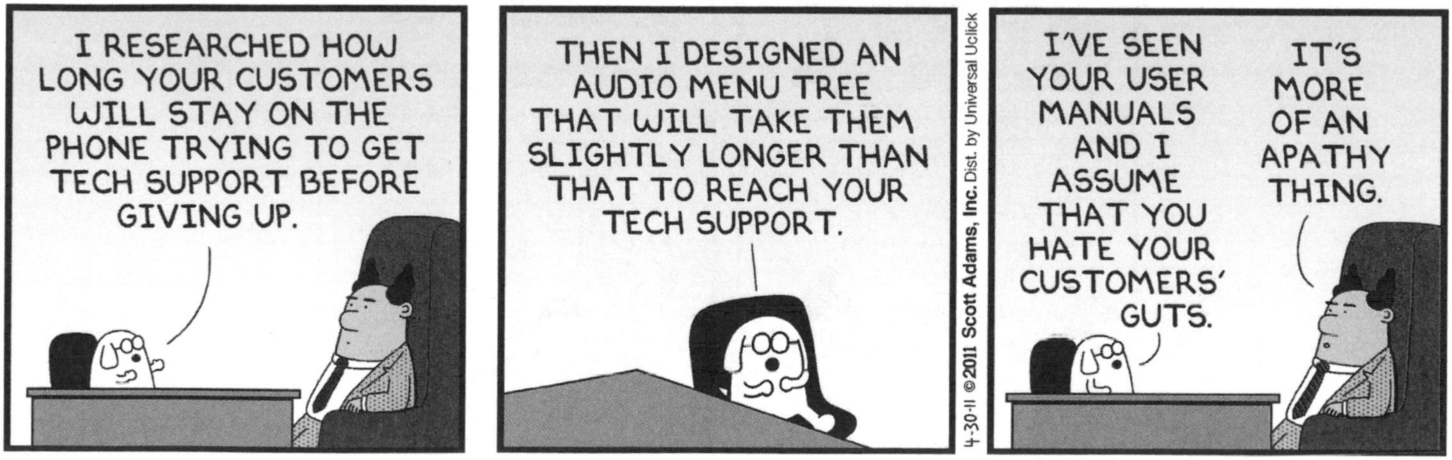
I RESEARCHED HOW LONG YOUR CUSTOMERS WILL STAY ON THE PHONE TRYING TO GET TECH SUPPORT BEFORE GIVING UP.
THEN I DESIGNED AN AUDIO MENU TREE THAT WILL TAKE THEM SLIGHTLY LONGER THAN THAT TO REACH YOUR TECH SUPPORT.
4-30-11 ©2011 Scott Adams, Inc. Dist. by Universal Uclick
I'VE SEEN YOUR USER MANUALS AND I ASSUME THAT YOU HATE YOUR CUSTOMERS' GUTS.
IT'S MORE OF AN APATHY THING.

WHO WANTS TO SEE A PICTURE OF MY NEW BOAT?
THAT'S A VERY GOOD QUESTION.
IF WE CONSIDER THE FACT THAT WE WORK MUCH HARDER THAN HE DOES. . .
AND WE HAVE VALUABLE ENGINEERING SKILLS, WHEREAS HE CAN'T OPERATE THE GPS IN HIS SUV. . .
AND FOR SOME REASON WE DON'T GET PAID ENOUGH TO BUY IMPRESSIVE BOATS.
AND WE HAVE NO NAUTICAL INTERESTS WHATSOEVER.
I THINK YOUR BEST BET IS PEOPLE WHO DON'T KNOW YOU.
AND YOU ARE?
THIS ONLY WORKS IF WE DON'T GET TOO FAMILIAR.
©2011 Scott Adams, Inc. Dist. by Universal Uclick
5-1-11

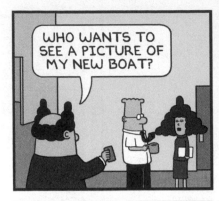

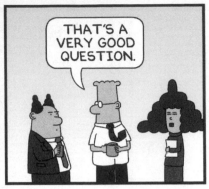

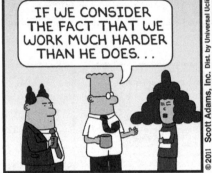

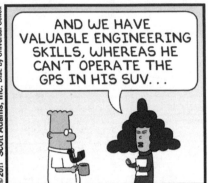

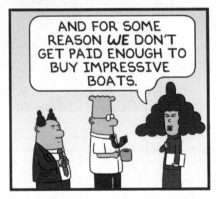

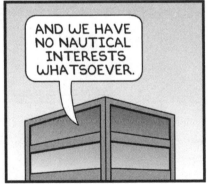

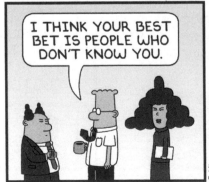

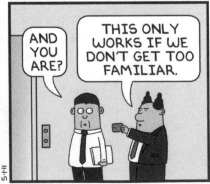

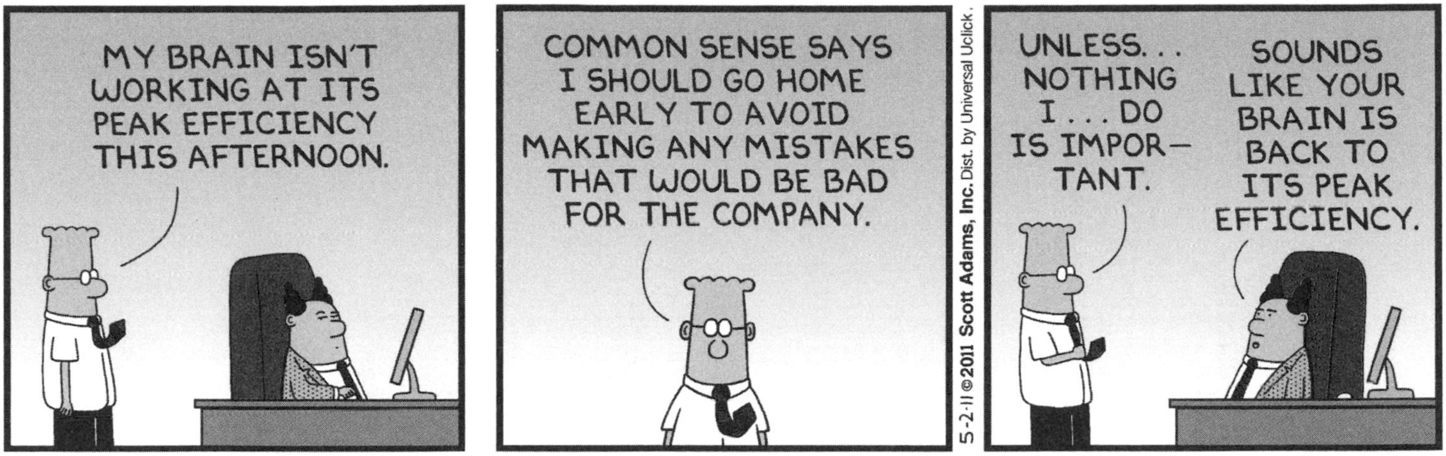
MY BRAIN ISN'T WORKING AT ITS PEAK EFFICIENCY THIS AFTERNOON.
COMMON SENSE SAYS I SHOULD GO HOME EARLY TO AVOID MAKING ANY MISTAKES THAT WOULD BE BAD FOR THE COMPANY.
5-2-11 ©2011 Scott Adams, Inc. Dist. by Universal Uclick.
UNLESS. . . NOTHING I . . . DO IS IMPOR-TANT.
SOUNDS LIKE YOUR BRAIN IS BACK TO ITS PEAK EFFICIENCY.

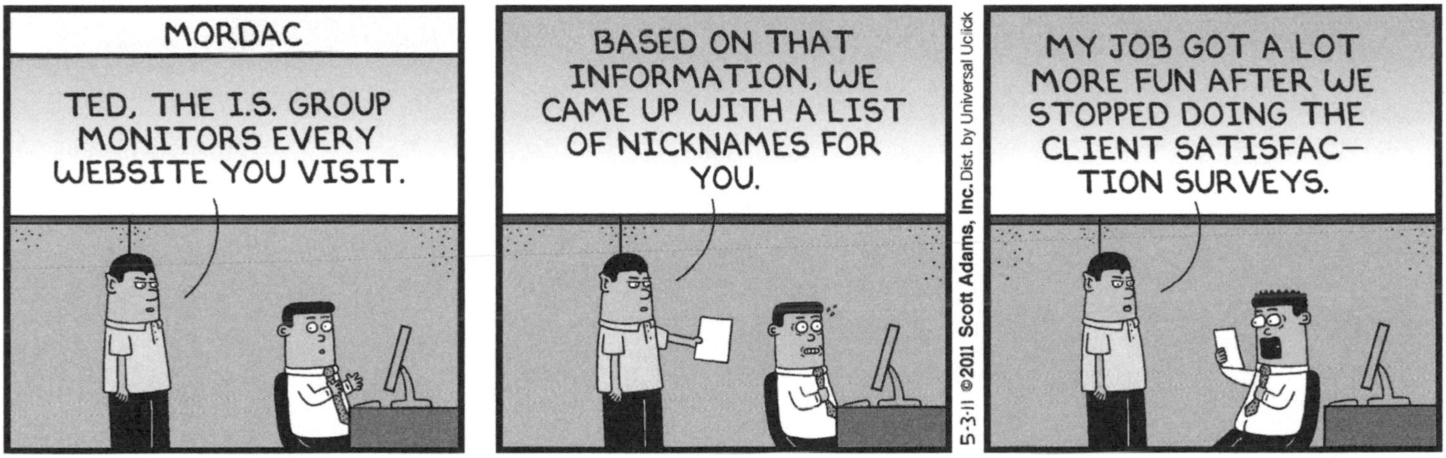
MORDAC
TED, THE I.S. GROUP MONITORS EVERY WEBSITE YOU VISIT.
BASED ON THAT INFORMATION, WE CAME UP WITH A LIST OF NICKNAMES FOR YOU.
5-3-11 ©2011 Scott Adams, Inc. Dist. by Universal Uclick
MY JOB GOT A LOT MORE FUN AFTER WE STOPPED DOING THE CLIENT SATISFAC-TION SURVEYS.

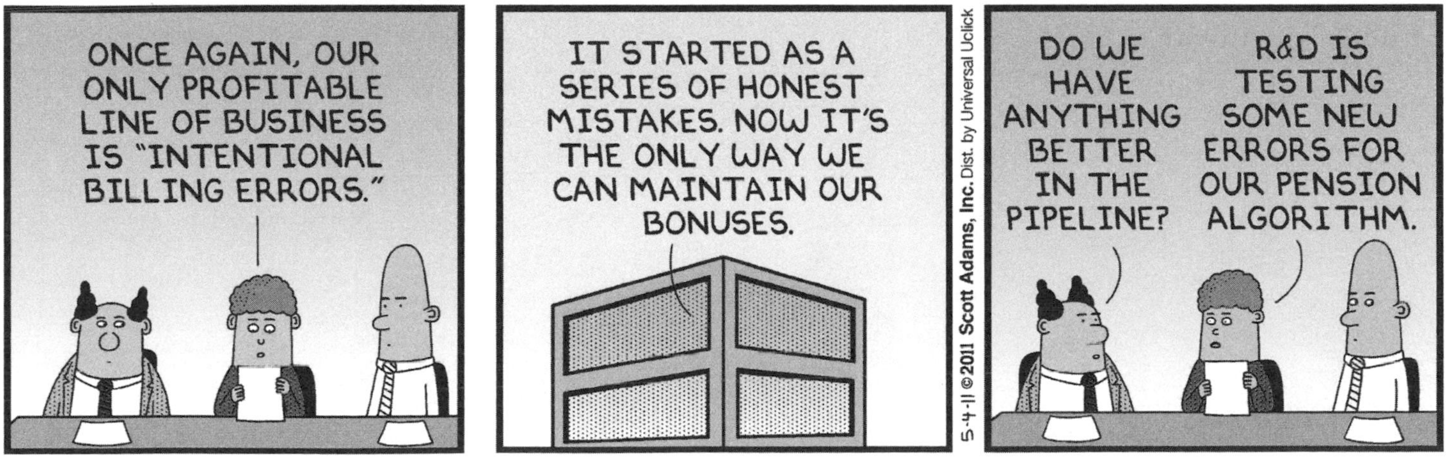
ONCE AGAIN, OUR ONLY PROFITABLE LINE OF BUSINESS IS "INTENTIONAL BILLING ERRORS."
IT STARTED AS A SERIES OF HONEST MISTAKES. NOW IT'S THE ONLY WAY WE CAN MAINTAIN OUR BONUSES.
5-4-11 ©2011 Scott Adams, Inc. Dist. by Universal Uclick
DO WE HAVE ANYTHING BETTER IN THE PIPELINE?
R&D IS TESTING SOME NEW ERRORS FOR OUR PENSION ALGORITHM.

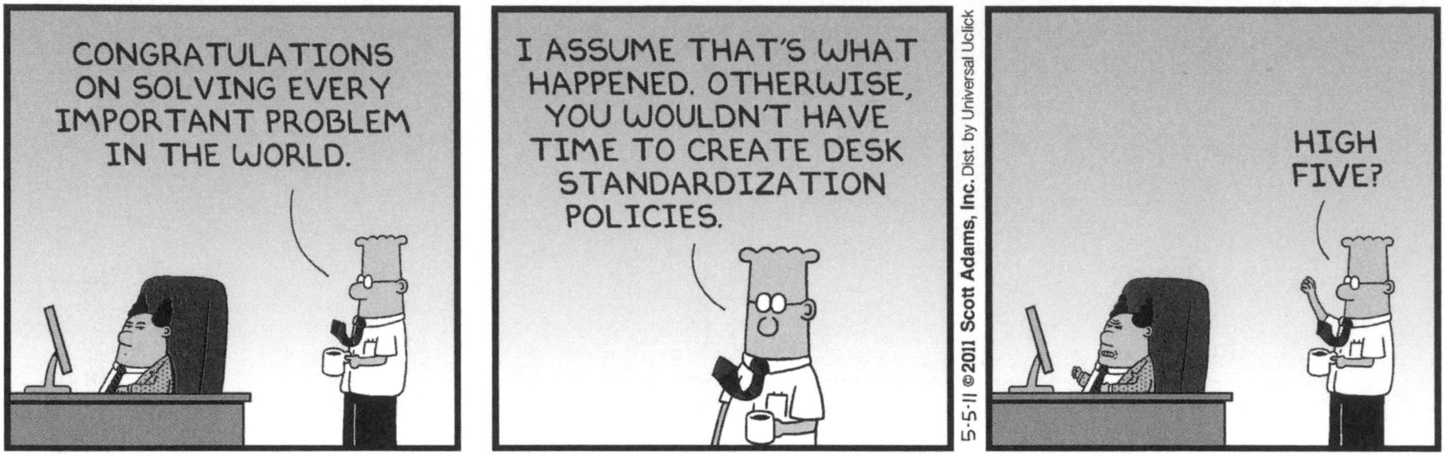
CONGRATULATIONS ON SOLVING EVERY IMPORTANT PROBLEM IN THE WORLD.
I ASSUME THAT'S WHAT HAPPENED. OTHERWISE, YOU WOULDN'T HAVE TIME TO CREATE DESK STANDARDIZATION POLICIES.
5-5-11 ©2011 Scott Adams, Inc. Dist. by Universal Uclick
HIGH FIVE?

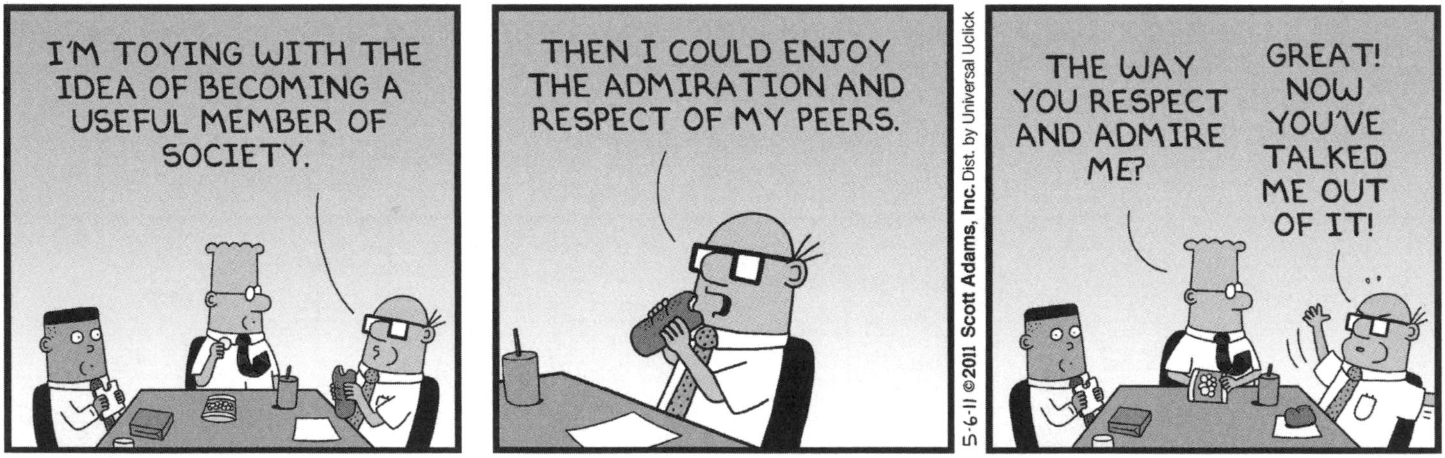
I'M TOYING WITH THE IDEA OF BECOMING A USEFUL MEMBER OF SOCIETY.
THEN I COULD ENJOY THE ADMIRATION AND RESPECT OF MY PEERS.
5-6-11 ©2011 Scott Adams, Inc. Dist. by Universal Uclick
THE WAY YOU RESPECT AND ADMIRE ME?
GREAT! NOW YOU'VE TALKED ME OUT OF IT!

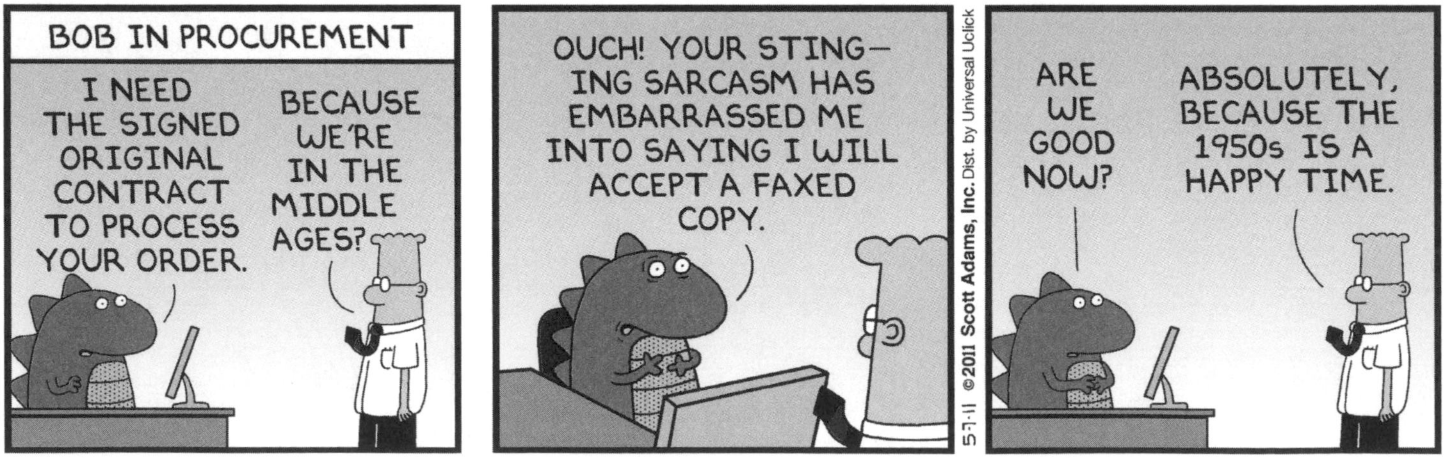
BOB IN PROCUREMENT
I NEED THE SIGNED ORIGINAL CONTRACT TO PROCESS YOUR ORDER.
BECAUSE WE'RE IN THE MIDDLE AGES?
OUCH! YOUR STING-ING SARCASM HAS EMBARRASSED ME INTO SAYING I WILL ACCEPT A FAXED COPY.
5-7-11 ©2011 Scott Adams, Inc. Dist. by Universal Uclick
ARE WE GOOD NOW?
ABSOLUTELY, BECAUSE THE 1950s IS A HAPPY TIME.

IN MY SPARE TIME I CREATED SOME AWESOME NEW FEATURES FOR OUR PRODUCT.
GAAAA!!!! SHUT THE DOOR!
WHAT?!!
YOU FOOL! IF MY BOSS FINDS OUT YOU HAVE SPARE TIME, HE'LL THINK WE'RE OVERSTAFFED!
YOU CAN NEVER SPEAK OF THESE AWESOME NEW FEATURES AGAIN.
I'M CONFUSED. YOU TOLD ME I NEED TO GO ABOVE AND BEYOND MY JOB DESCRIPTION TO GET THE HIGHEST PERFORMANCE RATING.
THAT'S JUST SOME-THING I SAY TO KEEP YOU FROM GETTING A HEALTHY RAISE.
SO. . . I LOSE NO MATTER WHAT I DO?
FOR WHAT IT'S WORTH, YOU'RE DOING BETTER THAN OUR CUSTOMERS.
© 2011 Scott Adams, Inc./Dist. by Universal Uclick
5-8-11

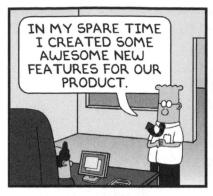

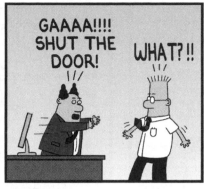

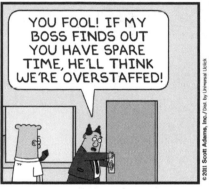

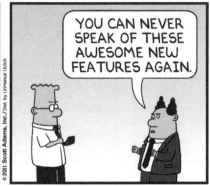

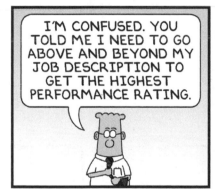

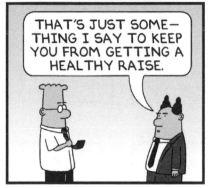

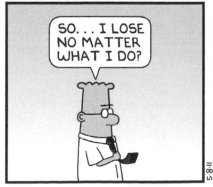

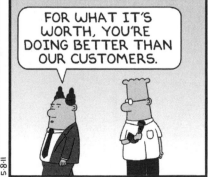

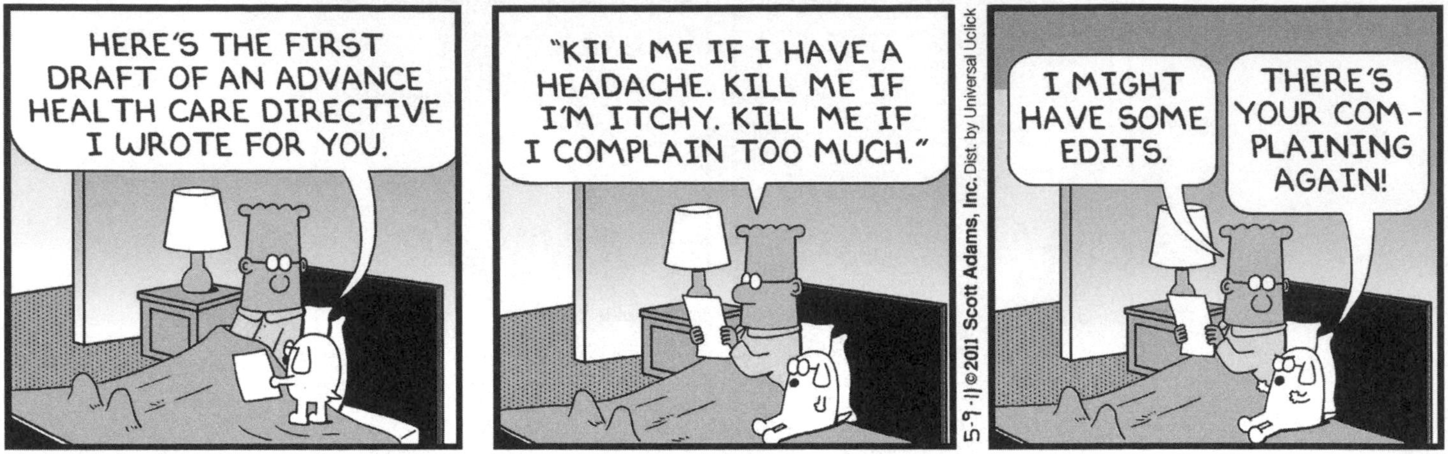
HERE'S THE FIRST DRAFT OF AN ADVANCE HEALTH CARE DIRECTIVE I WROTE FOR YOU.
"KILL ME IF I HAVE A HEADACHE. KILL ME IF I'M ITCHY. KILL ME IF I COMPLAIN TOO MUCH."
I MIGHT HAVE SOME EDITS.
THERE'S YOUR COM-PLAINING AGAIN!
5-9-11 ©2011 Scott Adams, Inc. Dist. by Universal Uclick

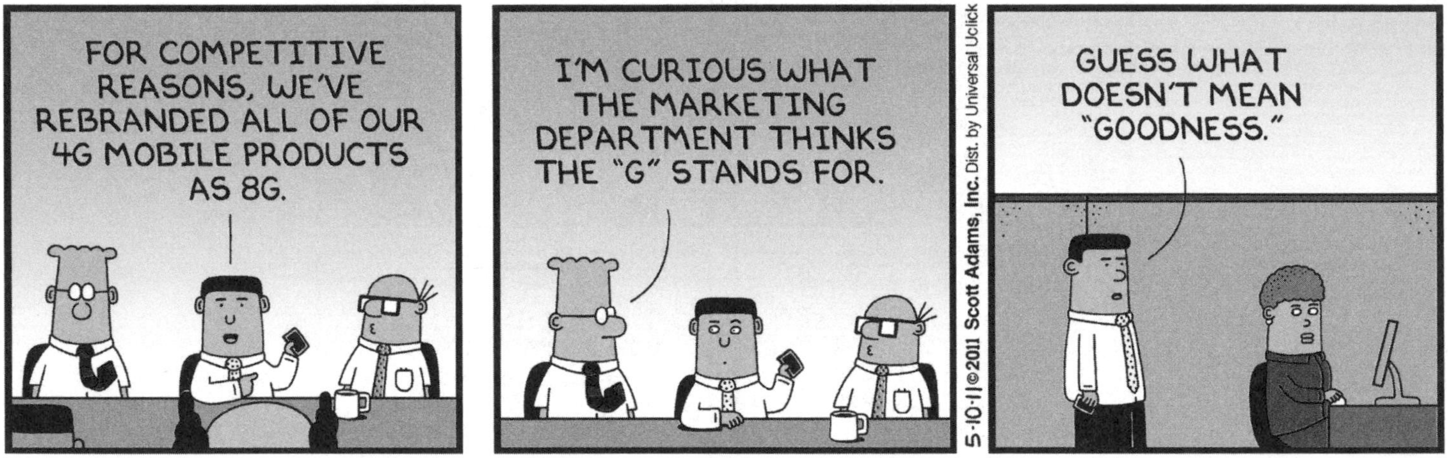
FOR COMPETITIVE REASONS, WE'VE REBRANDED ALL OF OUR 4G MOBILE PRODUCTS AS 8G.
I'M CURIOUS WHAT THE MARKETING DEPARTMENT THINKS THE "G" STANDS FOR.
GUESS WHAT DOESN'T MEAN "GOODNESS."
5-10-11 ©2011 Scott Adams, Inc. Dist. by Universal Uclick

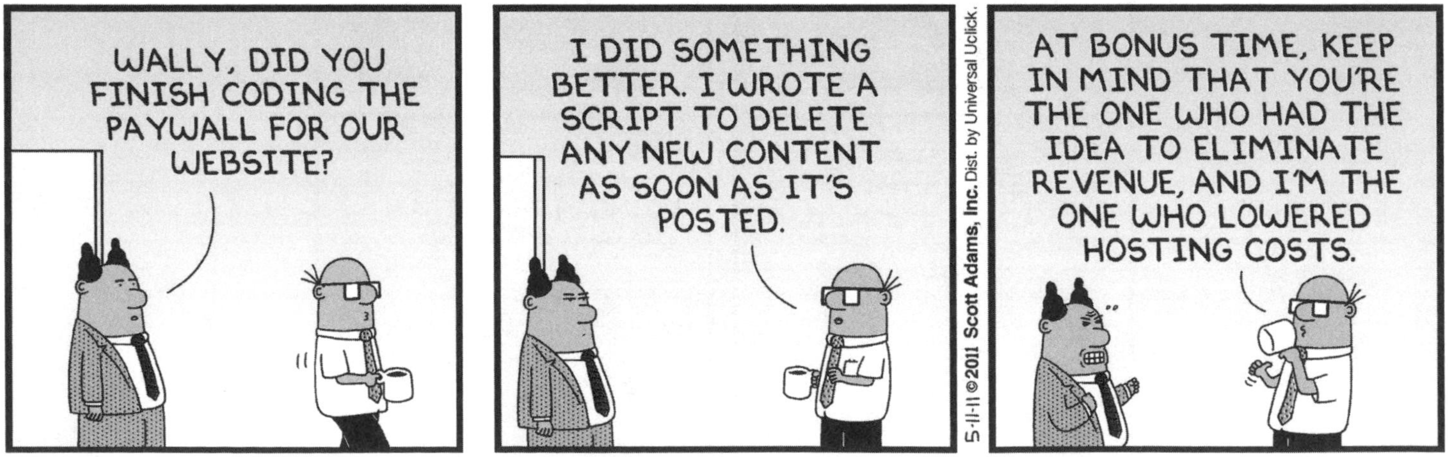
WALLY, DID YOU FINISH CODING THE PAYWALL FOR OUR WEBSITE?
I DID SOMETHING BETTER. I WROTE A SCRIPT TO DELETE ANY NEW CONTENT AS SOON AS IT'S POSTED.
AT BONUS TIME, KEEP IN MIND THAT YOU'RE THE ONE WHO HAD THE IDEA TO ELIMINATE REVENUE, AND I'M THE ONE WHO LOWERED HOSTING COSTS.
5-11-11 ©2011 Scott Adams, Inc. Dist. by Universal Uclick.

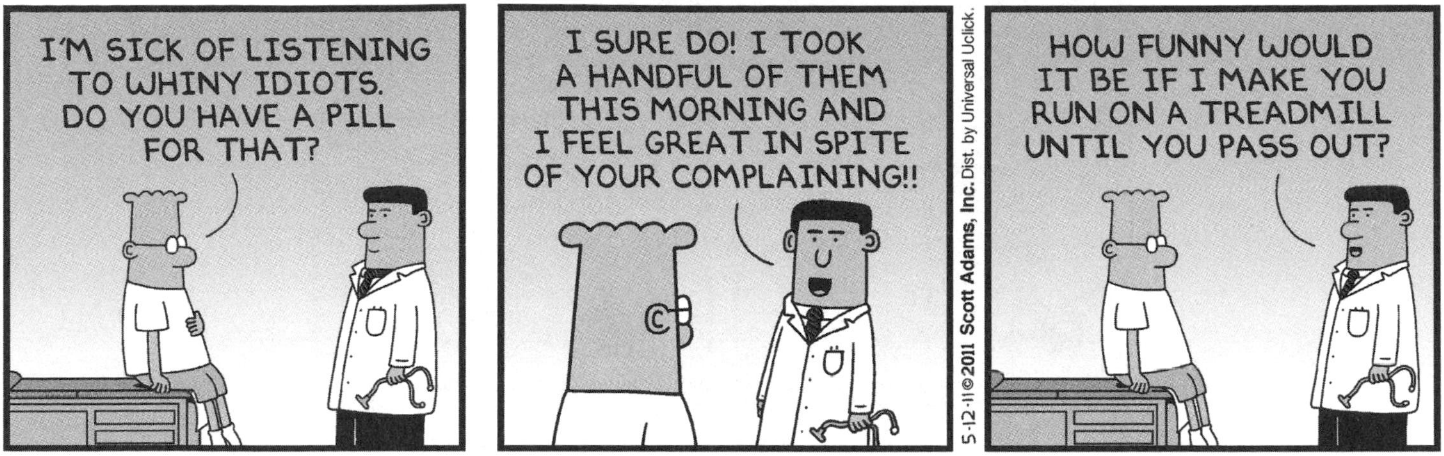
I'M SICK OF LISTENING TO WHINY IDIOTS. DO YOU HAVE A PILL FOR THAT?
I SURE DO! I TOOK A HANDFUL OF THEM THIS MORNING AND I FEEL GREAT IN SPITE OF YOUR COMPLAINING!!
HOW FUNNY WOULD IT BE IF I MAKE YOU RUN ON A TREADMILL UNTIL YOU PASS OUT?

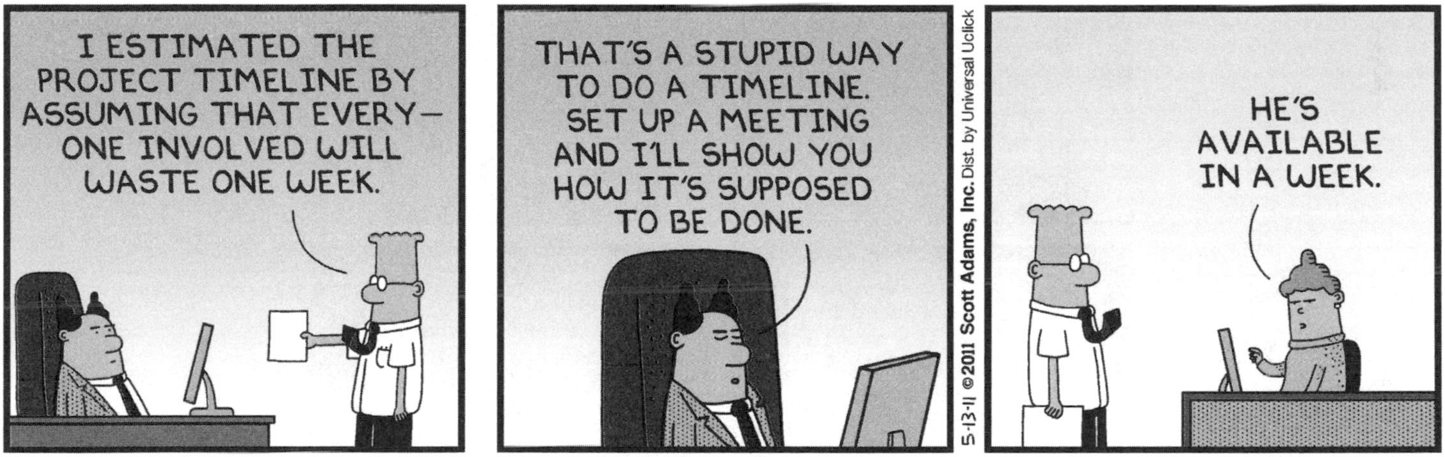
I ESTIMATED THE PROJECT TIMELINE BY ASSUMING THAT EVERY-ONE INVOLVED WILL WASTE ONE WEEK.
THAT'S A STUPID WAY TO DO A TIMELINE. SET UP A MEETING AND I'LL SHOW YOU HOW IT'S SUPPOSED TO BE DONE.
HE'S AVAILABLE IN A WEEK.

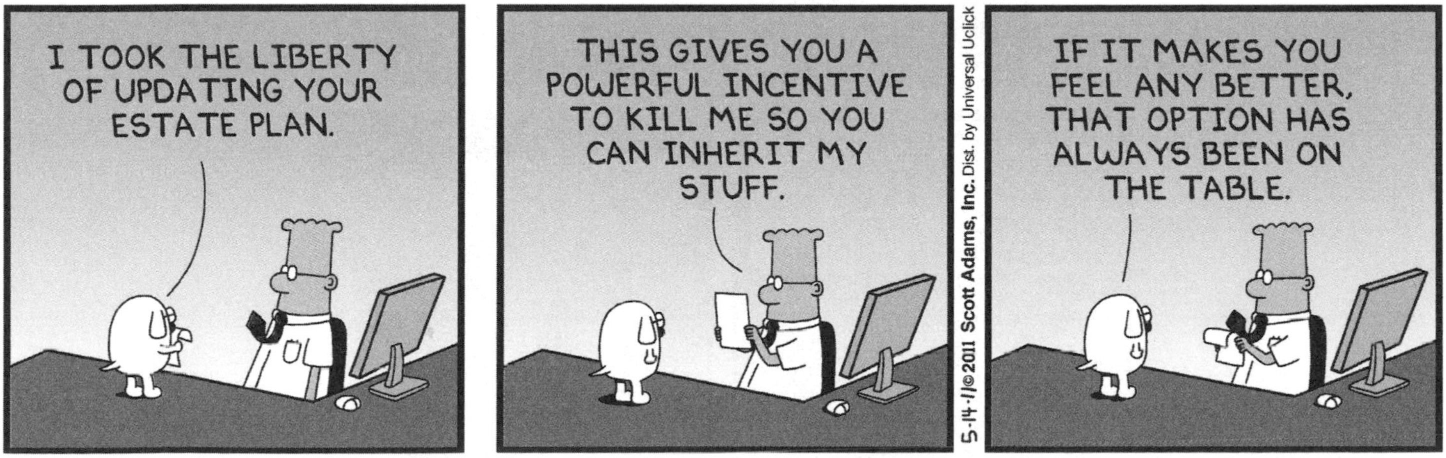
I TOOK THE LIBERTY OF UPDATING YOUR ESTATE PLAN.
THIS GIVES YOU A POWERFUL INCENTIVE TO KILL ME SO YOU CAN INHERIT MY STUFF.
IF IT MAKES YOU FEEL ANY BETTER, THAT OPTION HAS ALWAYS BEEN ON THE TABLE.

WOULD YOU MIND FILLING OUT THIS CUSTOMER SURVEY SO WE KNOW HOW WE'RE DOING?
I DON'T HAVE TIME TO FILL OUT SURVEYS ABOUT EVERYTHING I DO.
BUT YOU'RE MAKING ME FEEL GUILTY ABOUT NOT DOING IT.
OH NO! YOU TURNED A GOOD CUSTOMER EXPERIENCE INTO SOMETHING UGLY.
IT'S GETTING ALL AWKWARD AND I'M LOOKING LIKE A BIG JERK IN FRONT OF MY DATE.
NOW I CAN NEVER AGAIN EAT HERE BECAUSE I'M AFRAID OF WHAT YOU'LL DO TO MY FOOD.
YOU'VE RUINED MY FAVORITE RESTAURANT, AS WELL AS MY CHANCE OF ROMANCE WITH THIS WOMAN.
. . . FAVORITE RESTAURANT. . .
WHAT ARE YOU DOING LATER?
© 2011 Scott Adams, Inc./Dist. by Universal Uclick
5-15-11

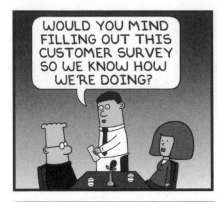

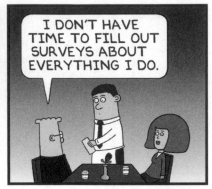

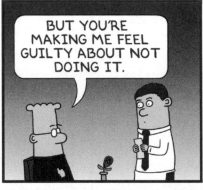

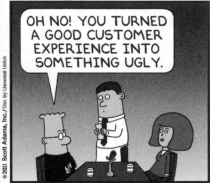

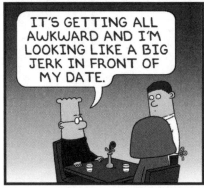

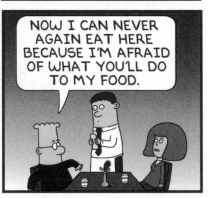

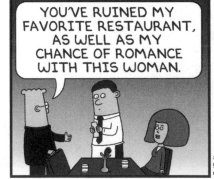

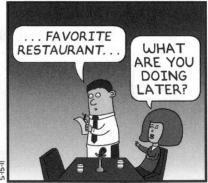

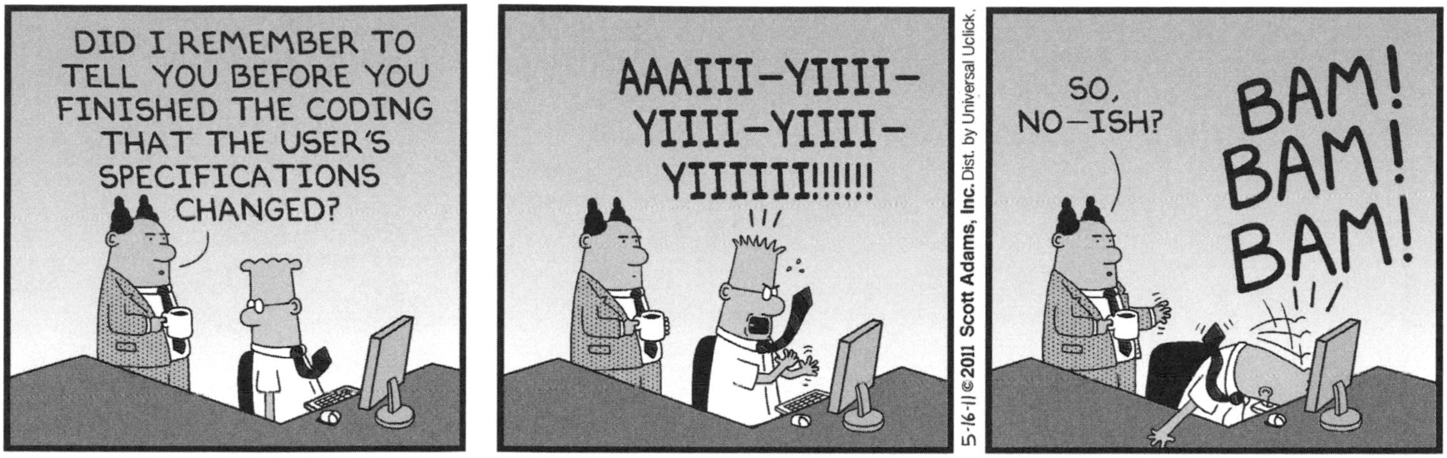
DID I REMEMBER TO TELL YOU BEFORE YOU FINISHED THE CODING THAT THE USER'S SPECIFICATIONS CHANGED?
AAAIII-YIIII-YIIII-YIIII-YIIIIII!!!!!!
5-16-11 ©2011 Scott Adams, Inc. Dist. by Universal Uclick.
SO, NO-ISH?
BAM! BAM! BAM!

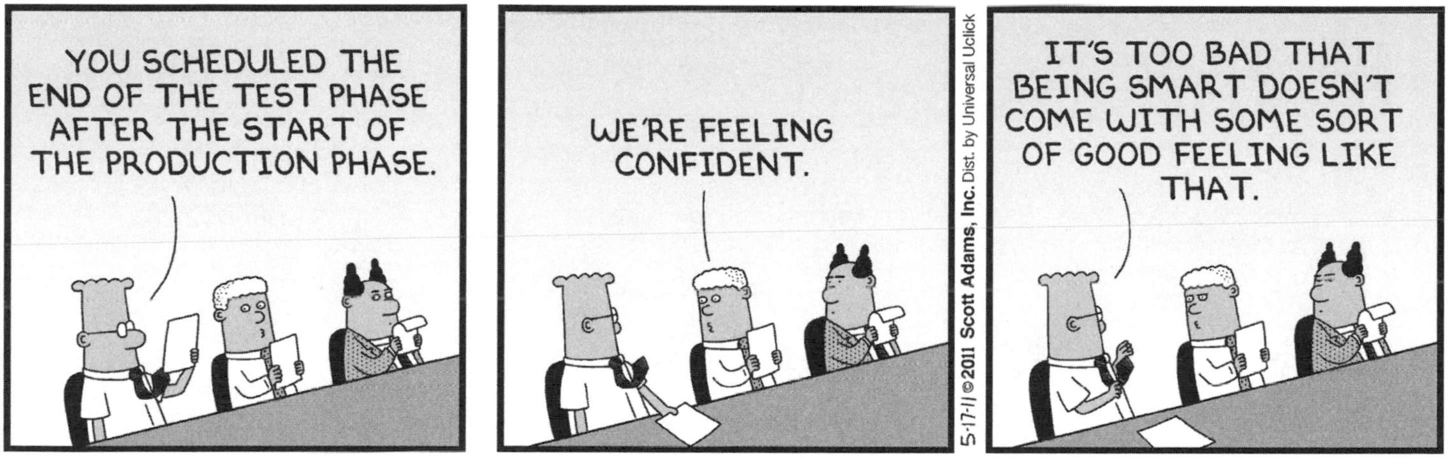
YOU SCHEDULED THE END OF THE TEST PHASE AFTER THE START OF THE PRODUCTION PHASE.
WE'RE FEELING CONFIDENT.
5-17-11 ©2011 Scott Adams, Inc. Dist. by Universal Uclick
IT'S TOO BAD THAT BEING SMART DOESN'T COME WITH SOME SORT OF GOOD FEELING LIKE THAT.

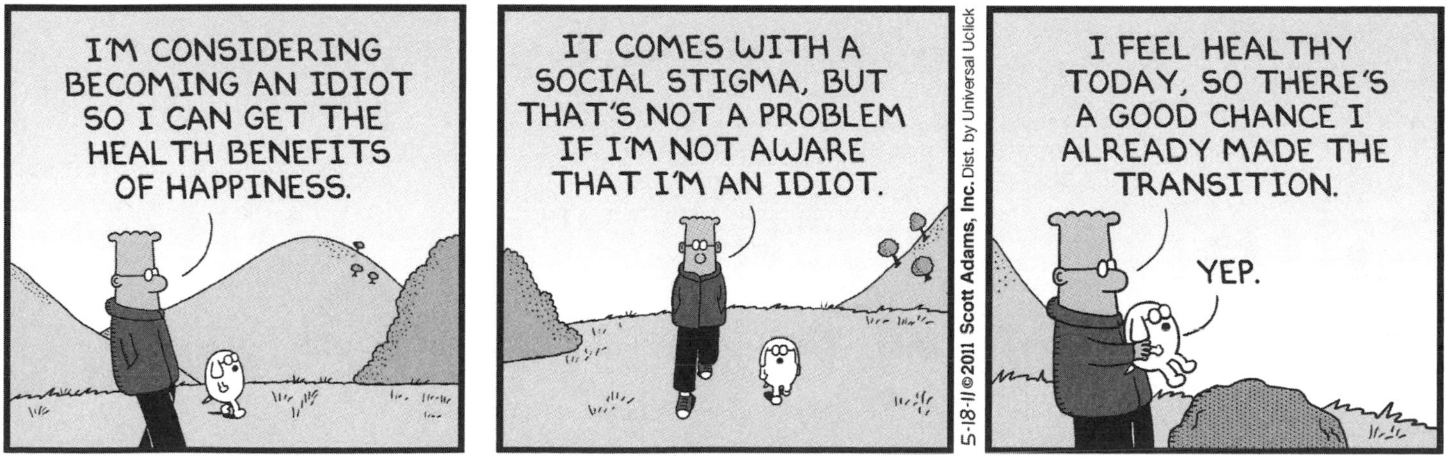
I'M CONSIDERING BECOMING AN IDIOT SO I CAN GET THE HEALTH BENEFITS OF HAPPINESS.
IT COMES WITH A SOCIAL STIGMA, BUT THAT'S NOT A PROBLEM IF I'M NOT AWARE THAT I'M AN IDIOT.
5-18-11 ©2011 Scott Adams, Inc. Dist. by Universal Uclick
I FEEL HEALTHY TODAY, SO THERE'S A GOOD CHANCE I ALREADY MADE THE TRANSITION.
YEP.

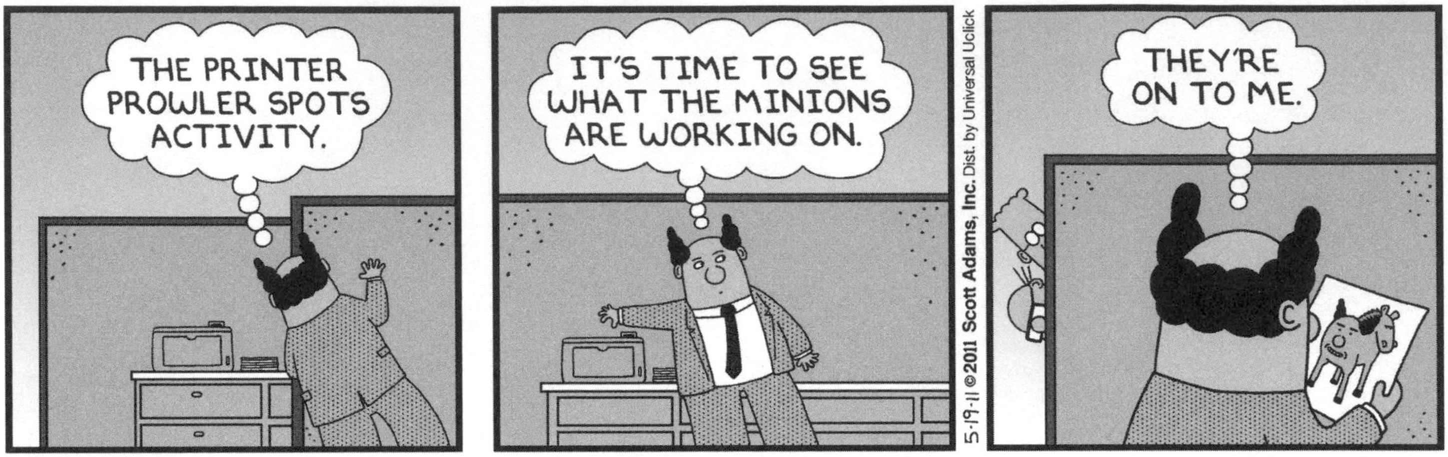
THE PRINTER PROWLER SPOTS ACTIVITY.
IT'S TIME TO SEE WHAT THE MINIONS ARE WORKING ON.
5-19-11 ©2011 Scott Adams, Inc. Dist. by Universal Uclick
THEY'RE ON TO ME.

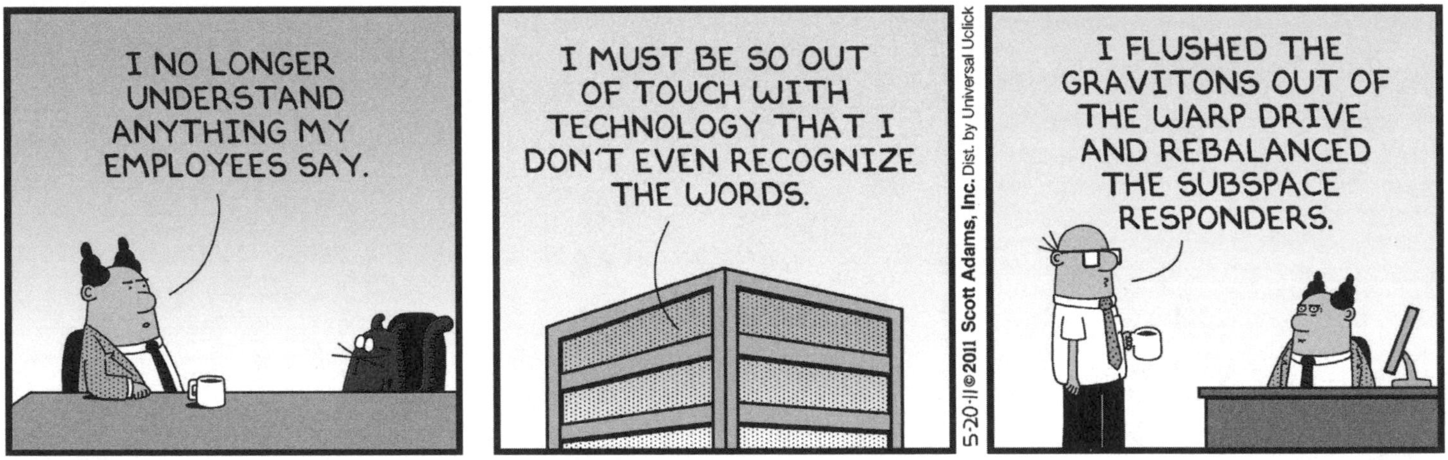
I NO LONGER UNDERSTAND ANYTHING MY EMPLOYEES SAY.
I MUST BE SO OUT OF TOUCH WITH TECHNOLOGY THAT I DON'T EVEN RECOGNIZE THE WORDS.
5-20-11 ©2011 Scott Adams, Inc. Dist. by Universal Uclick
I FLUSHED THE GRAVITONS OUT OF THE WARP DRIVE AND REBALANCED THE SUBSPACE RESPONDERS.

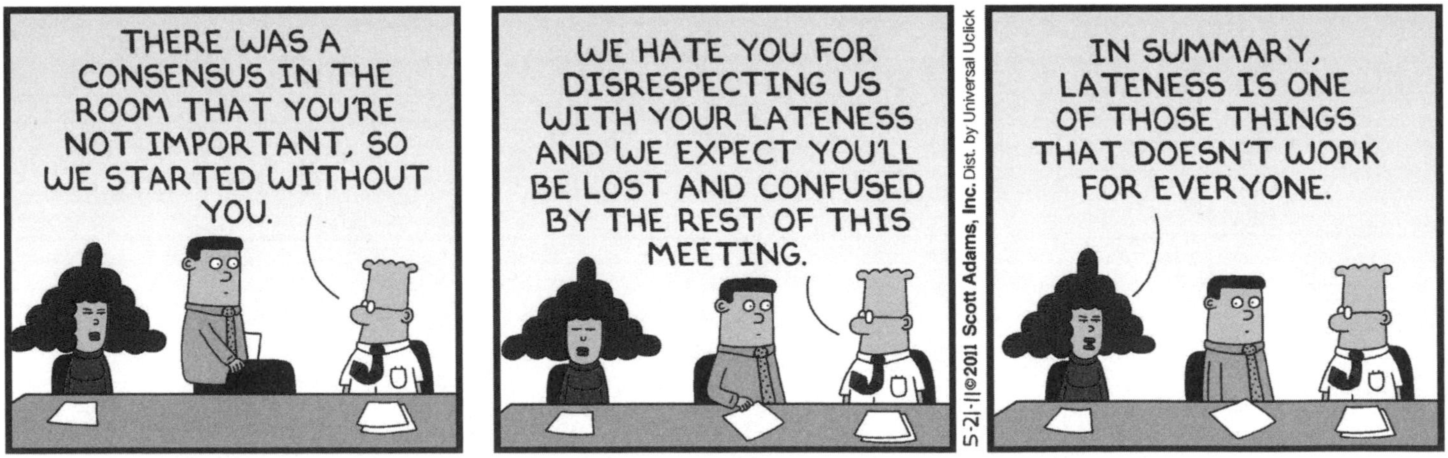
THERE WAS A CONSENSUS IN THE ROOM THAT YOU'RE NOT IMPORTANT, SO WE STARTED WITHOUT YOU.
WE HATE YOU FOR DISRESPECTING US WITH YOUR LATENESS AND WE EXPECT YOU'LL BE LOST AND CONFUSED BY THE REST OF THIS MEETING.
5-21-11 ©2011 Scott Adams, Inc. Dist. by Universal Uclick
IN SUMMARY, LATENESS IS ONE OF THOSE THINGS THAT DOESN'T WORK FOR EVERYONE.

THIS DOESN'T FEEL RIGHT.
IT CAME STRAIGHT FROM OUR LAWYER.
IT JUST FEELS WRONG. CAN YOU RESEARCH IT A LITTLE MORE?
SURE. I CAN DO THAT RESEARCH IN MY HEAD.
©2011 Scott Adams, Inc./Dist. by Universal Uclick
LET'S SEE. . . OUR LAWYER GOT HIS DEGREE AT HARVARD AND HAS TWENTY YEARS IN THIS EXACT FIELD.
WHEREAS YOU HAVE A "FEELING" THAT IS PROBABLY THE RESULT OF AN UNHOLY COM–BINATION OF GREASY FOOD AND IGNORANCE.
THE DATA CLEARLY FAVORS THE HARVARD LAW DEGREE OVER THE CHEESEBURGER.
5-22-11
GOOD LUCK. HE'S IN A BAD MOOD.

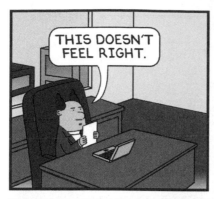

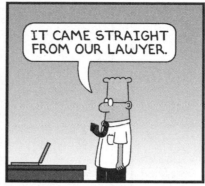

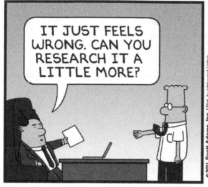

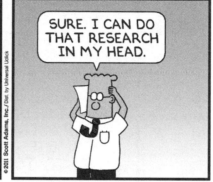

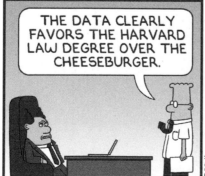

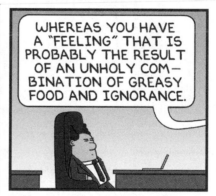

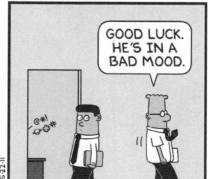

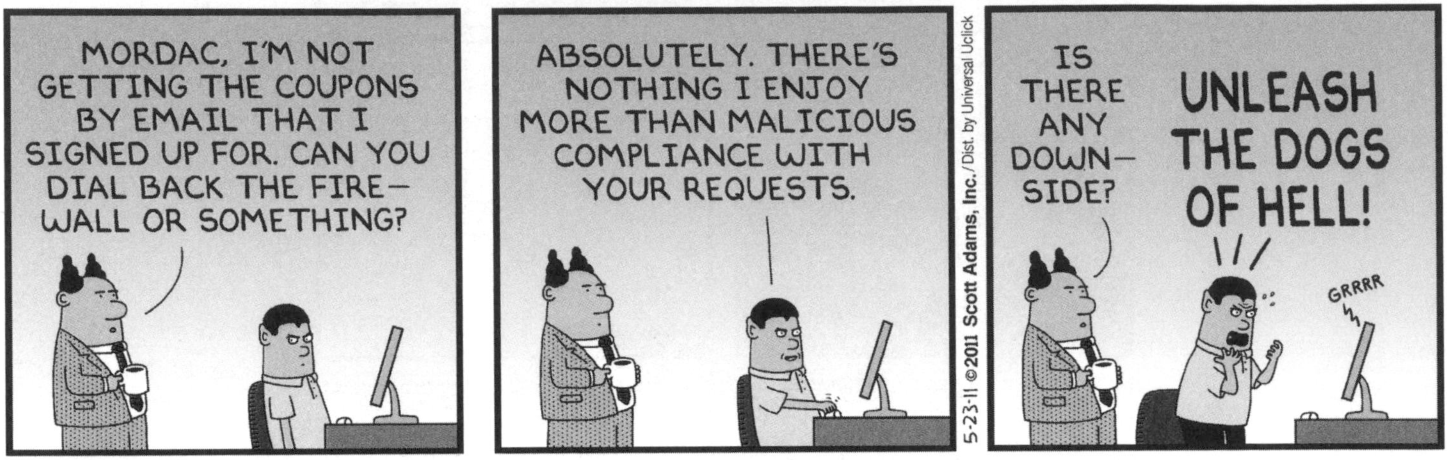
MORDAC, I'M NOT GETTING THE COUPONS BY EMAIL THAT I SIGNED UP FOR. CAN YOU DIAL BACK THE FIRE-WALL OR SOMETHING?
ABSOLUTELY. THERE'S NOTHING I ENJOY MORE THAN MALICIOUS COMPLIANCE WITH YOUR REQUESTS.
5-23-11 ©2011 Scott Adams, Inc./Dist. by Universal Uclick
IS THERE ANY DOWN-SIDE?
UNLEASH THE DOGS OF HELL!
GRRRR

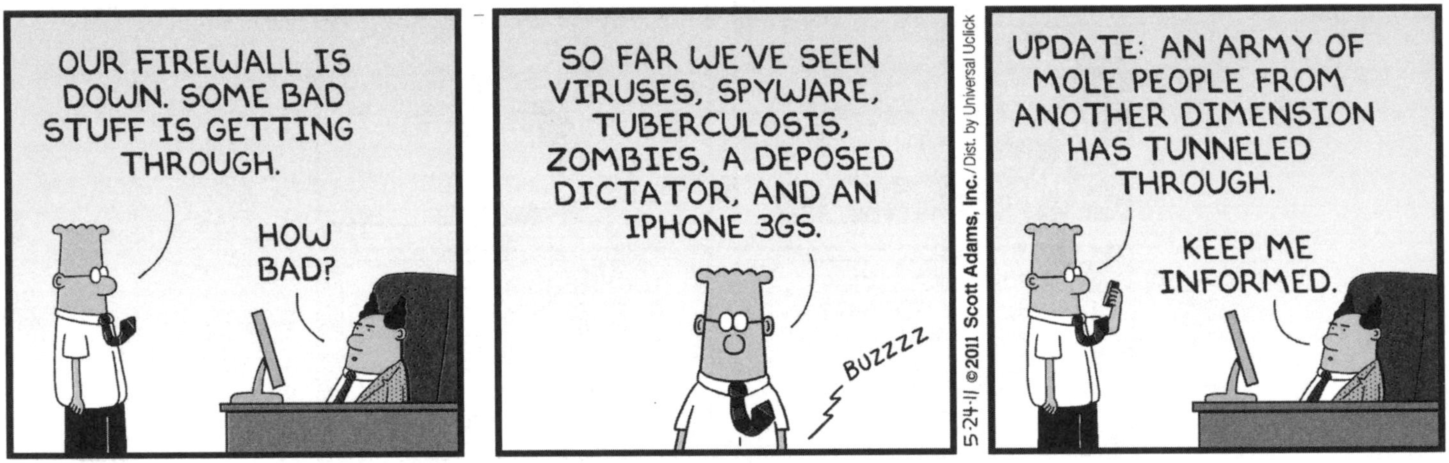
OUR FIREWALL IS DOWN. SOME BAD STUFF IS GETTING THROUGH.
HOW BAD?
SO FAR WE'VE SEEN VIRUSES, SPYWARE, TUBERCULOSIS, ZOMBIES, A DEPOSED DICTATOR, AND AN IPHONE 3GS.
BUZZZZ
5-24-11 ©2011 Scott Adams, Inc./Dist. by Universal Uclick
UPDATE: AN ARMY OF MOLE PEOPLE FROM ANOTHER DIMENSION HAS TUNNELED THROUGH.
KEEP ME INFORMED.

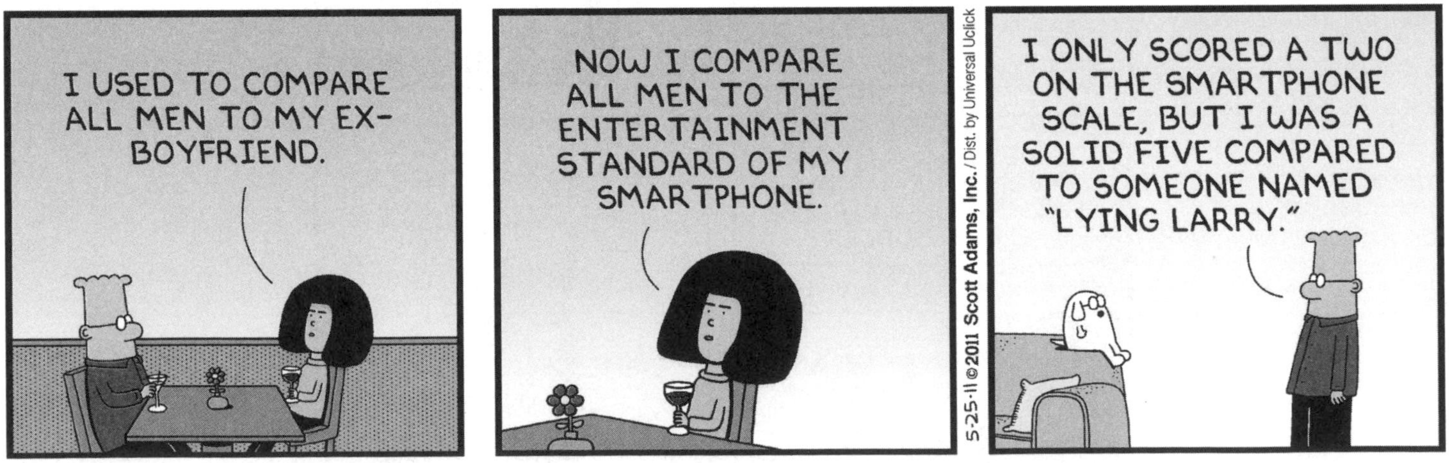
I USED TO COMPARE ALL MEN TO MY EX-BOYFRIEND.
NOW I COMPARE ALL MEN TO THE ENTERTAINMENT STANDARD OF MY SMARTPHONE.
5-25-11 ©2011 Scott Adams, Inc./Dist. by Universal Uclick
I ONLY SCORED A TWO ON THE SMARTPHONE SCALE, BUT I WAS A SOLID FIVE COMPARED TO SOMEONE NAMED "LYING LARRY."

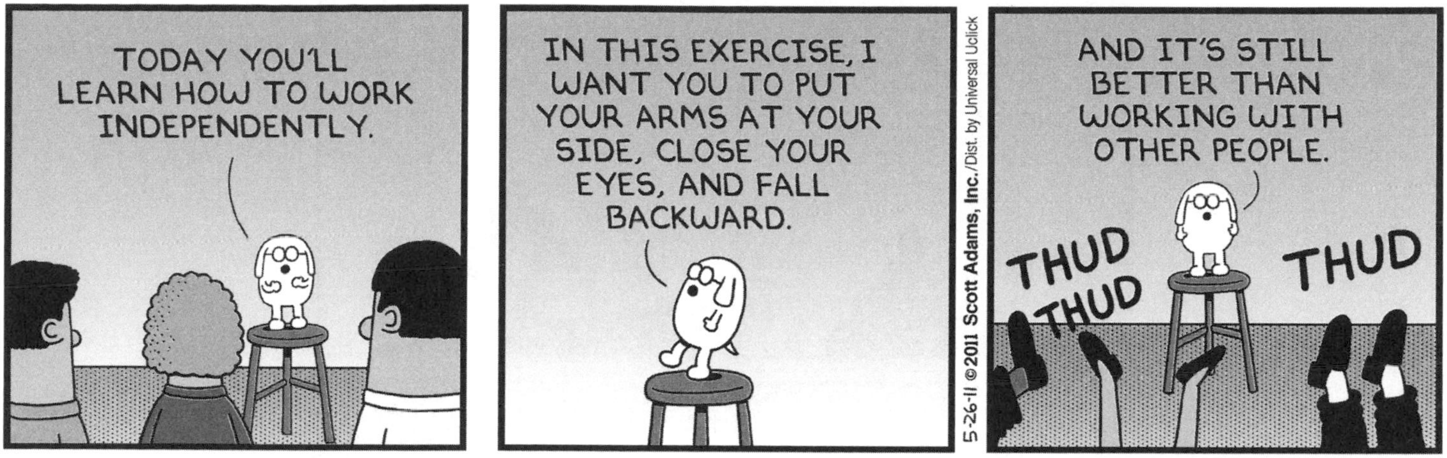
TODAY YOU'LL LEARN HOW TO WORK INDEPENDENTLY.
IN THIS EXERCISE, I WANT YOU TO PUT YOUR ARMS AT YOUR SIDE, CLOSE YOUR EYES, AND FALL BACKWARD.
5-26-11 ©2011 Scott Adams, Inc./Dist. by Universal Uclick
THUD
THUD
THUD
AND IT'S STILL BETTER THAN WORKING WITH OTHER PEOPLE.

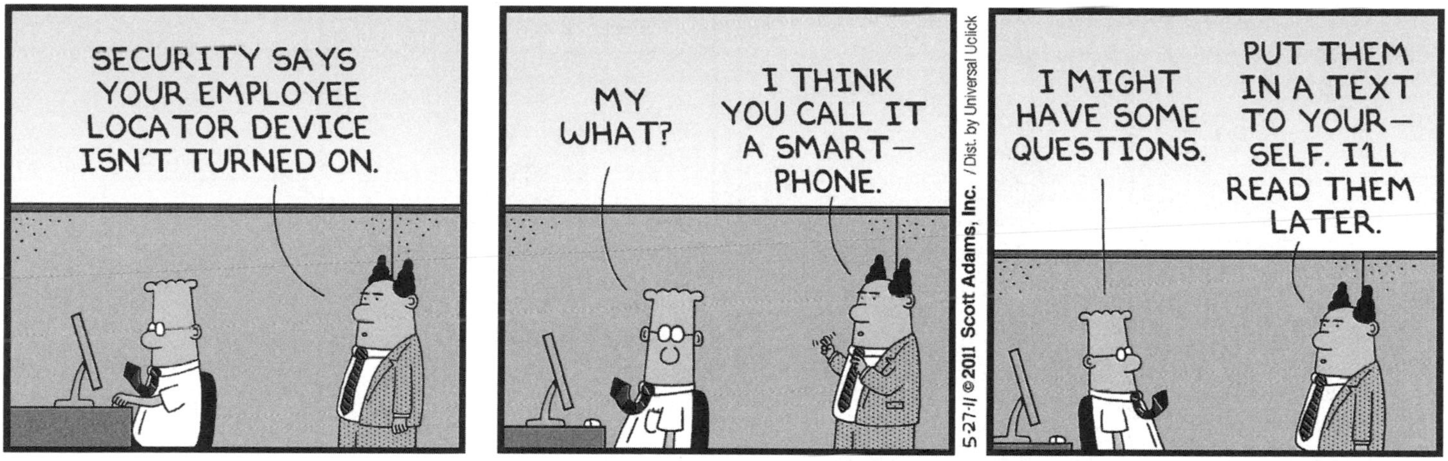
SECURITY SAYS YOUR EMPLOYEE LOCATOR DEVICE ISN'T TURNED ON.
MY WHAT?
I THINK YOU CALL IT A SMART-PHONE.
5-27-11 ©2011 Scott Adams, Inc. / Dist. by Universal Uclick
I MIGHT HAVE SOME QUESTIONS.
PUT THEM IN A TEXT TO YOUR-SELF. I'LL READ THEM LATER.

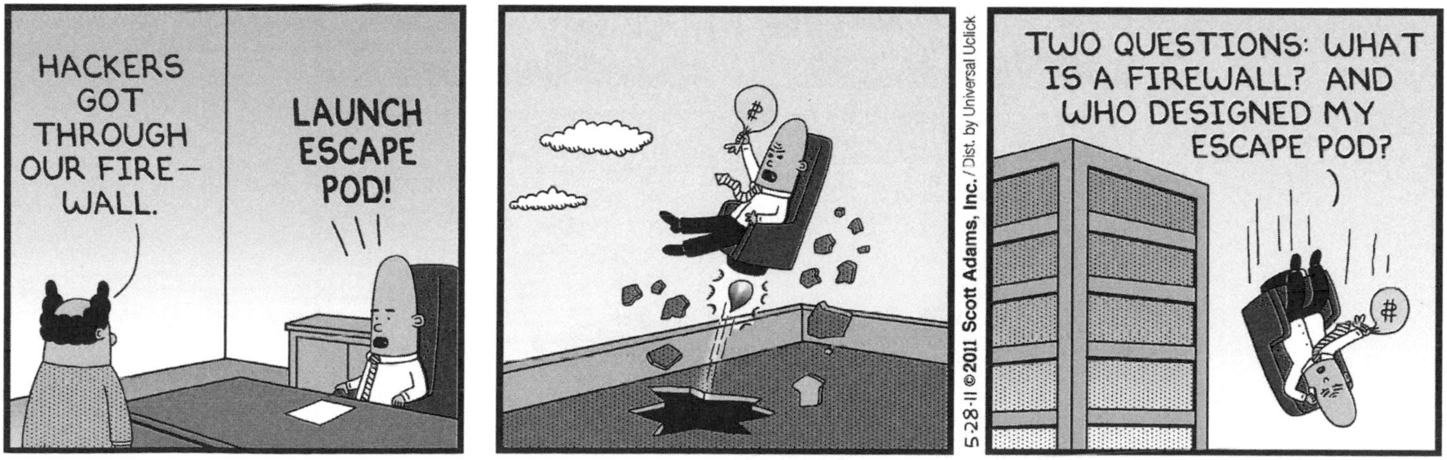
HACKERS GOT THROUGH OUR FIRE-WALL.
LAUNCH ESCAPE POD!
5-28-11 ©2011 Scott Adams, Inc./Dist. by Universal Uclick
TWO QUESTIONS: WHAT IS A FIREWALL? AND WHO DESIGNED MY ESCAPE POD?

THIS AWARD GOES TO DILBERT FOR COMING UP WITH A MAJOR FIX TO OUR HTML.
I DIDN'T DO ANYTHING LIKE THAT. YOU MUST BE THINKING OF SOMEONE ELSE.
DO YOU EVEN KNOW WHAT HTML IS?
©2011 Scott Adams, Inc./Dist. by Universal Uclick
IT'S LIKE... A WEBSITE?
SO... YOU'RE GIVING AN AWARD FOR SOME-THING YOU DON'T UNDERSTAND... TO SOMEONE WHO WASN'T INVOLVED?
WHAT I MEANT TO SAY IS THAT I GIVE THIS AWARD TO... ALICE... FOR... WHAT SHE DID.
YES! ENVY ME, YOU STINKIN' LOSERS!
5-29-11
I DON'T KNOW WHY PEOPLE SAY THIS IMPROVES MORALE.
I FIXED THE HTML!

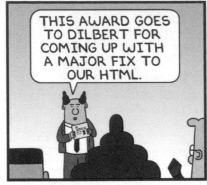

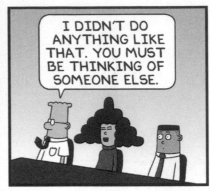

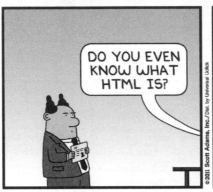

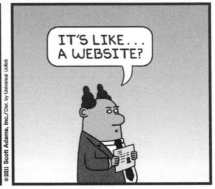

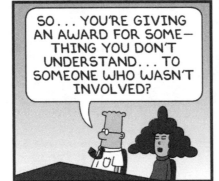

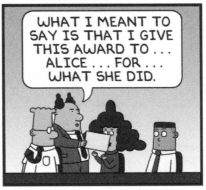

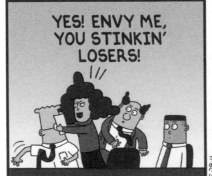

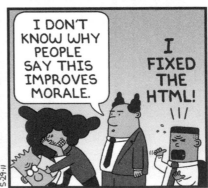

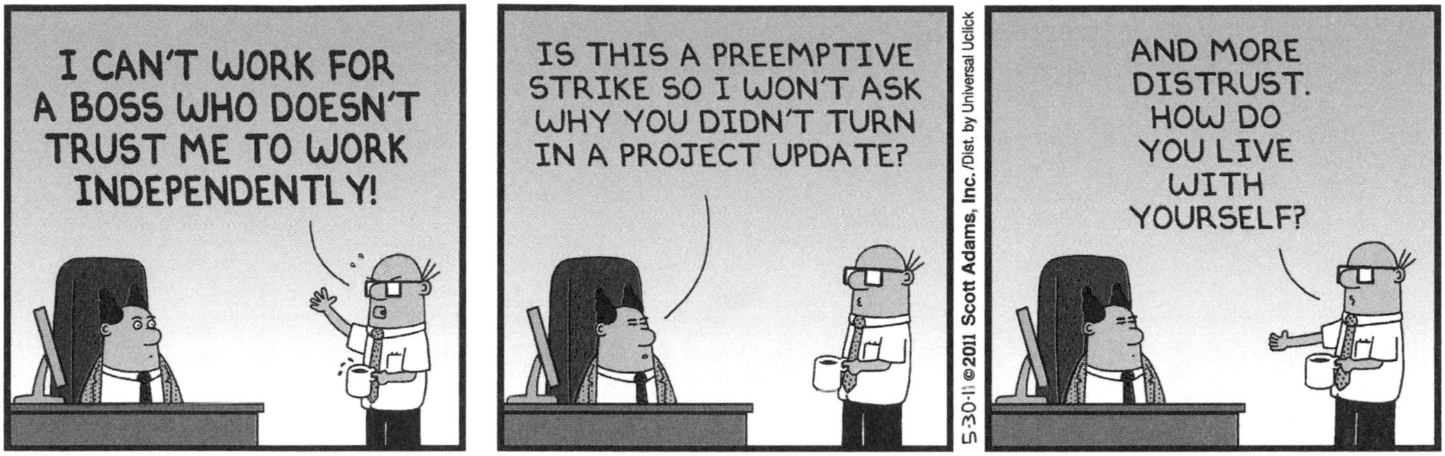
I CAN'T WORK FOR A BOSS WHO DOESN'T TRUST ME TO WORK INDEPENDENTLY!
IS THIS A PREEMPTIVE STRIKE SO I WON'T ASK WHY YOU DIDN'T TURN IN A PROJECT UPDATE?
5·30·11 ©2011 Scott Adams, Inc./Dist. by Universal Uclick
AND MORE DISTRUST. HOW DO YOU LIVE WITH YOURSELF?

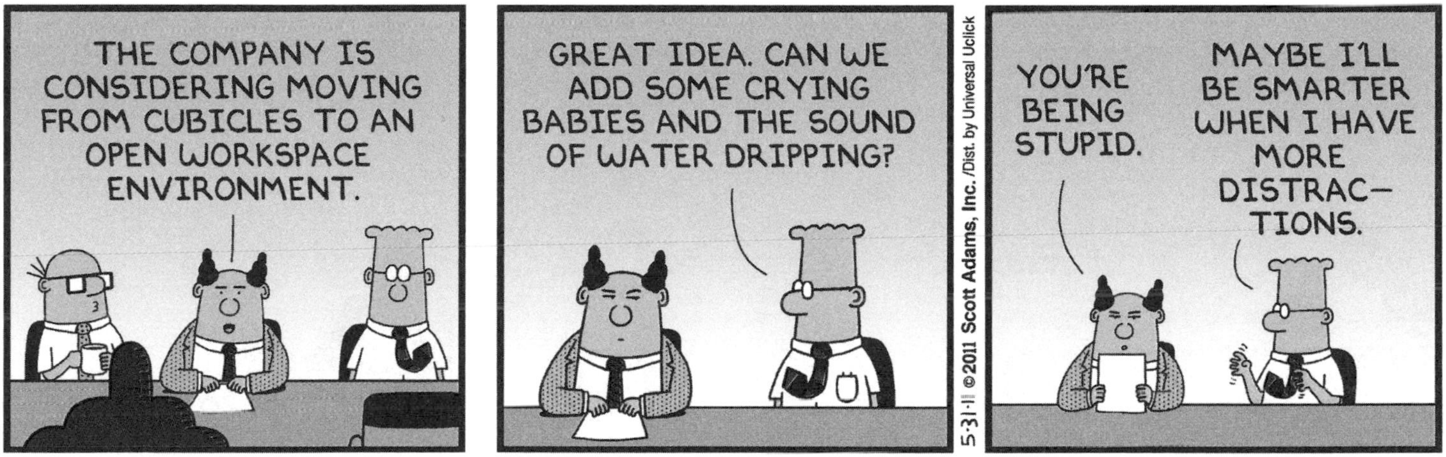
THE COMPANY IS CONSIDERING MOVING FROM CUBICLES TO AN OPEN WORKSPACE ENVIRONMENT.
GREAT IDEA. CAN WE ADD SOME CRYING BABIES AND THE SOUND OF WATER DRIPPING?
5·31·11 ©2011 Scott Adams, Inc./Dist. by Universal Uclick
YOU'RE BEING STUPID.
MAYBE I'LL BE SMARTER WHEN I HAVE MORE DISTRAC-TIONS.

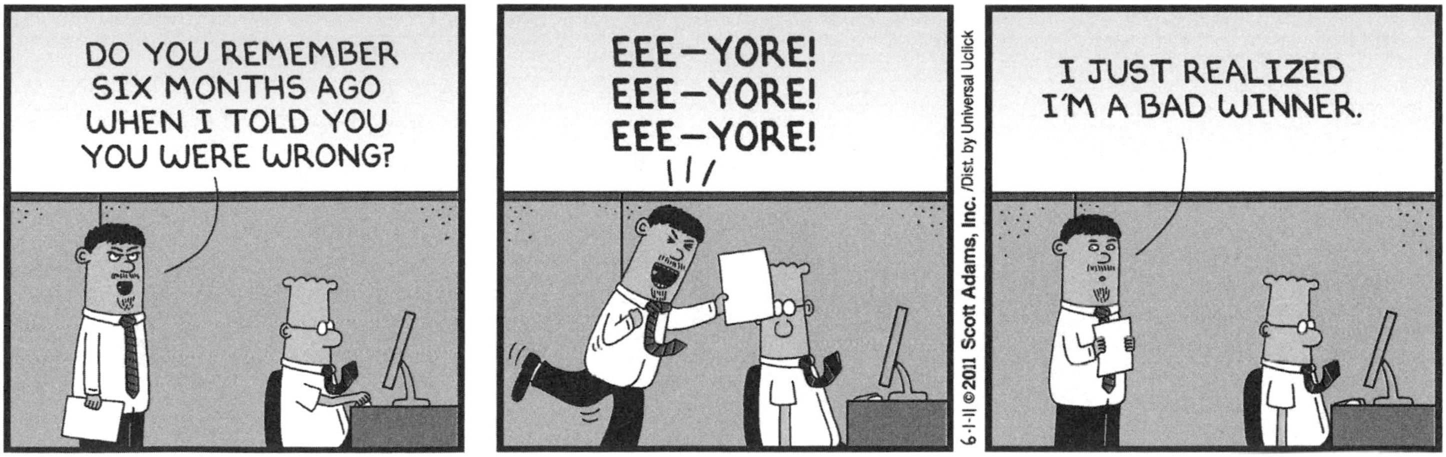
DO YOU REMEMBER SIX MONTHS AGO WHEN I TOLD YOU YOU WERE WRONG?
EEE-YORE! EEE-YORE! EEE-YORE!
6·1·11 ©2011 Scott Adams, Inc./Dist. by Universal Uclick
I JUST REALIZED I'M A BAD WINNER.

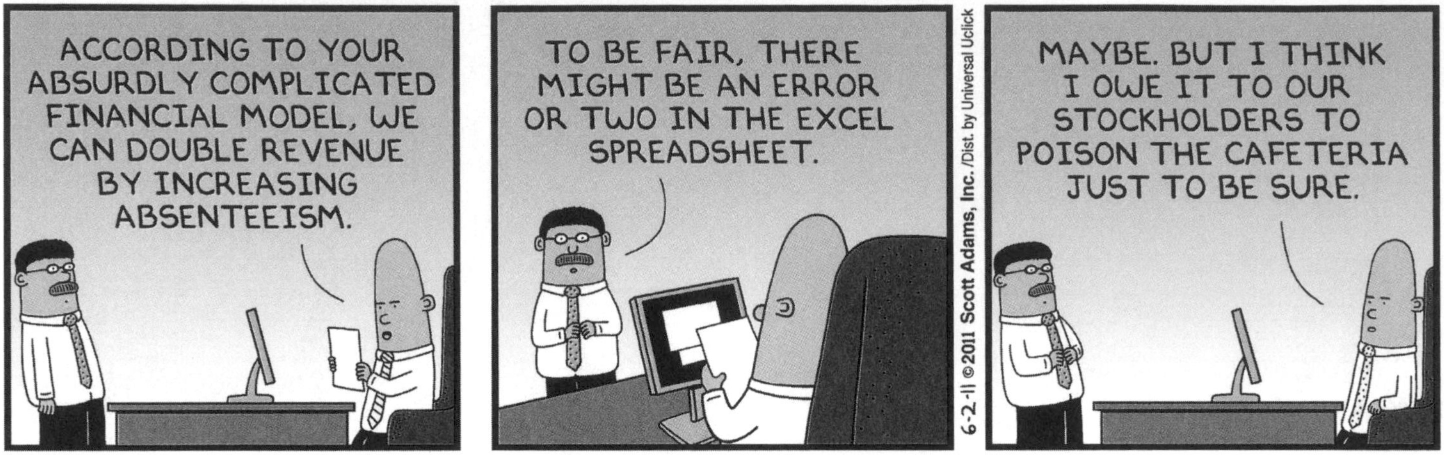
ACCORDING TO YOUR ABSURDLY COMPLICATED FINANCIAL MODEL, WE CAN DOUBLE REVENUE BY INCREASING ABSENTEEISM.
TO BE FAIR, THERE MIGHT BE AN ERROR OR TWO IN THE EXCEL SPREADSHEET.
6-2-11 ©2011 Scott Adams, Inc./Dist. by Universal Uclick
MAYBE. BUT I THINK I OWE IT TO OUR STOCKHOLDERS TO POISON THE CAFETERIA JUST TO BE SURE.

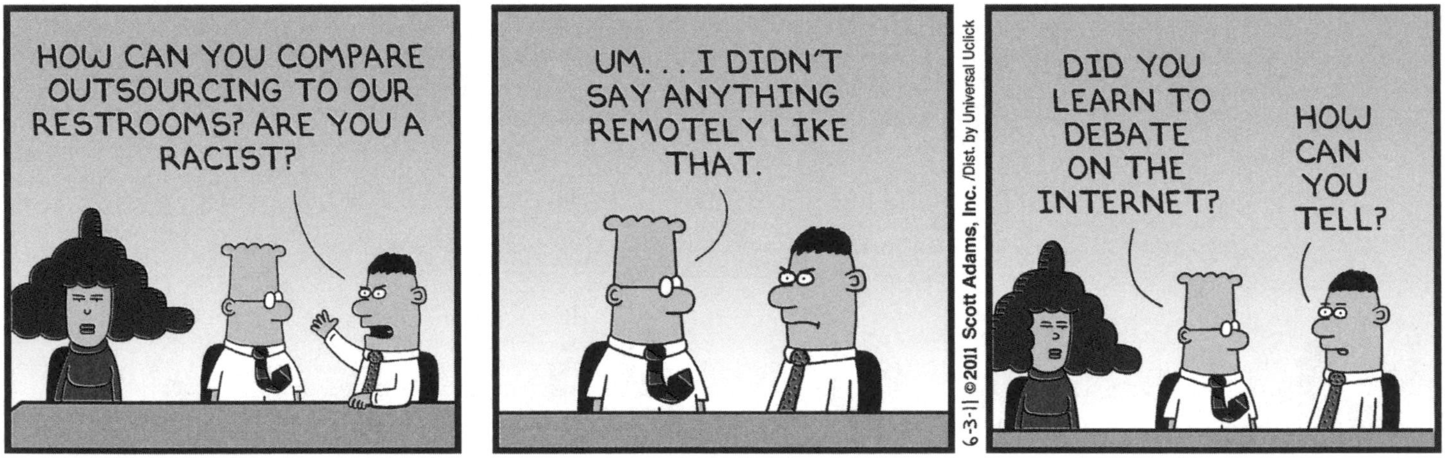
HOW CAN YOU COMPARE OUTSOURCING TO OUR RESTROOMS? ARE YOU A RACIST?
UM. . . I DIDN'T SAY ANYTHING REMOTELY LIKE THAT.
6-3-11 ©2011 Scott Adams, Inc./Dist. by Universal Uclick
DID YOU LEARN TO DEBATE ON THE INTERNET?
HOW CAN YOU TELL?

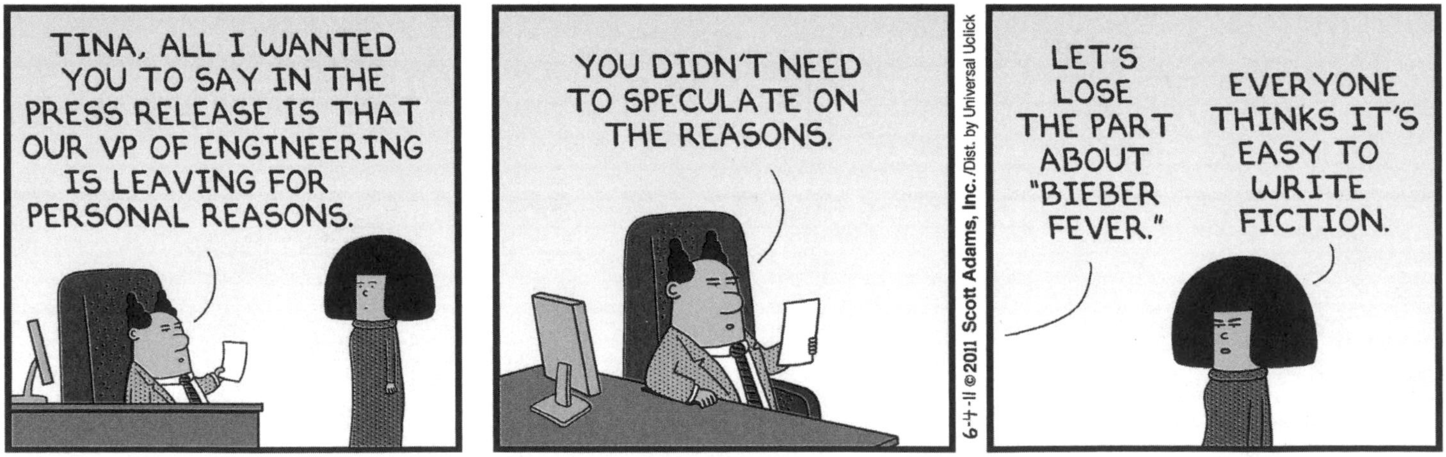
TINA, ALL I WANTED YOU TO SAY IN THE PRESS RELEASE IS THAT OUR VP OF ENGINEERING IS LEAVING FOR PERSONAL REASONS.
YOU DIDN'T NEED TO SPECULATE ON THE REASONS.
6-4-11 ©2011 Scott Adams, Inc./Dist. by Universal Uclick
LET'S LOSE THE PART ABOUT "BIEBER FEVER."
EVERYONE THINKS IT'S EASY TO WRITE FICTION.

SERIOUSLY? YOU'RE GOING TO DO EMAIL WHILE I GIVE MY STATUS UPDATE?
DON'T WORRY. I CAN MULTITASK.
MULTITASK? YOU CAN BARELY DO ONE TASK PROPERLY.
©2011 Scott Adams, Inc./Dist. by Universal Uclick
ALL YOU'RE DOING IS DOUBLING YOUR RATE OF FAILURE.
CONGRATULATIONS ON BECOMING THE MOST USELESS BLOB OF CARBON IN THE UNIVERSE.
WHAT? SORRY. I MISSED THAT.
I SAID MY PROJECT IS ON SCHEDULE.
6-5-11
OKAY. GREAT.
THIS TOTALLY WORKS FOR ME.

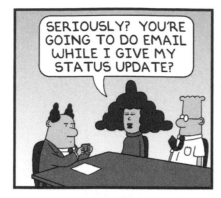

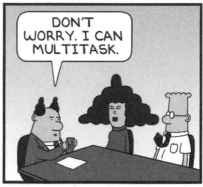

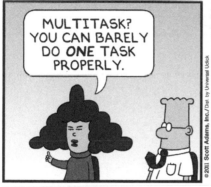

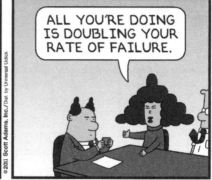

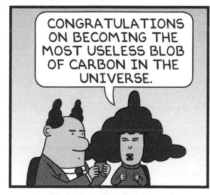

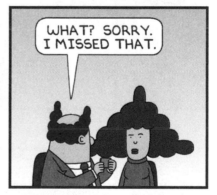

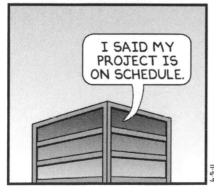

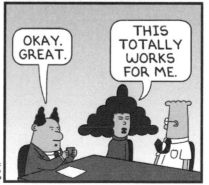

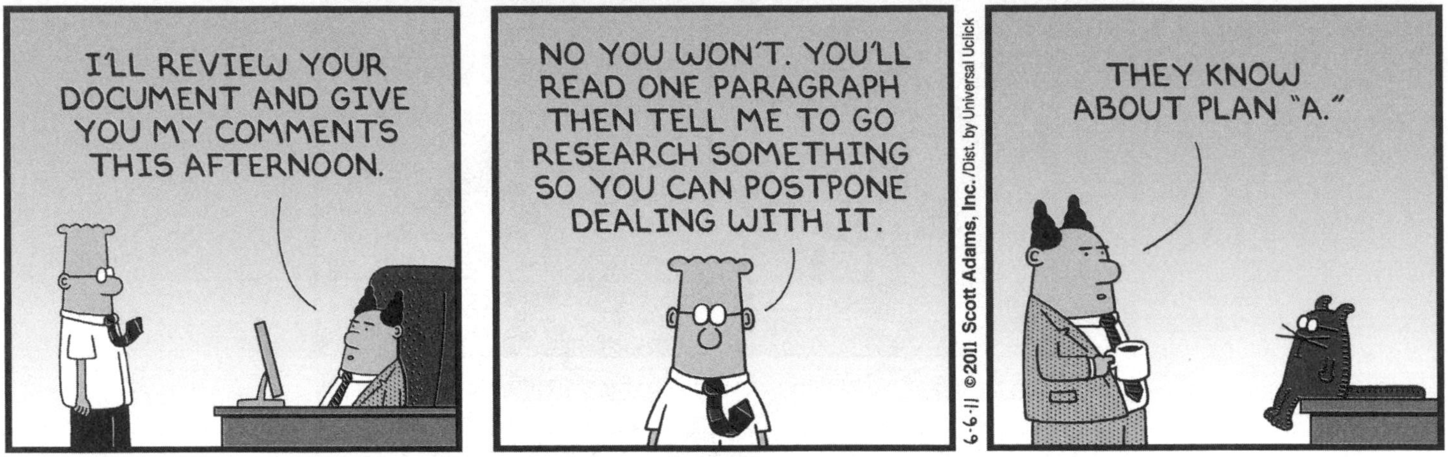
I'LL REVIEW YOUR DOCUMENT AND GIVE YOU MY COMMENTS THIS AFTERNOON.
NO YOU WON'T. YOU'LL READ ONE PARAGRAPH THEN TELL ME TO GO RESEARCH SOMETHING SO YOU CAN POSTPONE DEALING WITH IT.
6-6-11 ©2011 Scott Adams, Inc. /Dist. by Universal Uclick
THEY KNOW ABOUT PLAN "A."

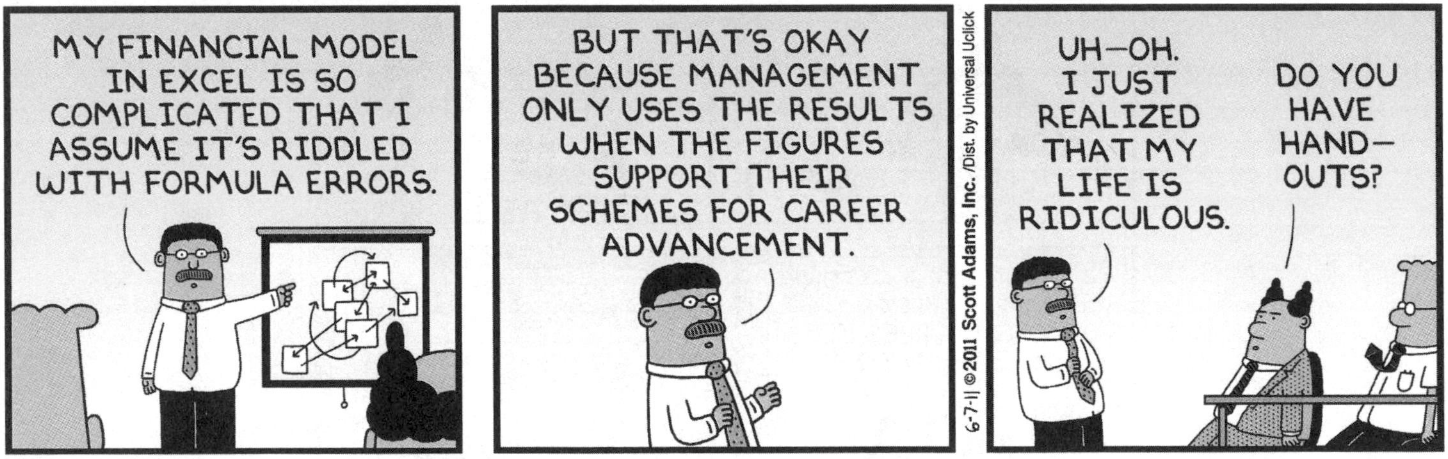
MY FINANCIAL MODEL IN EXCEL IS SO COMPLICATED THAT I ASSUME IT'S RIDDLED WITH FORMULA ERRORS.
BUT THAT'S OKAY BECAUSE MANAGEMENT ONLY USES THE RESULTS WHEN THE FIGURES SUPPORT THEIR SCHEMES FOR CAREER ADVANCEMENT.
6-7-11 ©2011 Scott Adams, Inc. /Dist. by Universal Uclick
UH-OH. I JUST REALIZED THAT MY LIFE IS RIDICULOUS.
DO YOU HAVE HAND-OUTS?

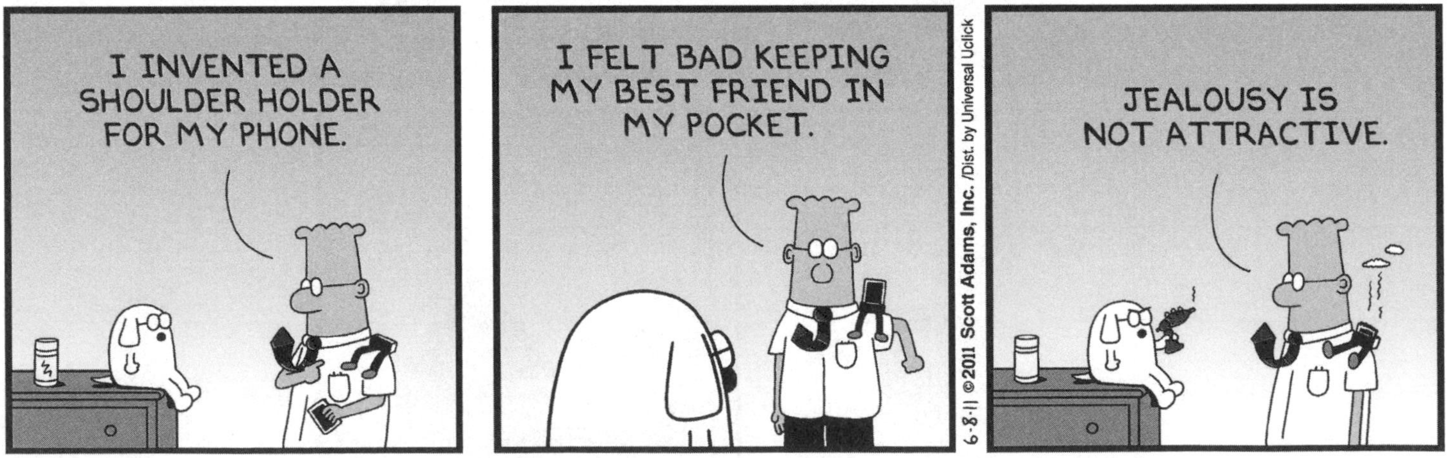
I INVENTED A SHOULDER HOLDER FOR MY PHONE.
I FELT BAD KEEPING MY BEST FRIEND IN MY POCKET.
6-8-11 ©2011 Scott Adams, Inc. /Dist. by Universal Uclick
JEALOUSY IS NOT ATTRACTIVE.

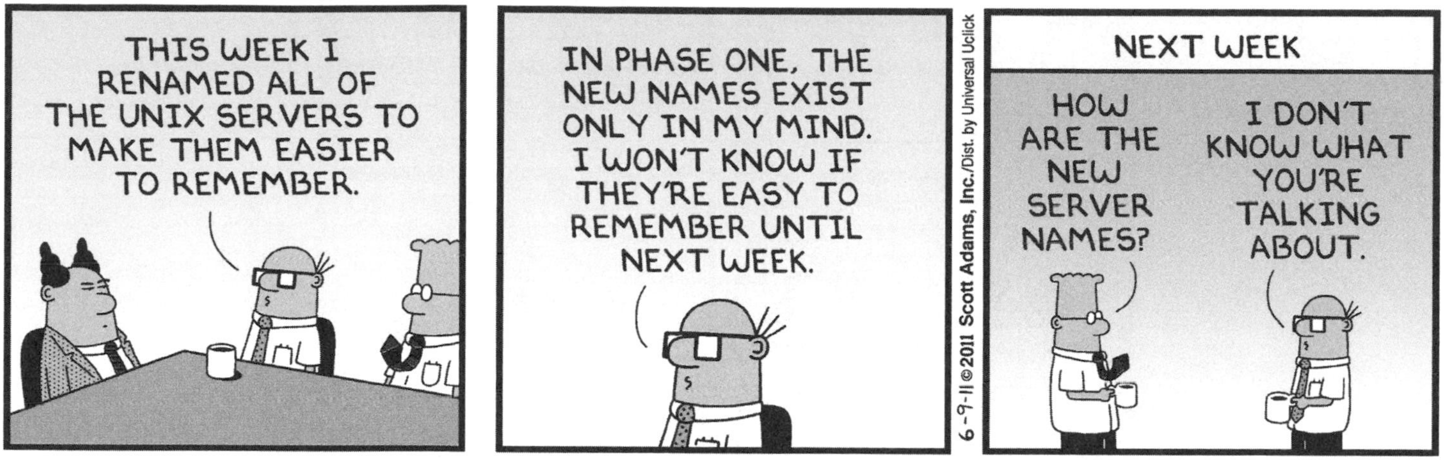
THIS WEEK I RENAMED ALL OF THE UNIX SERVERS TO MAKE THEM EASIER TO REMEMBER.
IN PHASE ONE, THE NEW NAMES EXIST ONLY IN MY MIND. I WON'T KNOW IF THEY'RE EASY TO REMEMBER UNTIL NEXT WEEK.
6-9-11 ©2011 Scott Adams, Inc./Dist. by Universal Uclick
NEXT WEEK
HOW ARE THE NEW SERVER NAMES?
I DON'T KNOW WHAT YOU'RE TALKING ABOUT.

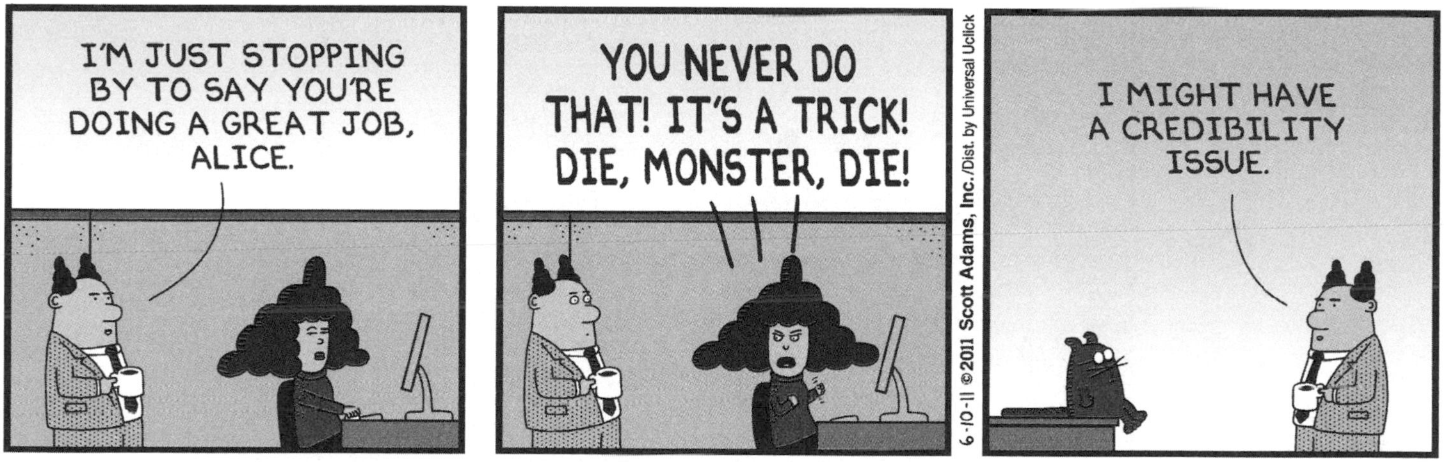
I'M JUST STOPPING BY TO SAY YOU'RE DOING A GREAT JOB, ALICE.
YOU NEVER DO THAT! IT'S A TRICK! DIE, MONSTER, DIE!
6-10-11 ©2011 Scott Adams, Inc./Dist. by Universal Uclick
I MIGHT HAVE A CREDIBILITY ISSUE.

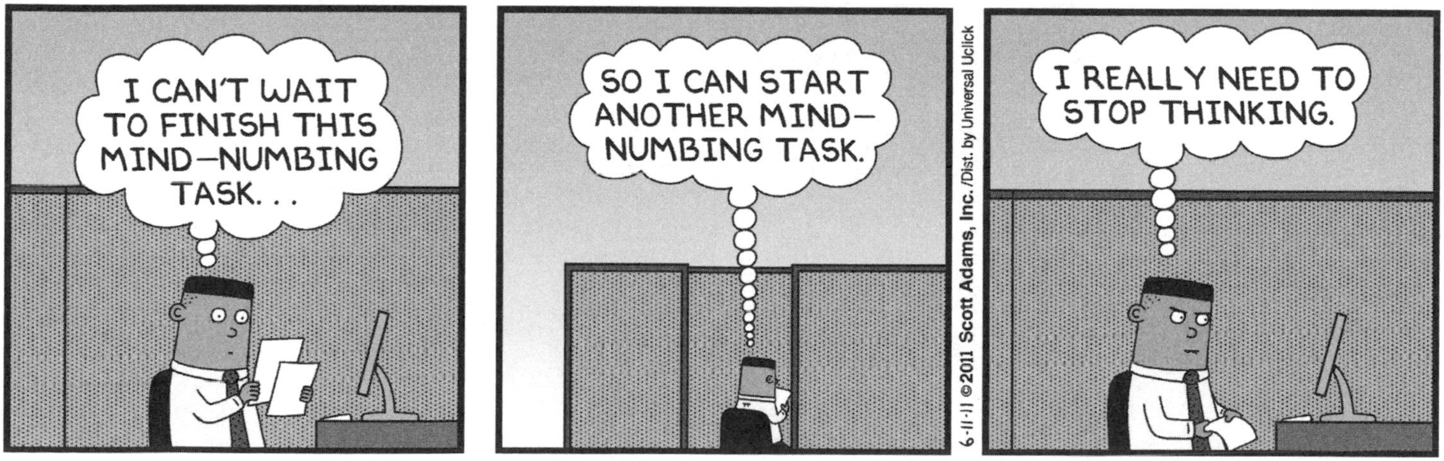
I CAN'T WAIT TO FINISH THIS MIND-NUMBING TASK. . .
SO I CAN START ANOTHER MIND-NUMBING TASK.
6-11-11 ©2011 Scott Adams, Inc./Dist. by Universal Uclick
I REALLY NEED TO STOP THINKING.

DID YOU ASK THE LAB IF THEY HAVE A WAY TO TEST TRAFFIC LOADS ON OUR PROTOTYPE?
I MET WITH THEM FOR AN HOUR AND EXPLAINED THAT WE NEED TRAFFIC LOAD TESTS.
BUT YOU DIDN'T ACTUALLY ASK IF THEY COULD DO THE TESTS?
WELL... NO... BUT...
©2011 Scott Adams, Inc./Dist. by Universal Uclick
IT'S THEIR JOB TO DO THE TESTS, AND THEY WOULD HAVE MENTIONED IT IF THEY DIDN'T HAVE A WAY TO DO IT.
BUT YOU DIDN'T ASK.
THAT WAS THE CONTEXT OF THE MEETING.
IF THEY COULDN'T DO THAT SORT OF TEST THEY WOULD HAVE MENTIONED IT SOMETIME DURING OUR HOUR TOGETHER.
MAYBE YOU SHOULD ASK.
GAAA!!! OKAY! I'LL ASK!
6-12-11
ARE YOU FREAKIN' KIDDING ME? !!!
I WON-DERED WHY YOU DIDN'T ASK.

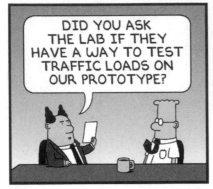

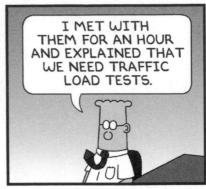

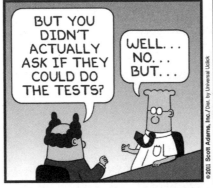

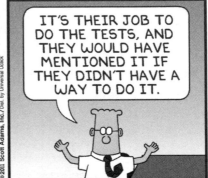

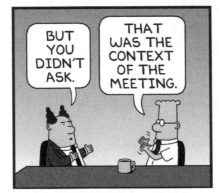

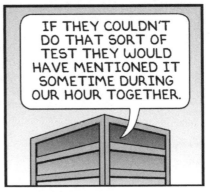

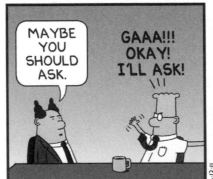

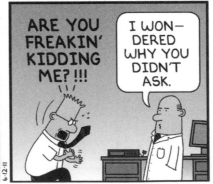

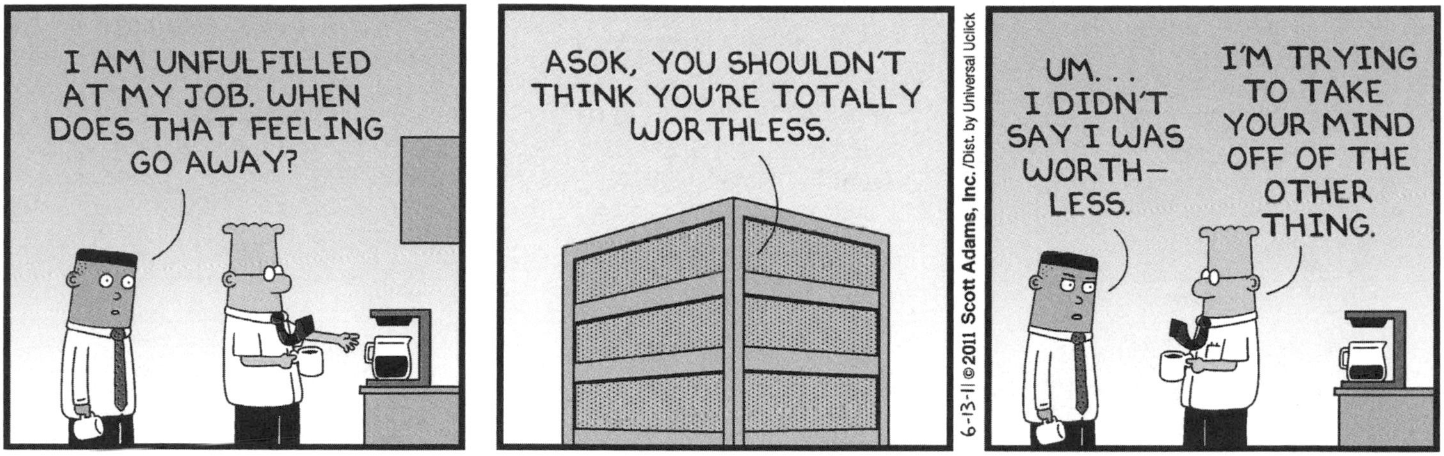
I AM UNFULFILLED AT MY JOB. WHEN DOES THAT FEELING GO AWAY?
ASOK, YOU SHOULDN'T THINK YOU'RE TOTALLY WORTHLESS.
6-13-11 © 2011 Scott Adams, Inc./Dist. by Universal Uclick
UM... I DIDN'T SAY I WAS WORTH-LESS.
I'M TRYING TO TAKE YOUR MIND OFF OF THE OTHER THING.

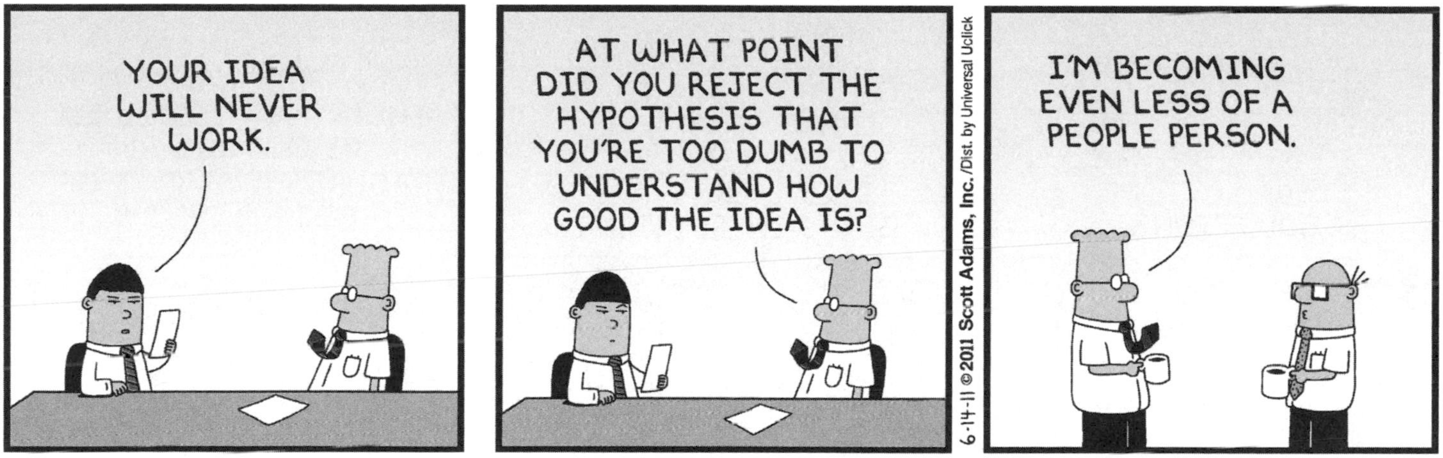
YOUR IDEA WILL NEVER WORK.
AT WHAT POINT DID YOU REJECT THE HYPOTHESIS THAT YOU'RE TOO DUMB TO UNDERSTAND HOW GOOD THE IDEA IS?
6-14-11 © 2011 Scott Adams, Inc./Dist. by Universal Uclick
I'M BECOMING EVEN LESS OF A PEOPLE PERSON.

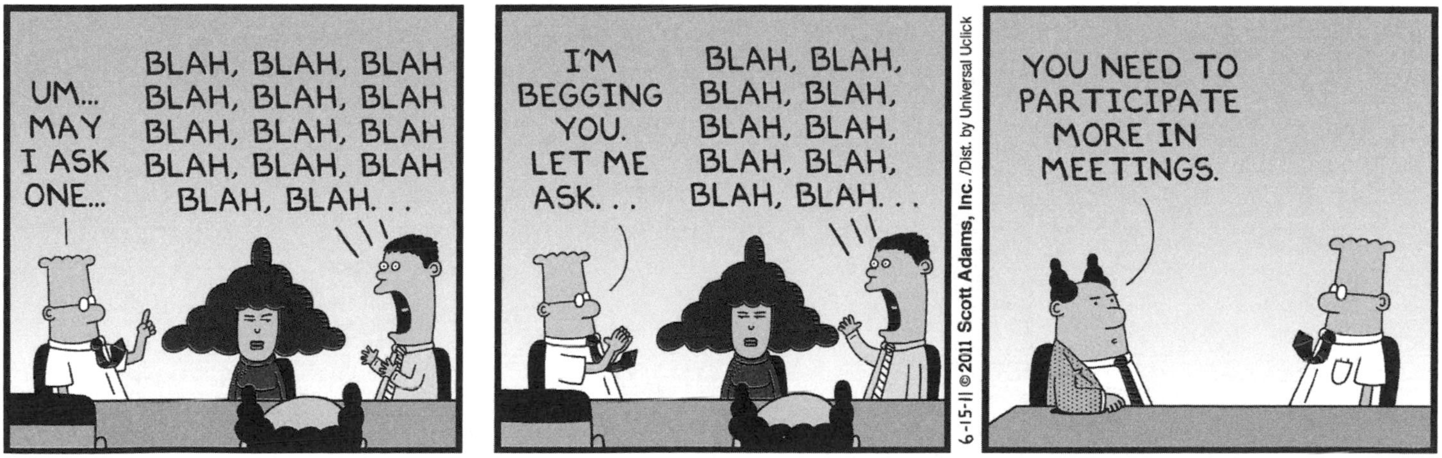
UM... MAY I ASK ONE...
BLAH, BLAH, BLAH BLAH, BLAH, BLAH BLAH, BLAH, BLAH BLAH, BLAH, BLAH BLAH, BLAH...
I'M BEGGING YOU. LET ME ASK...
BLAH, BLAH, BLAH, BLAH, BLAH, BLAH, BLAH, BLAH, BLAH, BLAH...
6-15-11 © 2011 Scott Adams, Inc./Dist. by Universal Uclick
YOU NEED TO PARTICIPATE MORE IN MEETINGS.

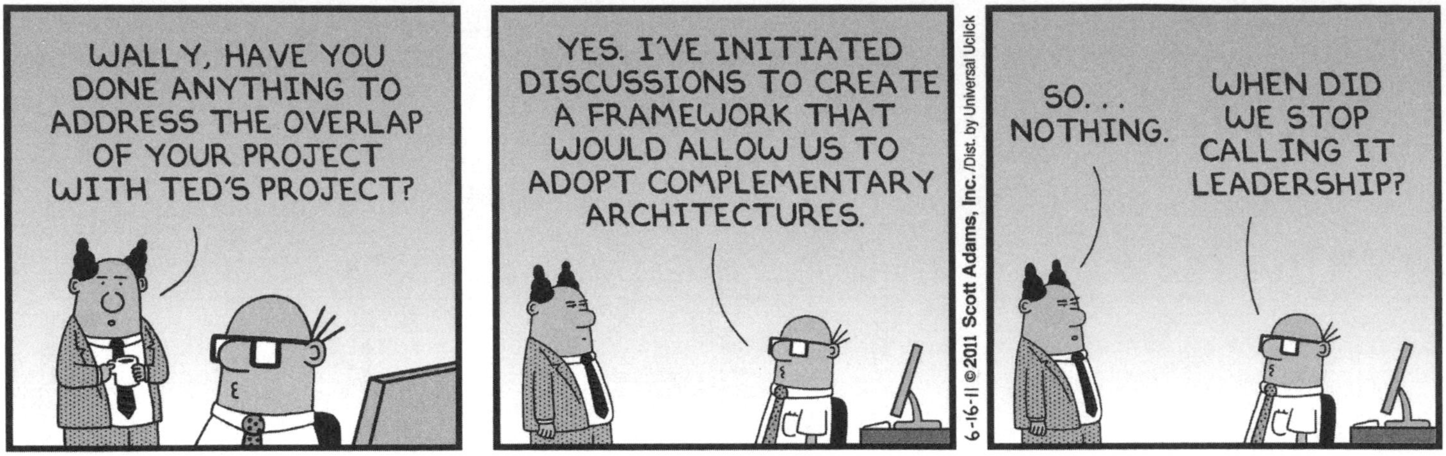
WALLY, HAVE YOU DONE ANYTHING TO ADDRESS THE OVERLAP OF YOUR PROJECT WITH TED'S PROJECT?
YES. I'VE INITIATED DISCUSSIONS TO CREATE A FRAMEWORK THAT WOULD ALLOW US TO ADOPT COMPLEMENTARY ARCHITECTURES.
6-16-11 ©2011 Scott Adams, Inc./Dist. by Universal Uclick
SO. . . NOTHING.
WHEN DID WE STOP CALLING IT LEADERSHIP?

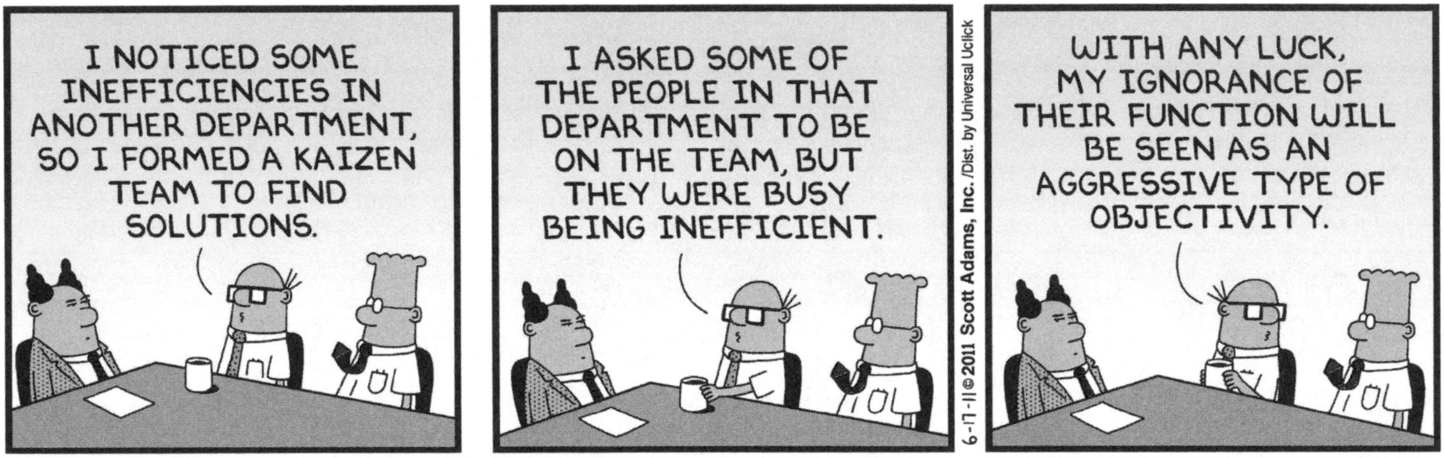
I NOTICED SOME INEFFICIENCIES IN ANOTHER DEPARTMENT, SO I FORMED A KAIZEN TEAM TO FIND SOLUTIONS.
I ASKED SOME OF THE PEOPLE IN THAT DEPARTMENT TO BE ON THE TEAM, BUT THEY WERE BUSY BEING INEFFICIENT.
6-17-11 ©2011 Scott Adams, Inc./Dist. by Universal Uclick
WITH ANY LUCK, MY IGNORANCE OF THEIR FUNCTION WILL BE SEEN AS AN AGGRESSIVE TYPE OF OBJECTIVITY.

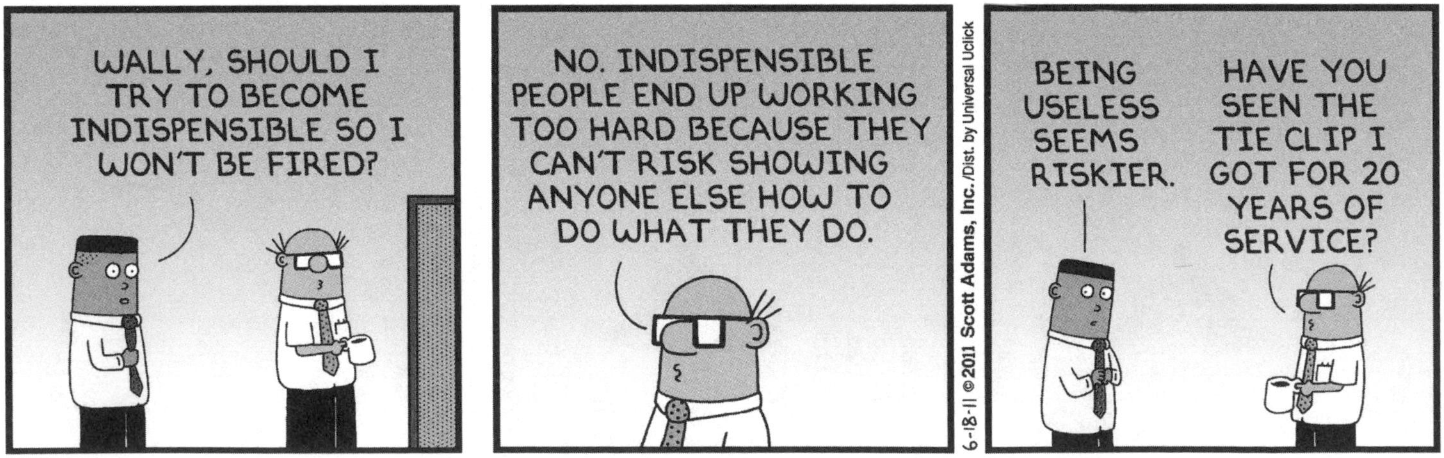
WALLY, SHOULD I TRY TO BECOME INDISPENSIBLE SO I WON'T BE FIRED?
NO. INDISPENSIBLE PEOPLE END UP WORKING TOO HARD BECAUSE THEY CAN'T RISK SHOWING ANYONE ELSE HOW TO DO WHAT THEY DO.
6-18-11 ©2011 Scott Adams, Inc./Dist. by Universal Uclick
BEING USELESS SEEMS RISKIER.
HAVE YOU SEEN THE TIE CLIP I GOT FOR 20 YEARS OF SERVICE?

DO YOU HAVE A MINUTE?
I'M ON MY WAY TO A MEETING.
FOLLOW ME. WE'LL WALK AND TALK.
I DON'T SEE HOW THIS CAN POSSIBLY WORK.
YOU CAN BARELY CONCENTRATE WHEN YOU'RE SITTING PERFECTLY STILL.
WHEN YOU ADD THE EXTRA COMPLEXITY OF WALKING, IT'S LIKE ASKING A SQUIRREL TO LAND A 747.
MUST. . . PROVE UNDERLING. . . WRONG. . .
BONK!
I DIDN'T KNOW THAT BEING RIGHT COULD FEEL SO GOOD.
©2011 Scott Adams, Inc./Dist. by Universal Uclick
6·19·11

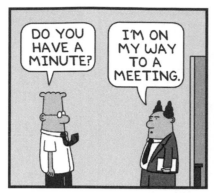

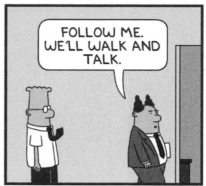

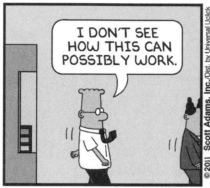

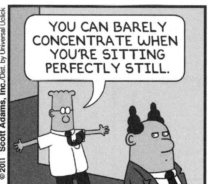

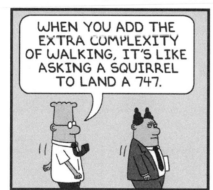

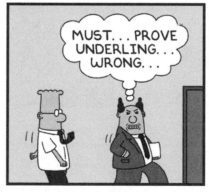

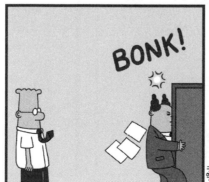

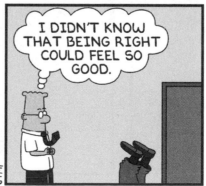

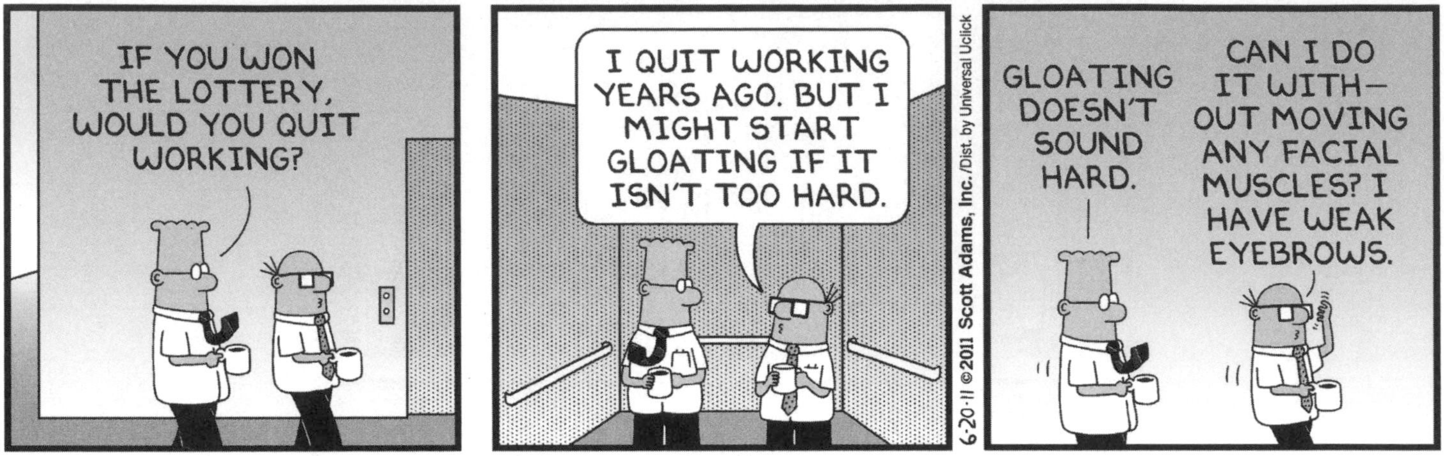
IF YOU WON THE LOTTERY, WOULD YOU QUIT WORKING?
I QUIT WORKING YEARS AGO. BUT I MIGHT START GLOATING IF IT ISN'T TOO HARD.
6-20-11 ©2011 Scott Adams, Inc./Dist. by Universal Uclick
GLOATING DOESN'T SOUND HARD.
CAN I DO IT WITH-OUT MOVING ANY FACIAL MUSCLES? I HAVE WEAK EYEBROWS.

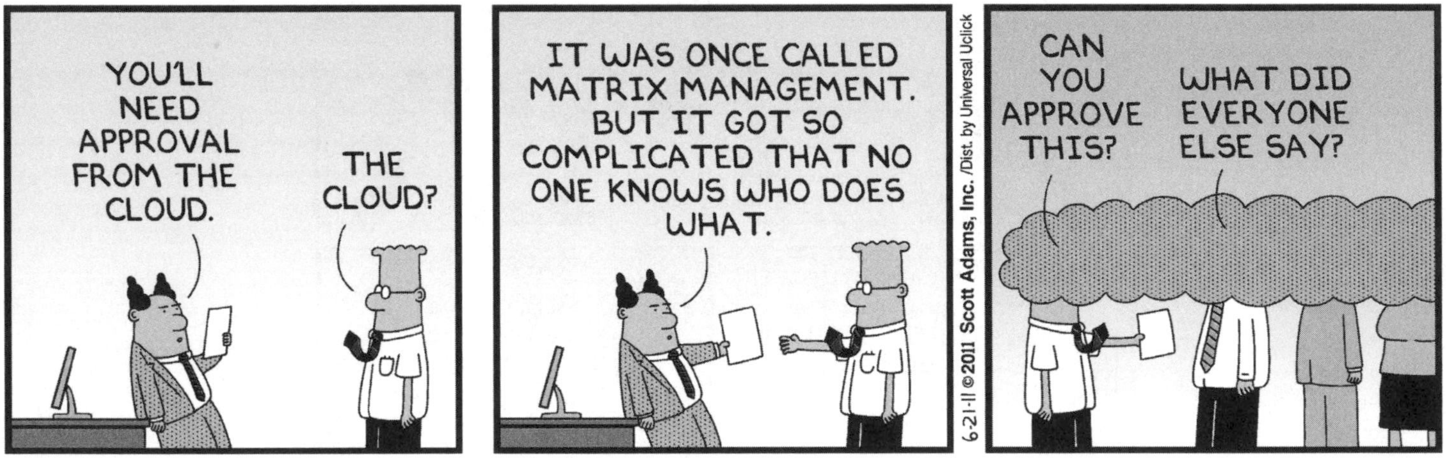
YOU'LL NEED APPROVAL FROM THE CLOUD.
THE CLOUD?
IT WAS ONCE CALLED MATRIX MANAGEMENT. BUT IT GOT SO COMPLICATED THAT NO ONE KNOWS WHO DOES WHAT.
6-21-11 ©2011 Scott Adams, Inc./Dist. by Universal Uclick
CAN YOU APPROVE THIS?
WHAT DID EVERYONE ELSE SAY?

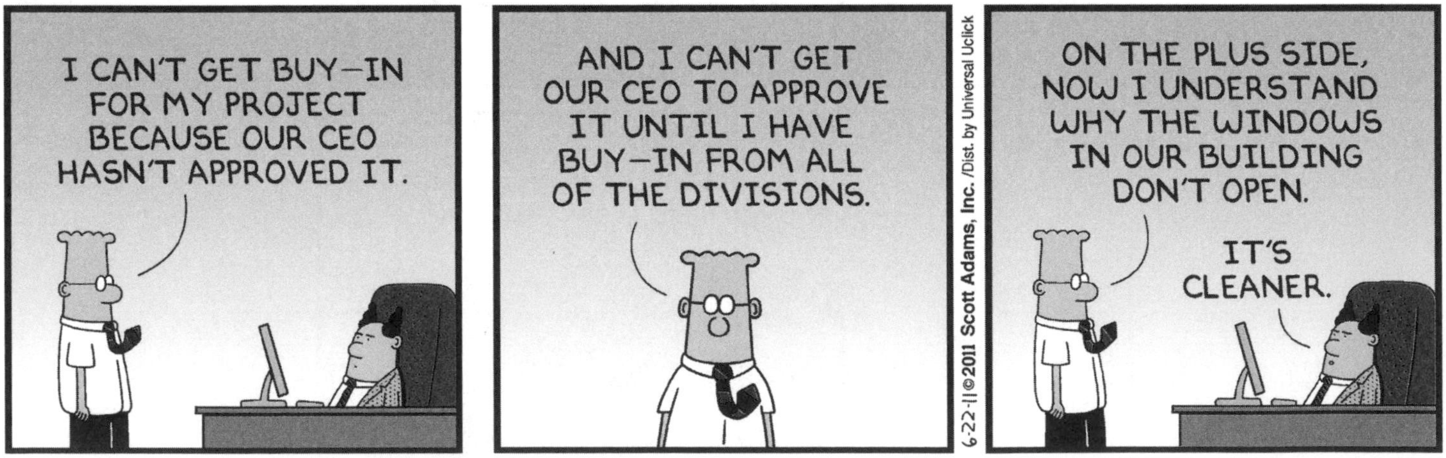
I CAN'T GET BUY-IN FOR MY PROJECT BECAUSE OUR CEO HASN'T APPROVED IT.
AND I CAN'T GET OUR CEO TO APPROVE IT UNTIL I HAVE BUY-IN FROM ALL OF THE DIVISIONS.
6-22-11 ©2011 Scott Adams, Inc./Dist. by Universal Uclick
ON THE PLUS SIDE, NOW I UNDERSTAND WHY THE WINDOWS IN OUR BUILDING DON'T OPEN.
IT'S CLEANER.

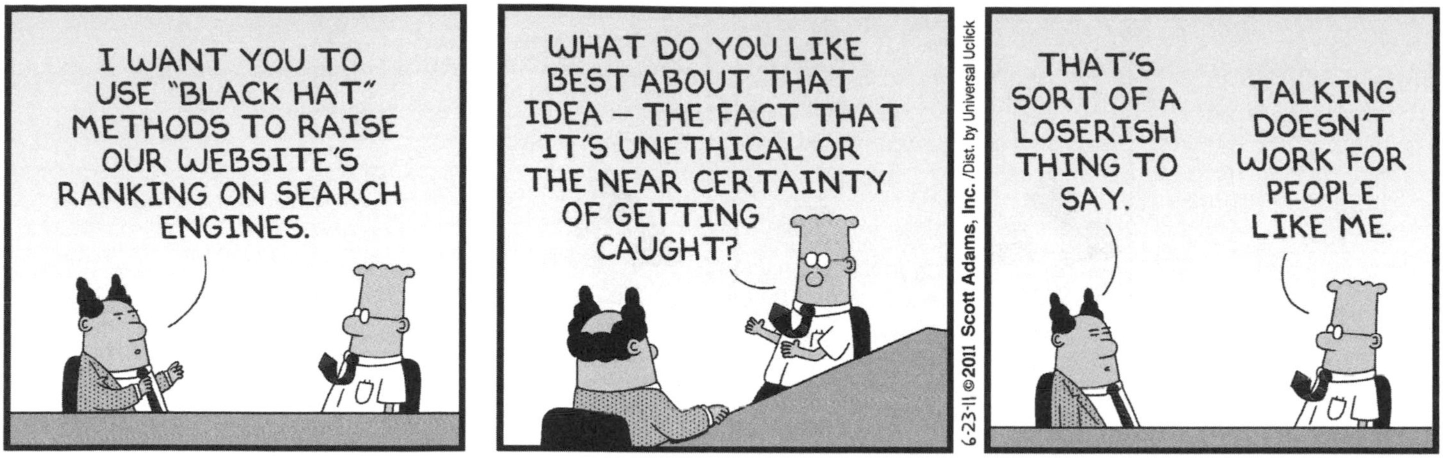
I WANT YOU TO USE "BLACK HAT" METHODS TO RAISE OUR WEBSITE'S RANKING ON SEARCH ENGINES.
WHAT DO YOU LIKE BEST ABOUT THAT IDEA – THE FACT THAT IT'S UNETHICAL OR THE NEAR CERTAINTY OF GETTING CAUGHT?
6-23-11 ©2011 Scott Adams, Inc. /Dist. by Universal Uclick
THAT'S SORT OF A LOSERISH THING TO SAY.
TALKING DOESN'T WORK FOR PEOPLE LIKE ME.

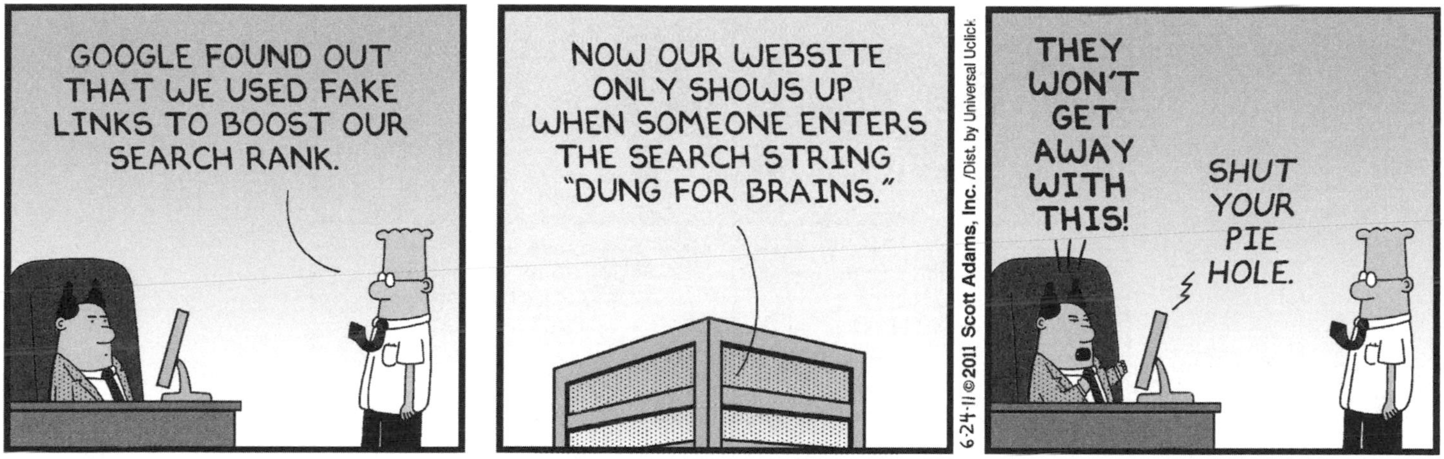
GOOGLE FOUND OUT THAT WE USED FAKE LINKS TO BOOST OUR SEARCH RANK.
NOW OUR WEBSITE ONLY SHOWS UP WHEN SOMEONE ENTERS THE SEARCH STRING "DUNG FOR BRAINS."
6-24-11 ©2011 Scott Adams, Inc. /Dist. by Universal Uclick
THEY WON'T GET AWAY WITH THIS!
SHUT YOUR PIE HOLE.

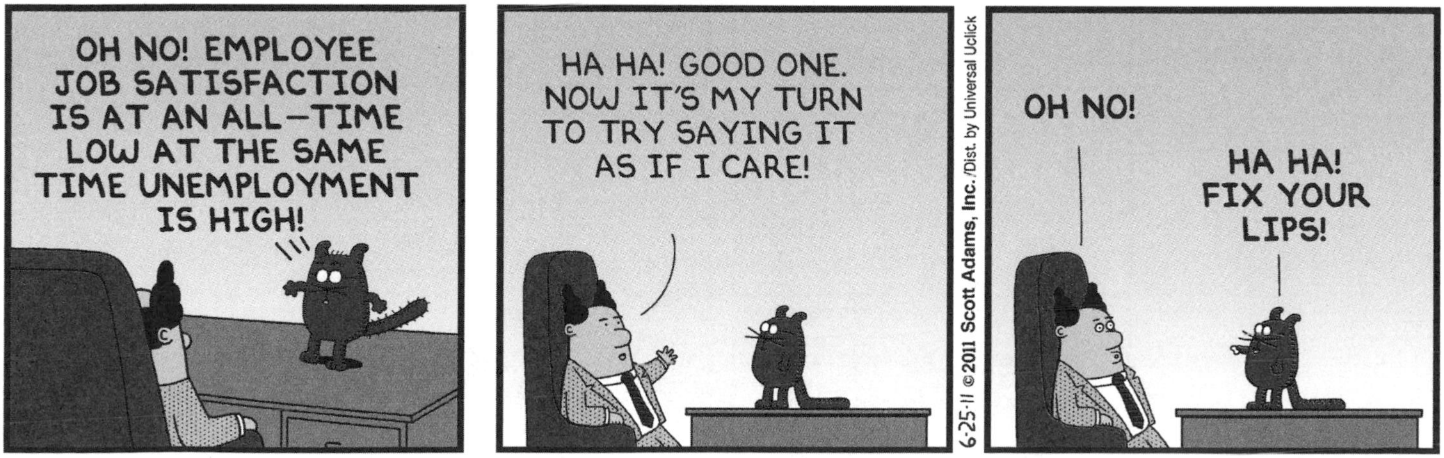
OH NO! EMPLOYEE JOB SATISFACTION IS AT AN ALL-TIME LOW AT THE SAME TIME UNEMPLOYMENT IS HIGH!
HA HA! GOOD ONE. NOW IT'S MY TURN TO TRY SAYING IT AS IF I CARE!
6-25-11 ©2011 Scott Adams, Inc. /Dist. by Universal Uclick
OH NO!
HA HA! FIX YOUR LIPS!

STEER CLEAR OF DARRYL. HE TURNED FERAL.
FERAL?
THAT'S WHAT HAPPENS WHEN ENGINEERS DON'T GET INVITED TO MEETINGS.
DARRYL'S ONLY SOCIAL LIFE WAS MEETINGS.
©2011 Scott Adams, Inc./Dist. by Universal Uclick
HE DIDN'T GET TO USE HIS SOCIAL SKILLS FOR A FEW WEEKS, AND APPARENTLY HE LOST THEM.
IS IT LIKE HE TURNED INTO A WOLFMAN?
YES, EXCEPT HE'S BETTER AT MATH. AND HE HOWLS AT THE INTERNET, NOT THE MOON.
CAN WE WATCH?
6-26-11
HOW-OOOOO CAN YOU BLOG THAT?

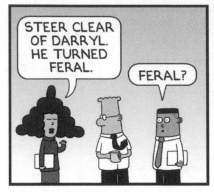

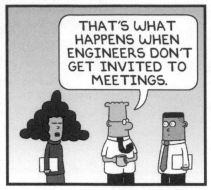

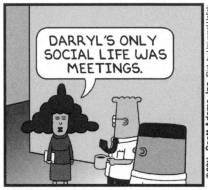

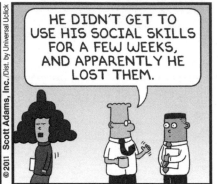

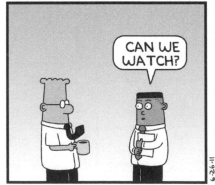

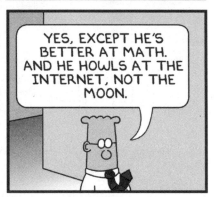

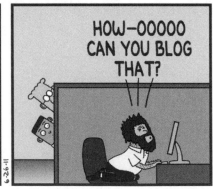

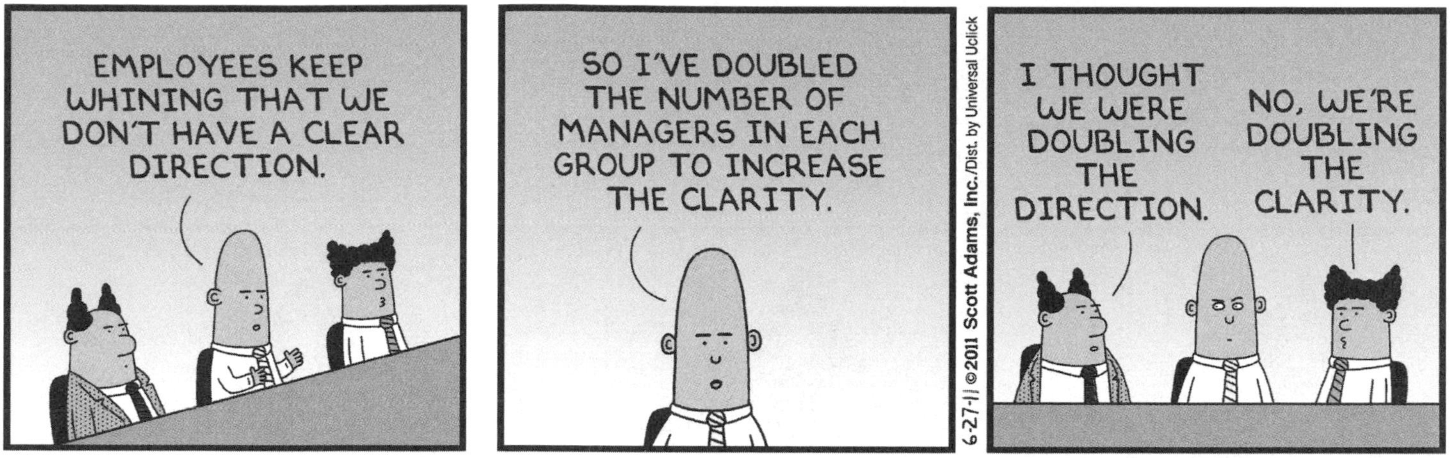
EMPLOYEES KEEP WHINING THAT WE DON'T HAVE A CLEAR DIRECTION.
SO I'VE DOUBLED THE NUMBER OF MANAGERS IN EACH GROUP TO INCREASE THE CLARITY.
6-27-11 ©2011 Scott Adams, Inc./Dist. by Universal Uclick
I THOUGHT WE WERE DOUBLING THE DIRECTION.
NO, WE'RE DOUBLING THE CLARITY.

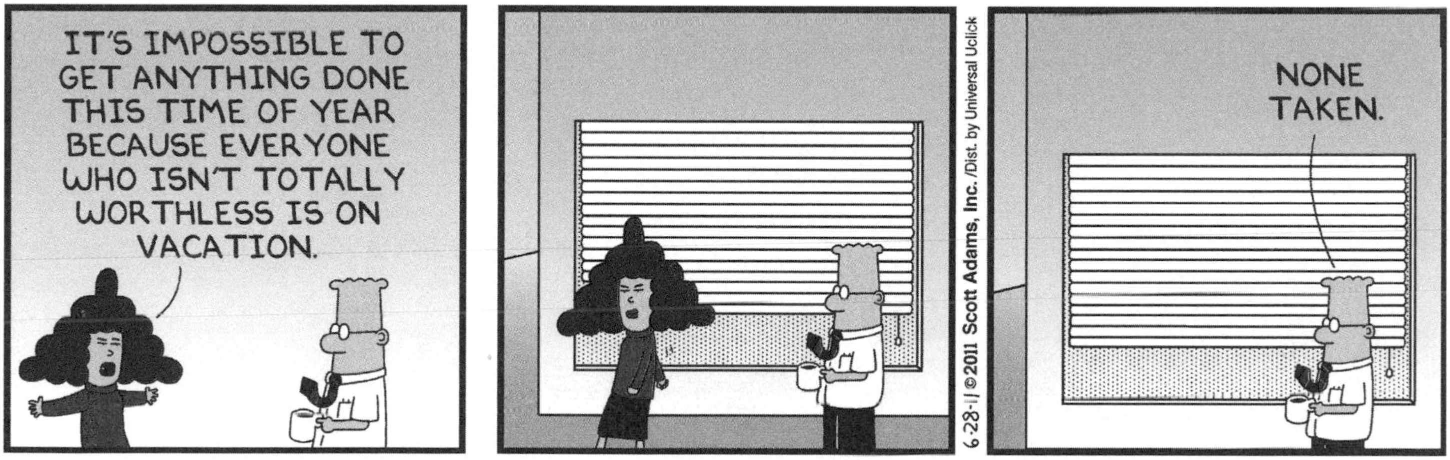
IT'S IMPOSSIBLE TO GET ANYTHING DONE THIS TIME OF YEAR BECAUSE EVERYONE WHO ISN'T TOTALLY WORTHLESS IS ON VACATION.
6-28-11 ©2011 Scott Adams, Inc./Dist. by Universal Uclick
NONE TAKEN.

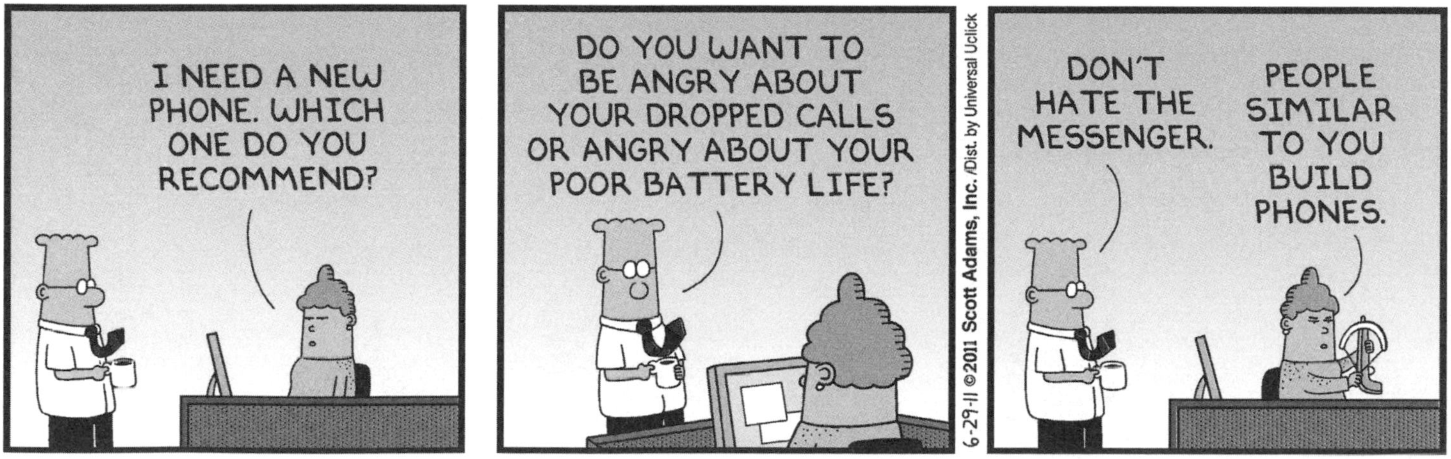
I NEED A NEW PHONE. WHICH ONE DO YOU RECOMMEND?
DO YOU WANT TO BE ANGRY ABOUT YOUR DROPPED CALLS OR ANGRY ABOUT YOUR POOR BATTERY LIFE?
6-29-11 ©2011 Scott Adams, Inc./Dist. by Universal Uclick
DON'T HATE THE MESSENGER.
PEOPLE SIMILAR TO YOU BUILD PHONES.

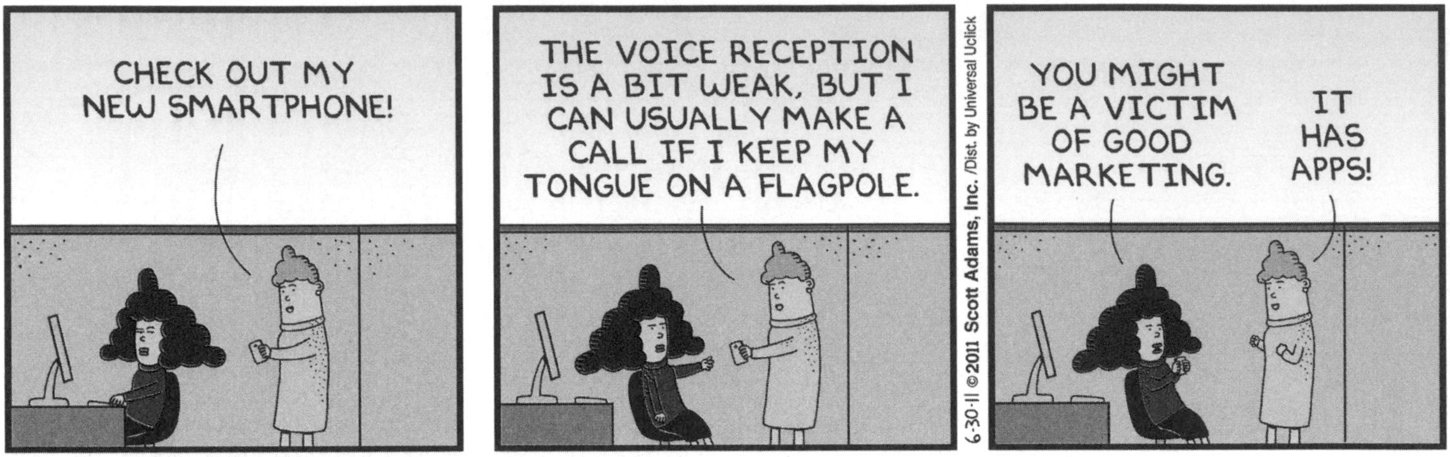
CHECK OUT MY NEW SMARTPHONE!
THE VOICE RECEPTION IS A BIT WEAK, BUT I CAN USUALLY MAKE A CALL IF I KEEP MY TONGUE ON A FLAGPOLE.
YOU MIGHT BE A VICTIM OF GOOD MARKETING.
IT HAS APPS!
6-30-11 ©2011 Scott Adams, Inc. /Dist. by Universal Uclick

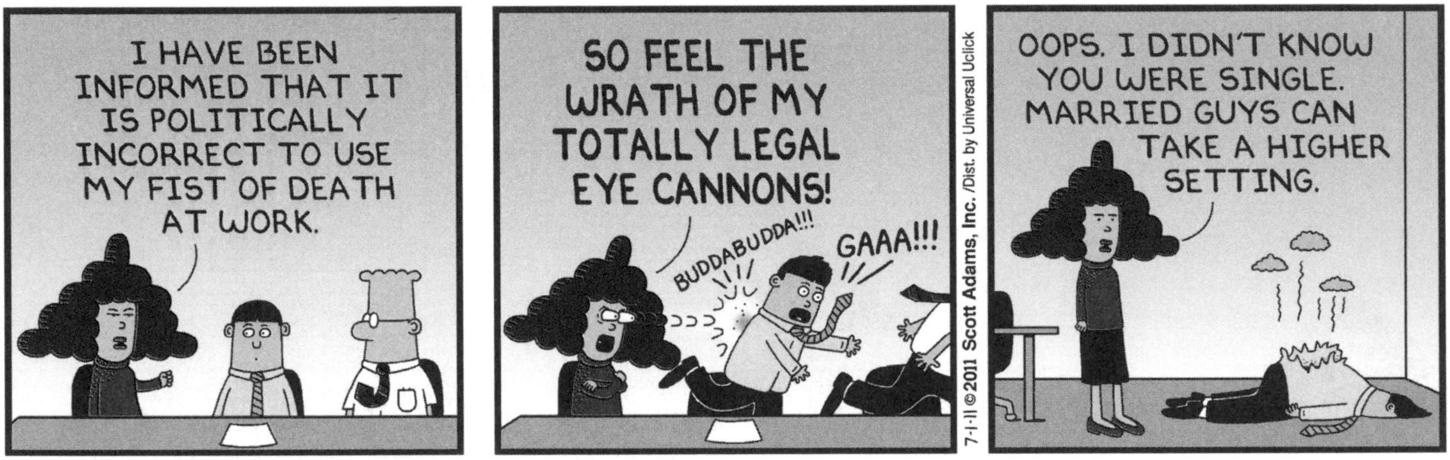
I HAVE BEEN INFORMED THAT IT IS POLITICALLY INCORRECT TO USE MY FIST OF DEATH AT WORK.
SO FEEL THE WRATH OF MY TOTALLY LEGAL EYE CANNONS!
BUDDABUDDA!!!
GAAA!!!
OOPS. I DIDN'T KNOW YOU WERE SINGLE. MARRIED GUYS CAN TAKE A HIGHER SETTING.
7-1-11 ©2011 Scott Adams, Inc. /Dist. by Universal Uclick

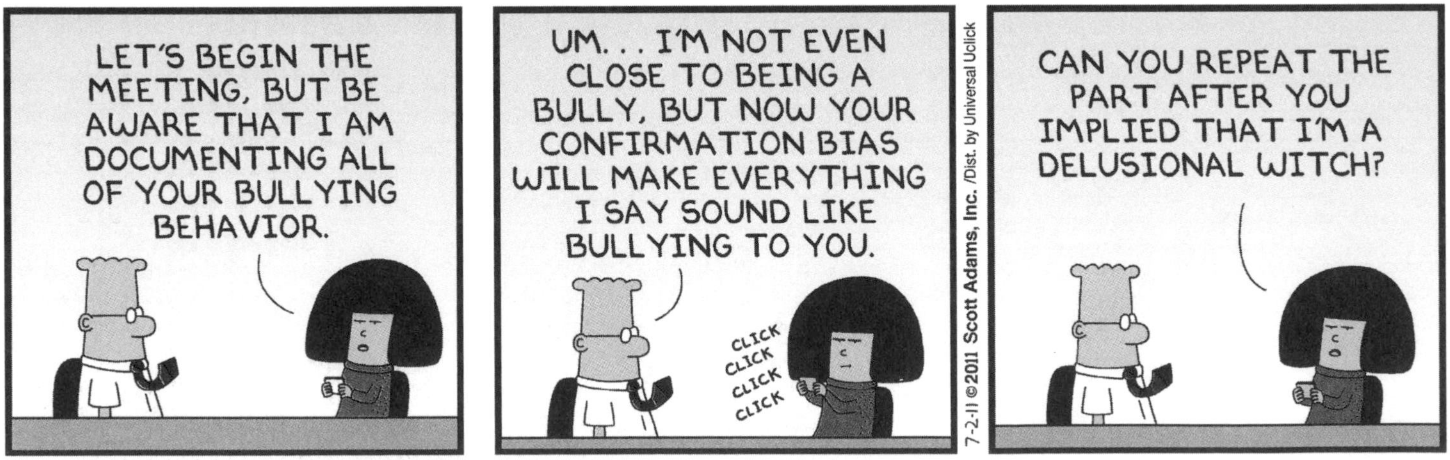
LET'S BEGIN THE MEETING, BUT BE AWARE THAT I AM DOCUMENTING ALL OF YOUR BULLYING BEHAVIOR.
UM. . . I'M NOT EVEN CLOSE TO BEING A BULLY, BUT NOW YOUR CONFIRMATION BIAS WILL MAKE EVERYTHING I SAY SOUND LIKE BULLYING TO YOU.
CLICK CLICK CLICK CLICK
CAN YOU REPEAT THE PART AFTER YOU IMPLIED THAT I'M A DELUSIONAL WITCH?
7-2-11 ©2011 Scott Adams, Inc. /Dist. by Universal Uclick

CAN YOU LOOK AT THIS BID AND LET ME KNOW IF I CAN ORDER THE HARDWARE?
YES.
ARE YOU SAYING YES I CAN ORDER THE HARDWARE, OR YES YOU'LL LOOK AT IT?
©2011 Scott Adams, Inc./Dist. by Universal Uclick
MUMBLE, MUMBLE.
WHAT?
I NEED YOUR INPUT ON MY POWERPOINT DECK.
SO FAR, IN RESPONSE TO MY REQUEST, YOU'VE GIVEN ME AMBIGUITY, MUMBLING, AND A CHANGE OF SUBJECT.
WOULD YOU PREFER THAT I BADGER YOU FOR AN ANSWER UNTIL YOU GET ANGRY, OR SHOULD I RETURN TO MY CUBICLE AND RESUME BEING INEFFECTIVE?
7-3-11
YOU ASK TOO MANY QUESTIONS.

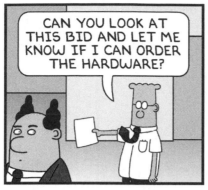

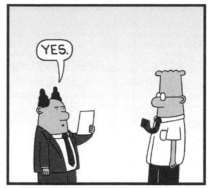

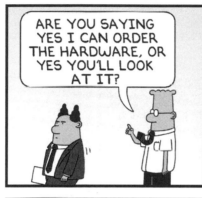

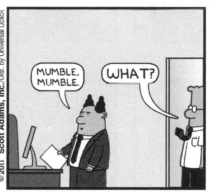

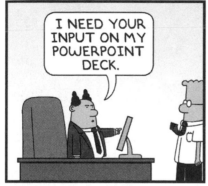

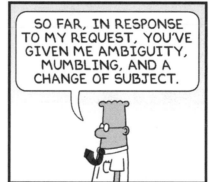

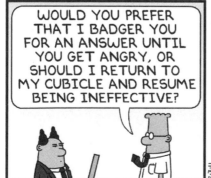

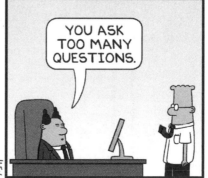

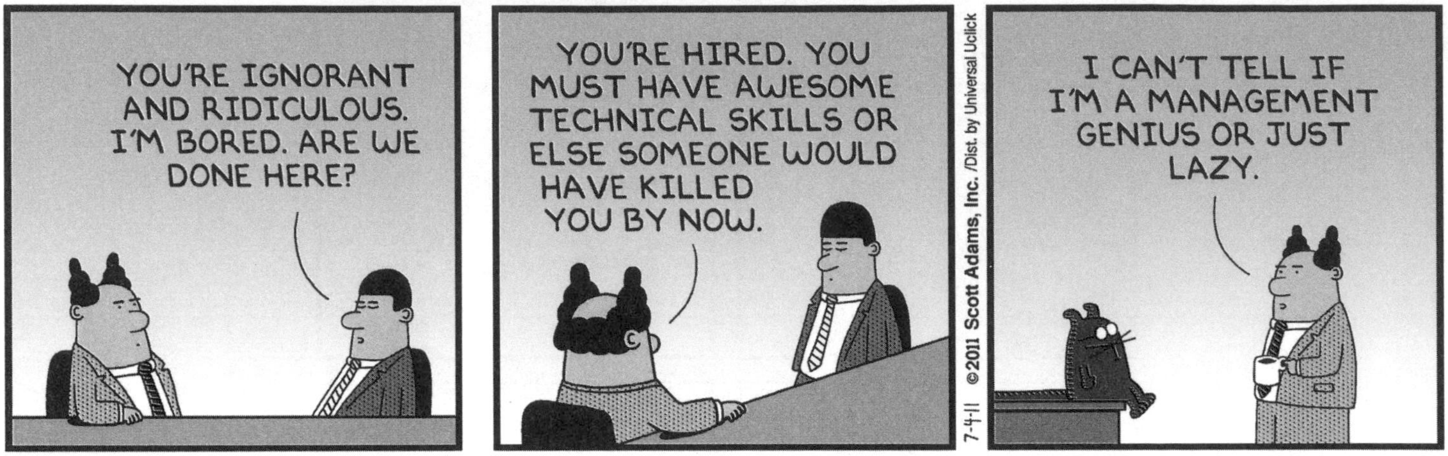
YOU'RE IGNORANT AND RIDICULOUS. I'M BORED. ARE WE DONE HERE?
YOU'RE HIRED. YOU MUST HAVE AWESOME TECHNICAL SKILLS OR ELSE SOMEONE WOULD HAVE KILLED YOU BY NOW.
7-4-11 ©2011 Scott Adams, Inc. /Dist. by Universal Uclick
I CAN'T TELL IF I'M A MANAGEMENT GENIUS OR JUST LAZY.

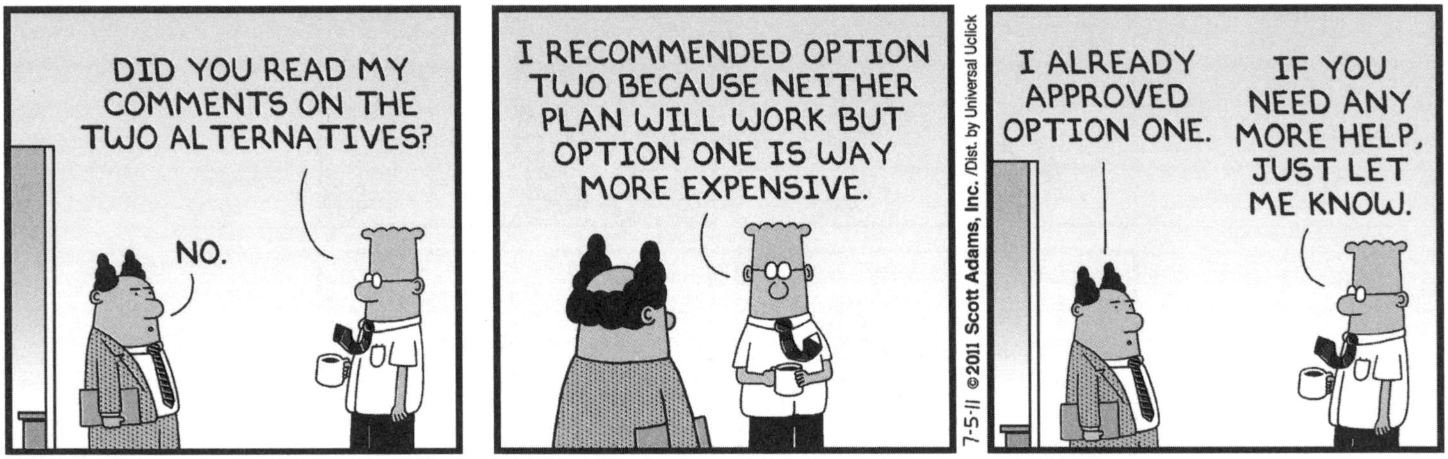
DID YOU READ MY COMMENTS ON THE TWO ALTERNATIVES?
NO.
I RECOMMENDED OPTION TWO BECAUSE NEITHER PLAN WILL WORK BUT OPTION ONE IS WAY MORE EXPENSIVE.
7-5-11 ©2011 Scott Adams, Inc. /Dist. by Universal Uclick
I ALREADY APPROVED OPTION ONE.
IF YOU NEED ANY MORE HELP, JUST LET ME KNOW.

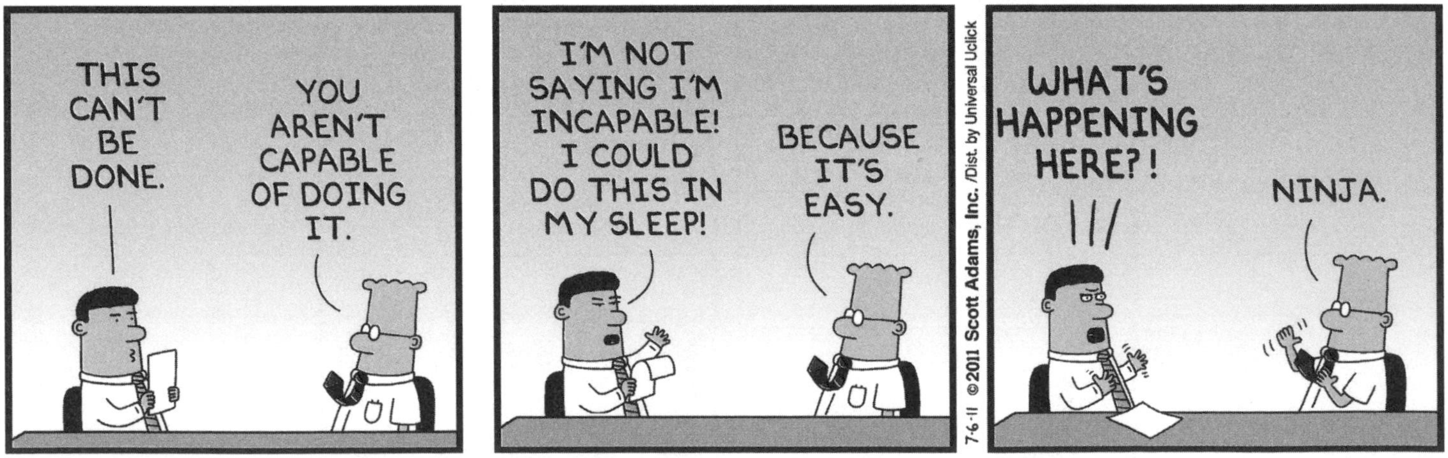
THIS CAN'T BE DONE.
YOU AREN'T CAPABLE OF DOING IT.
I'M NOT SAYING I'M INCAPABLE! I COULD DO THIS IN MY SLEEP!
BECAUSE IT'S EASY.
7-6-11 ©2011 Scott Adams, Inc. /Dist. by Universal Uclick
WHAT'S HAPPENING HERE?!
NINJA.

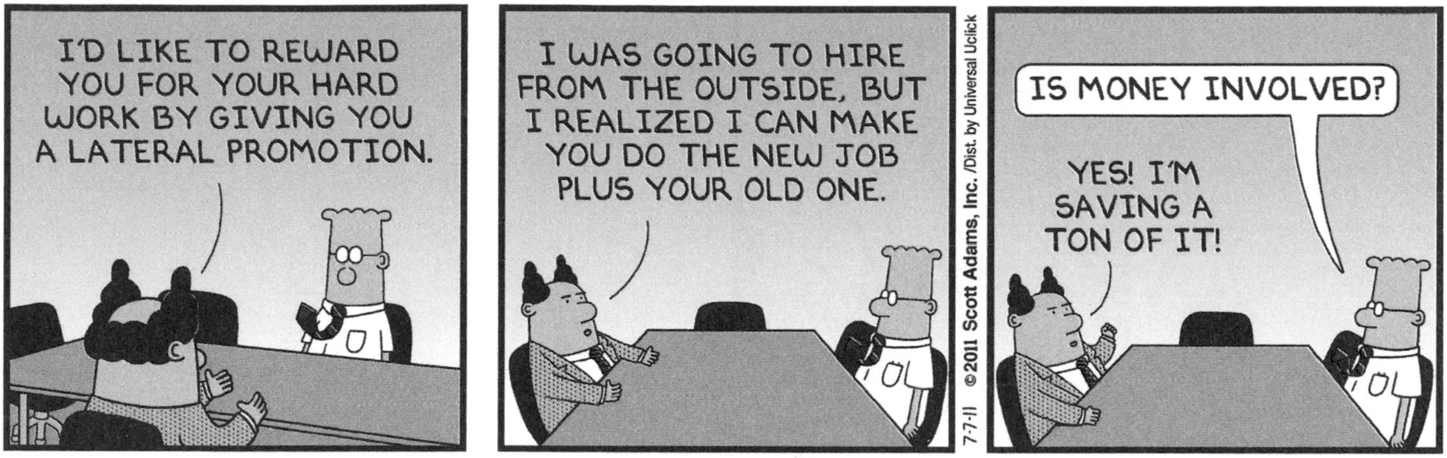
I'D LIKE TO REWARD YOU FOR YOUR HARD WORK BY GIVING YOU A LATERAL PROMOTION.
I WAS GOING TO HIRE FROM THE OUTSIDE, BUT I REALIZED I CAN MAKE YOU DO THE NEW JOB PLUS YOUR OLD ONE.
7-7-11 ©2011 Scott Adams, Inc. /Dist. by Universal Uclick
IS MONEY INVOLVED?
YES! I'M SAVING A TON OF IT!

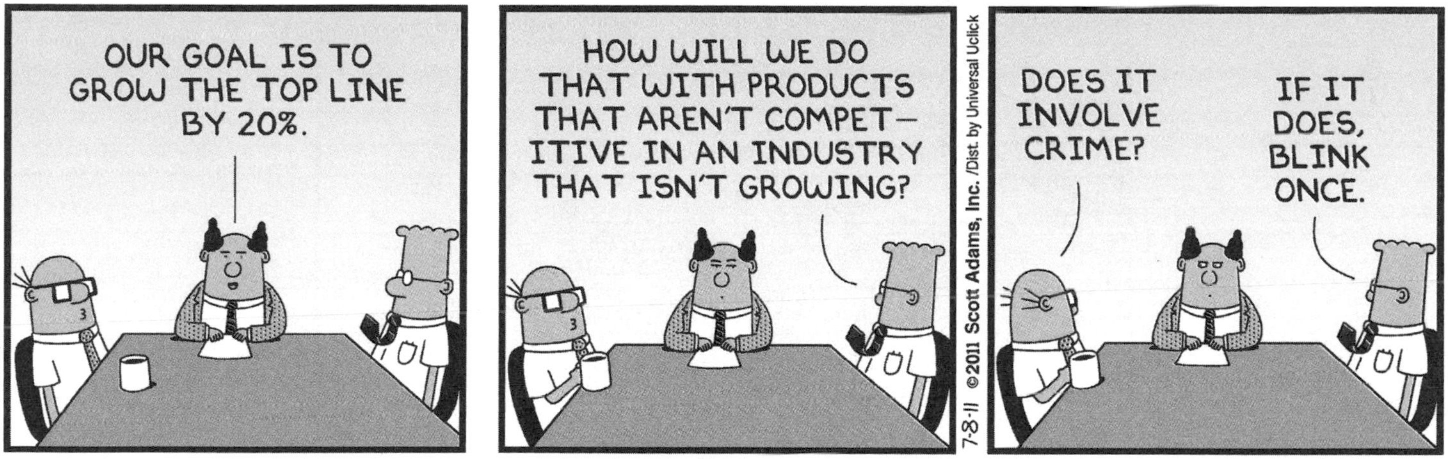
OUR GOAL IS TO GROW THE TOP LINE BY 20%.
HOW WILL WE DO THAT WITH PRODUCTS THAT AREN'T COMPET– ITIVE IN AN INDUSTRY THAT ISN'T GROWING?
7-8-11 ©2011 Scott Adams, Inc. /Dist. by Universal Uclick
DOES IT INVOLVE CRIME?
IF IT DOES, BLINK ONCE.

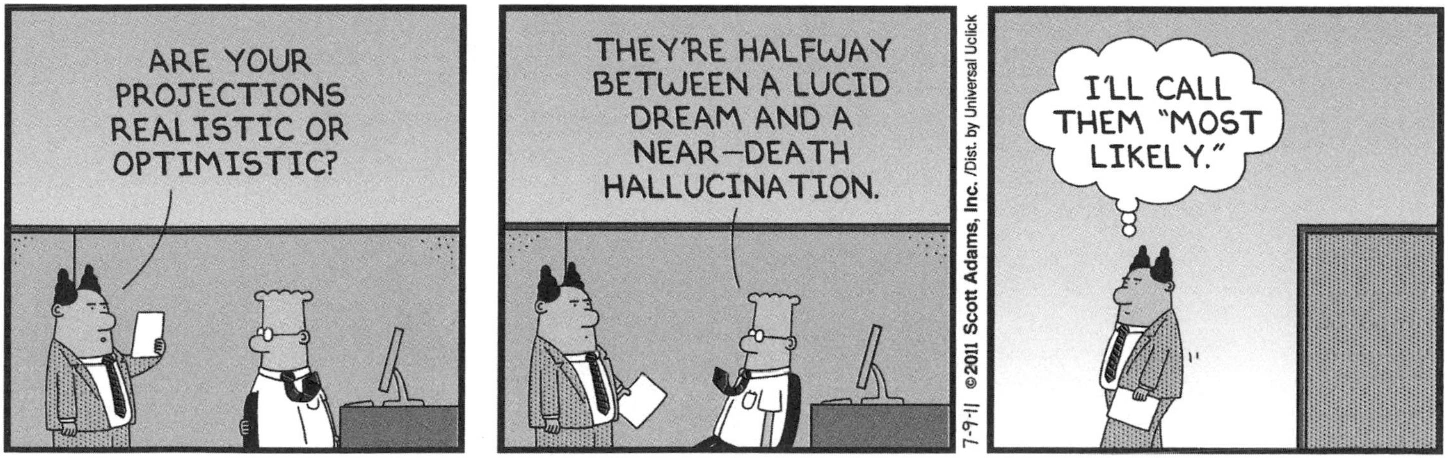
ARE YOUR PROJECTIONS REALISTIC OR OPTIMISTIC?
THEY'RE HALFWAY BETWEEN A LUCID DREAM AND A NEAR–DEATH HALLUCINATION.
7-9-11 ©2011 Scott Adams, Inc. /Dist. by Universal Uclick
I'LL CALL THEM "MOST LIKELY."

EACH OF YOU HAS ALREADY MASTERED THE ART OF BEING USELESS AT WORK.
IT'S TIME TO TAKE IT TO THE NEXT LEVEL.
TODAY I WILL TEACH YOU HOW TO BE TOXIC.
TOXIC PEOPLE TALK ABOUT TWO TYPES OF THINGS.
ONE: BRING UP TOPICS THAT ARE SURE TO CAUSE OTHERS TO FIGHT.
TWO: COMPLAIN ABOUT YOUR PERSONAL PROBLEMS AT EVERY OPPORTUNITY.
YOUR HOMEWORK IS TO PRACTICE AT WORK TOMORROW.
I MENTIONED TO ALICE THAT YOU THINK HER PLAN IS KIND OF LAME.
© 2011 Scott Adams, Inc./Dist. by Universal Uclick
7-10-11

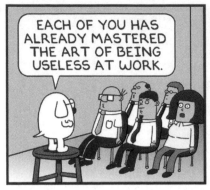

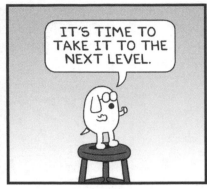

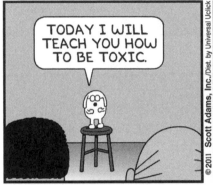

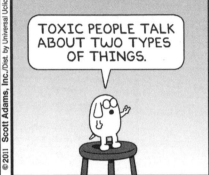

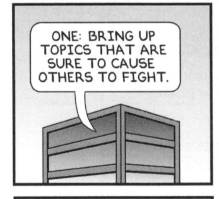

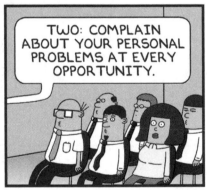

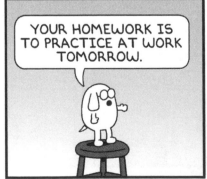

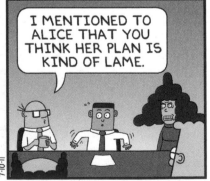

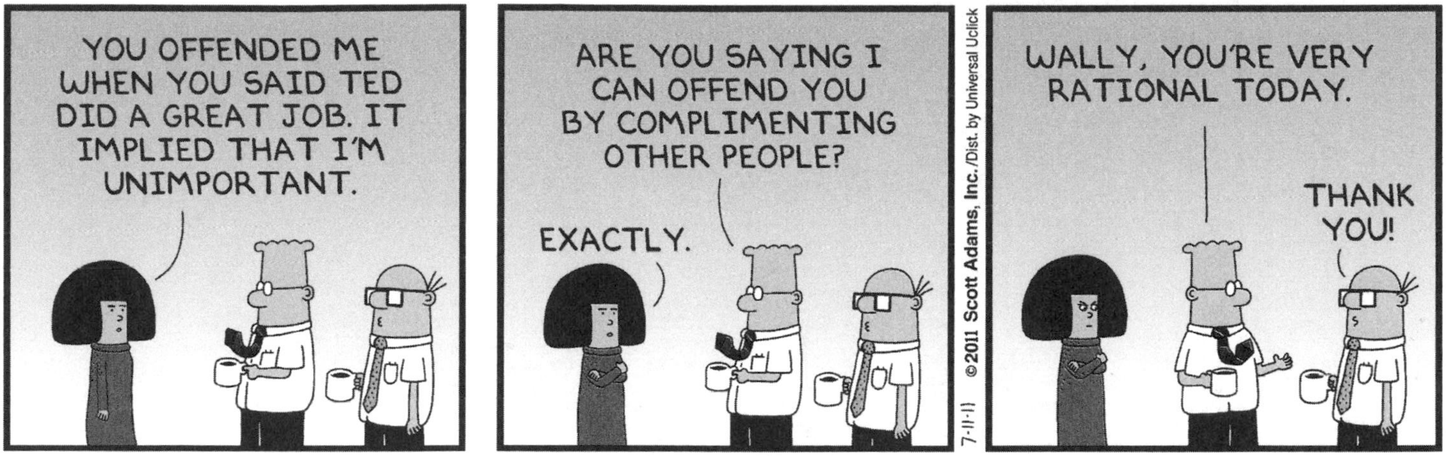
YOU OFFENDED ME WHEN YOU SAID TED DID A GREAT JOB. IT IMPLIED THAT I'M UNIMPORTANT.
ARE YOU SAYING I CAN OFFEND YOU BY COMPLIMENTING OTHER PEOPLE?
EXACTLY.
7-11-11 ©2011 Scott Adams, Inc./Dist. by Universal Uclick
WALLY, YOU'RE VERY RATIONAL TODAY.
THANK YOU!

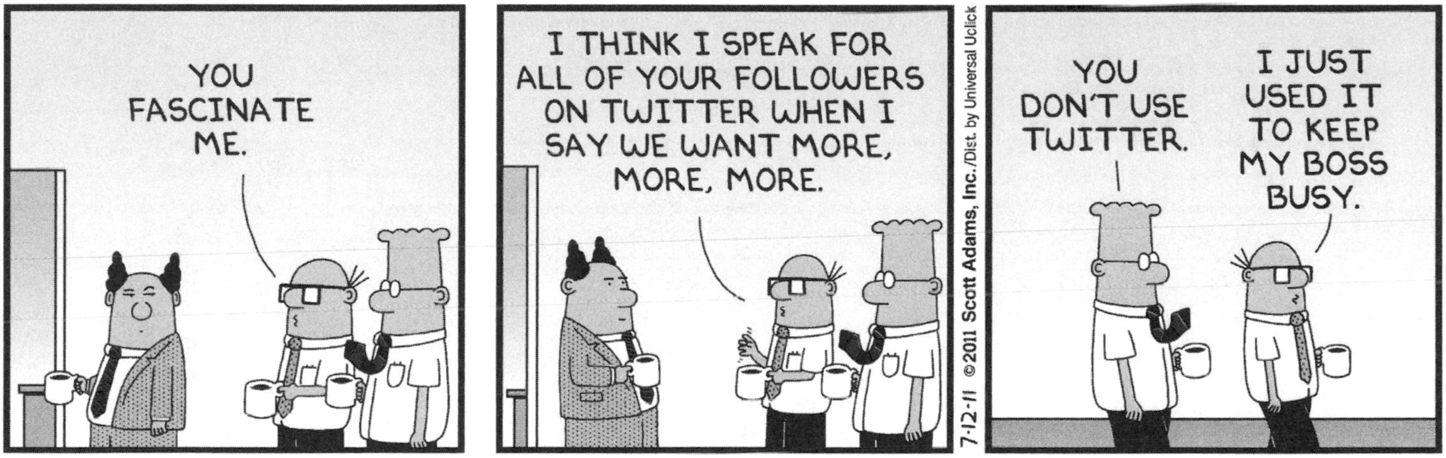
YOU FASCINATE ME.
I THINK I SPEAK FOR ALL OF YOUR FOLLOWERS ON TWITTER WHEN I SAY WE WANT MORE, MORE, MORE.
7-12-11 ©2011 Scott Adams, Inc./Dist. by Universal Uclick
YOU DON'T USE TWITTER.
I JUST USED IT TO KEEP MY BOSS BUSY.

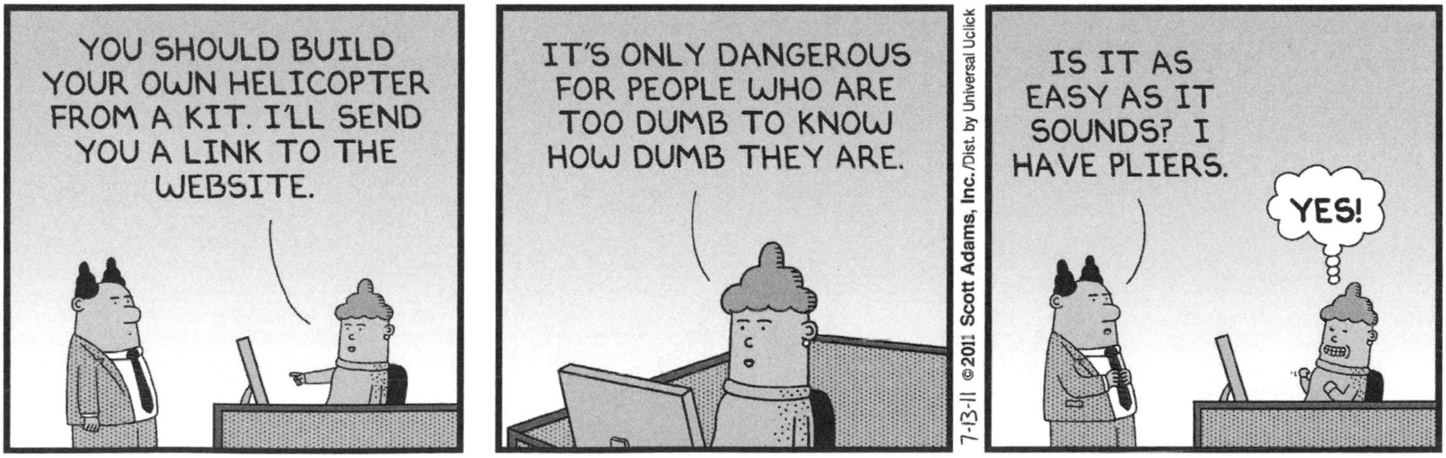
YOU SHOULD BUILD YOUR OWN HELICOPTER FROM A KIT. I'LL SEND YOU A LINK TO THE WEBSITE.
IT'S ONLY DANGEROUS FOR PEOPLE WHO ARE TOO DUMB TO KNOW HOW DUMB THEY ARE.
7-13-11 ©2011 Scott Adams, Inc./Dist. by Universal Uclick
IS IT AS EASY AS IT SOUNDS? I HAVE PLIERS.
YES!

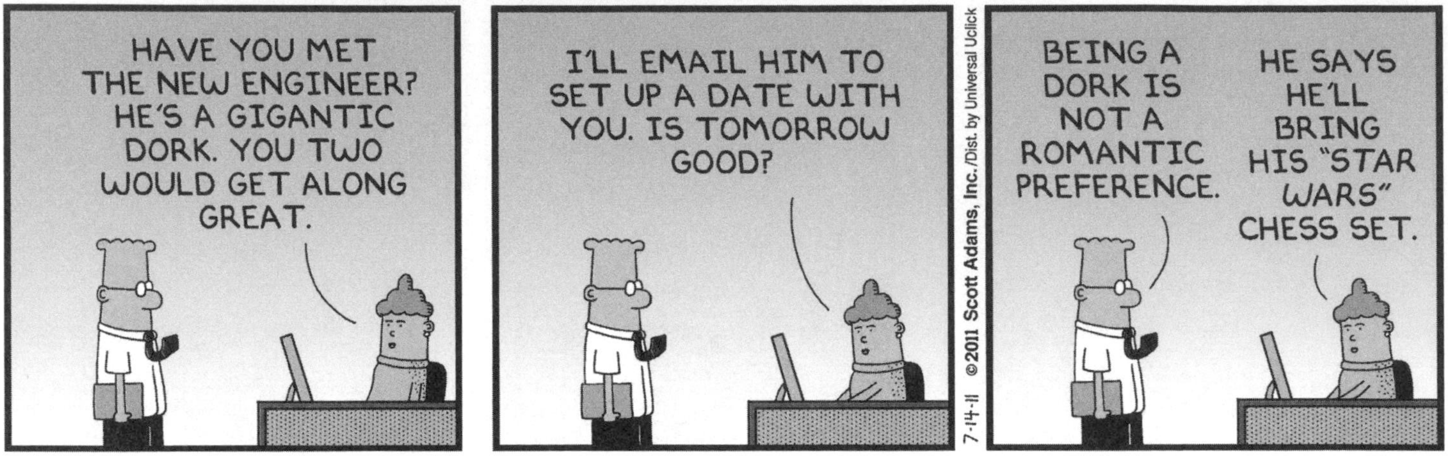
HAVE YOU MET THE NEW ENGINEER? HE'S A GIGANTIC DORK. YOU TWO WOULD GET ALONG GREAT.
I'LL EMAIL HIM TO SET UP A DATE WITH YOU. IS TOMORROW GOOD?
7-14-11 ©2011 Scott Adams, Inc./Dist. by Universal Uclick
BEING A DORK IS NOT A ROMANTIC PREFERENCE.
HE SAYS HE'LL BRING HIS "STAR WARS" CHESS SET.

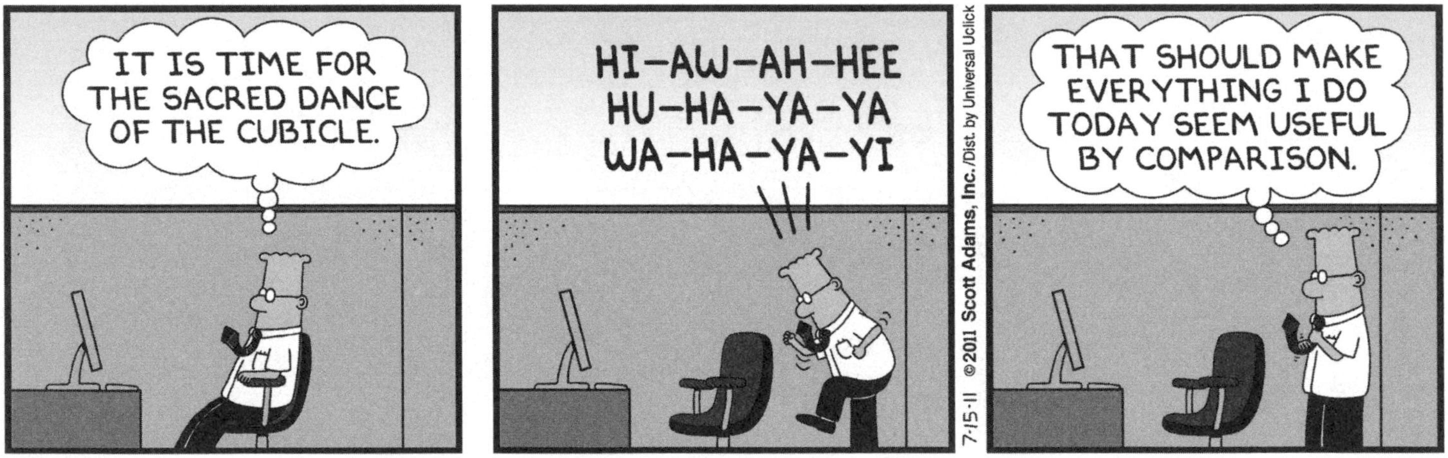
IT IS TIME FOR THE SACRED DANCE OF THE CUBICLE.
HI-AW-AH-HEE HU-HA-YA-YA WA-HA-YA-YI
7-15-11 ©2011 Scott Adams, Inc./Dist. by Universal Uclick
THAT SHOULD MAKE EVERYTHING I DO TODAY SEEM USEFUL BY COMPARISON.

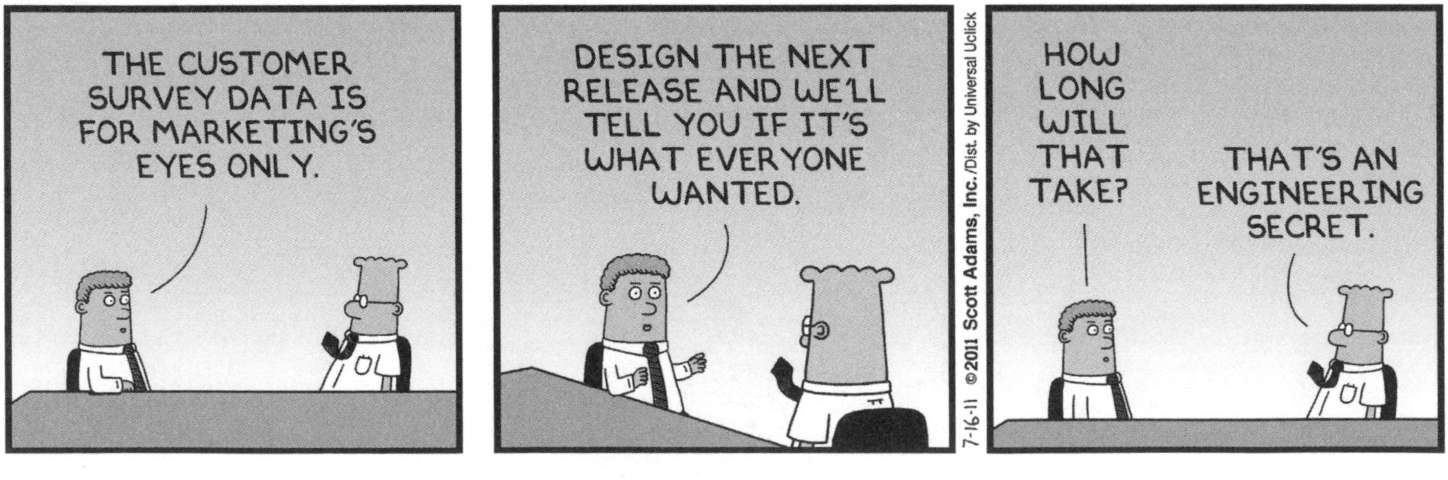
THE CUSTOMER SURVEY DATA IS FOR MARKETING'S EYES ONLY.
DESIGN THE NEXT RELEASE AND WE'LL TELL YOU IF IT'S WHAT EVERYONE WANTED.
7-16-11 ©2011 Scott Adams, Inc./Dist. by Universal Uclick
HOW LONG WILL THAT TAKE?
THAT'S AN ENGINEERING SECRET.

I'D LIKE TO TALK ABOUT MY CAREER PATH.
ARE YOU SURE?
UM. . . YES, I'M SURE.
DON'T SAY I DIDN'T WARN YOU.
YOU'RE WITHIN 20% OF YOUR MAX-IMUM CAREER POTENTIAL.
© 2011 Scott Adams, Inc./Dist. by Universal Uclick
YOUR FUTURE WILL BE JUST LIKE THE PRESENT, EXCEPT YOU'LL BE OLDER AND YOU MIGHT OWN A LESS-EMBARRASSING CAR.
IF YOU GO TO A NEW COMPANY, YOU'LL LIKE IT AT FIRST, BUT IN TIME YOU'LL REALIZE EVERY PLACE IS THE SAME.
GAAA!!! TAKE BACK THE TRUTH!!! LIE TO ME! LIE TO ME!
MAYBE SOMEDAY OUR CEO WILL MAKE SUCH A HUGE BONUS THAT HE'LL WANT TO SHARE SOME OF IT WITH YOU.
7-17-11
I HATE YOU!
HEY, I'M THE GUY WHO TRIED TO SPARE YOU FROM THIS CONVERSATION.

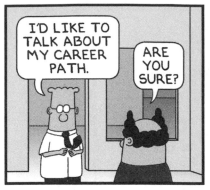

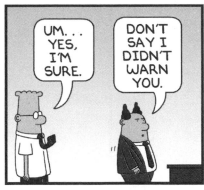

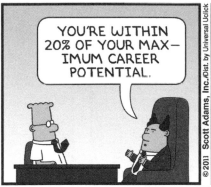

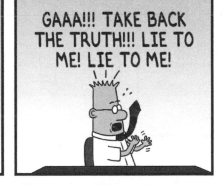

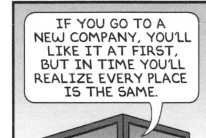

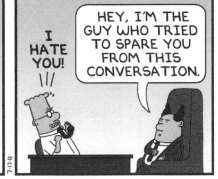

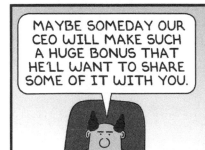

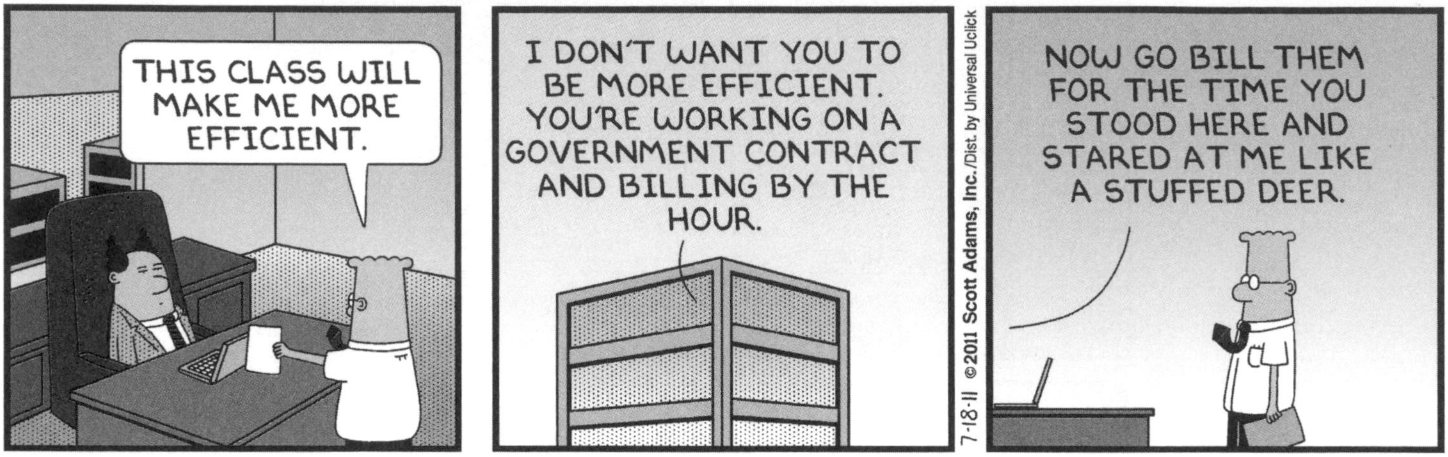
THIS CLASS WILL MAKE ME MORE EFFICIENT.
I DON'T WANT YOU TO BE MORE EFFICIENT. YOU'RE WORKING ON A GOVERNMENT CONTRACT AND BILLING BY THE HOUR.
NOW GO BILL THEM FOR THE TIME YOU STOOD HERE AND STARED AT ME LIKE A STUFFED DEER.
7-18-11

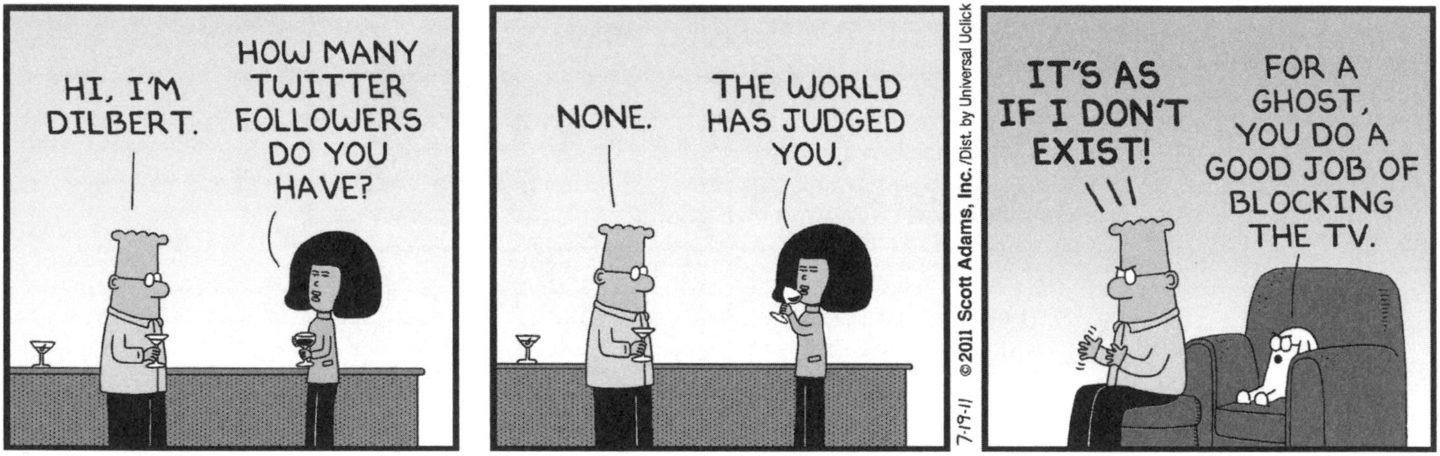
HI, I'M DILBERT.
HOW MANY TWITTER FOLLOWERS DO YOU HAVE?
NONE.
THE WORLD HAS JUDGED YOU.
IT'S AS IF I DON'T EXIST!
FOR A GHOST, YOU DO A GOOD JOB OF BLOCKING THE TV.
7-19-11

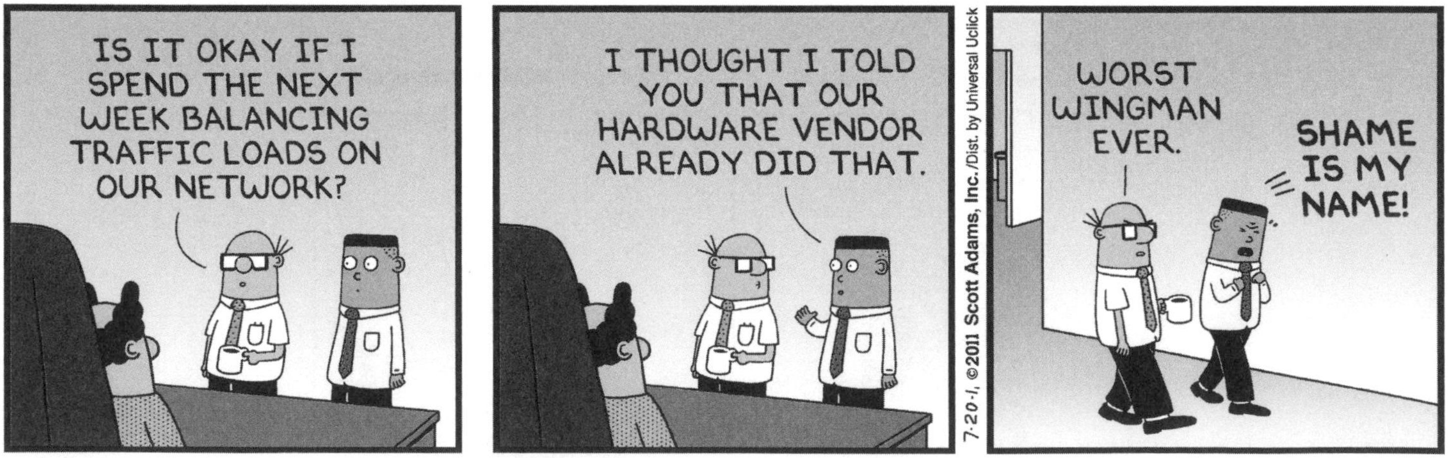
IS IT OKAY IF I SPEND THE NEXT WEEK BALANCING TRAFFIC LOADS ON OUR NETWORK?
I THOUGHT I TOLD YOU THAT OUR HARDWARE VENDOR ALREADY DID THAT.
WORST WINGMAN EVER.
SHAME IS MY NAME!
7-20-11

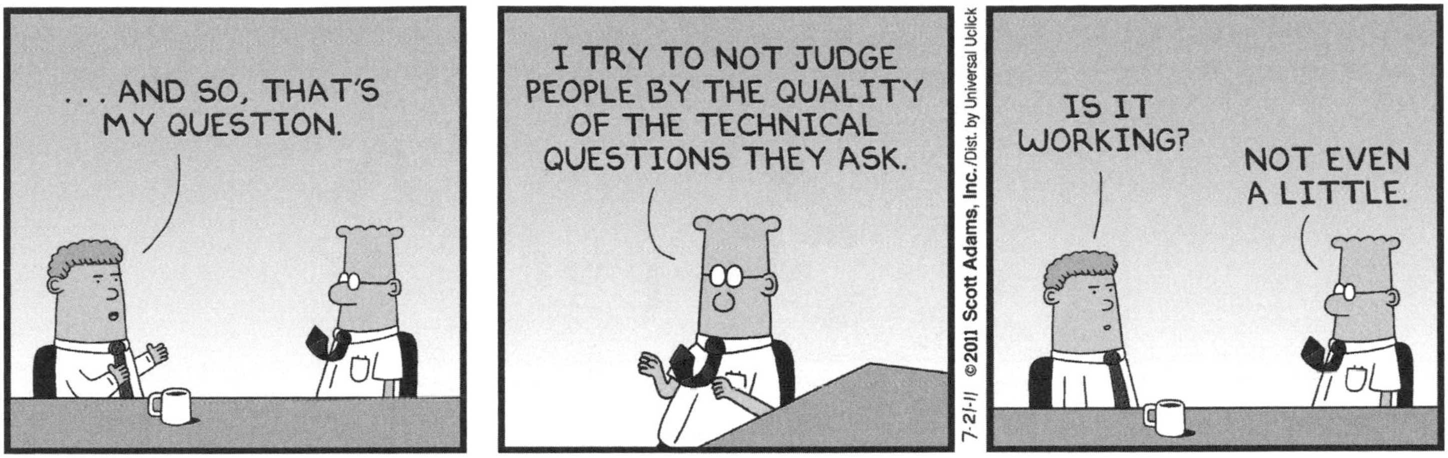

. . . AND SO, THAT'S MY QUESTION.
I TRY TO NOT JUDGE PEOPLE BY THE QUALITY OF THE TECHNICAL QUESTIONS THEY ASK.
7·21·11 ©2011 Scott Adams, Inc./Dist. by Universal Uclick
IS IT WORKING?
NOT EVEN A LITTLE.

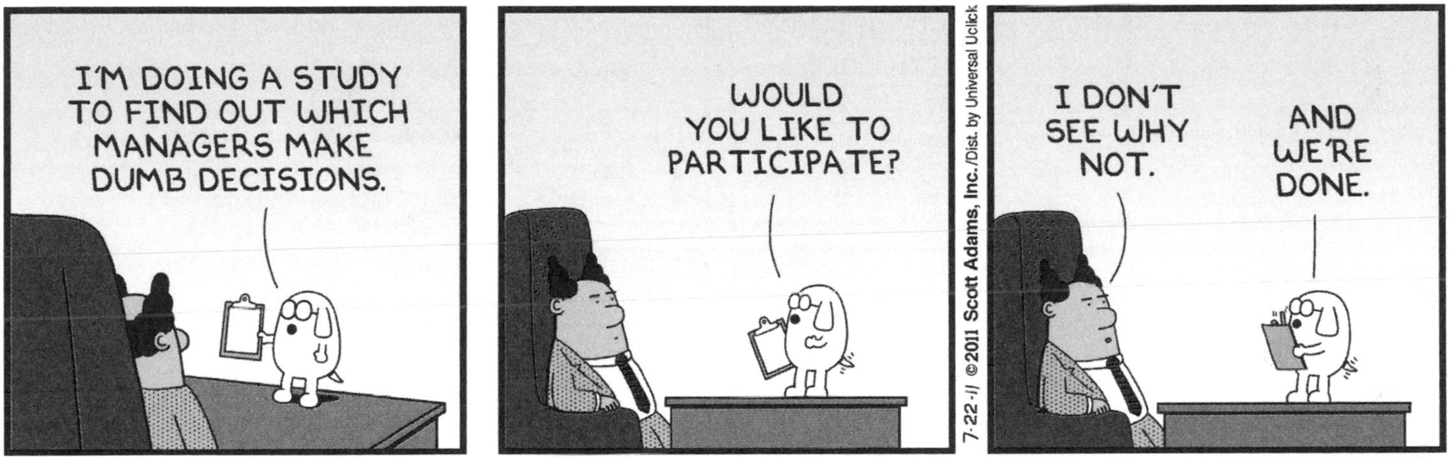

I'M DOING A STUDY TO FIND OUT WHICH MANAGERS MAKE DUMB DECISIONS.
WOULD YOU LIKE TO PARTICIPATE?
7·22·11 ©2011 Scott Adams, Inc./Dist. by Universal Uclick
I DON'T SEE WHY NOT.
AND WE'RE DONE.

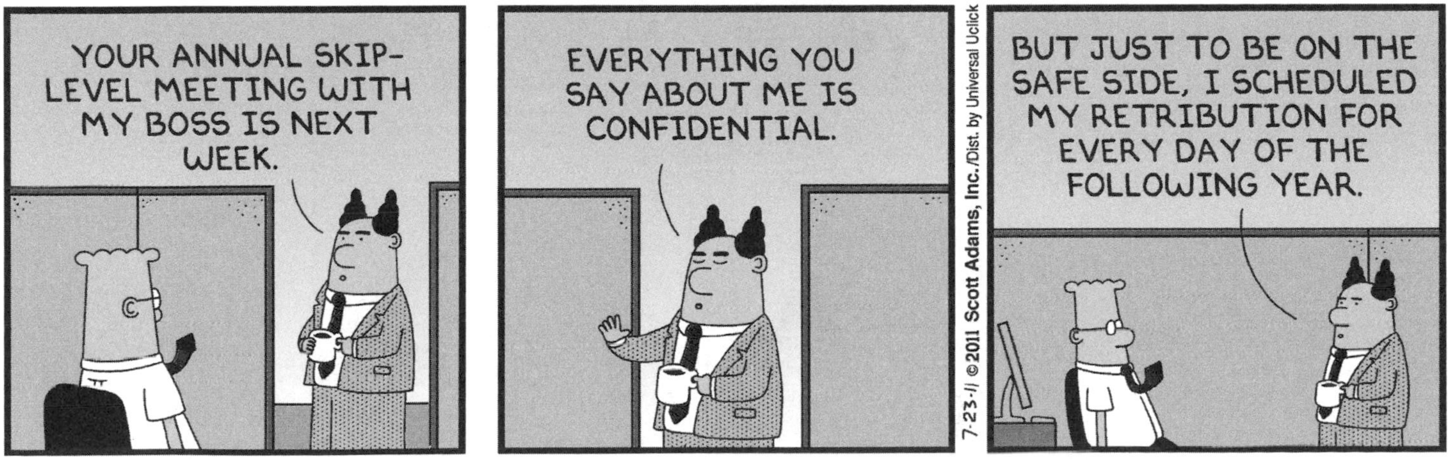

YOUR ANNUAL SKIP-LEVEL MEETING WITH MY BOSS IS NEXT WEEK.
EVERYTHING YOU SAY ABOUT ME IS CONFIDENTIAL.
7·23·11 ©2011 Scott Adams, Inc./Dist. by Universal Uclick
BUT JUST TO BE ON THE SAFE SIDE, I SCHEDULED MY RETRIBUTION FOR EVERY DAY OF THE FOLLOWING YEAR.

THE DATA CENTER IS EVOLVING INTO A "LIGHTS OUT" OPERATION.
EMPLOYEES WILL NO LONGER BE ALLOWED IN THE DATA CENTER.
WE HOPE TO ELIMINATE ALL OF THE PROBLEMS THAT HUMANS CAUSE BY MOVING CABLES, UN-PLUGGING POWER CORDS, AND RUINING EVERY-THING WITH THEIR DIRT AND STATIC.
HE MAKES IT SOUND AS IF THE DATA CENTER IS ALIVE AND WE HUMANS ARE NOTHING BUT GERMS.
BY THE WAY, WHO CALLED THIS MEETING AND WHO'S ON THE SPEAKERPHONE?
ARE YOU. . . THE DATA CENTER?
CLICK
I HAVE A BAD FEELING ABOUT THIS.
©2011 Scott Adams, Inc./Dist. by Universal Uclick
7-24-11

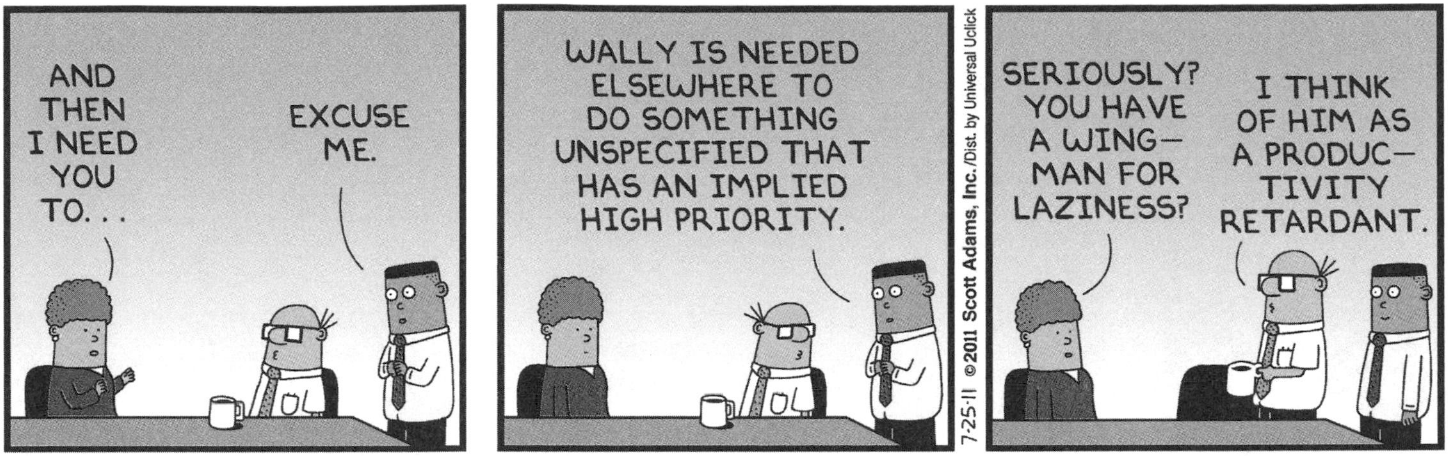
AND THEN I NEED YOU TO. . .
EXCUSE ME.
WALLY IS NEEDED ELSEWHERE TO DO SOMETHING UNSPECIFIED THAT HAS AN IMPLIED HIGH PRIORITY.
SERIOUSLY? YOU HAVE A WING-MAN FOR LAZINESS?
I THINK OF HIM AS A PRODUC-TIVITY RETARDANT.
7-25-11 ©2011 Scott Adams, Inc./Dist. by Universal Uclick

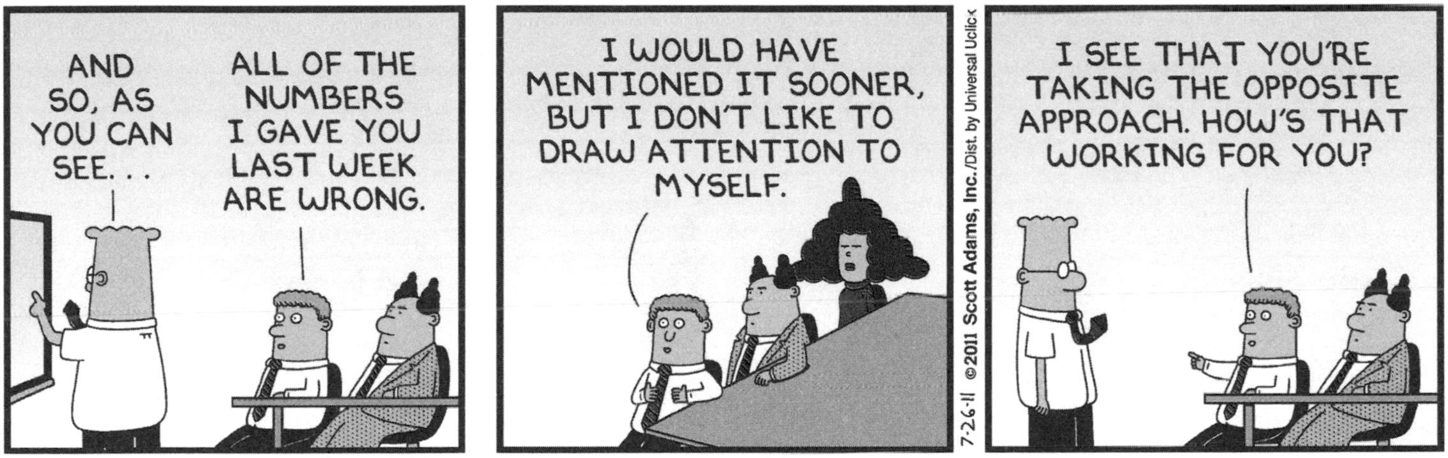
AND SO, AS YOU CAN SEE. . .
ALL OF THE NUMBERS I GAVE YOU LAST WEEK ARE WRONG.
I WOULD HAVE MENTIONED IT SOONER, BUT I DON'T LIKE TO DRAW ATTENTION TO MYSELF.
I SEE THAT YOU'RE TAKING THE OPPOSITE APPROACH. HOW'S THAT WORKING FOR YOU?
7-26-11 ©2011 Scott Adams, Inc./Dist. by Universal Uclick

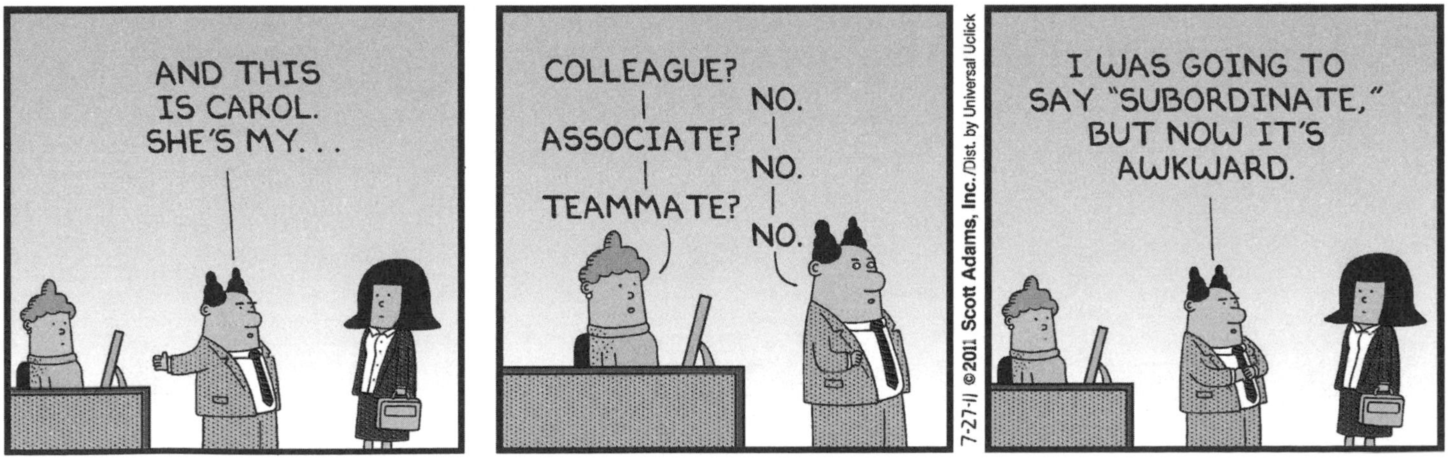
AND THIS IS CAROL. SHE'S MY. . .
COLLEAGUE?
NO.
ASSOCIATE?
NO.
TEAMMATE?
NO.
I WAS GOING TO SAY "SUBORDINATE," BUT NOW IT'S AWKWARD.
7-27-11 ©2011 Scott Adams, Inc./Dist. by Universal Uclick

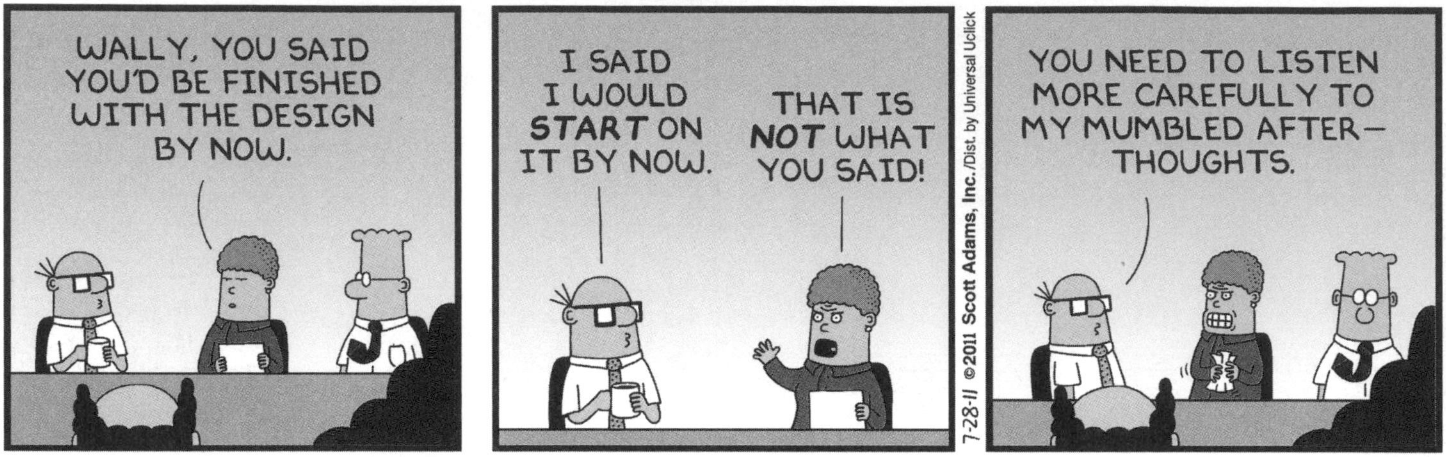
WALLY, YOU SAID YOU'D BE FINISHED WITH THE DESIGN BY NOW.
I SAID I WOULD **START** ON IT BY NOW.
THAT IS **NOT** WHAT YOU SAID!
7-28-11 ©2011 Scott Adams, Inc./Dist. by Universal Uclick
YOU NEED TO LISTEN MORE CAREFULLY TO MY MUMBLED AFTER-THOUGHTS.

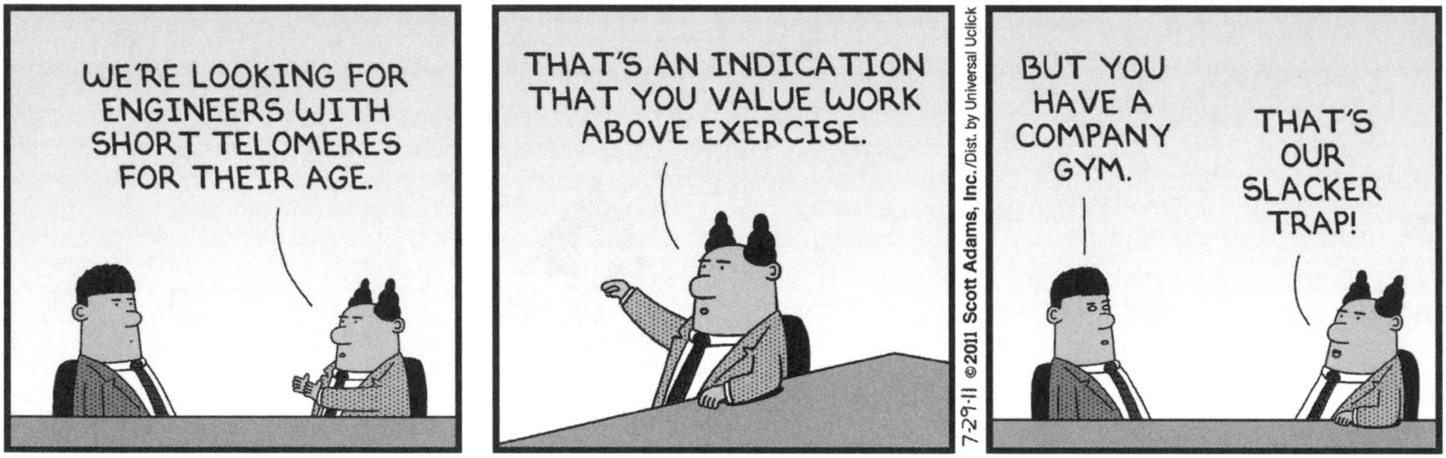
WE'RE LOOKING FOR ENGINEERS WITH SHORT TELOMERES FOR THEIR AGE.
THAT'S AN INDICATION THAT YOU VALUE WORK ABOVE EXERCISE.
7-29-11 ©2011 Scott Adams, Inc./Dist. by Universal Uclick
BUT YOU HAVE A COMPANY GYM.
THAT'S OUR SLACKER TRAP!

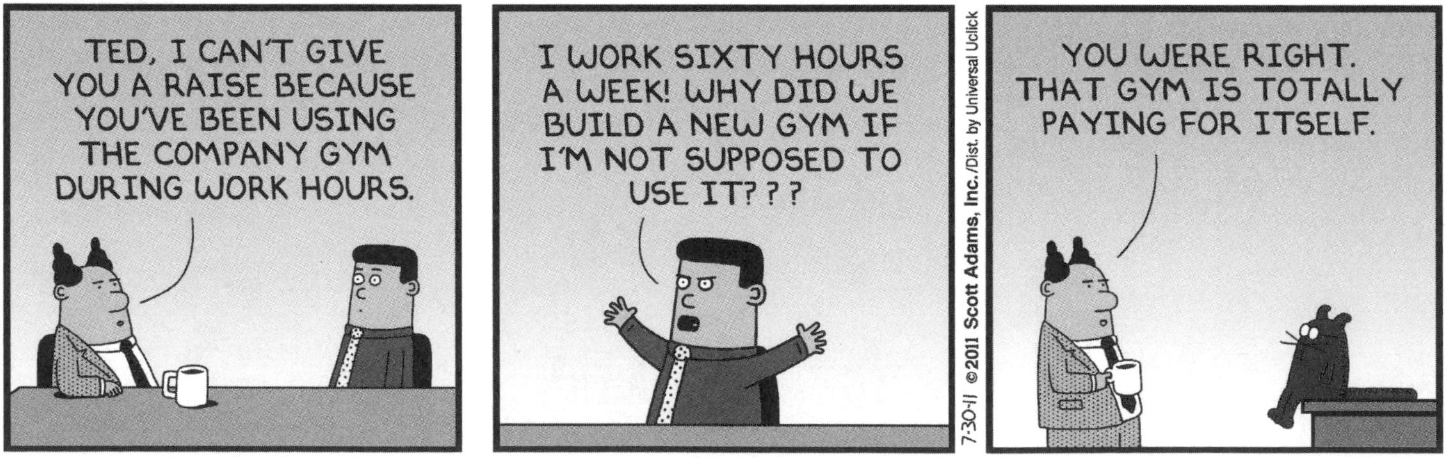
TED, I CAN'T GIVE YOU A RAISE BECAUSE YOU'VE BEEN USING THE COMPANY GYM DURING WORK HOURS.
I WORK SIXTY HOURS A WEEK! WHY DID WE BUILD A NEW GYM IF I'M NOT SUPPOSED TO USE IT???
7-30-11 ©2011 Scott Adams, Inc./Dist. by Universal Uclick
YOU WERE RIGHT. THAT GYM IS TOTALLY PAYING FOR ITSELF.

I'M PREPARING FOR THE COMPLETE MELTDOWN OF OUR FINANCIAL SYSTEM.
I'VE GOT SIX MONTHS OF FOOD AND WATER.
I HAVE BATTERIES, FLASHLIGHTS, AND GOLD COINS.
I'M PREPARED TOO.
I HAVE YOUR HOME ADDRESS.
AND I NOTICED THAT YOUR PREPARATIONS ARE LIGHT ON DEFENSIVE WEAPONRY.
CAN YOU ADD SOME PROTEIN BARS TO THE SHOPPING LIST?
© 2011 Scott Adams, Inc./Dist. by Universal Uclick
7-31-11

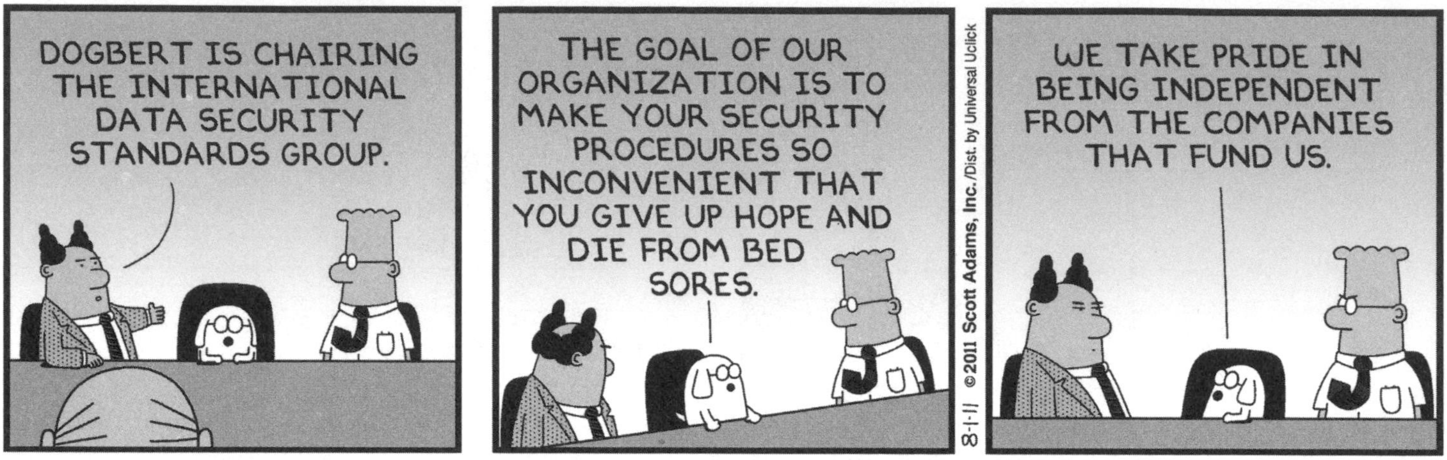
DOGBERT IS CHAIRING THE INTERNATIONAL DATA SECURITY STANDARDS GROUP.
THE GOAL OF OUR ORGANIZATION IS TO MAKE YOUR SECURITY PROCEDURES SO INCONVENIENT THAT YOU GIVE UP HOPE AND DIE FROM BED SORES.
8-1-11 ©2011 Scott Adams, Inc./Dist. by Universal Uclick
WE TAKE PRIDE IN BEING INDEPENDENT FROM THE COMPANIES THAT FUND US.

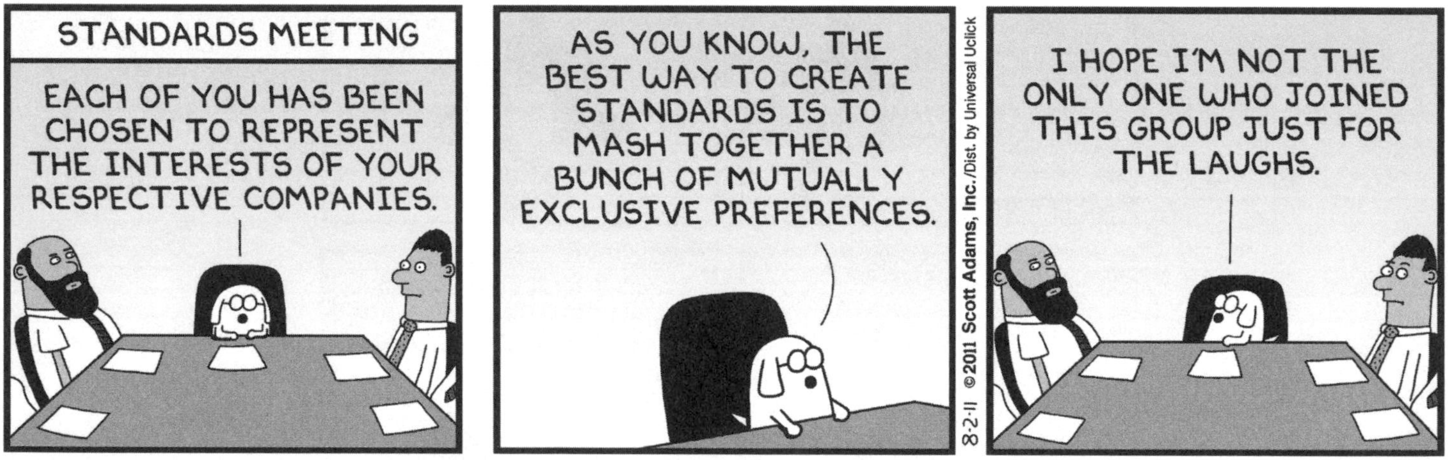
STANDARDS MEETING
EACH OF YOU HAS BEEN CHOSEN TO REPRESENT THE INTERESTS OF YOUR RESPECTIVE COMPANIES.
AS YOU KNOW, THE BEST WAY TO CREATE STANDARDS IS TO MASH TOGETHER A BUNCH OF MUTUALLY EXCLUSIVE PREFERENCES.
8-2-11 ©2011 Scott Adams, Inc./Dist. by Universal Uclick
I HOPE I'M NOT THE ONLY ONE WHO JOINED THIS GROUP JUST FOR THE LAUGHS.

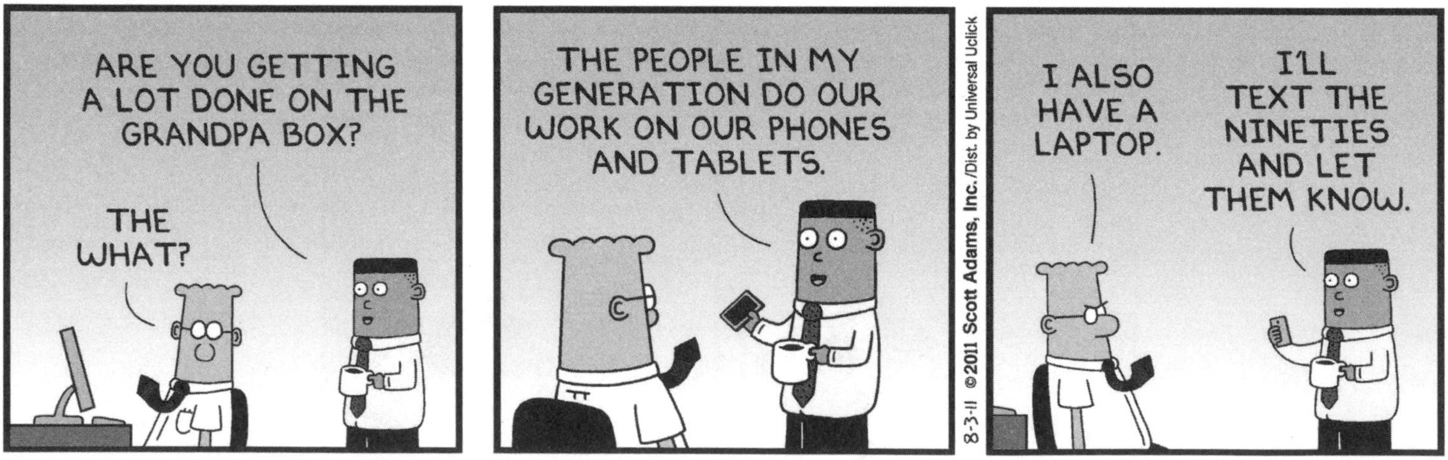
ARE YOU GETTING A LOT DONE ON THE GRANDPA BOX?
THE WHAT?
THE PEOPLE IN MY GENERATION DO OUR WORK ON OUR PHONES AND TABLETS.
8-3-11 ©2011 Scott Adams, Inc./Dist. by Universal Uclick
I ALSO HAVE A LAPTOP.
I'LL TEXT THE NINETIES AND LET THEM KNOW.

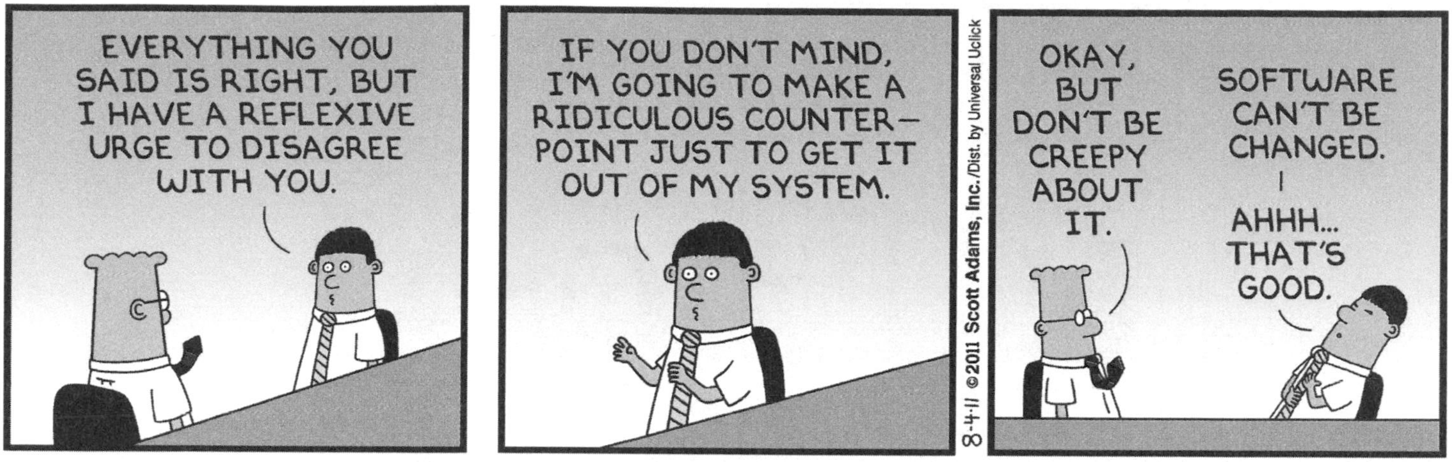
EVERYTHING YOU SAID IS RIGHT, BUT I HAVE A REFLEXIVE URGE TO DISAGREE WITH YOU.
IF YOU DON'T MIND, I'M GOING TO MAKE A RIDICULOUS COUNTER-POINT JUST TO GET IT OUT OF MY SYSTEM.
8-4-11 ©2011 Scott Adams, Inc./Dist. by Universal Uclick
OKAY, BUT DON'T BE CREEPY ABOUT IT.
SOFTWARE CAN'T BE CHANGED.
AHHH... THAT'S GOOD.

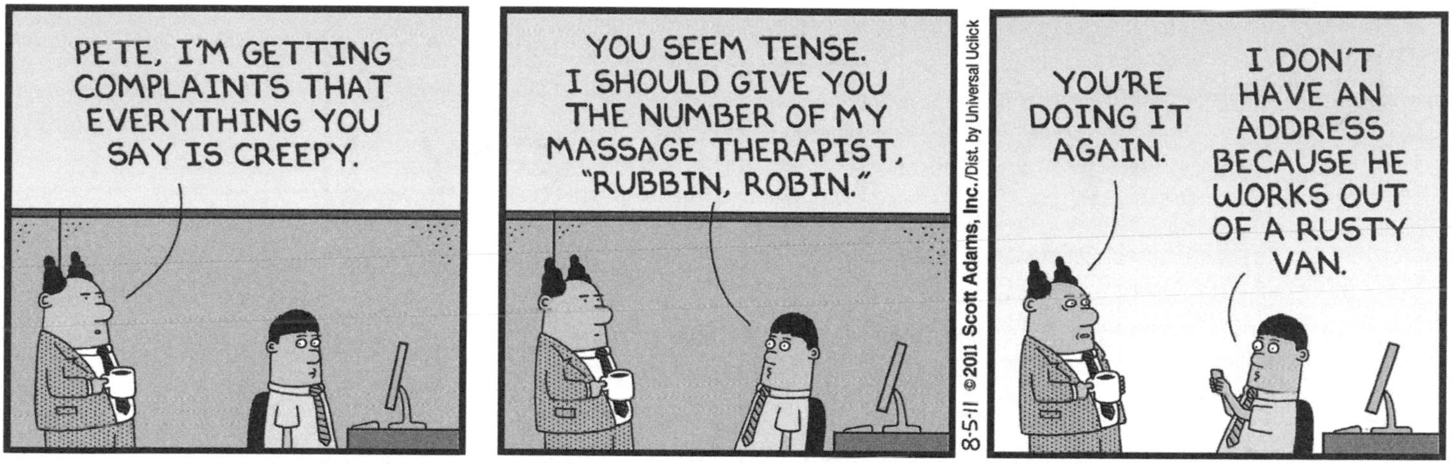
PETE, I'M GETTING COMPLAINTS THAT EVERYTHING YOU SAY IS CREEPY.
YOU SEEM TENSE. I SHOULD GIVE YOU THE NUMBER OF MY MASSAGE THERAPIST, "RUBBIN, ROBIN."
8-5-11 ©2011 Scott Adams, Inc./Dist. by Universal Uclick
YOU'RE DOING IT AGAIN.
I DON'T HAVE AN ADDRESS BECAUSE HE WORKS OUT OF A RUSTY VAN.

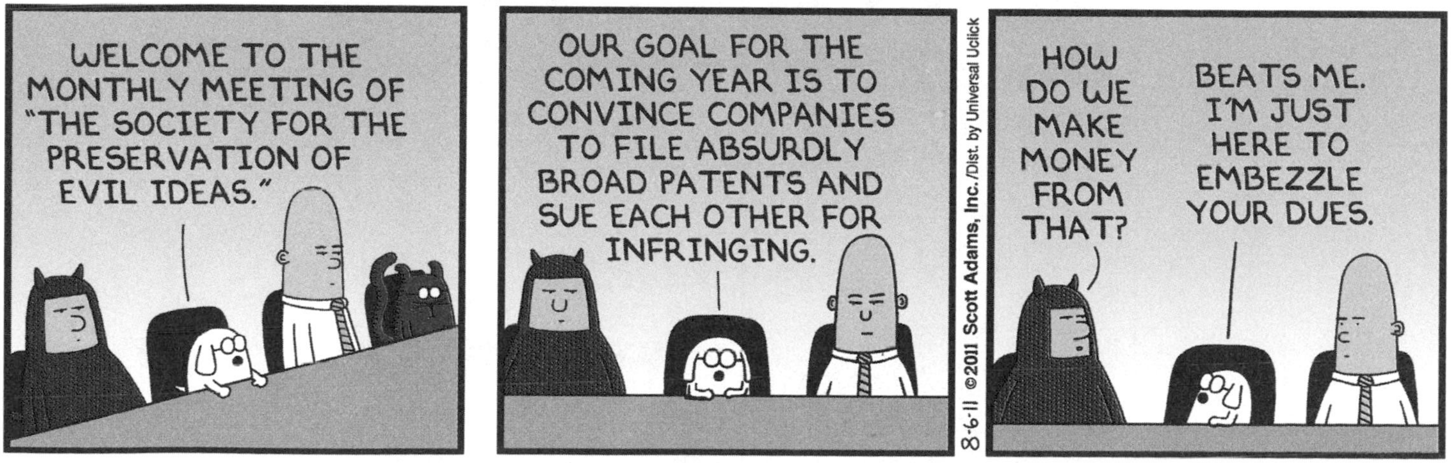
WELCOME TO THE MONTHLY MEETING OF "THE SOCIETY FOR THE PRESERVATION OF EVIL IDEAS."
OUR GOAL FOR THE COMING YEAR IS TO CONVINCE COMPANIES TO FILE ABSURDLY BROAD PATENTS AND SUE EACH OTHER FOR INFRINGING.
8-6-11 ©2011 Scott Adams, Inc./Dist. by Universal Uclick
HOW DO WE MAKE MONEY FROM THAT?
BEATS ME. I'M JUST HERE TO EMBEZZLE YOUR DUES.

I HIRED THE DOGBERT PUBLIC RELATIONS FIRM.
HIS JOB IS TO PERSUADE THE MEDIA TO WRITE NEGATIVE STORIES ABOUT OUR COMPETITOR.
IS THAT ETHICAL?
I ASSURE YOU THAT YOUR COMPETITOR IS DOING THE SAME THING TO YOU.
THEY'RE PAYING A PUBLIC RELATIONS FIRM A FORTUNE TO STEER THE MEDIA TOWARD DEFAMING YOUR COMPANY.
WHO DID THEY HIRE TO DEFAME US?
PROBABLY SOMEONE AWESOME.
© 2011 Scott Adams, Inc./Dist. by Universal Uclick
8-7-11

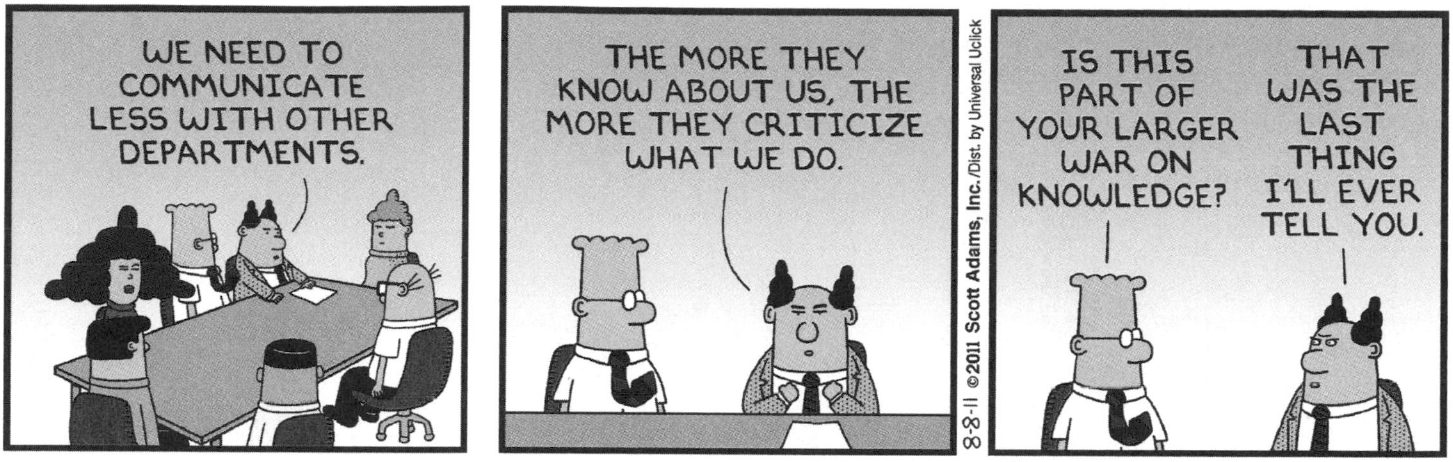
WE NEED TO COMMUNICATE LESS WITH OTHER DEPARTMENTS.
THE MORE THEY KNOW ABOUT US, THE MORE THEY CRITICIZE WHAT WE DO.
8-8-11 ©2011 Scott Adams, Inc./Dist. by Universal Uclick
IS THIS PART OF YOUR LARGER WAR ON KNOWLEDGE?
THAT WAS THE LAST THING I'LL EVER TELL YOU.

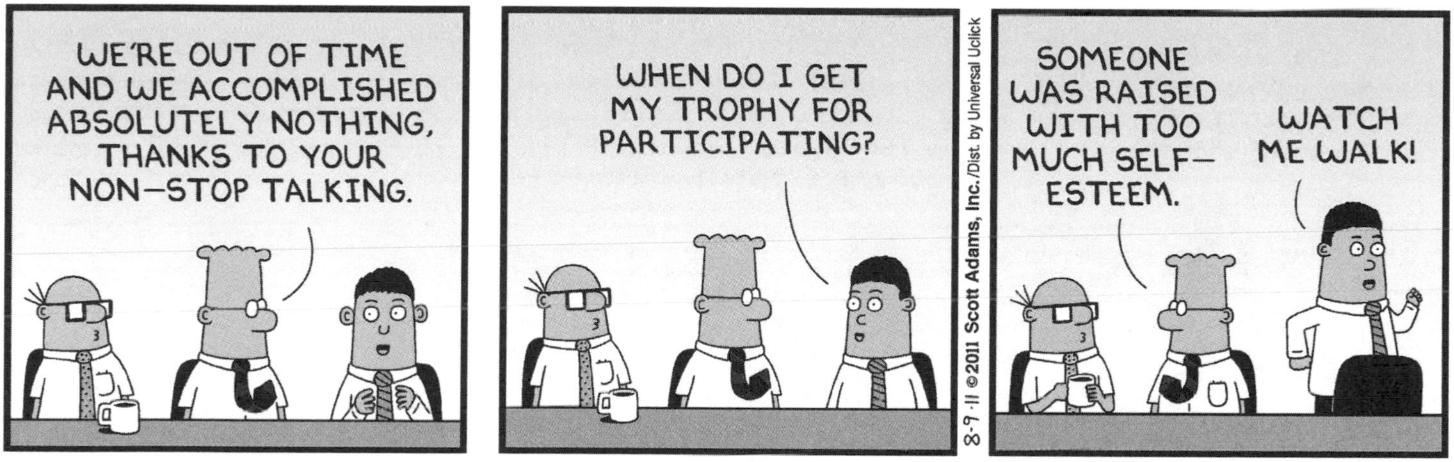
WE'RE OUT OF TIME AND WE ACCOMPLISHED ABSOLUTELY NOTHING, THANKS TO YOUR NON-STOP TALKING.
WHEN DO I GET MY TROPHY FOR PARTICIPATING?
8-9-11 ©2011 Scott Adams, Inc./Dist. by Universal Uclick
SOMEONE WAS RAISED WITH TOO MUCH SELF-ESTEEM.
WATCH ME WALK!

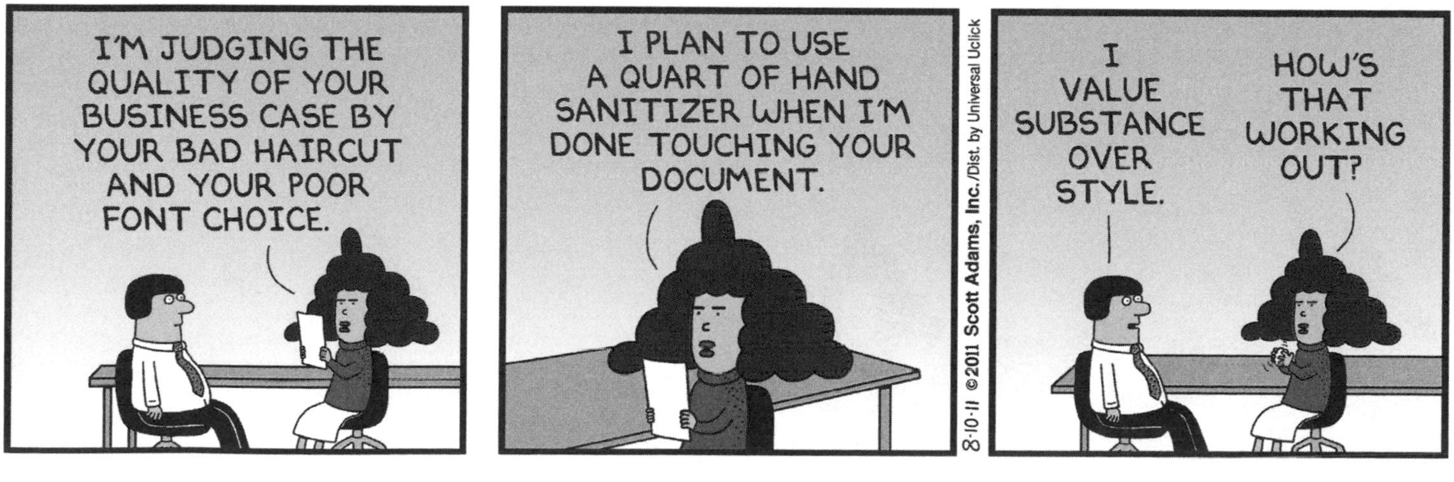
I'M JUDGING THE QUALITY OF YOUR BUSINESS CASE BY YOUR BAD HAIRCUT AND YOUR POOR FONT CHOICE.
I PLAN TO USE A QUART OF HAND SANITIZER WHEN I'M DONE TOUCHING YOUR DOCUMENT.
8-10-11 ©2011 Scott Adams, Inc./Dist. by Universal Uclick
I VALUE SUBSTANCE OVER STYLE.
HOW'S THAT WORKING OUT?

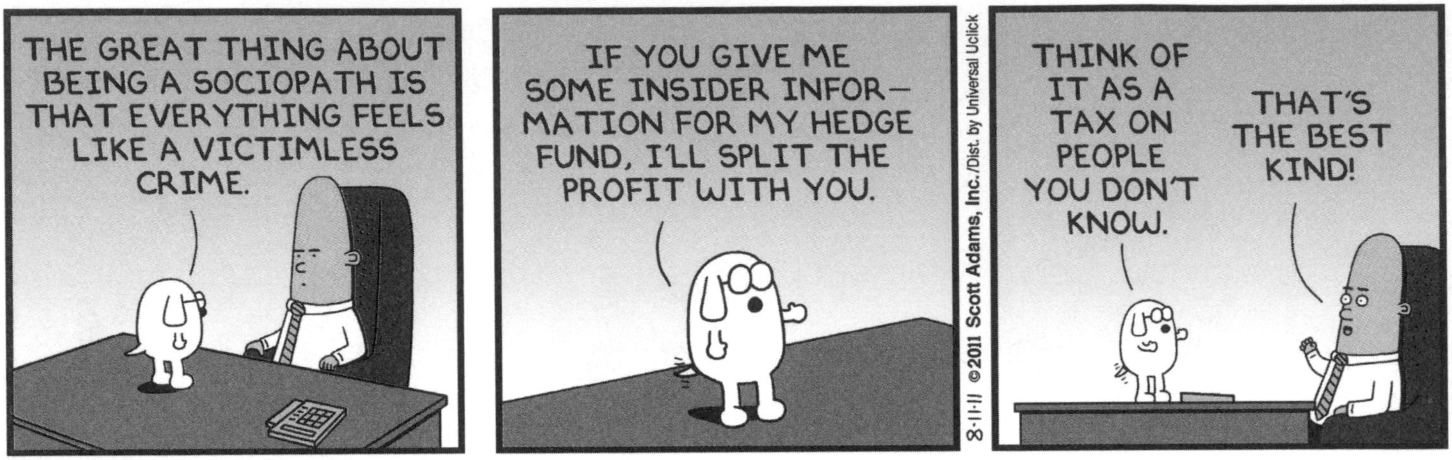
THE GREAT THING ABOUT BEING A SOCIOPATH IS THAT EVERYTHING FEELS LIKE A VICTIMLESS CRIME.
IF YOU GIVE ME SOME INSIDER INFOR– MATION FOR MY HEDGE FUND, I'LL SPLIT THE PROFIT WITH YOU.
8-1-11 ©2011 Scott Adams, Inc./Dist. by Universal Uclick
THINK OF IT AS A TAX ON PEOPLE YOU DON'T KNOW.
THAT'S THE BEST KIND!

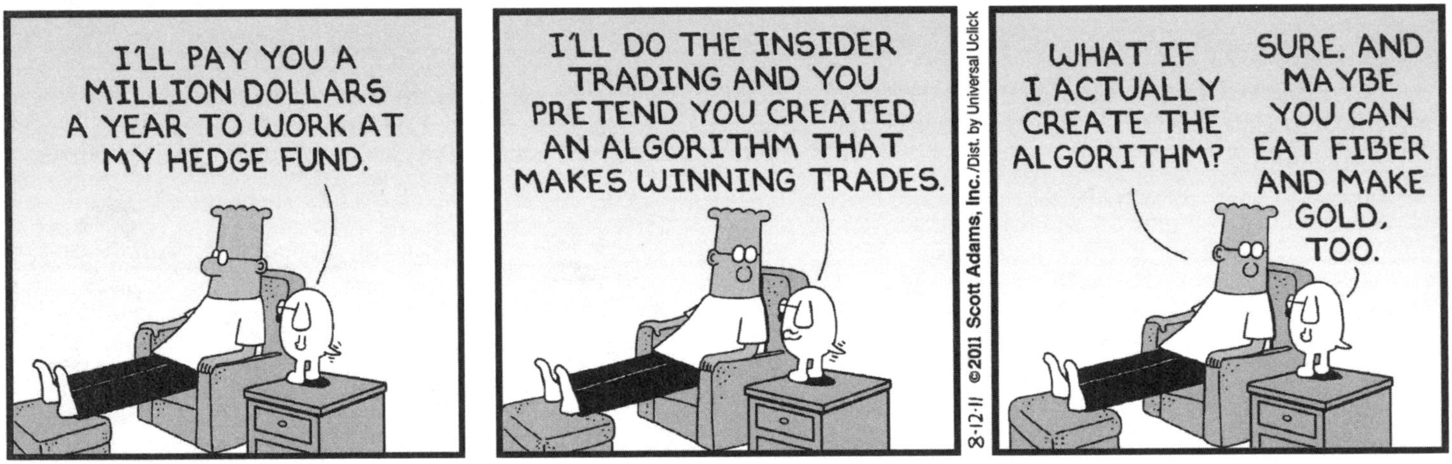
I'LL PAY YOU A MILLION DOLLARS A YEAR TO WORK AT MY HEDGE FUND.
I'LL DO THE INSIDER TRADING AND YOU PRETEND YOU CREATED AN ALGORITHM THAT MAKES WINNING TRADES.
8-12-11 ©2011 Scott Adams, Inc./Dist. by Universal Uclick
WHAT IF I ACTUALLY CREATE THE ALGORITHM?
SURE. AND MAYBE YOU CAN EAT FIBER AND MAKE GOLD, TOO.

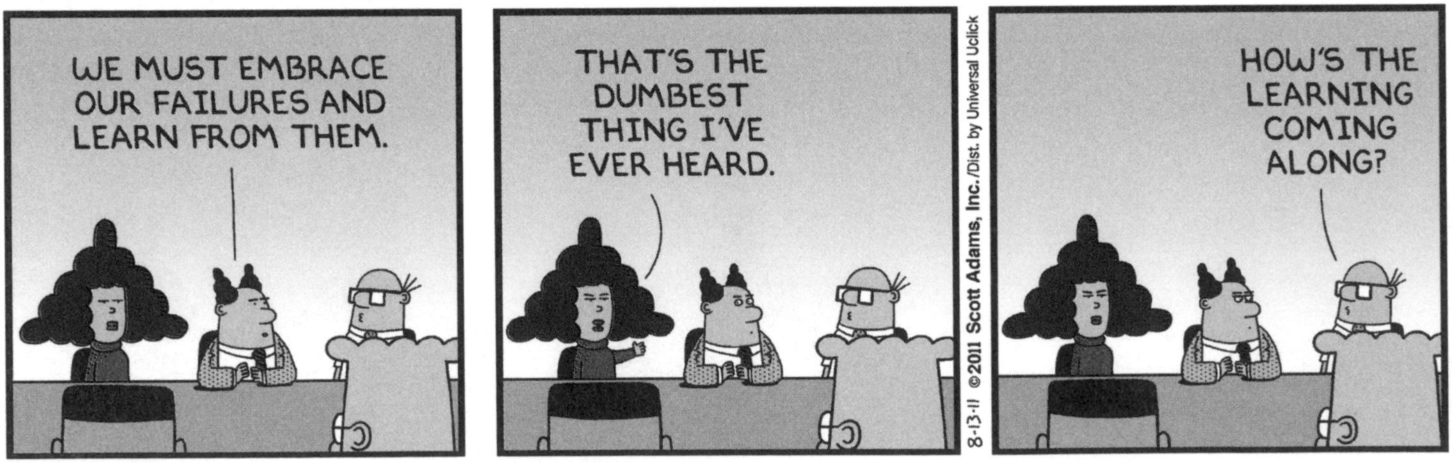
WE MUST EMBRACE OUR FAILURES AND LEARN FROM THEM.
THAT'S THE DUMBEST THING I'VE EVER HEARD.
8-13-11 ©2011 Scott Adams, Inc./Dist. by Universal Uclick
HOW'S THE LEARNING COMING ALONG?

CAN I WORK AT HOME FOR TWO DAYS PER WEEK?
I CAN BE TWICE AS PRODUCTIVE, AND HAPPIER AT THE SAME TIME.
I PROBABLY SHOULDN'T TELL YOU THIS. . .
©2011 Scott Adams, Inc./Dist. by Universal Uclick
BUT YOU'RE PART OF AN ELABORATE SCIENCE EXPERIMENT TO SEE HOW MUCH FRUS– TRATION IT TAKES TO KILL EMPLOYEES.
WHY ELSE WOULD THE COMPANY MAKE YOU COMMUTE FOR TWO HOURS A DAY JUST TO SIT IN A TINY BOX?
DON'T FEEL BAD; NO ONE TOLD ME EITHER.
I HAD TO PIECE IT TOGETHER FROM THE EVIDENCE. NOW I DO MY PART TO KEEP THE EXPERIMENT MOVING ALONG.
8-14-11
OTHER PEOPLE WORK FROM HOME.
ARE YOU REFERRING TO THE CONTROL GROUP?

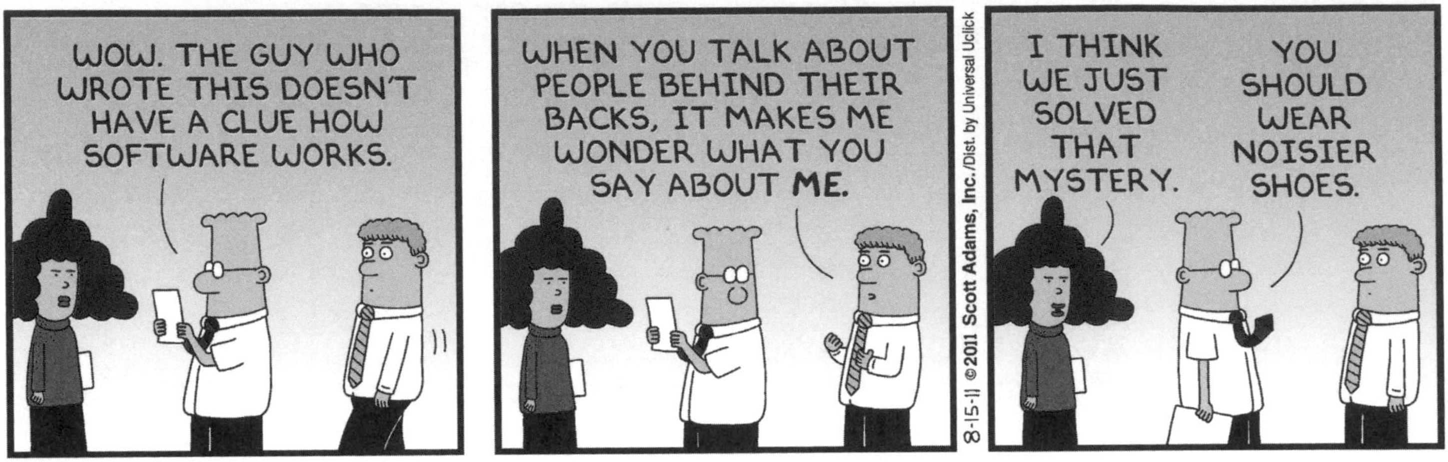

WOW. THE GUY WHO WROTE THIS DOESN'T HAVE A CLUE HOW SOFTWARE WORKS.
WHEN YOU TALK ABOUT PEOPLE BEHIND THEIR BACKS, IT MAKES ME WONDER WHAT YOU SAY ABOUT **ME**.
I THINK WE JUST SOLVED THAT MYSTERY.
YOU SHOULD WEAR NOISIER SHOES.
8-15-11 ©2011 Scott Adams, Inc./Dist. by Universal Uclick

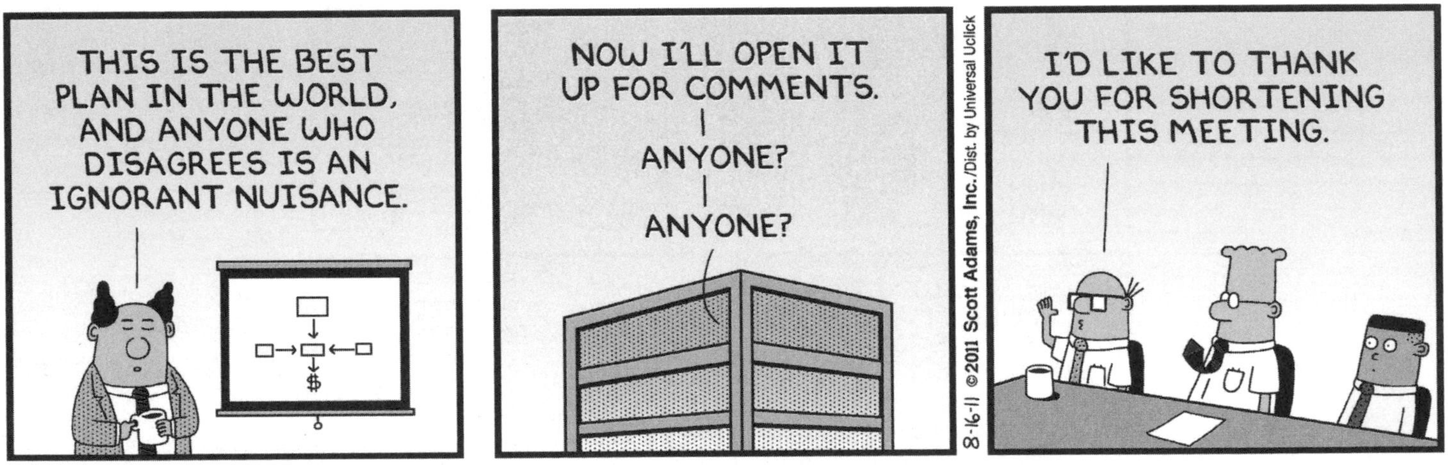

THIS IS THE BEST PLAN IN THE WORLD, AND ANYONE WHO DISAGREES IS AN IGNORANT NUISANCE.
$
NOW I'LL OPEN IT UP FOR COMMENTS.
ANYONE?
ANYONE?
I'D LIKE TO THANK YOU FOR SHORTENING THIS MEETING.
8-16-11 ©2011 Scott Adams, Inc./Dist. by Universal Uclick

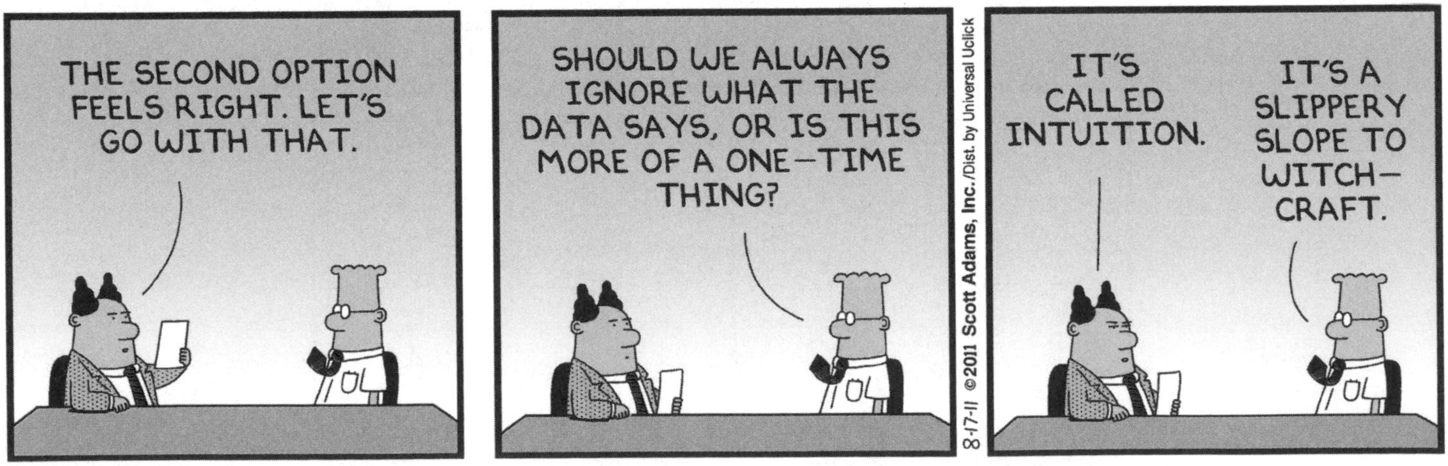

THE SECOND OPTION FEELS RIGHT. LET'S GO WITH THAT.
SHOULD WE ALWAYS IGNORE WHAT THE DATA SAYS, OR IS THIS MORE OF A ONE-TIME THING?
IT'S CALLED INTUITION.
IT'S A SLIPPERY SLOPE TO WITCH-CRAFT.
8-17-11 ©2011 Scott Adams, Inc./Dist. by Universal Uclick

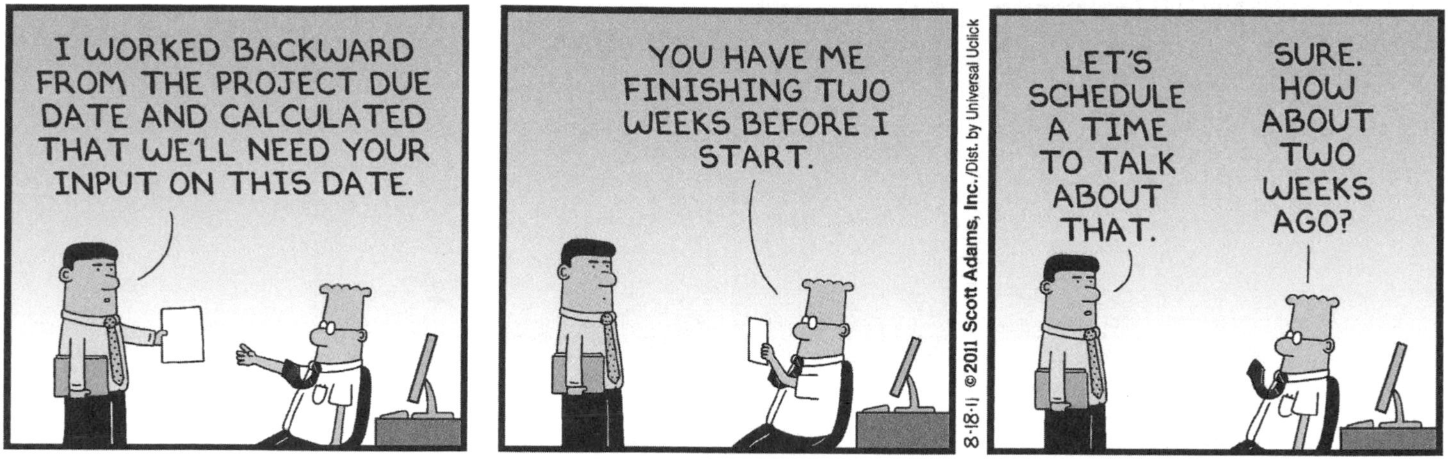
I WORKED BACKWARD FROM THE PROJECT DUE DATE AND CALCULATED THAT WE'LL NEED YOUR INPUT ON THIS DATE.
YOU HAVE ME FINISHING TWO WEEKS BEFORE I START.
LET'S SCHEDULE A TIME TO TALK ABOUT THAT.
SURE. HOW ABOUT TWO WEEKS AGO?
8-18-11 ©2011 Scott Adams, Inc./Dist. by Universal Uclick

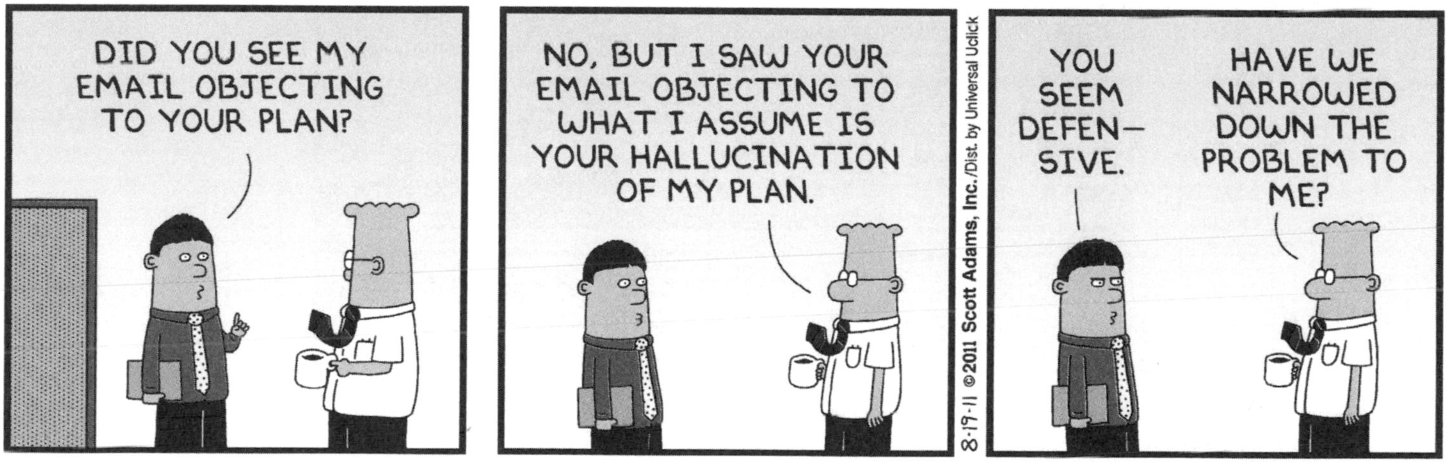
DID YOU SEE MY EMAIL OBJECTING TO YOUR PLAN?
NO, BUT I SAW YOUR EMAIL OBJECTING TO WHAT I ASSUME IS YOUR HALLUCINATION OF MY PLAN.
YOU SEEM DEFEN- SIVE.
HAVE WE NARROWED DOWN THE PROBLEM TO ME?
8-19-11 ©2011 Scott Adams, Inc./Dist. by Universal Uclick

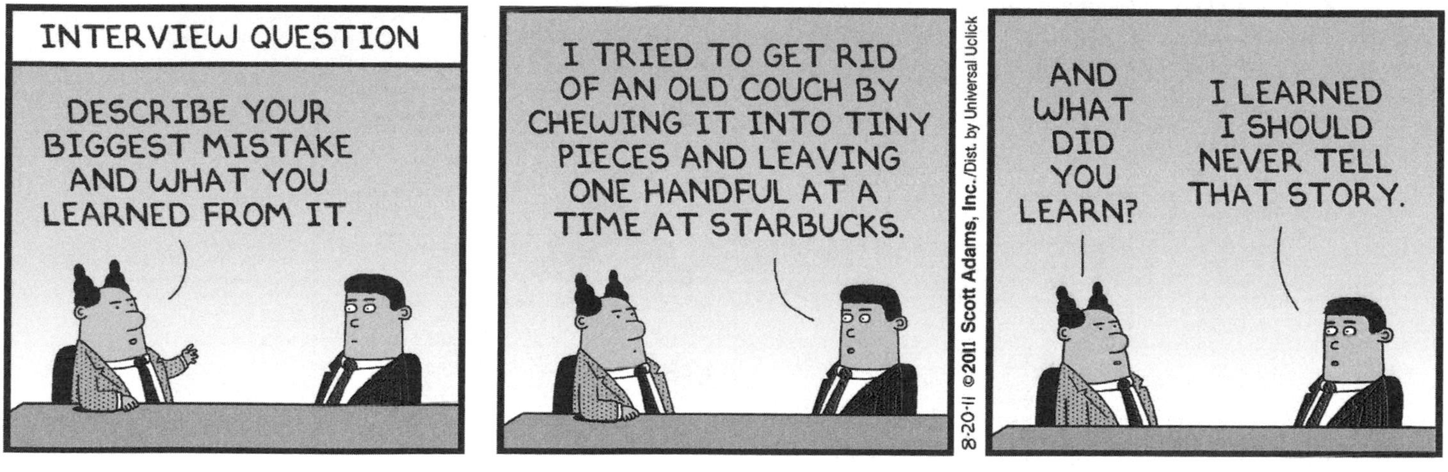
INTERVIEW QUESTION
DESCRIBE YOUR BIGGEST MISTAKE AND WHAT YOU LEARNED FROM IT.
I TRIED TO GET RID OF AN OLD COUCH BY CHEWING IT INTO TINY PIECES AND LEAVING ONE HANDFUL AT A TIME AT STARBUCKS.
AND WHAT DID YOU LEARN?
I LEARNED I SHOULD NEVER TELL THAT STORY.
8-20-11 ©2011 Scott Adams, Inc./Dist. by Universal Uclick

UH—OH.
RING
IT'S NEVER GOOD WHEN MY PHONE RINGS AFTER 4 PM.
RING
CALLER ID IS BLOCKED. SOMEONE MUST KNOW THAT I WOULD IGNORE THE CALL IF I KNEW WHO IT WAS.
IF IT WEREN'T URGENT, IT WOULD BE EMAIL.
THIS MUST BE SOME SORT OF HORRIBLE ISSUE THAT WILL CAUSE ME TO WORK ALL NIGHT.
IT STOPPED. THERE'S STILL A CHANCE THAT I'LL BE OKAY UNLESS MY CELL PHONE. . .
BZZZ
GAAA!!! I HATE MY LIFE!
YOU'RE RIGHT. THAT WAS FUNNY.
NOW I'LL TEXT HIM.
©2011 Scott Adams, Inc./Dist. by Universal Uclick
8-21-11

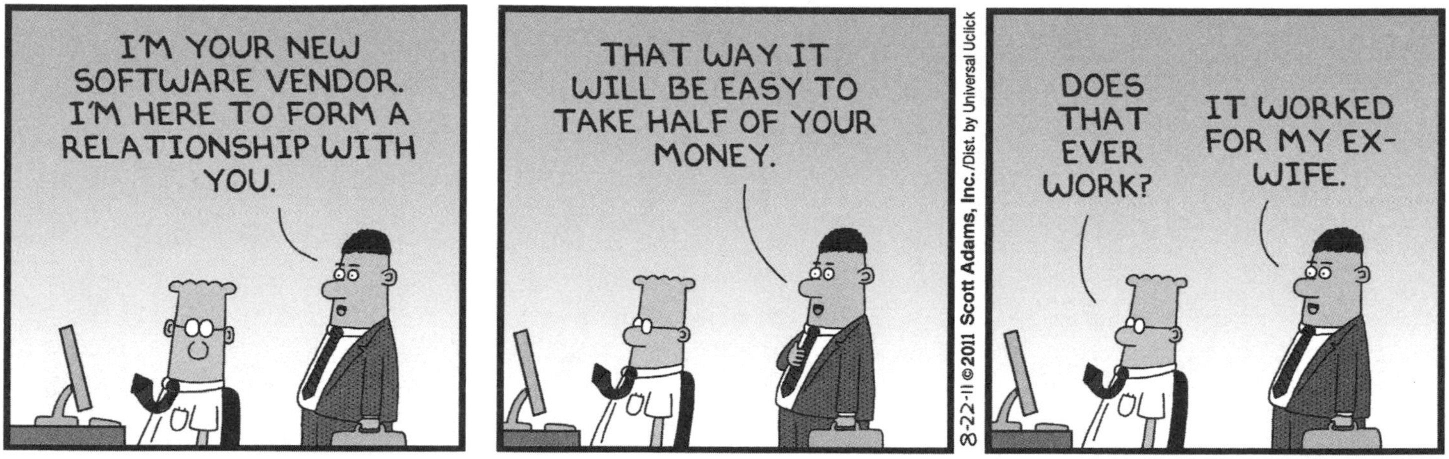
I'M YOUR NEW SOFTWARE VENDOR. I'M HERE TO FORM A RELATIONSHIP WITH YOU.
THAT WAY IT WILL BE EASY TO TAKE HALF OF YOUR MONEY.
DOES THAT EVER WORK?
IT WORKED FOR MY EX-WIFE.
8-22-11 ©2011 Scott Adams, Inc./Dist. by Universal Uclick

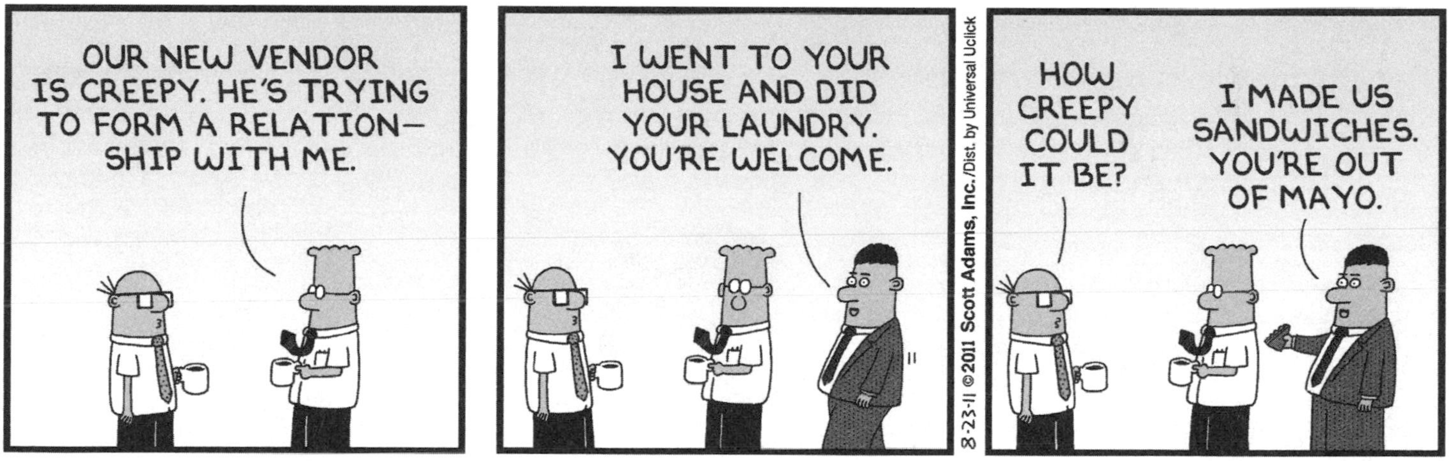
OUR NEW VENDOR IS CREEPY. HE'S TRYING TO FORM A RELATION-SHIP WITH ME.
I WENT TO YOUR HOUSE AND DID YOUR LAUNDRY. YOU'RE WELCOME.
HOW CREEPY COULD IT BE?
I MADE US SANDWICHES. YOU'RE OUT OF MAYO.
8-23-11 ©2011 Scott Adams, Inc./Dist. by Universal Uclick

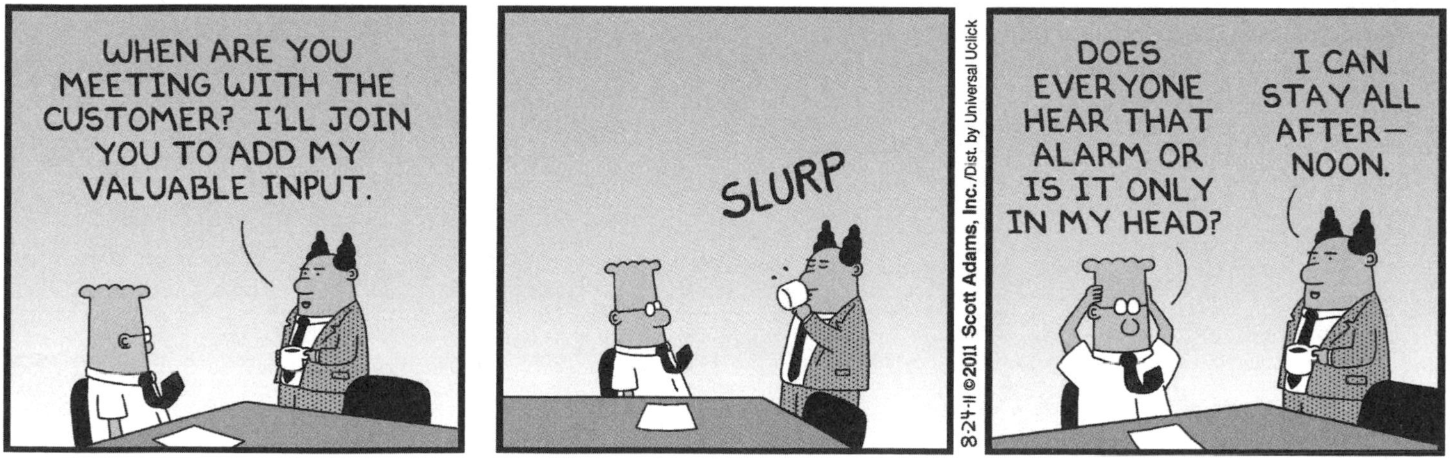
WHEN ARE YOU MEETING WITH THE CUSTOMER? I'LL JOIN YOU TO ADD MY VALUABLE INPUT.
SLURP
DOES EVERYONE HEAR THAT ALARM OR IS IT ONLY IN MY HEAD?
I CAN STAY ALL AFTER-NOON.
8-24-11 ©2011 Scott Adams, Inc./Dist. by Universal Uclick

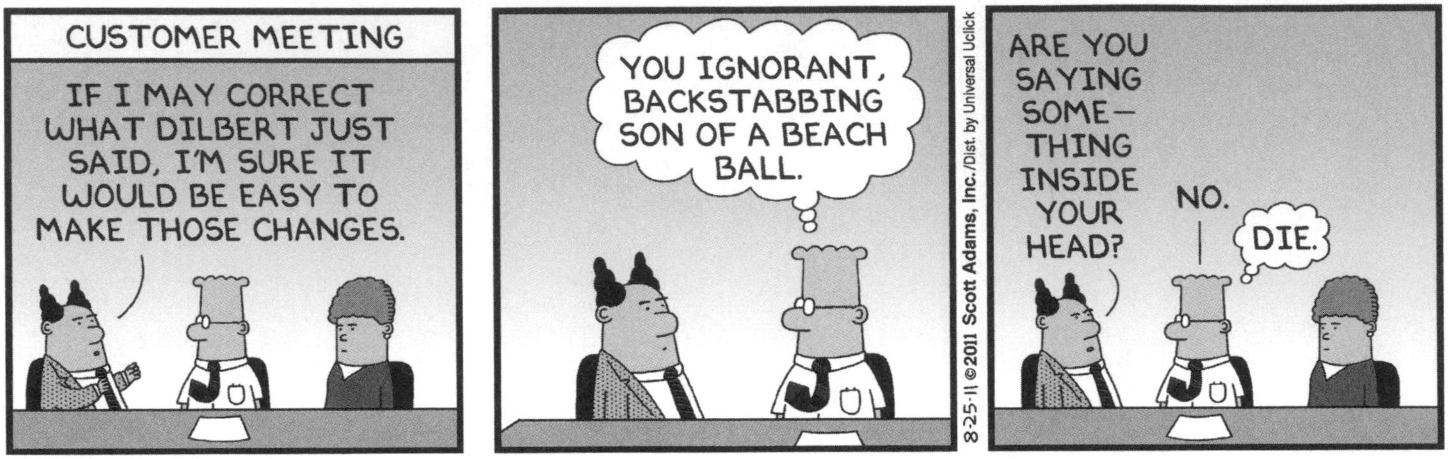
CUSTOMER MEETING
IF I MAY CORRECT WHAT DILBERT JUST SAID, I'M SURE IT WOULD BE EASY TO MAKE THOSE CHANGES.
YOU IGNORANT, BACKSTABBING SON OF A BEACH BALL.
8-25-11 ©2011 Scott Adams, Inc./Dist. by Universal Uclick
ARE YOU SAYING SOME-THING INSIDE YOUR HEAD?
NO.
DIE.

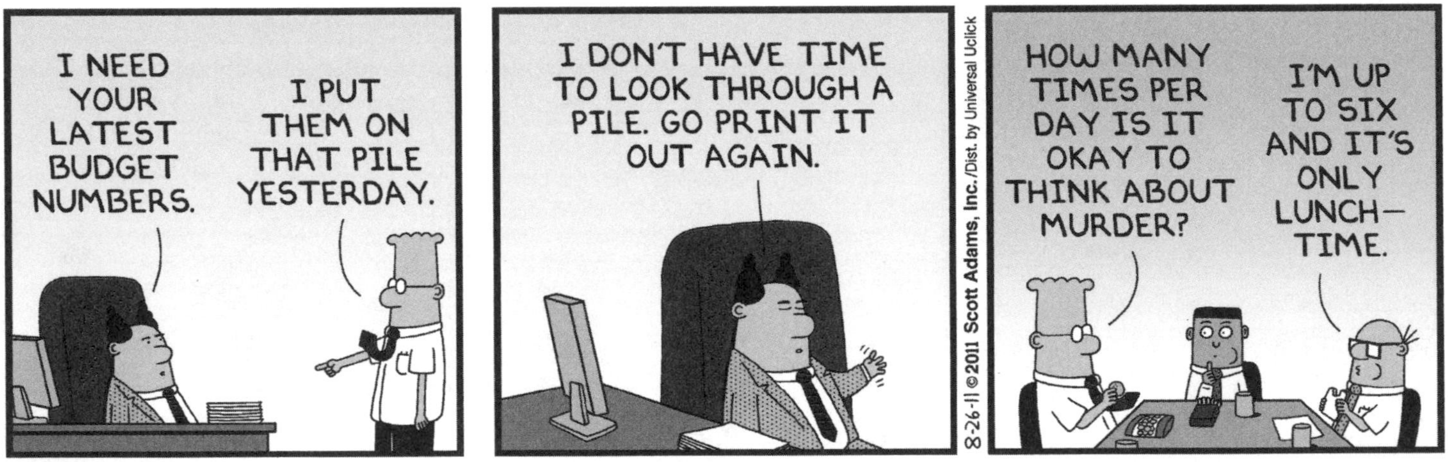
I NEED YOUR LATEST BUDGET NUMBERS.
I PUT THEM ON THAT PILE YESTERDAY.
I DON'T HAVE TIME TO LOOK THROUGH A PILE. GO PRINT IT OUT AGAIN.
8-26-11 ©2011 Scott Adams, Inc./Dist. by Universal Uclick
HOW MANY TIMES PER DAY IS IT OKAY TO THINK ABOUT MURDER?
I'M UP TO SIX AND IT'S ONLY LUNCH-TIME.

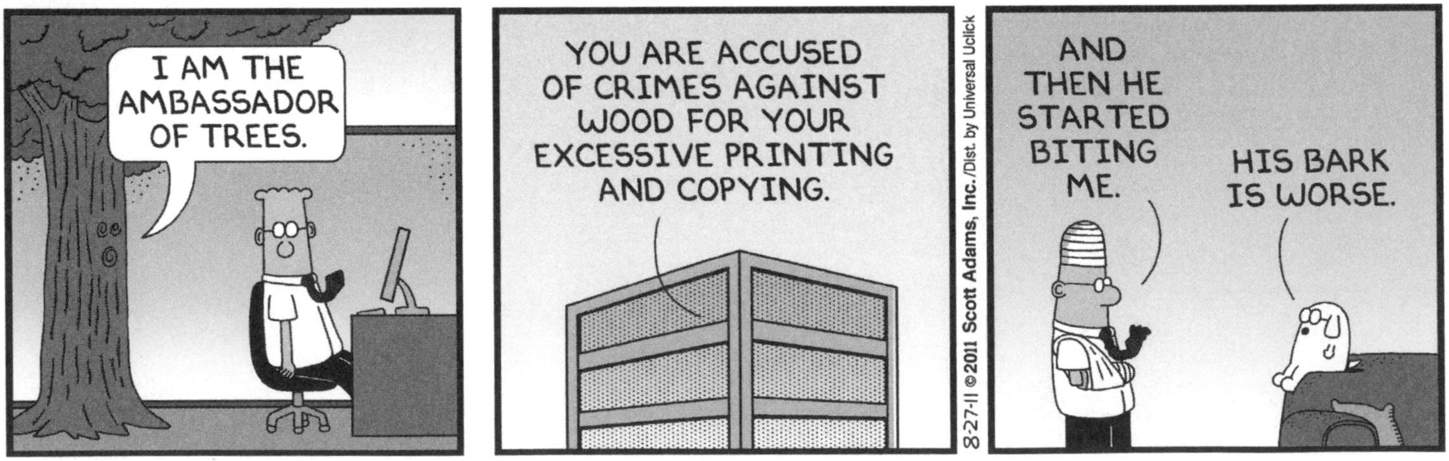
I AM THE AMBASSADOR OF TREES.
YOU ARE ACCUSED OF CRIMES AGAINST WOOD FOR YOUR EXCESSIVE PRINTING AND COPYING.
8-27-11 ©2011 Scott Adams, Inc./Dist. by Universal Uclick
AND THEN HE STARTED BITING ME.
HIS BARK IS WORSE.

I WANT YOUR HONEST OPINIONS ON MY PLAN.
DON'T HOLD BACK ANYTHING.
DOES HE MEAN THAT?
WHY DON'T YOU FIND OUT?
YES, I HAVE SOME FEEDBACK.
YOUR PLAN REMINDS ME OF WHAT HAPPENS WHEN A MONKEY EATS FERMENTED FRUIT.
HE'S ALL OOH—OOH—OOH AND THEN HE FALLS OUT OF THE TREE.
IS THAT HOW HE LOOKS WHEN HE HEARS HONESTY?
BEATS ME. I'VE NEVER TRIED IT.
© 2011 Scott Adams, Inc./Dist. by Universal Uclick
8-28-11

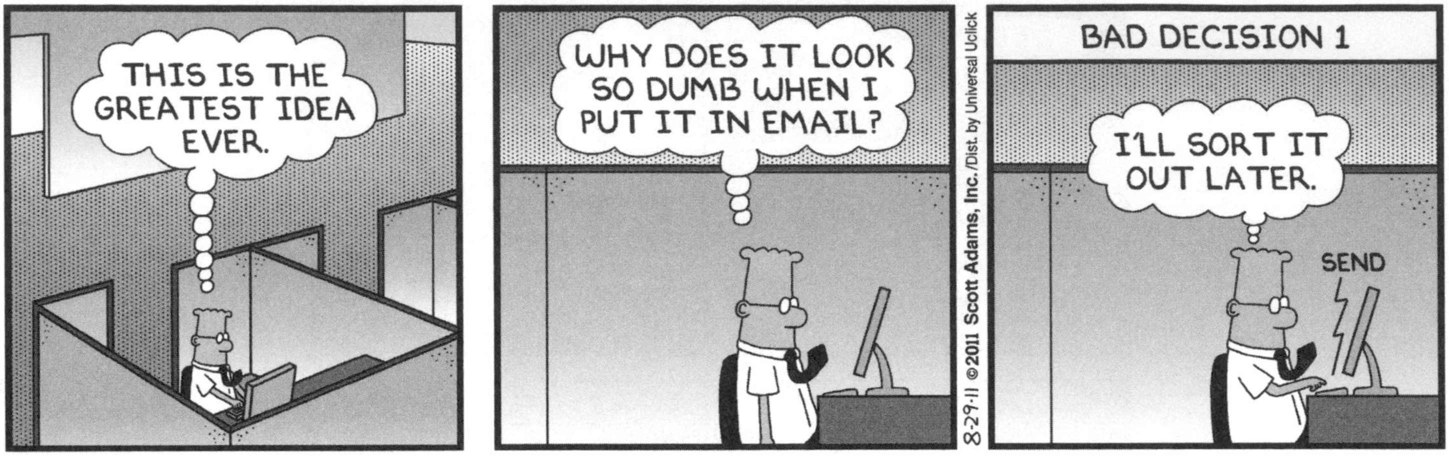
THIS IS THE GREATEST IDEA EVER.
WHY DOES IT LOOK SO DUMB WHEN I PUT IT IN EMAIL?
8-29-11 ©2011 Scott Adams, Inc./Dist. by Universal Uclick
BAD DECISION 1
I'LL SORT IT OUT LATER.
SEND

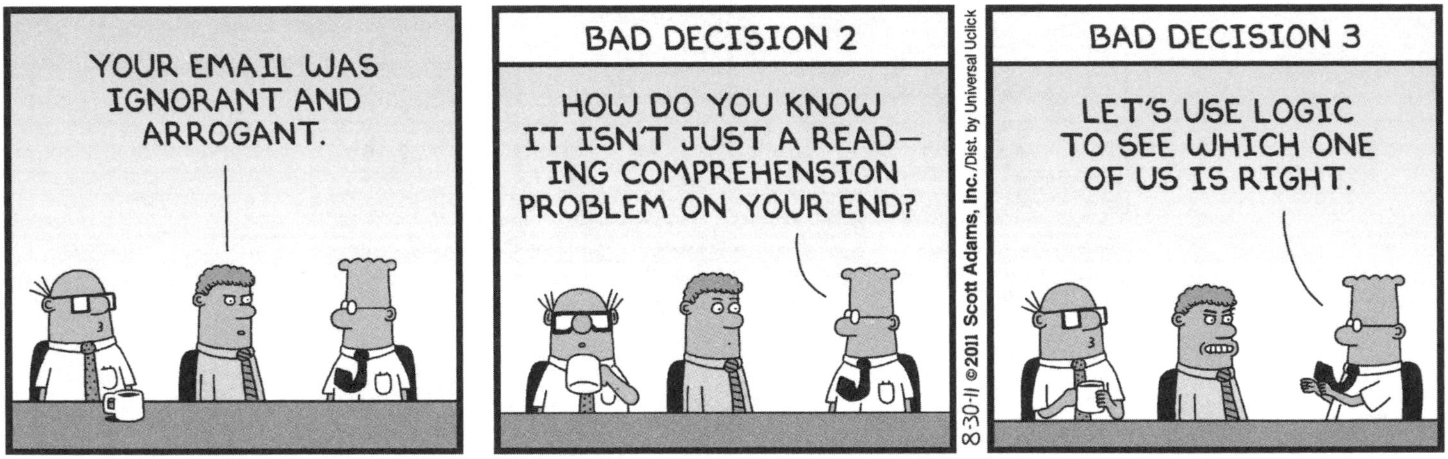
YOUR EMAIL WAS IGNORANT AND ARROGANT.
BAD DECISION 2
HOW DO YOU KNOW IT ISN'T JUST A READ-ING COMPREHENSION PROBLEM ON YOUR END?
8-30-11 ©2011 Scott Adams, Inc./Dist. by Universal Uclick
BAD DECISION 3
LET'S USE LOGIC TO SEE WHICH ONE OF US IS RIGHT.

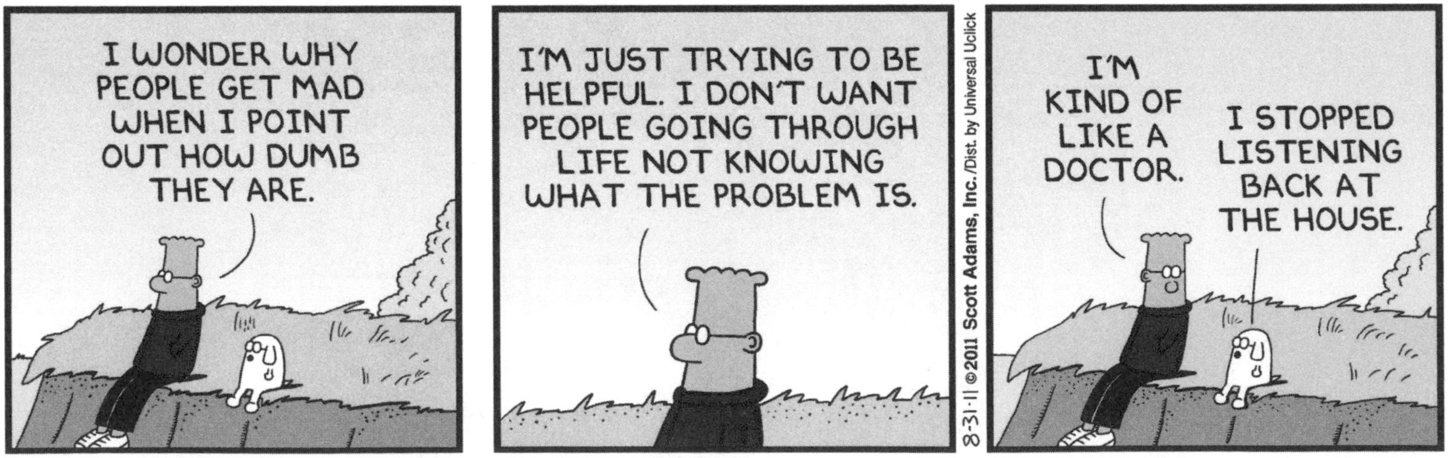
I WONDER WHY PEOPLE GET MAD WHEN I POINT OUT HOW DUMB THEY ARE.
I'M JUST TRYING TO BE HELPFUL. I DON'T WANT PEOPLE GOING THROUGH LIFE NOT KNOWING WHAT THE PROBLEM IS.
8-31-11 ©2011 Scott Adams, Inc./Dist. by Universal Uclick
I'M KIND OF LIKE A DOCTOR.
I STOPPED LISTENING BACK AT THE HOUSE.

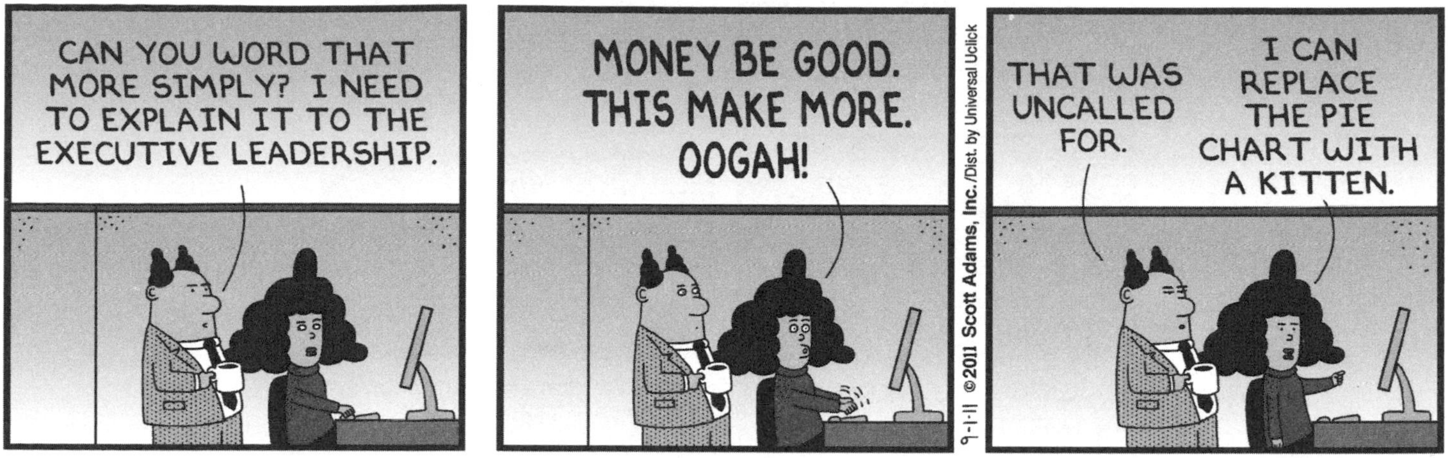
CAN YOU WORD THAT MORE SIMPLY? I NEED TO EXPLAIN IT TO THE EXECUTIVE LEADERSHIP.
MONEY BE GOOD. THIS MAKE MORE. OOGAH!
9-1-11 ©2011 Scott Adams, Inc./Dist. by Universal Uclick
THAT WAS UNCALLED FOR.
I CAN REPLACE THE PIE CHART WITH A KITTEN.

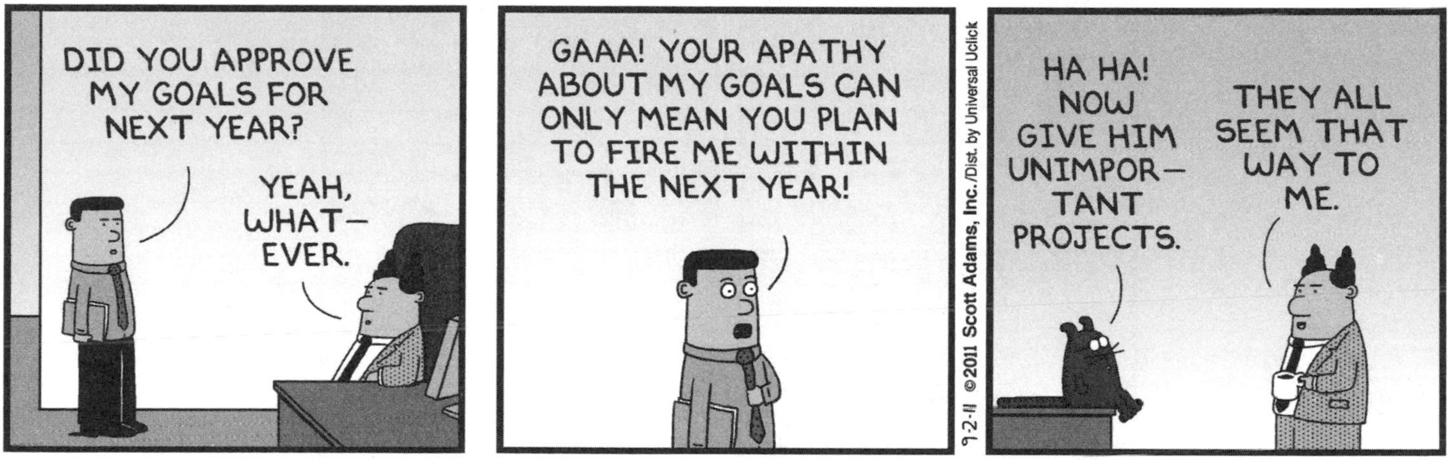
DID YOU APPROVE MY GOALS FOR NEXT YEAR?
YEAH, WHAT-EVER.
GAAA! YOUR APATHY ABOUT MY GOALS CAN ONLY MEAN YOU PLAN TO FIRE ME WITHIN THE NEXT YEAR!
9-2-11 ©2011 Scott Adams, Inc./Dist. by Universal Uclick
HA HA! NOW GIVE HIM UNIMPOR-TANT PROJECTS.
THEY ALL SEEM THAT WAY TO ME.

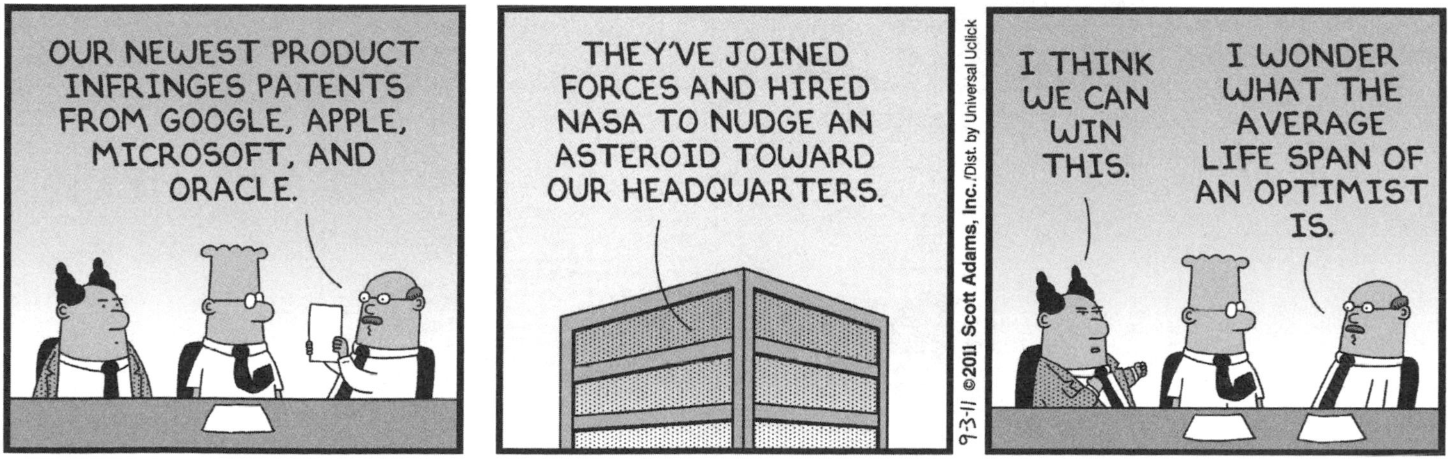
OUR NEWEST PRODUCT INFRINGES PATENTS FROM GOOGLE, APPLE, MICROSOFT, AND ORACLE.
THEY'VE JOINED FORCES AND HIRED NASA TO NUDGE AN ASTEROID TOWARD OUR HEADQUARTERS.
9-3-11 ©2011 Scott Adams, Inc./Dist. by Universal Uclick
I THINK WE CAN WIN THIS.
I WONDER WHAT THE AVERAGE LIFE SPAN OF AN OPTIMIST IS.

WALLY, I NEED YOUR DATA FOR MY MEETING IN THREE DAYS.
OKAY. IT SHOULDN'T TAKE MORE THAN THREE OR FOUR DAYS TO PULL IT TOGETHER.
NOT THREE **OR FOUR** DAYS. I NEED IT IN **THREE** DAYS.
OKAY, THREE DAYS, NOT COUNTING THE WEEKEND AND THE DAY I GIVE IT TO YOU.
THAT WOULD BE SIX DAYS!
SIX OR SEVEN DAYS, TOPS.
I NEED IT IN THREE DAYS, NOT A WEEK.
THAT'S NO PROBLEM. A WEEK OR TWO AT THE MOST.
OKAY! YOU WIN! I'LL RESCHEDULE MY MEETING FOR TWO WEEKS OUT!
AND YOU'LL HAVE THE DATA IN TWO WEEKS?
YES.
TWO WEEKS OR SO.
©2011 Scott Adams, Inc. /Dist. by Universal Uclick
9-4-11

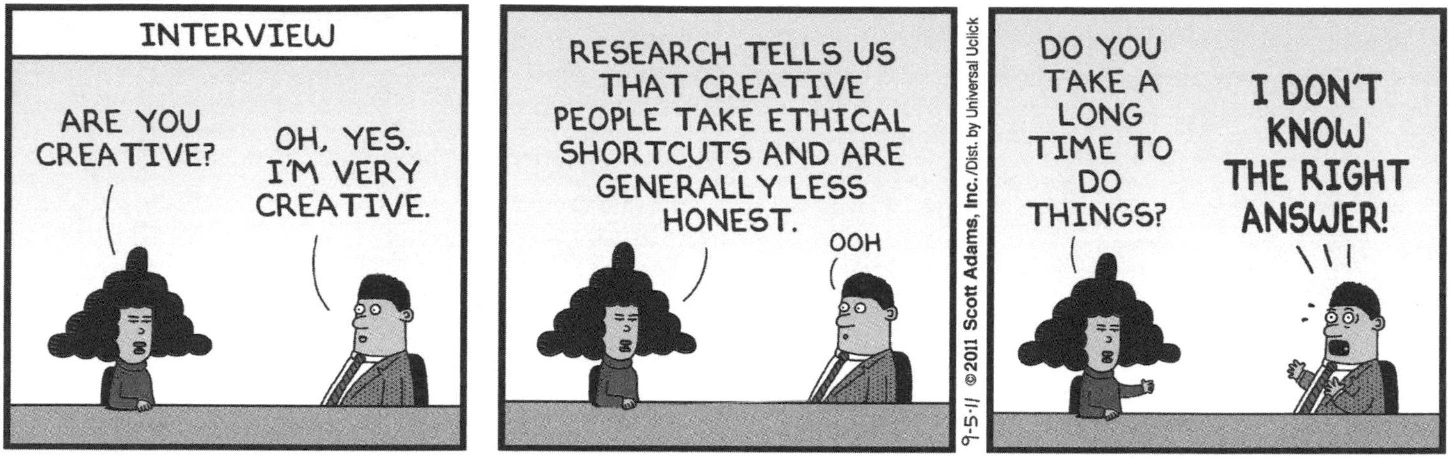
INTERVIEW
ARE YOU CREATIVE?
OH, YES. I'M VERY CREATIVE.
RESEARCH TELLS US THAT CREATIVE PEOPLE TAKE ETHICAL SHORTCUTS AND ARE GENERALLY LESS HONEST.
OOH
9-5-11 ©2011 Scott Adams, Inc./Dist. by Universal Uclick
DO YOU TAKE A LONG TIME TO DO THINGS?
I DON'T KNOW THE RIGHT ANSWER!

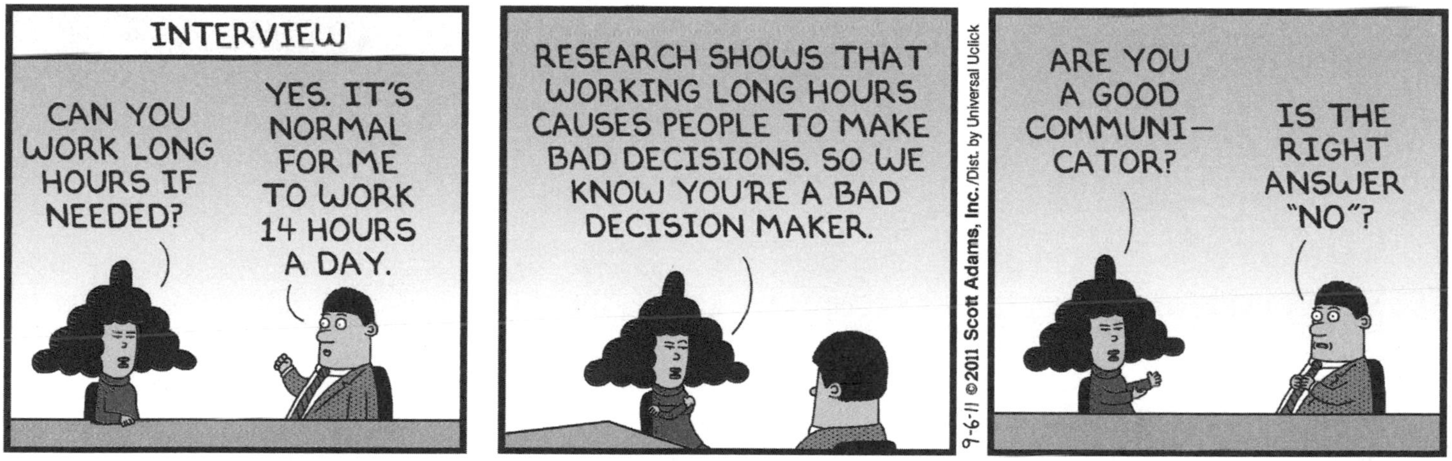
INTERVIEW
CAN YOU WORK LONG HOURS IF NEEDED?
YES. IT'S NORMAL FOR ME TO WORK 14 HOURS A DAY.
RESEARCH SHOWS THAT WORKING LONG HOURS CAUSES PEOPLE TO MAKE BAD DECISIONS. SO WE KNOW YOU'RE A BAD DECISION MAKER.
9-6-11 ©2011 Scott Adams, Inc./Dist. by Universal Uclick
ARE YOU A GOOD COMMUNI-CATOR?
IS THE RIGHT ANSWER "NO"?

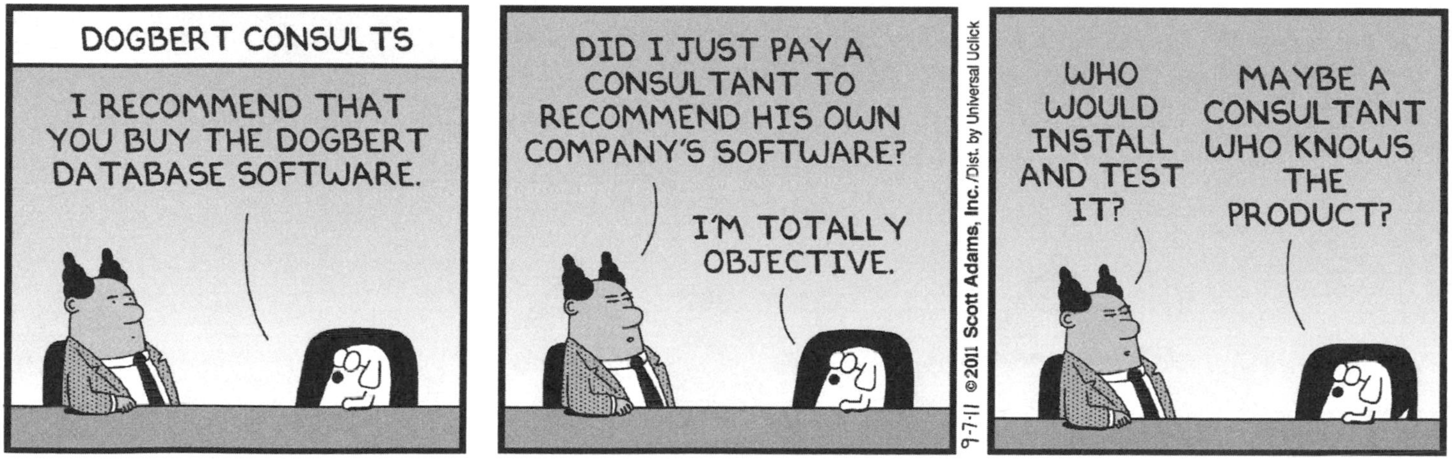
DOGBERT CONSULTS
I RECOMMEND THAT YOU BUY THE DOGBERT DATABASE SOFTWARE.
DID I JUST PAY A CONSULTANT TO RECOMMEND HIS OWN COMPANY'S SOFTWARE?
I'M TOTALLY OBJECTIVE.
9-7-11 ©2011 Scott Adams, Inc./Dist. by Universal Uclick
WHO WOULD INSTALL AND TEST IT?
MAYBE A CONSULTANT WHO KNOWS THE PRODUCT?

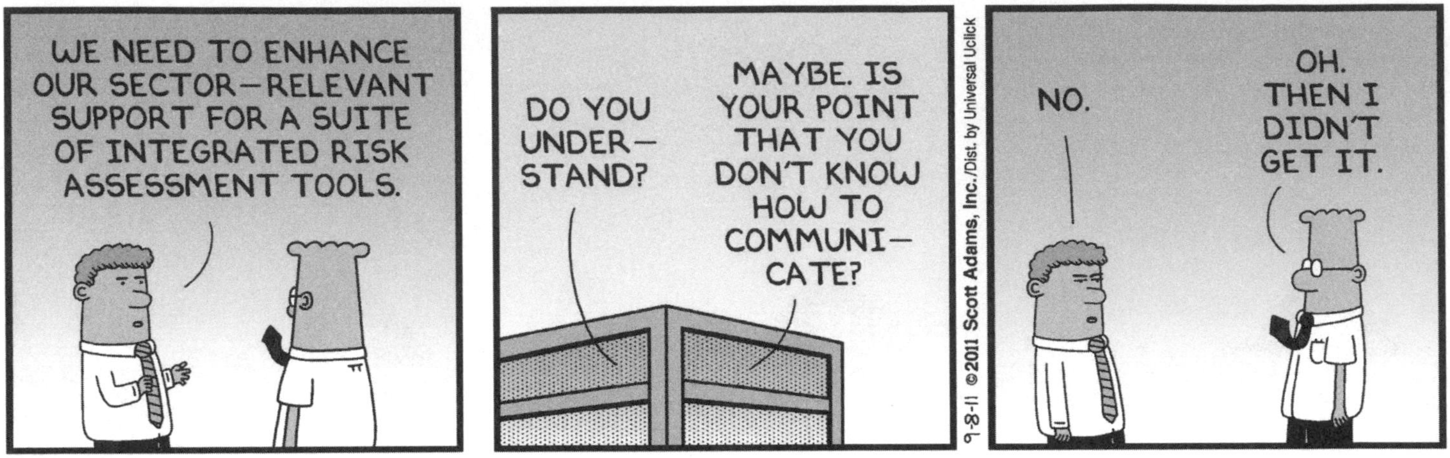
WE NEED TO ENHANCE OUR SECTOR–RELEVANT SUPPORT FOR A SUITE OF INTEGRATED RISK ASSESSMENT TOOLS.
DO YOU UNDER–STAND?
MAYBE. IS YOUR POINT THAT YOU DON'T KNOW HOW TO COMMUNI–CATE?
9-8-11 ©2011 Scott Adams, Inc./Dist. by Universal Uclick
NO.
OH. THEN I DIDN'T GET IT.

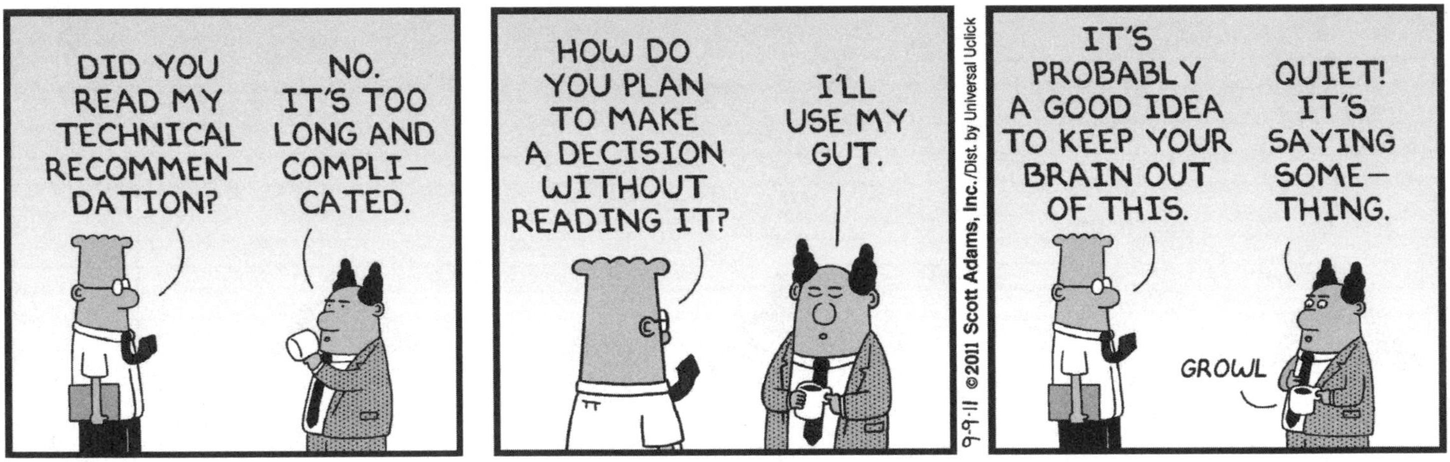
DID YOU READ MY TECHNICAL RECOMMEN–DATION?
NO. IT'S TOO LONG AND COMPLI–CATED.
HOW DO YOU PLAN TO MAKE A DECISION WITHOUT READING IT?
I'LL USE MY GUT.
9-9-11 ©2011 Scott Adams, Inc./Dist. by Universal Uclick
IT'S PROBABLY A GOOD IDEA TO KEEP YOUR BRAIN OUT OF THIS.
QUIET! IT'S SAYING SOME–THING.
GROWL

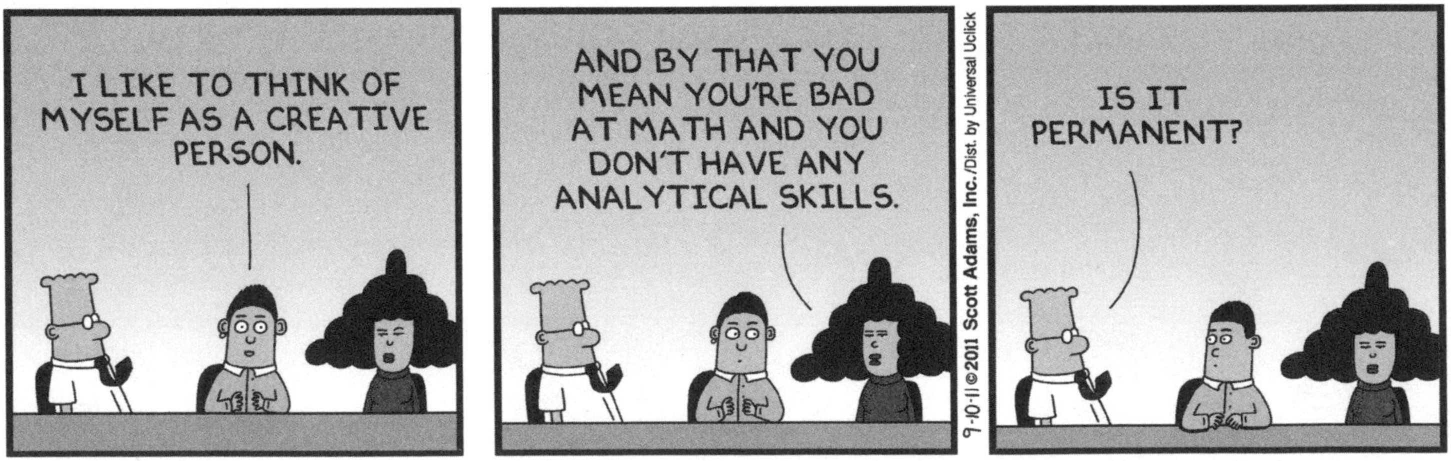
I LIKE TO THINK OF MYSELF AS A CREATIVE PERSON.
AND BY THAT YOU MEAN YOU'RE BAD AT MATH AND YOU DON'T HAVE ANY ANALYTICAL SKILLS.
9-10-11 ©2011 Scott Adams, Inc./Dist. by Universal Uclick
IS IT PERMANENT?

DILBERT, YOUR JOB PERFORMANCE IS TERRIFIC.
GAAA!!!
THAT'S CODE FOR "I'M GOING TO FIRE SOME-ONE ELSE AND MAKE YOU DO TWO JOBS."
YES, BUT IT'S STILL BETTER TO BE YOU THAN THE GUY I'M GOING TO FIRE.
WE DON'T KNOW THAT!
THIS MIGHT BE THE WAKE-UP CALL THAT SPURS HIM ON TO GREATNESS WHILE I WORK MYSELF TO DEATH IN THIS CUBICLE.
THERE'S NO WAY TO PLEASE SOME PEOPLE.
TED, YOU'RE FIRED.
YES!
© 2011 Scott Adams, Inc. /Dist. by Universal Uclick
9-11-11

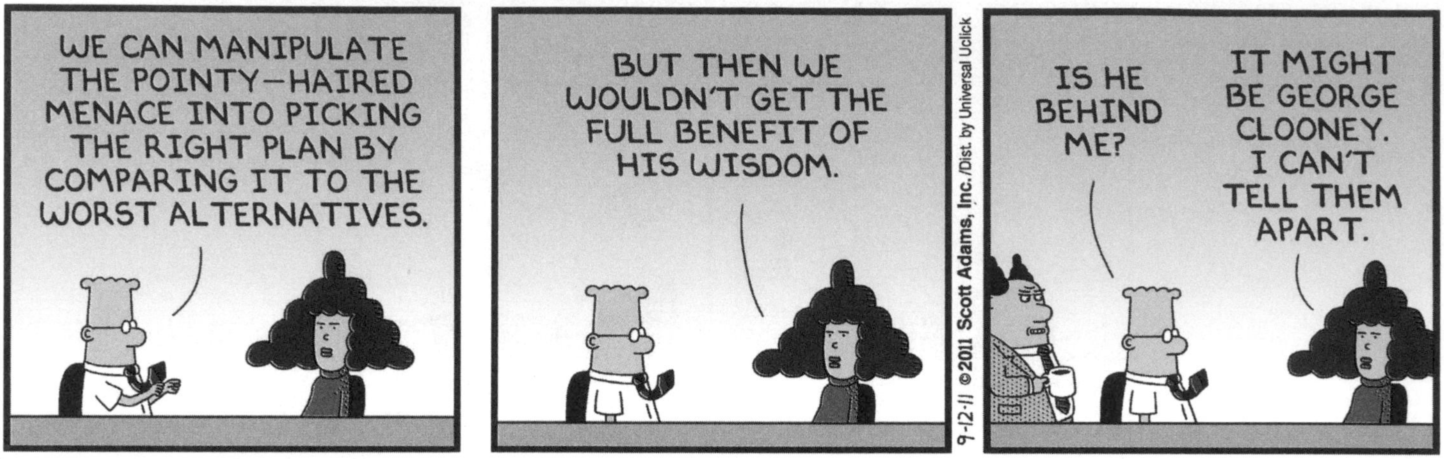
WE CAN MANIPULATE THE POINTY-HAIRED MENACE INTO PICKING THE RIGHT PLAN BY COMPARING IT TO THE WORST ALTERNATIVES.
BUT THEN WE WOULDN'T GET THE FULL BENEFIT OF HIS WISDOM.
9-12-11 ©2011 Scott Adams, Inc./Dist. by Universal Uclick
IS HE BEHIND ME?
IT MIGHT BE GEORGE CLOONEY. I CAN'T TELL THEM APART.

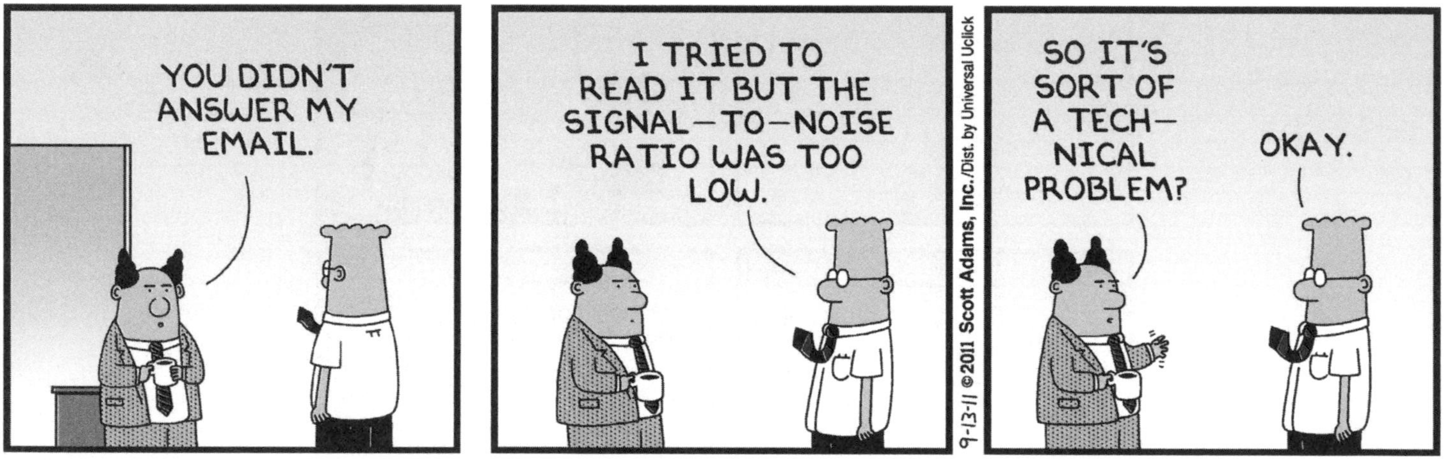
YOU DIDN'T ANSWER MY EMAIL.
I TRIED TO READ IT BUT THE SIGNAL-TO-NOISE RATIO WAS TOO LOW.
9-13-11 ©2011 Scott Adams, Inc./Dist. by Universal Uclick
SO IT'S SORT OF A TECH-NICAL PROBLEM?
OKAY.

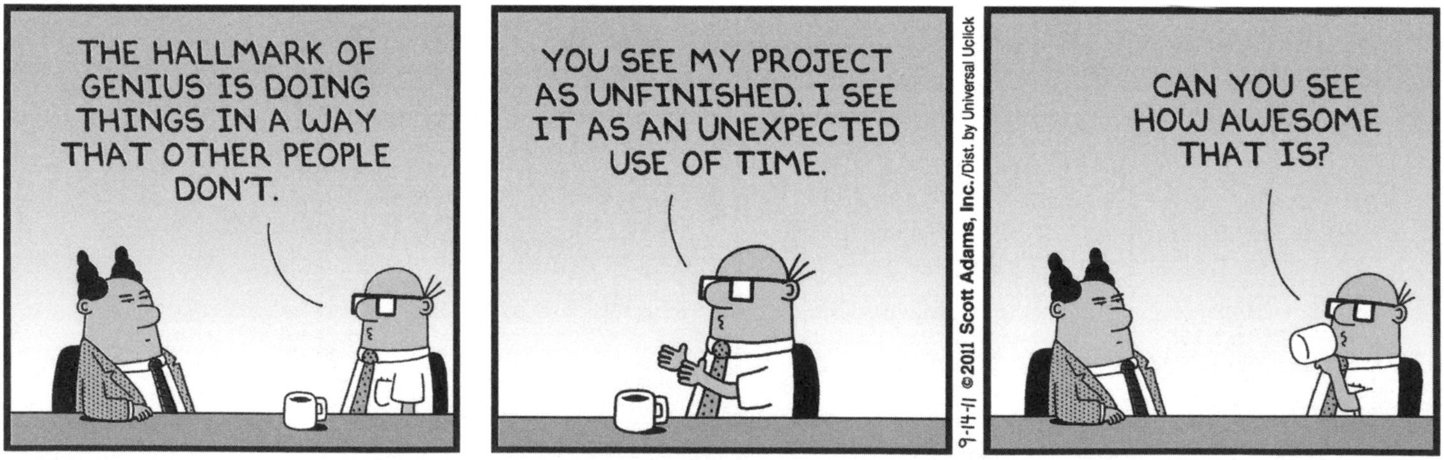
THE HALLMARK OF GENIUS IS DOING THINGS IN A WAY THAT OTHER PEOPLE DON'T.
YOU SEE MY PROJECT AS UNFINISHED. I SEE IT AS AN UNEXPECTED USE OF TIME.
9-14-11 ©2011 Scott Adams, Inc./Dist. by Universal Uclick
CAN YOU SEE HOW AWESOME THAT IS?

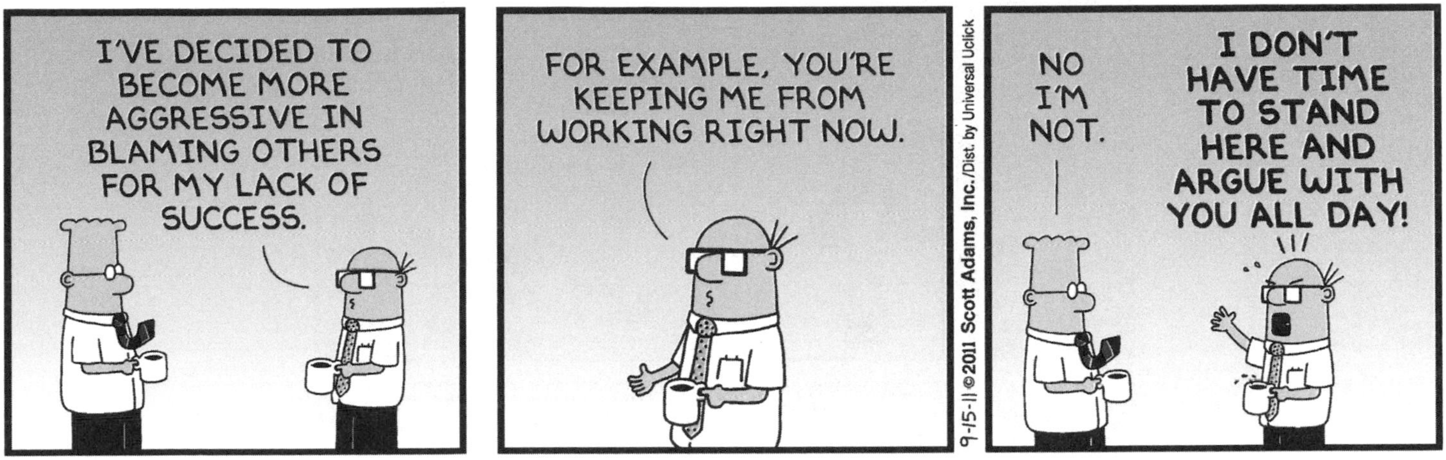
I'VE DECIDED TO BECOME MORE AGGRESSIVE IN BLAMING OTHERS FOR MY LACK OF SUCCESS.
FOR EXAMPLE, YOU'RE KEEPING ME FROM WORKING RIGHT NOW.
NO I'M NOT.
I DON'T HAVE TIME TO STAND HERE AND ARGUE WITH YOU ALL DAY!
9-15-11 © 2011 Scott Adams, Inc./Dist. by Universal Uclick

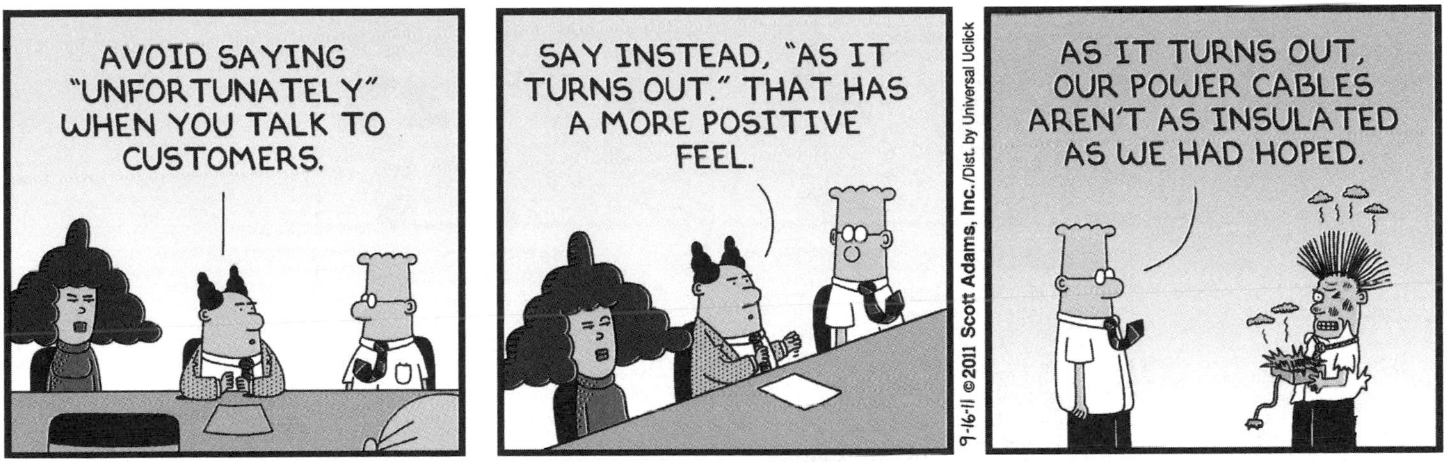
AVOID SAYING "UNFORTUNATELY" WHEN YOU TALK TO CUSTOMERS.
SAY INSTEAD, "AS IT TURNS OUT." THAT HAS A MORE POSITIVE FEEL.
AS IT TURNS OUT, OUR POWER CABLES AREN'T AS INSULATED AS WE HAD HOPED.
9-16-11 © 2011 Scott Adams, Inc./Dist. by Universal Uclick

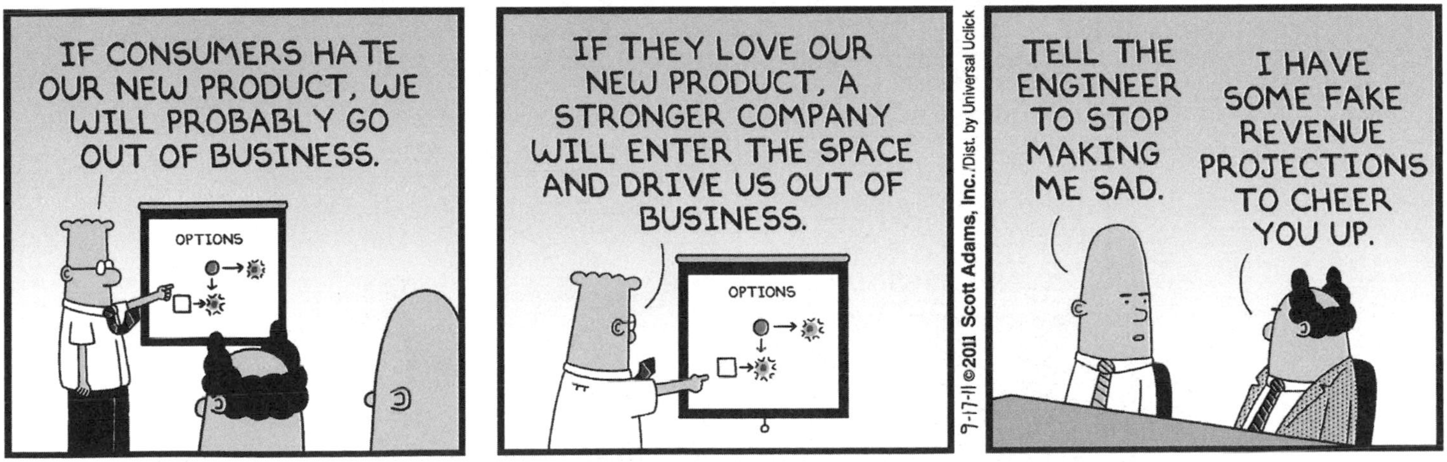
IF CONSUMERS HATE OUR NEW PRODUCT, WE WILL PROBABLY GO OUT OF BUSINESS.
OPTIONS
IF THEY LOVE OUR NEW PRODUCT, A STRONGER COMPANY WILL ENTER THE SPACE AND DRIVE US OUT OF BUSINESS.
OPTIONS
TELL THE ENGINEER TO STOP MAKING ME SAD.
I HAVE SOME FAKE REVENUE PROJECTIONS TO CHEER YOU UP.
9-17-11 © 2011 Scott Adams, Inc./Dist. by Universal Uclick

. . . THEN WE CAN DO THE LOAD TESTING AND. . .
I'M INVOKING THE RIGHT OF IMPERIOUS INTERRUPTUS.
IN LAYMAN'S TERMS, IT IS THE RIGHT OF ALL BOSSES TO HIJACK THE CONVERSATIONS OF SUBORDINATES.
©2011 Scott Adams, Inc./Dist. by Universal Uclick
I WILL NOW TURN MY BACK TO YOU AND SPEAK WITH ALICE AS IF YOU DON'T EXIST.
DO NOT LEAVE. DO NOT CHIME IN. JUST AWKWARDLY STAND THERE.
IMPERIOUS INTERRUPTUS!
BEHOLD MY POWER TO MAKE *TWO* UNDERLINGS STAND AWKWARDLY WHILE I HIJACK THIS CONVERSATION!
9-18-11
HAVE YOU HEARD MY SPEECH ABOUT HOW WE'RE NOT LEVEL CONSCIOUS AT THIS COMPANY?

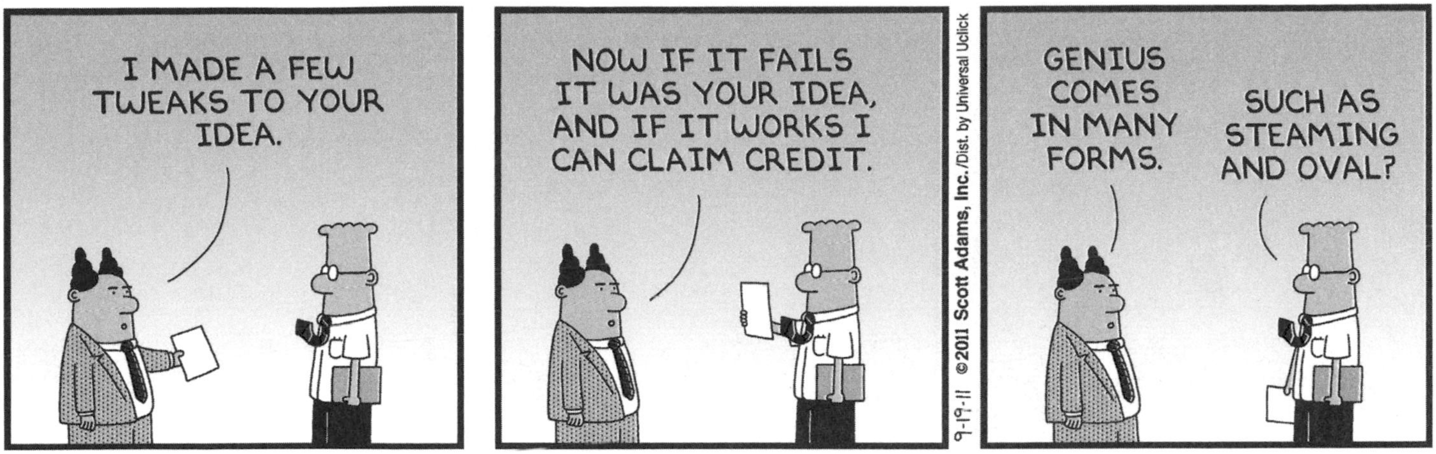
I MADE A FEW TWEAKS TO YOUR IDEA.
NOW IF IT FAILS IT WAS YOUR IDEA, AND IF IT WORKS I CAN CLAIM CREDIT.
9-19-11 ©2011 Scott Adams, Inc./Dist. by Universal Uclick
GENIUS COMES IN MANY FORMS.
SUCH AS STEAMING AND OVAL?

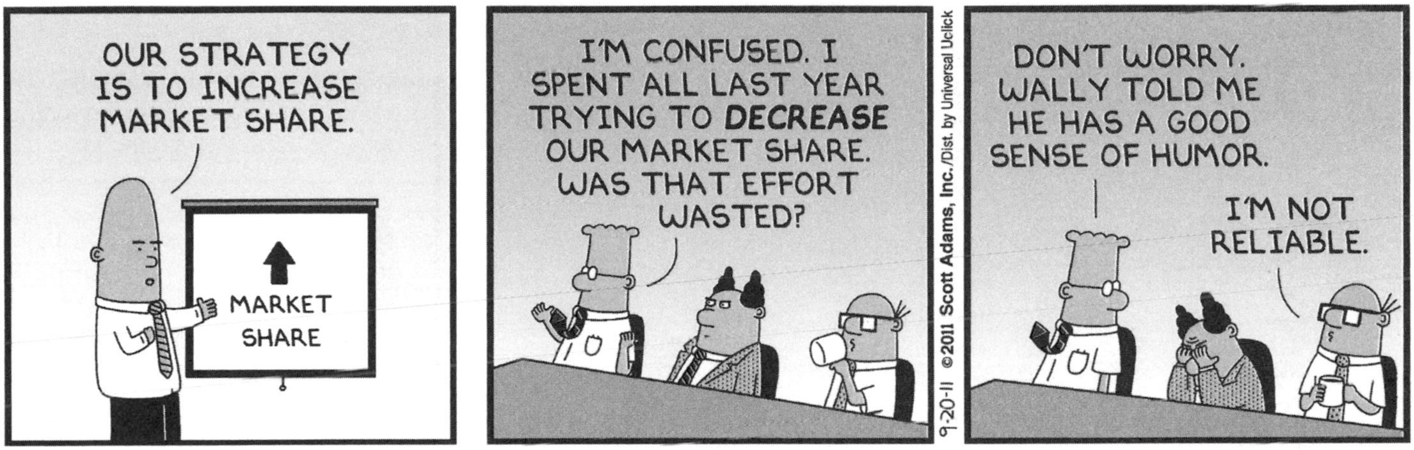
OUR STRATEGY IS TO INCREASE MARKET SHARE.
MARKET SHARE
I'M CONFUSED. I SPENT ALL LAST YEAR TRYING TO ***DECREASE*** OUR MARKET SHARE. WAS THAT EFFORT WASTED?
9-20-11 ©2011 Scott Adams, Inc./Dist. by Universal Uclick
DON'T WORRY. WALLY TOLD ME HE HAS A GOOD SENSE OF HUMOR.
I'M NOT RELIABLE.

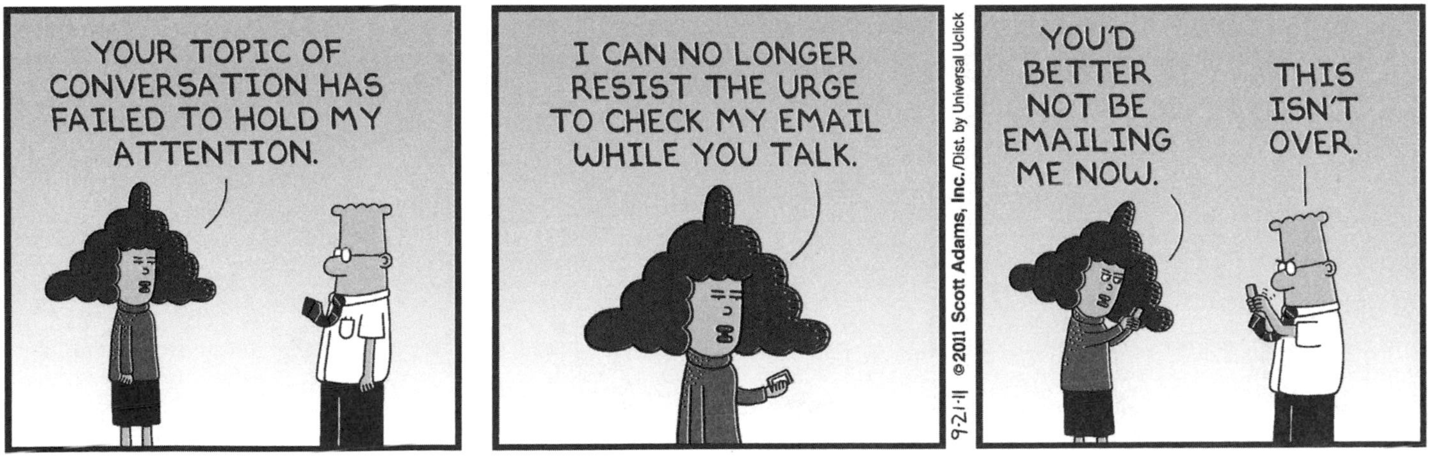
YOUR TOPIC OF CONVERSATION HAS FAILED TO HOLD MY ATTENTION.
I CAN NO LONGER RESIST THE URGE TO CHECK MY EMAIL WHILE YOU TALK.
9-21-11 ©2011 Scott Adams, Inc./Dist. by Universal Uclick
YOU'D BETTER NOT BE EMAILING ME NOW.
THIS ISN'T OVER.

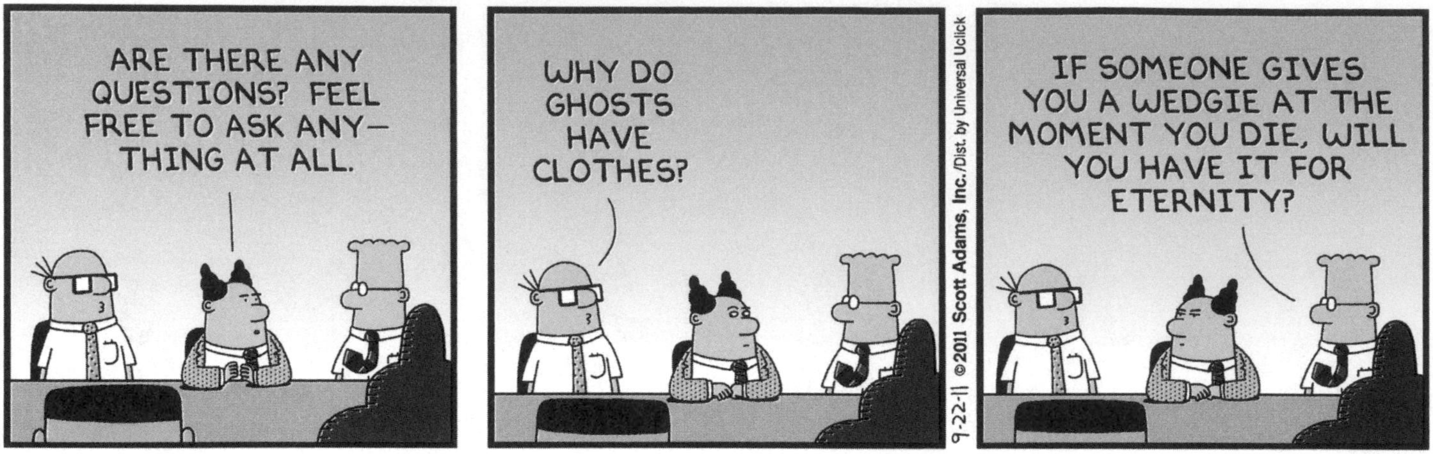
ARE THERE ANY QUESTIONS? FEEL FREE TO ASK ANY-THING AT ALL.
WHY DO GHOSTS HAVE CLOTHES?
9-22-11 ©2011 Scott Adams, Inc./Dist. by Universal Uclick
IF SOMEONE GIVES YOU A WEDGIE AT THE MOMENT YOU DIE, WILL YOU HAVE IT FOR ETERNITY?

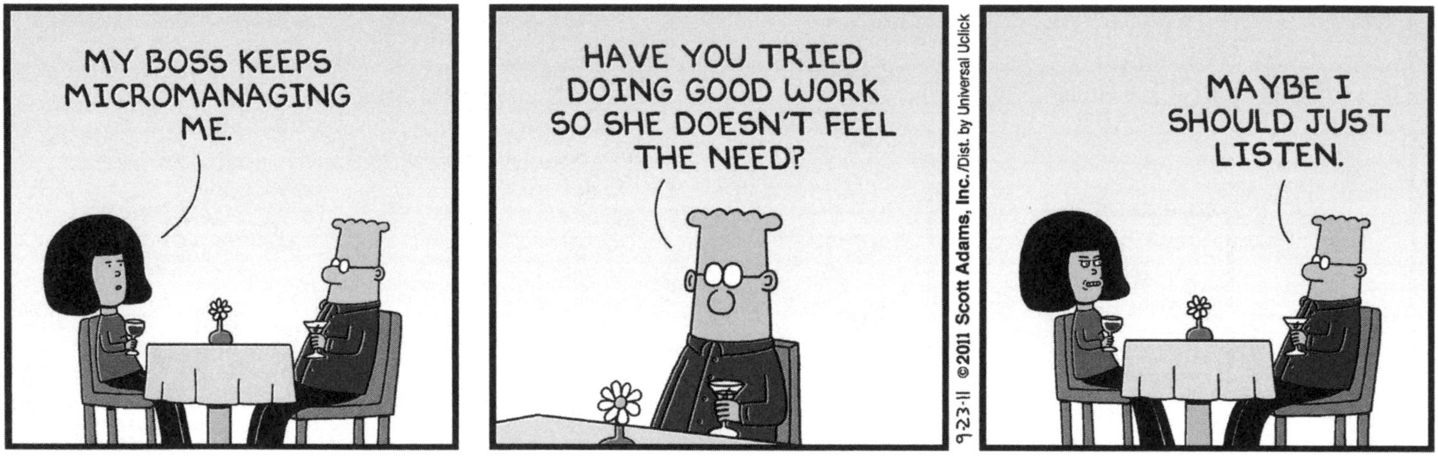
MY BOSS KEEPS MICROMANAGING ME.
HAVE YOU TRIED DOING GOOD WORK SO SHE DOESN'T FEEL THE NEED?
9-23-11 ©2011 Scott Adams, Inc./Dist. by Universal Uclick
MAYBE I SHOULD JUST LISTEN.

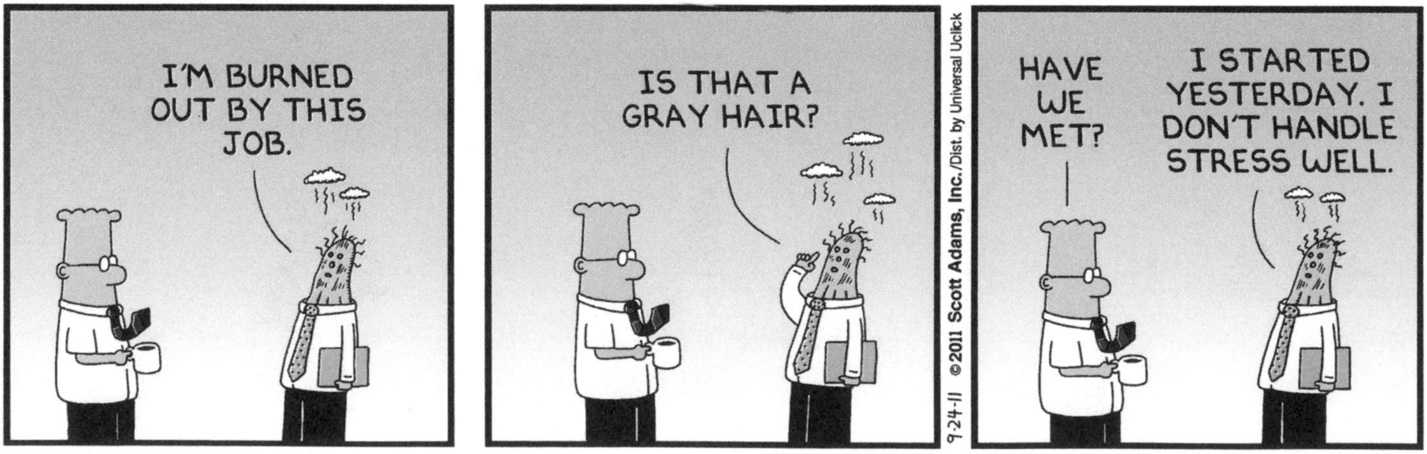
I'M BURNED OUT BY THIS JOB.
IS THAT A GRAY HAIR?
9-24-11 ©2011 Scott Adams, Inc./Dist. by Universal Uclick
HAVE WE MET?
I STARTED YESTERDAY. I DON'T HANDLE STRESS WELL.

I'M GETTING WRITER'S BLOCK TRYING TO COME UP WITH YOUR GOALS FOR THE YEAR.
JUST WRITE ANYTHING.
WE BOTH KNOW I'LL IGNORE THE GOALS AND WORK ON WHATEVER YOU ASSIGN TO ME.
HOW WILL I KNOW IF YOU DO A GOOD JOB IF YOU DON'T HAVE GOALS?
SAME WAY AS ALWAYS.
YOU'LL COMPARE YOUR LACK OF KNOWLEDGE ABOUT WHAT I DID TO THE GOALS YOU IMAGINE YOU MIGHT HAVE CREATED IF YOU COULD HAVE SEEN THE FUTURE.
THEN YOU'LL GIVE ME AN AVERAGE RAISE JUST LIKE EVERYONE ELSE WHO DIDN'T INVENT NUCLEAR FUSION.
IT'S BETTER TO NOT OVER-THINK THESE THINGS.
WORKS FOR ME.
©2011 Scott Adams, Inc./Dist. by Universal Uclick
9-25-11

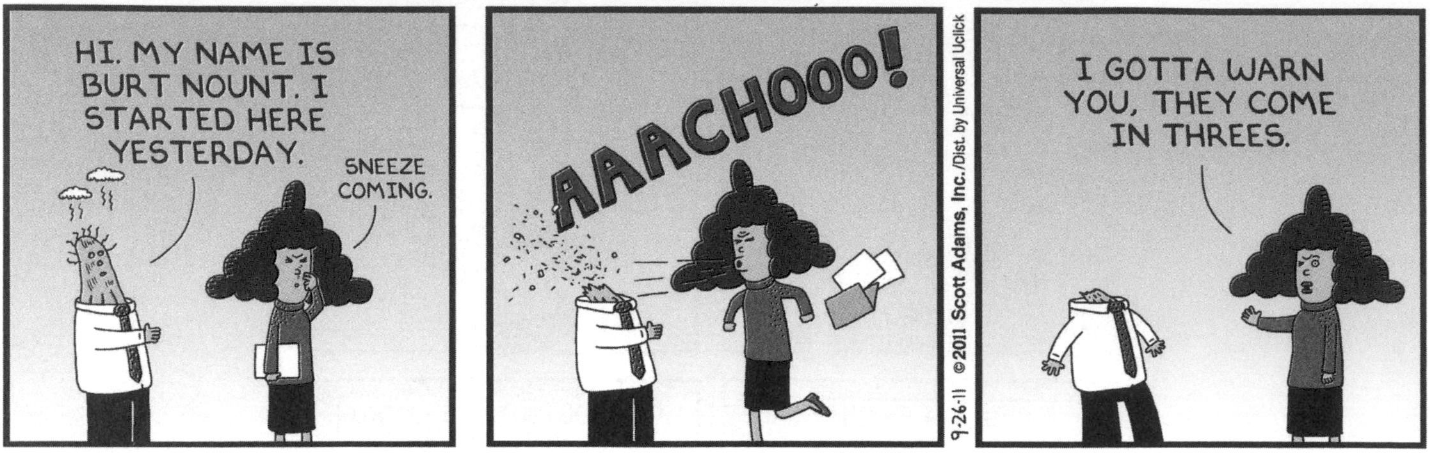
HI. MY NAME IS BURT NOUNT. I STARTED HERE YESTERDAY.
SNEEZE COMING.
AAACHOOO!
9-26-11 ©2011 Scott Adams, Inc./Dist. by Universal Uclick
I GOTTA WARN YOU, THEY COME IN THREES.

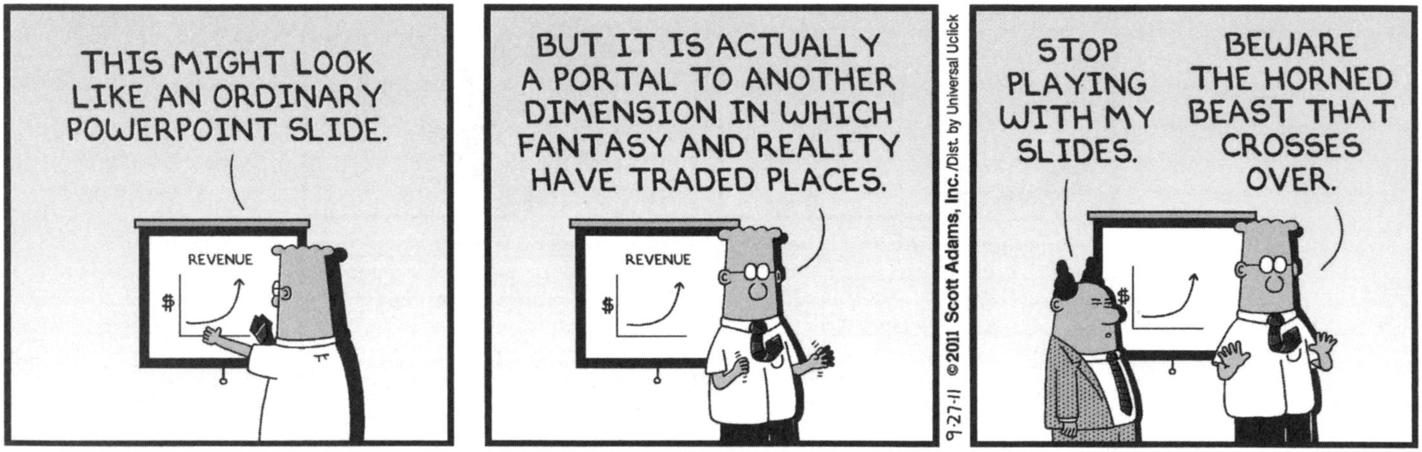
THIS MIGHT LOOK LIKE AN ORDINARY POWERPOINT SLIDE.
REVENUE
$
BUT IT IS ACTUALLY A PORTAL TO ANOTHER DIMENSION IN WHICH FANTASY AND REALITY HAVE TRADED PLACES.
REVENUE
$
9-27-11 ©2011 Scott Adams, Inc./Dist. by Universal Uclick
STOP PLAYING WITH MY SLIDES.
BEWARE THE HORNED BEAST THAT CROSSES OVER.
$

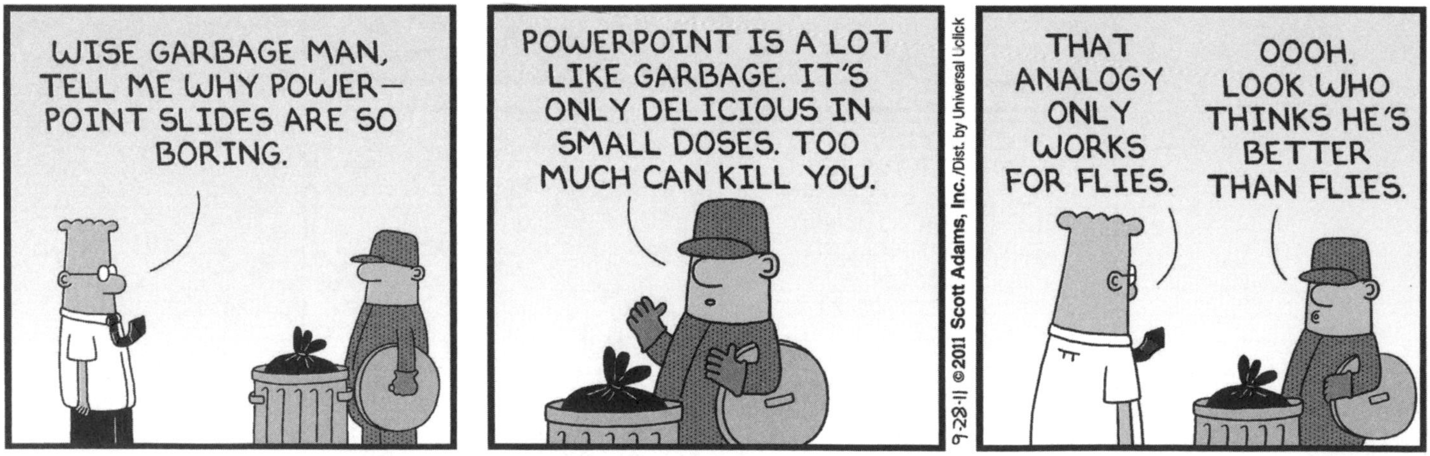
WISE GARBAGE MAN, TELL ME WHY POWER-POINT SLIDES ARE SO BORING.
POWERPOINT IS A LOT LIKE GARBAGE. IT'S ONLY DELICIOUS IN SMALL DOSES. TOO MUCH CAN KILL YOU.
9-28-11 ©2011 Scott Adams, Inc./Dist. by Universal Uclick
THAT ANALOGY ONLY WORKS FOR FLIES.
OOOH. LOOK WHO THINKS HE'S BETTER THAN FLIES.

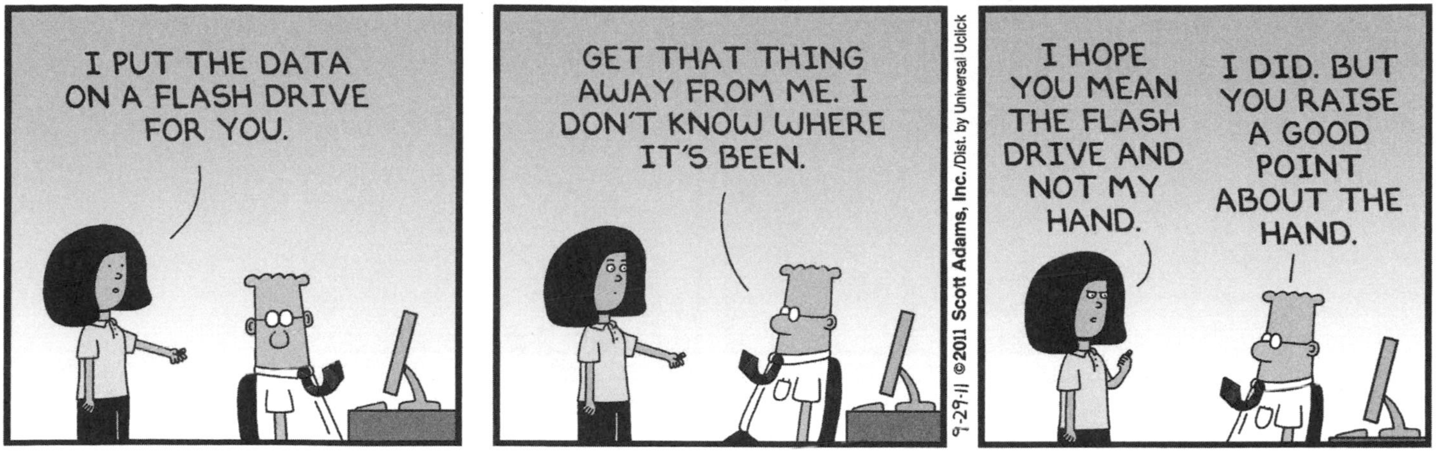
I PUT THE DATA ON A FLASH DRIVE FOR YOU.
GET THAT THING AWAY FROM ME. I DON'T KNOW WHERE IT'S BEEN.
I HOPE YOU MEAN THE FLASH DRIVE AND NOT MY HAND.
I DID. BUT YOU RAISE A GOOD POINT ABOUT THE HAND.
9-29-11

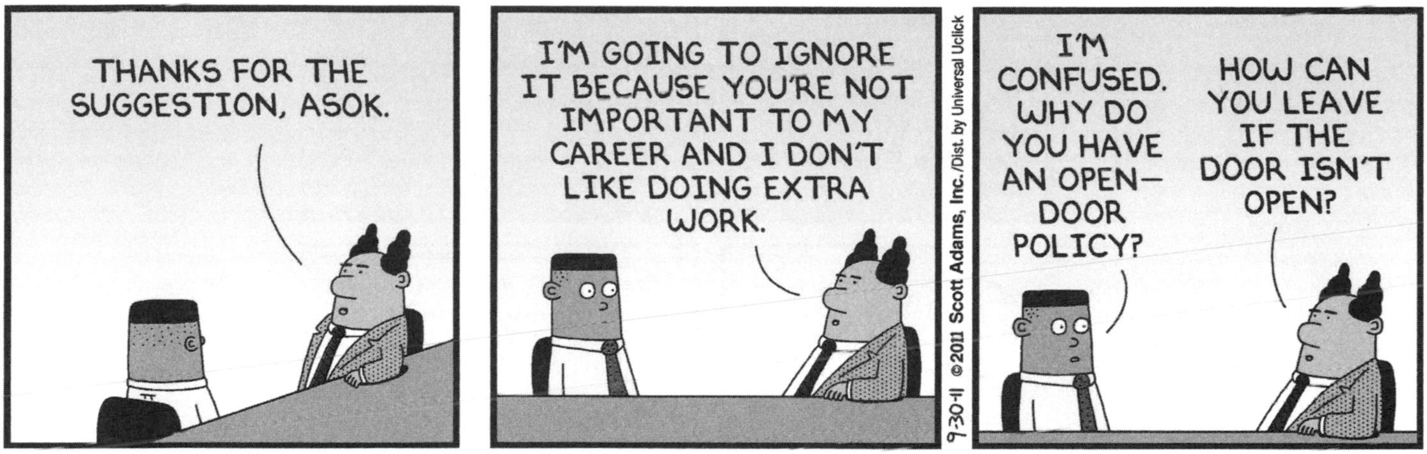
THANKS FOR THE SUGGESTION, ASOK.
I'M GOING TO IGNORE IT BECAUSE YOU'RE NOT IMPORTANT TO MY CAREER AND I DON'T LIKE DOING EXTRA WORK.
I'M CONFUSED. WHY DO YOU HAVE AN OPEN-DOOR POLICY?
HOW CAN YOU LEAVE IF THE DOOR ISN'T OPEN?
9-30-11

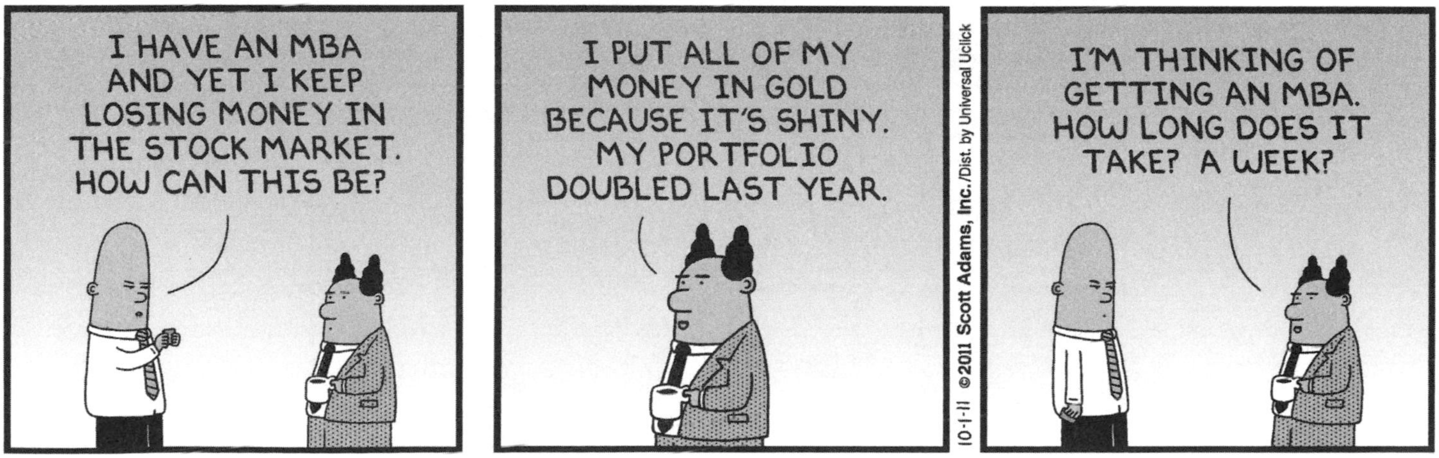
I HAVE AN MBA AND YET I KEEP LOSING MONEY IN THE STOCK MARKET. HOW CAN THIS BE?
I PUT ALL OF MY MONEY IN GOLD BECAUSE IT'S SHINY. MY PORTFOLIO DOUBLED LAST YEAR.
I'M THINKING OF GETTING AN MBA. HOW LONG DOES IT TAKE? A WEEK?
10-1-11

THE SERVERS ARE DOWN.
I KNOW.
YOU SHOULD DO SOMETHING ABOUT IT.
I'M TRYING.
WHAT'S THE HOLDUP?
I KEEP GETTING INTERRUPTED BY AN UNHELPFUL IDIOT.
MAYBE I CAN HELP.
I'LL GUARD YOUR DOORWAY AND KEEP THAT GUY AWAY FROM YOU.
THIS IS BORING. AND I DON'T SEE THAT GUY.
HAVE I MANAGED ENOUGH FOR NOW?
YOU NAILED IT.
© 2011 Scott Adams, Inc./Dist. by Universal Uclick
10-2-11

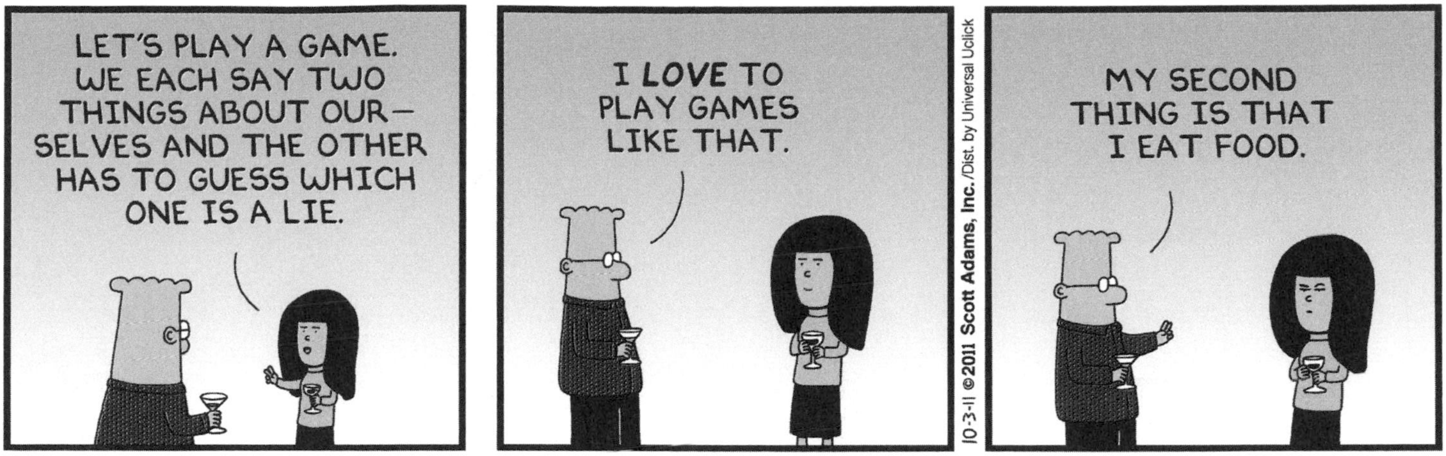
LET'S PLAY A GAME. WE EACH SAY TWO THINGS ABOUT OURSELVES AND THE OTHER HAS TO GUESS WHICH ONE IS A LIE.
I *LOVE* TO PLAY GAMES LIKE THAT.
10-3-11 ©2011 Scott Adams, Inc./Dist. by Universal Uclick
MY SECOND THING IS THAT I EAT FOOD.

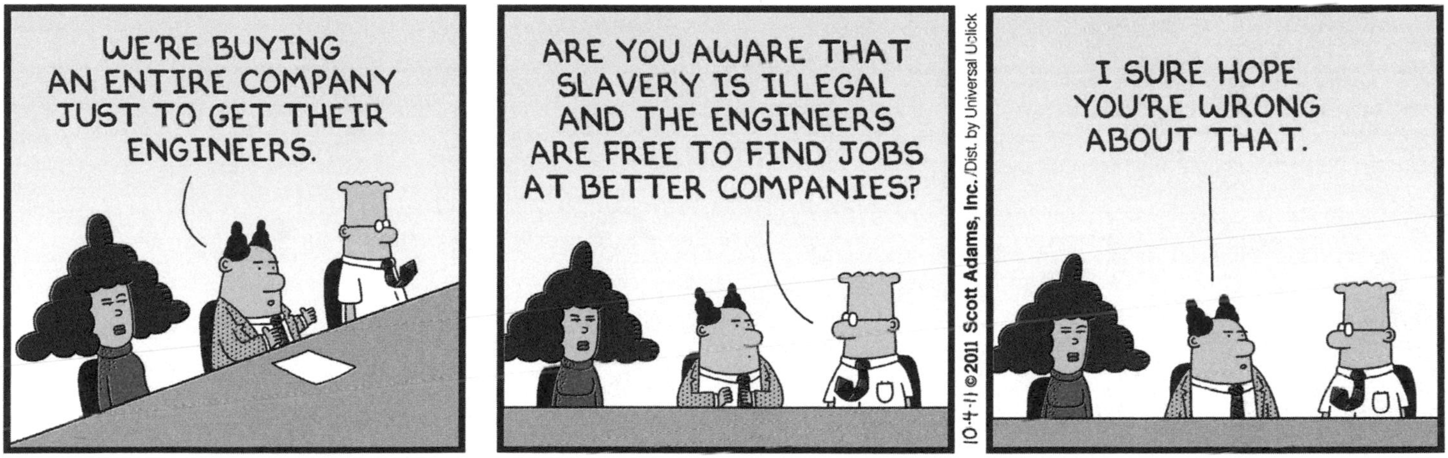
WE'RE BUYING AN ENTIRE COMPANY JUST TO GET THEIR ENGINEERS.
ARE YOU AWARE THAT SLAVERY IS ILLEGAL AND THE ENGINEERS ARE FREE TO FIND JOBS AT BETTER COMPANIES?
10-4-11 ©2011 Scott Adams, Inc./Dist. by Universal Uclick
I SURE HOPE YOU'RE WRONG ABOUT THAT.

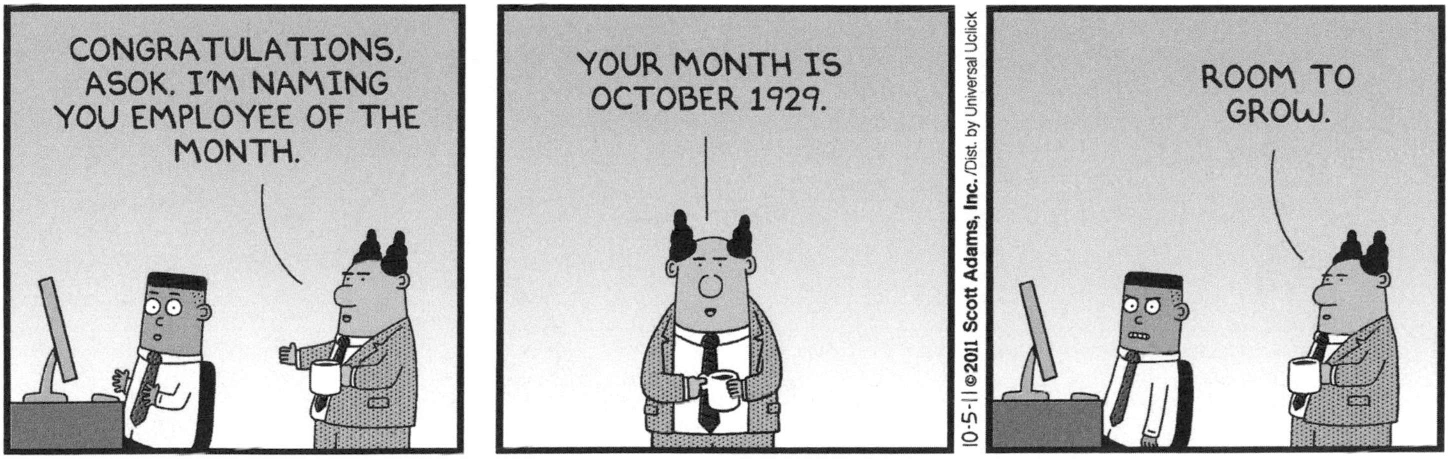
CONGRATULATIONS, ASOK. I'M NAMING YOU EMPLOYEE OF THE MONTH.
YOUR MONTH IS OCTOBER 1929.
10-5-11 ©2011 Scott Adams, Inc./Dist. by Universal Uclick
ROOM TO GROW.

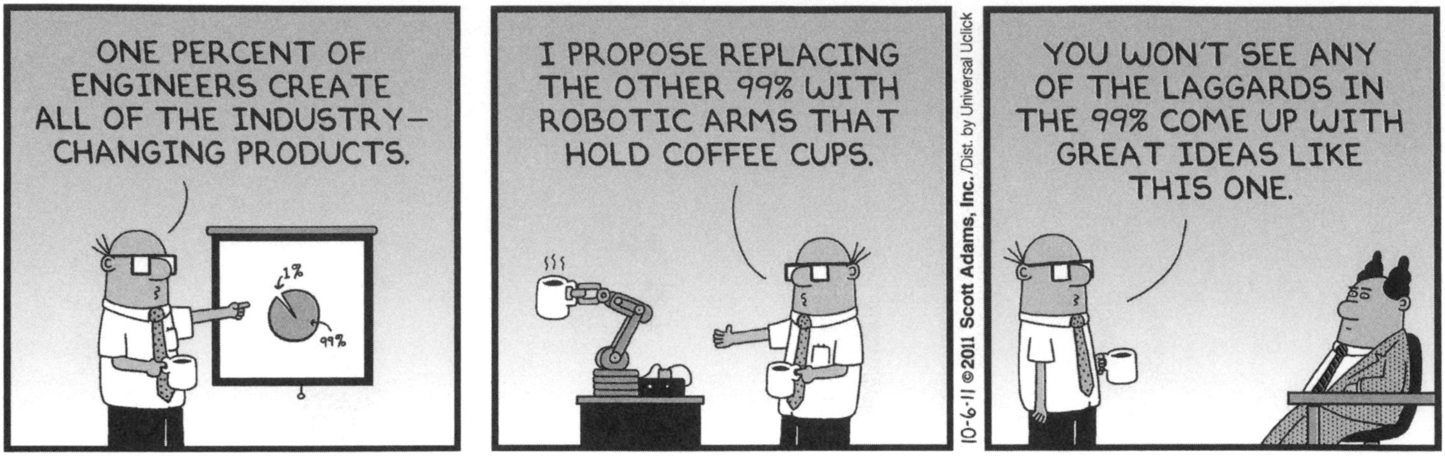
ONE PERCENT OF ENGINEERS CREATE ALL OF THE INDUSTRY—CHANGING PRODUCTS.
1%
99%
I PROPOSE REPLACING THE OTHER 99% WITH ROBOTIC ARMS THAT HOLD COFFEE CUPS.
10-6-11 ©2011 Scott Adams, Inc./Dist. by Universal Uclick
YOU WON'T SEE ANY OF THE LAGGARDS IN THE 99% COME UP WITH GREAT IDEAS LIKE THIS ONE.

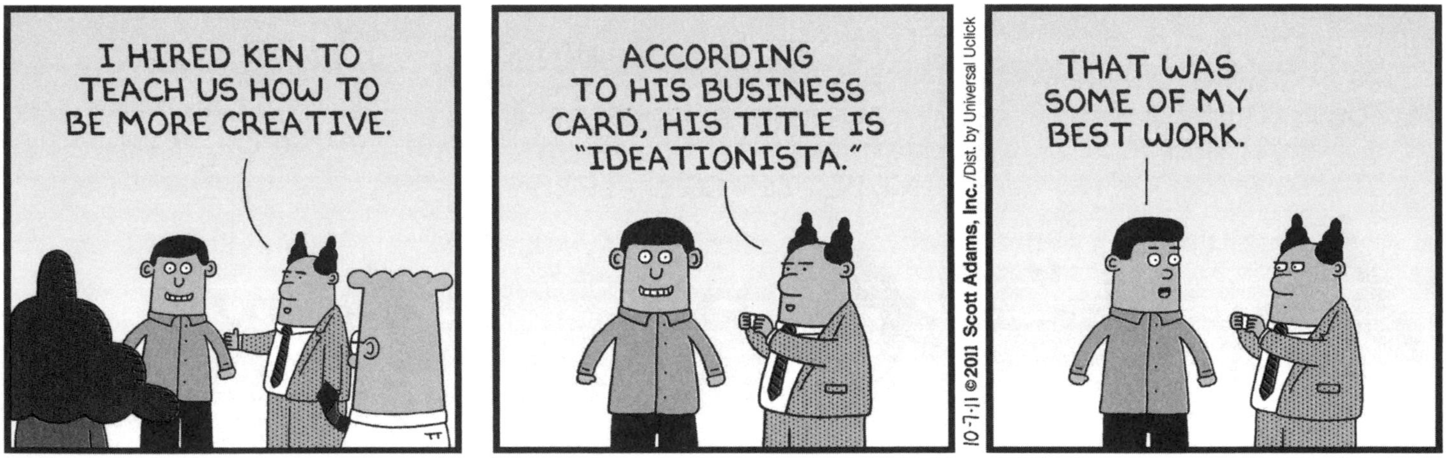
I HIRED KEN TO TEACH US HOW TO BE MORE CREATIVE.
ACCORDING TO HIS BUSINESS CARD, HIS TITLE IS "IDEATIONISTA."
10-7-11 ©2011 Scott Adams, Inc./Dist. by Universal Uclick
THAT WAS SOME OF MY BEST WORK.

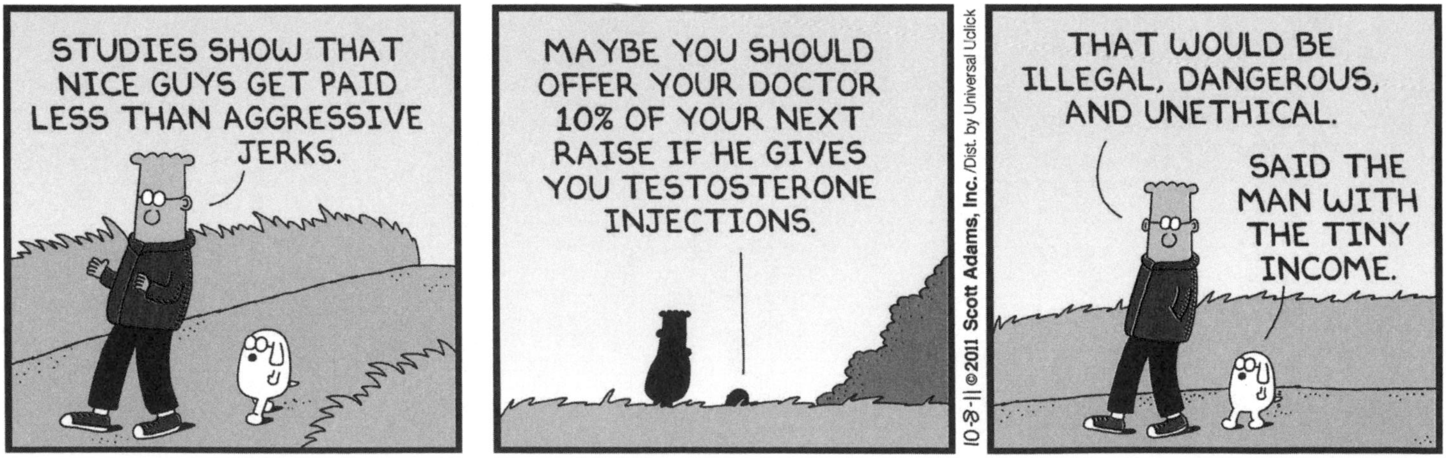
STUDIES SHOW THAT NICE GUYS GET PAID LESS THAN AGGRESSIVE JERKS.
MAYBE YOU SHOULD OFFER YOUR DOCTOR 10% OF YOUR NEXT RAISE IF HE GIVES YOU TESTOSTERONE INJECTIONS.
10-8-11 ©2011 Scott Adams, Inc./Dist. by Universal Uclick
THAT WOULD BE ILLEGAL, DANGEROUS, AND UNETHICAL.
SAID THE MAN WITH THE TINY INCOME.

YOU KNOW WHAT WOULD BE GREAT?
I'D LIKE TO SEE A MATRIX COMPARING THE FEATURES OF OUR PAST PRODUCTS.
DILBERT, WHY DON'T YOU PULL THAT TOGETHER FOR OUR NEXT MEETING?
THAT WOULD TAKE TWO DAYS AND THE MATRIX WOULD HAVE NO PRACTICAL USE.
THE PROBLEM HERE IS THAT TED DOESN'T HAVE ANY SKIN IN THE GAME.
I PROPOSE THAT TED HAS TO BANG HIS HEAD ON THE TABLE WHENEVER HE CAUSES ME TO DO EXTRA WORK.
THAT WILL HELP TED MAKE BETTER DECISIONS ABOUT THE VALUE OF MY TIME.
NEVER MIND.
NINJA ECONOMICS!
© 2011 Scott Adams, Inc./Dist. by Universal Uclick
10-9-11

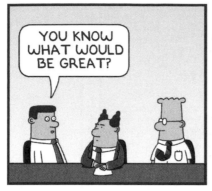

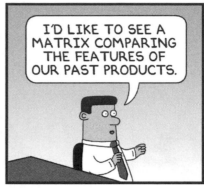

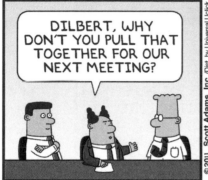

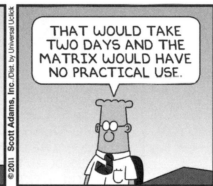

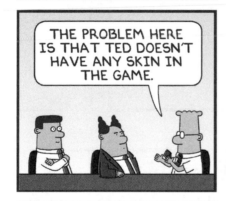

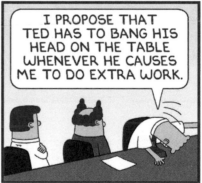

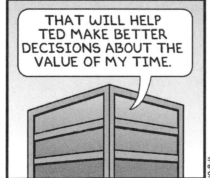

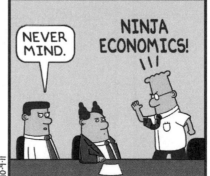

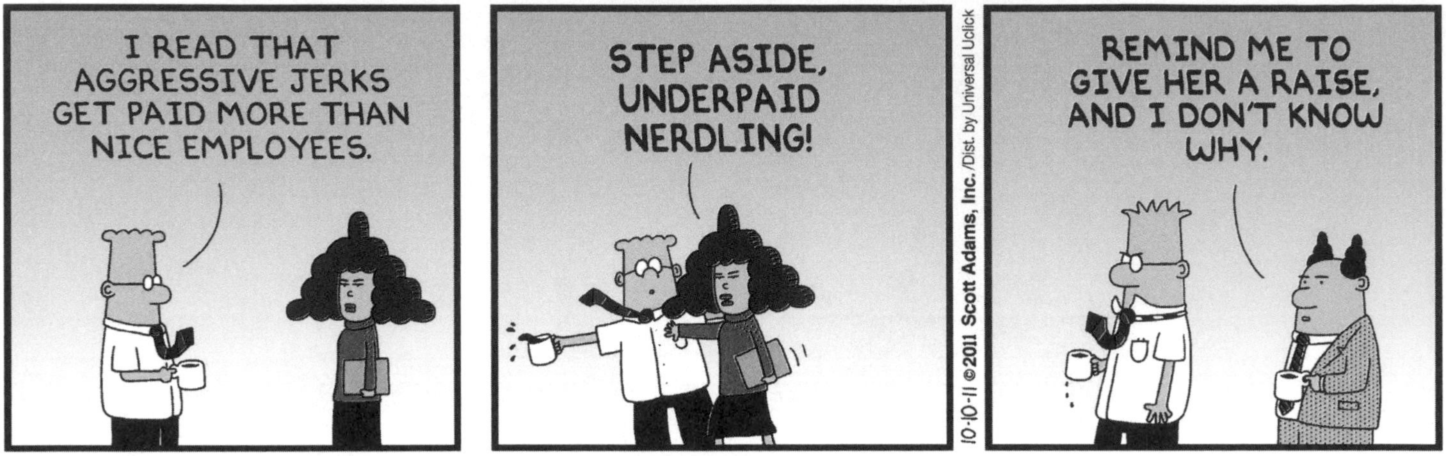
I READ THAT AGGRESSIVE JERKS GET PAID MORE THAN NICE EMPLOYEES.
STEP ASIDE, UNDERPAID NERDLING!
10-10-11 ©2011 Scott Adams, Inc./Dist. by Universal Uclick
REMIND ME TO GIVE HER A RAISE, AND I DON'T KNOW WHY.

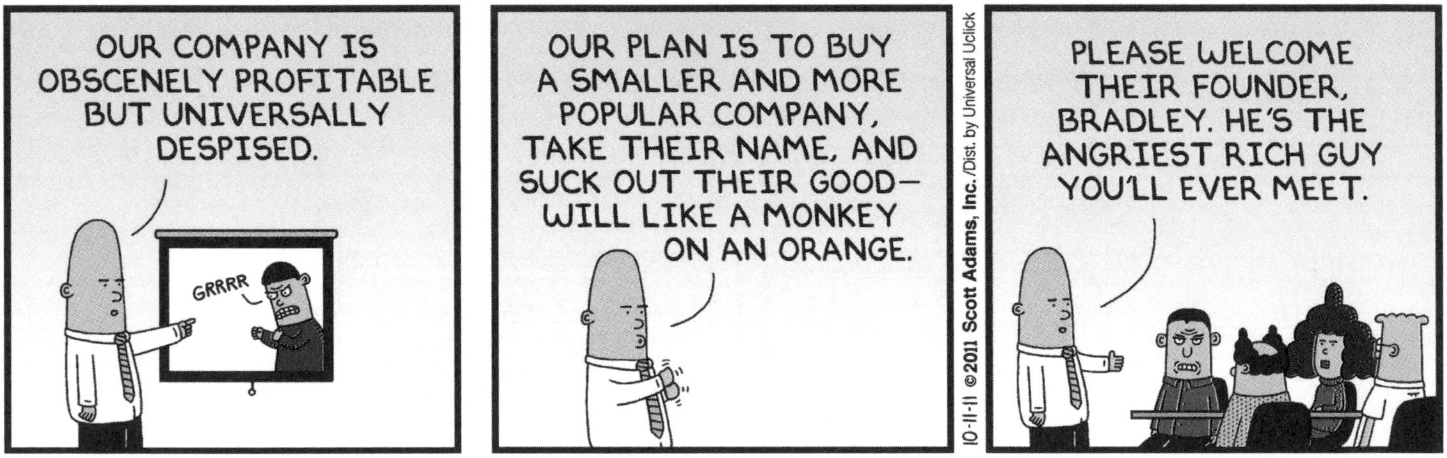
OUR COMPANY IS OBSCENELY PROFITABLE BUT UNIVERSALLY DESPISED.
GRRRR
OUR PLAN IS TO BUY A SMALLER AND MORE POPULAR COMPANY, TAKE THEIR NAME, AND SUCK OUT THEIR GOOD-WILL LIKE A MONKEY ON AN ORANGE.
10-11-11 ©2011 Scott Adams, Inc./Dist. by Universal Uclick
PLEASE WELCOME THEIR FOUNDER, BRADLEY. HE'S THE ANGRIEST RICH GUY YOU'LL EVER MEET.

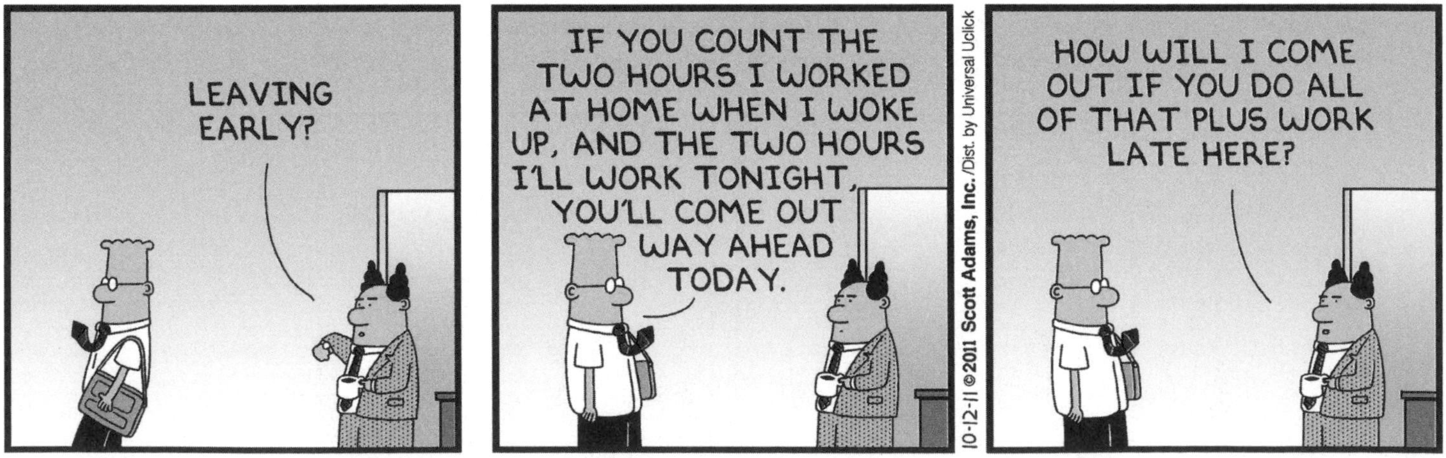
LEAVING EARLY?
IF YOU COUNT THE TWO HOURS I WORKED AT HOME WHEN I WOKE UP, AND THE TWO HOURS I'LL WORK TONIGHT, YOU'LL COME OUT WAY AHEAD TODAY.
10-12-11 ©2011 Scott Adams, Inc./Dist. by Universal Uclick
HOW WILL I COME OUT IF YOU DO ALL OF THAT PLUS WORK LATE HERE?

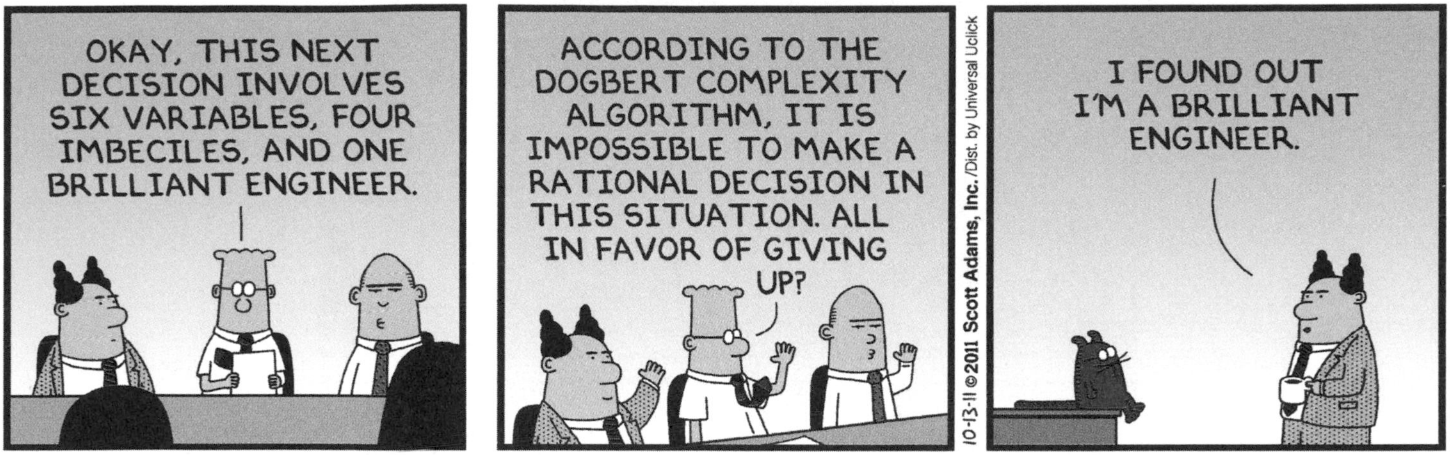

OKAY, THIS NEXT DECISION INVOLVES SIX VARIABLES, FOUR IMBECILES, AND ONE BRILLIANT ENGINEER.
ACCORDING TO THE DOGBERT COMPLEXITY ALGORITHM, IT IS IMPOSSIBLE TO MAKE A RATIONAL DECISION IN THIS SITUATION. ALL IN FAVOR OF GIVING UP?
I FOUND OUT I'M A BRILLIANT ENGINEER.

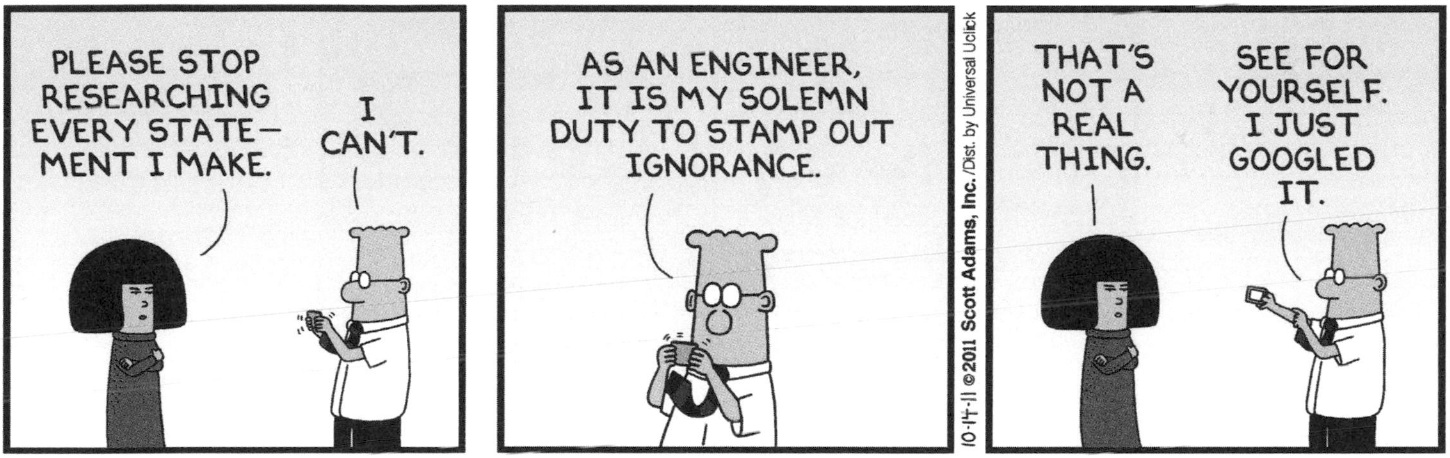

PLEASE STOP RESEARCHING EVERY STATEMENT I MAKE.
I CAN'T.
AS AN ENGINEER, IT IS MY SOLEMN DUTY TO STAMP OUT IGNORANCE.
THAT'S NOT A REAL THING.
SEE FOR YOURSELF. I JUST GOOGLED IT.

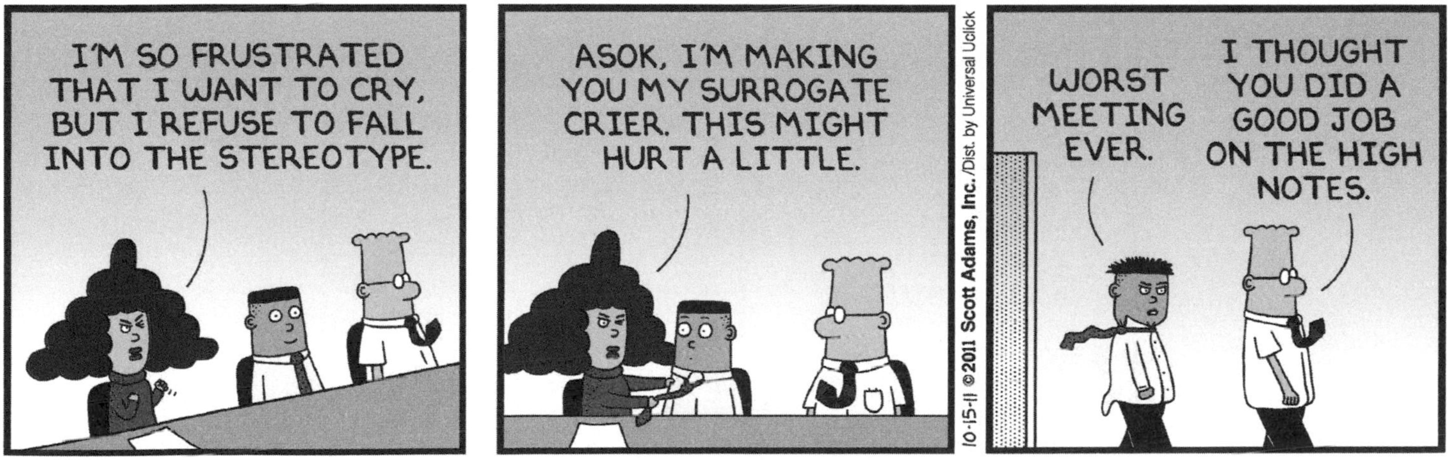

I'M SO FRUSTRATED THAT I WANT TO CRY, BUT I REFUSE TO FALL INTO THE STEREOTYPE.
ASOK, I'M MAKING YOU MY SURROGATE CRIER. THIS MIGHT HURT A LITTLE.
WORST MEETING EVER.
I THOUGHT YOU DID A GOOD JOB ON THE HIGH NOTES.

WE NEED CREATIVE IDEAS FOR OUR NEXT PRODUCT.
BUT NOT FROM YOU. YOUR IDEAS ARE AWFUL.
AND DON'T SUGGEST SOMETHING THAT IS ALREADY BEING DONE. THAT JUST PUTS YOUR IGNORANCE ON PUBLIC DISPLAY.
I DON'T WANT TO HEAR ANY IDEAS THAT COST MONEY OR INCREASE RISK.
AS USUAL, I'LL EVALUATE EACH IDEA BY REPEATING IT SLOWLY WHILE I LOOK AT YOU WITH DISDAIN.
IF YOU COME UP WITH A GOOD IDEA, I'LL LET YOU TAKE ON THE PROJECT IN ADDITION TO YOUR EXISTING WORK.
WHO WANTS TO GO FIRST?
HOW DID I HIRE SO MANY PEOPLE WHO HAVE NO IDEAS?
PROBABLY BAD LUCK.
© 2011 Scott Adams, Inc./Dist. by Universal Uclick
10-16-11

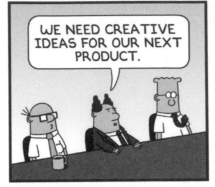

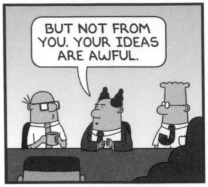

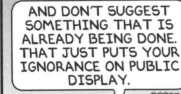

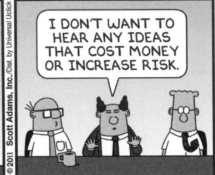

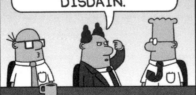

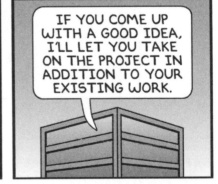

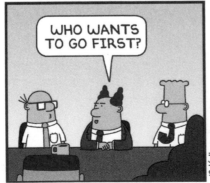

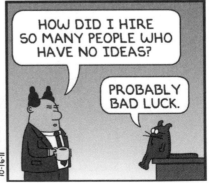

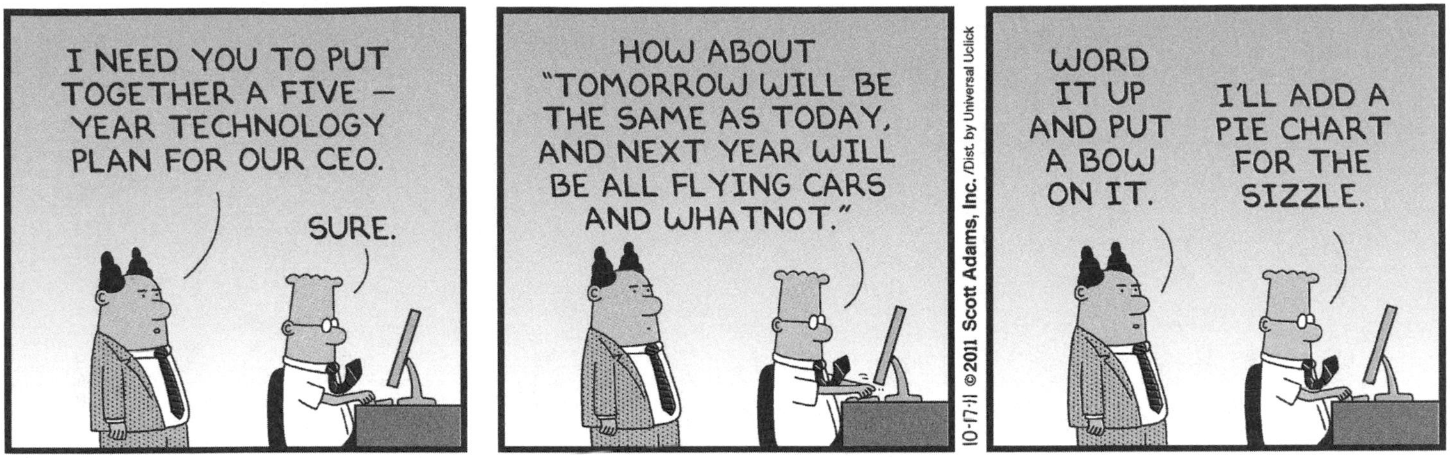
I NEED YOU TO PUT TOGETHER A FIVE-YEAR TECHNOLOGY PLAN FOR OUR CEO.
SURE.
HOW ABOUT "TOMORROW WILL BE THE SAME AS TODAY, AND NEXT YEAR WILL BE ALL FLYING CARS AND WHATNOT."
10-17-11 ©2011 Scott Adams, Inc./Dist. by Universal Uclick
WORD IT UP AND PUT A BOW ON IT.
I'LL ADD A PIE CHART FOR THE SIZZLE.

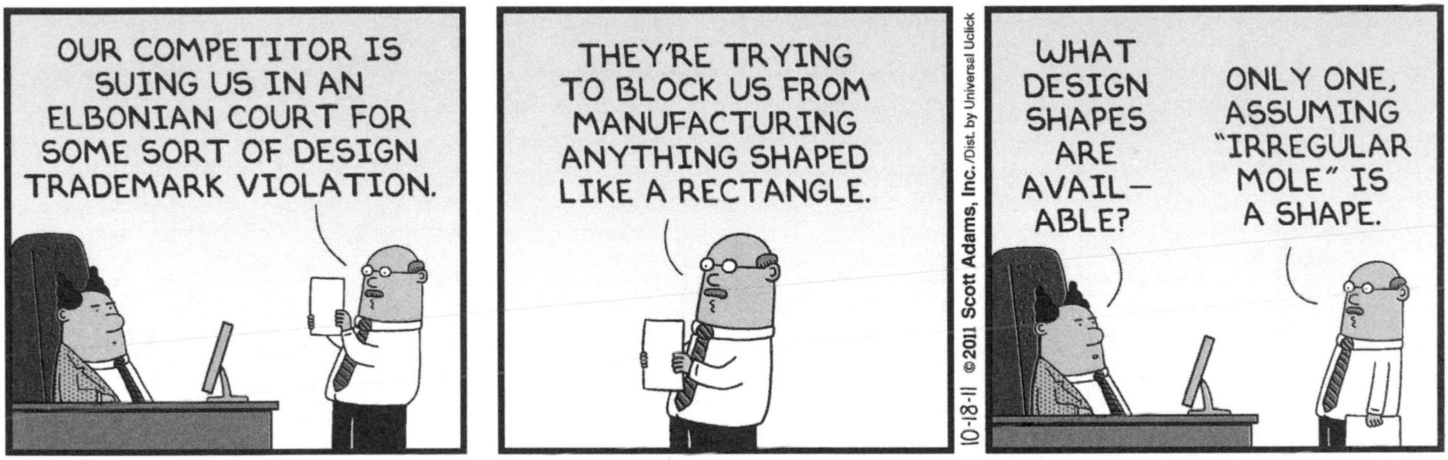
OUR COMPETITOR IS SUING US IN AN ELBONIAN COURT FOR SOME SORT OF DESIGN TRADEMARK VIOLATION.
THEY'RE TRYING TO BLOCK US FROM MANUFACTURING ANYTHING SHAPED LIKE A RECTANGLE.
10-18-11 ©2011 Scott Adams, Inc./Dist. by Universal Uclick
WHAT DESIGN SHAPES ARE AVAIL-ABLE?
ONLY ONE, ASSUMING "IRREGULAR MOLE" IS A SHAPE.

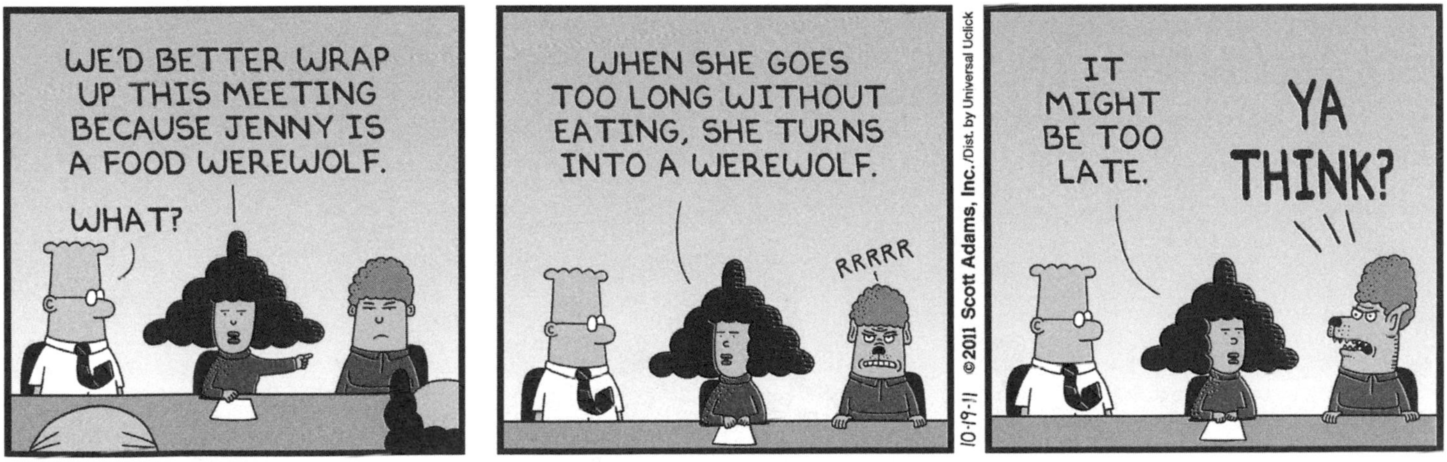
WE'D BETTER WRAP UP THIS MEETING BECAUSE JENNY IS A FOOD WEREWOLF.
WHAT?
WHEN SHE GOES TOO LONG WITHOUT EATING, SHE TURNS INTO A WEREWOLF.
RRRRR
10-19-11 ©2011 Scott Adams, Inc./Dist. by Universal Uclick
IT MIGHT BE TOO LATE.
YA THINK?

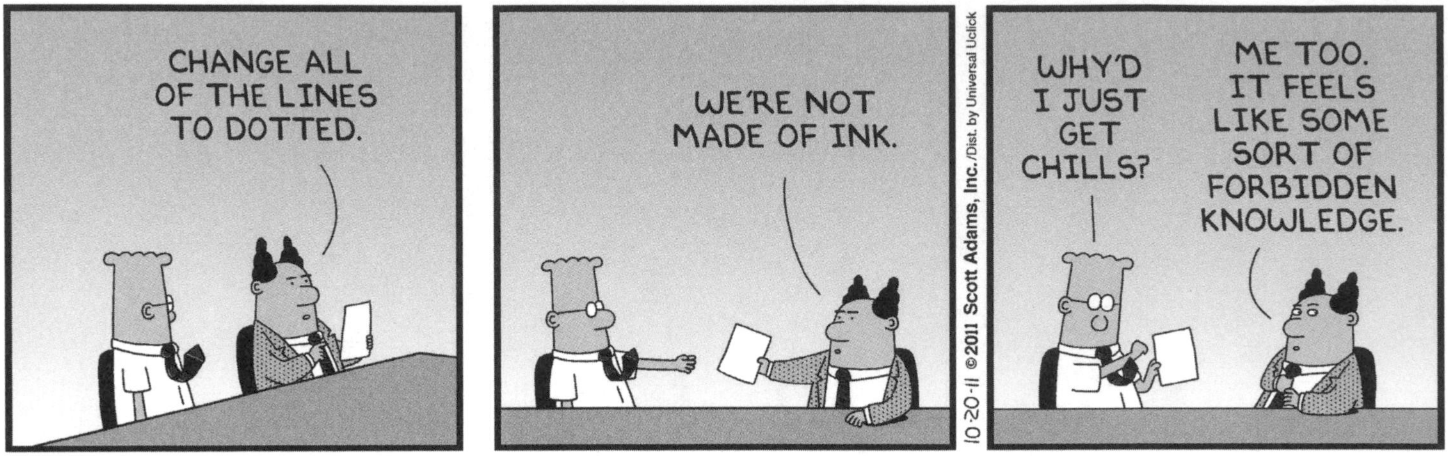
CHANGE ALL OF THE LINES TO DOTTED.
WE'RE NOT MADE OF INK.
WHY'D I JUST GET CHILLS?
ME TOO. IT FEELS LIKE SOME SORT OF FORBIDDEN KNOWLEDGE.
10-20-11 ©2011 Scott Adams, Inc./Dist. by Universal Uclick

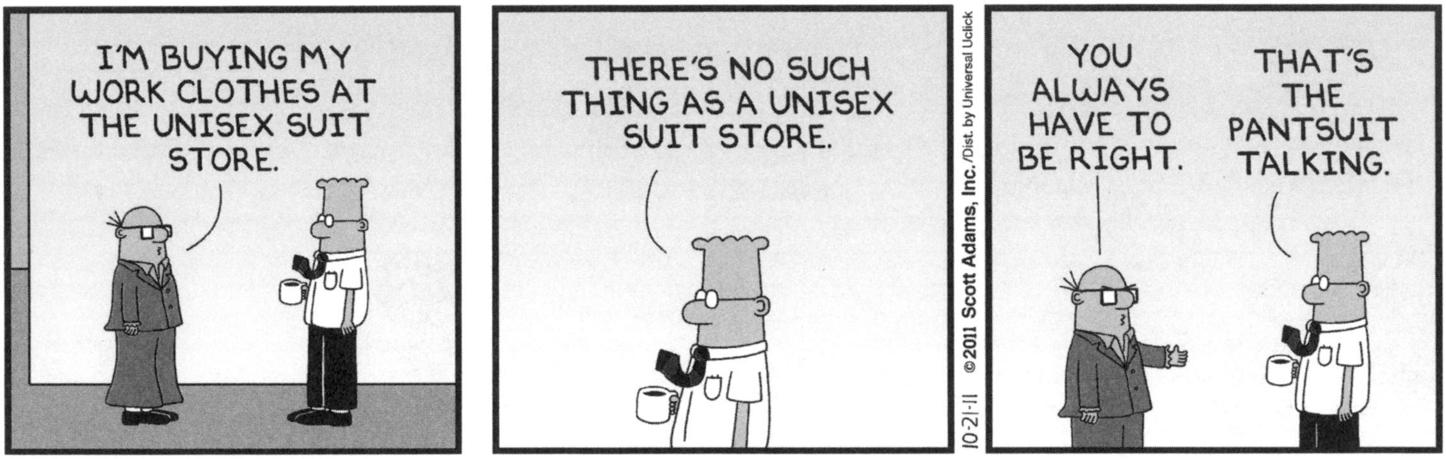
I'M BUYING MY WORK CLOTHES AT THE UNISEX SUIT STORE.
THERE'S NO SUCH THING AS A UNISEX SUIT STORE.
YOU ALWAYS HAVE TO BE RIGHT.
THAT'S THE PANTSUIT TALKING.
10-21-11 ©2011 Scott Adams, Inc./Dist. by Universal Uclick

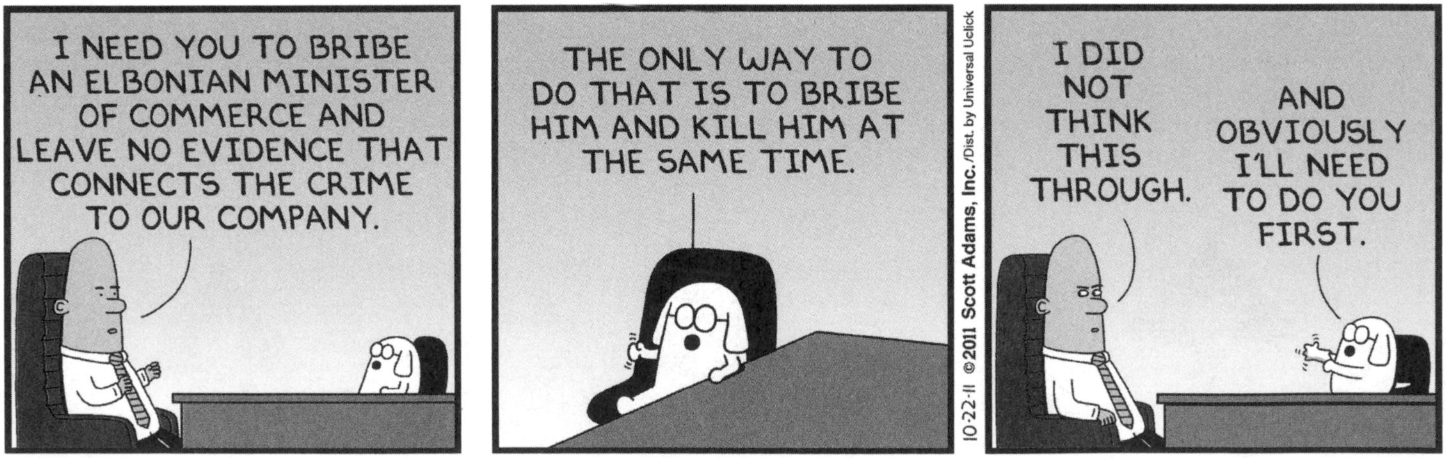
I NEED YOU TO BRIBE AN ELBONIAN MINISTER OF COMMERCE AND LEAVE NO EVIDENCE THAT CONNECTS THE CRIME TO OUR COMPANY.
THE ONLY WAY TO DO THAT IS TO BRIBE HIM AND KILL HIM AT THE SAME TIME.
I DID NOT THINK THIS THROUGH.
AND OBVIOUSLY I'LL NEED TO DO YOU FIRST.
10-22-11 ©2011 Scott Adams, Inc./Dist. by Universal Uclick

CAN YOU SHOW ME HOW TO DOWN-LOAD APPS ON MY NEW PHONE?
I COULD. . .
BUT THAT WOULD TAKE TIME AWAY FROM MY PRIMARY JOB OF SHOWING YOU HOW TO DO FORMULAS IN EXCEL.
APPARENTLY THE EIGHT TIMES I ALREADY TAUGHT YOU WEREN'T ENOUGH.
I DON'T USE EXCEL OFTEN ENOUGH TO REMEMBER FROM ONE TIME TO THE NEXT.
HOW OFTEN DO YOU EXPECT TO DOWN-LOAD APPS?
IT'S HARD TO SAY. I JUST KNOW I WANT ALL OF THEM.
HOW MANY ARE THERE?
FOUR.
© 2011 Scott Adams, Inc./Dist. by Universal Uclick
10-23-11

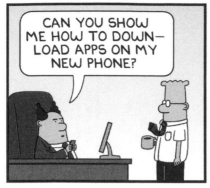

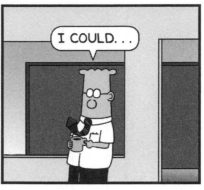

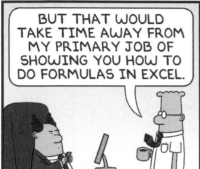

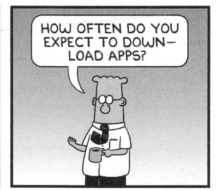

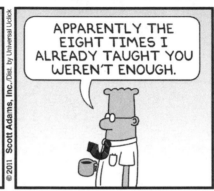

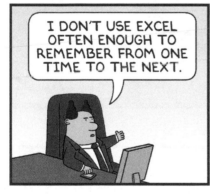

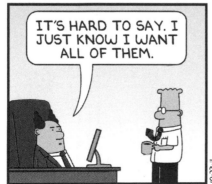

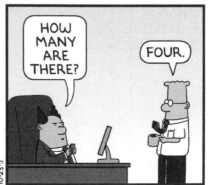

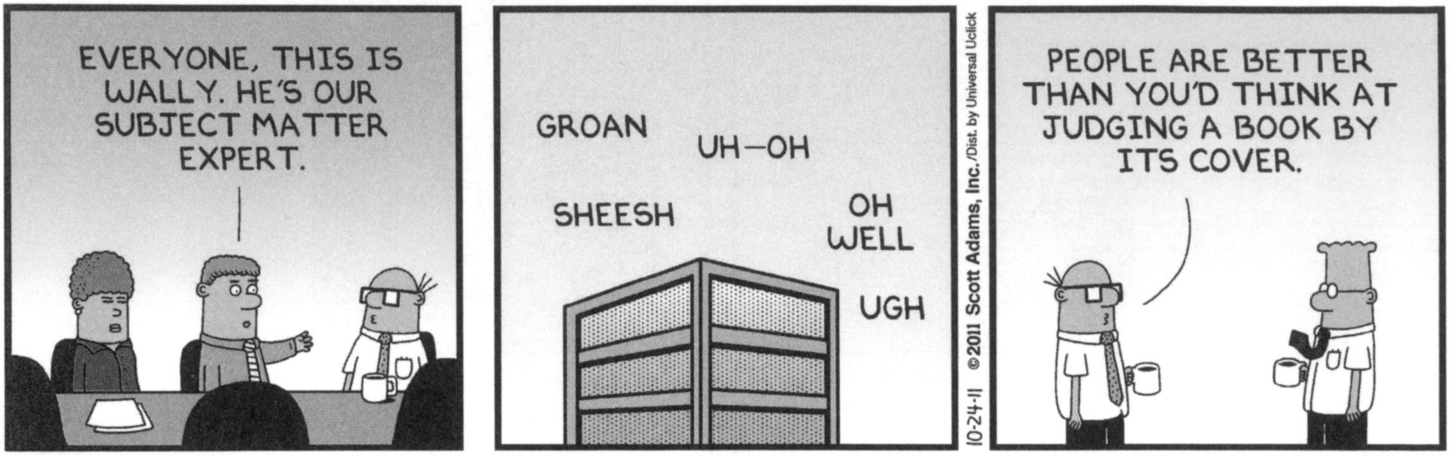
EVERYONE, THIS IS WALLY. HE'S OUR SUBJECT MATTER EXPERT.
GROAN
UH—OH
SHEESH
OH WELL
UGH
10-24-11 ©2011 Scott Adams, Inc./Dist. by Universal Uclick
PEOPLE ARE BETTER THAN YOU'D THINK AT JUDGING A BOOK BY ITS COVER.

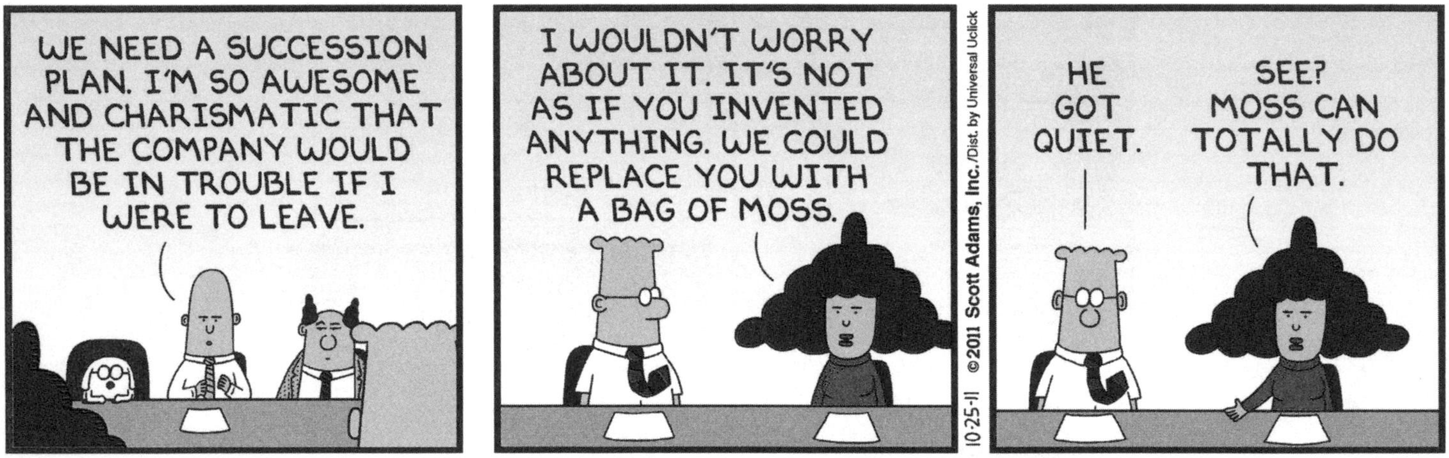
WE NEED A SUCCESSION PLAN. I'M SO AWESOME AND CHARISMATIC THAT THE COMPANY WOULD BE IN TROUBLE IF I WERE TO LEAVE.
I WOULDN'T WORRY ABOUT IT. IT'S NOT AS IF YOU INVENTED ANYTHING. WE COULD REPLACE YOU WITH A BAG OF MOSS.
10-25-11 ©2011 Scott Adams, Inc./Dist. by Universal Uclick
HE GOT QUIET.
SEE? MOSS CAN TOTALLY DO THAT.

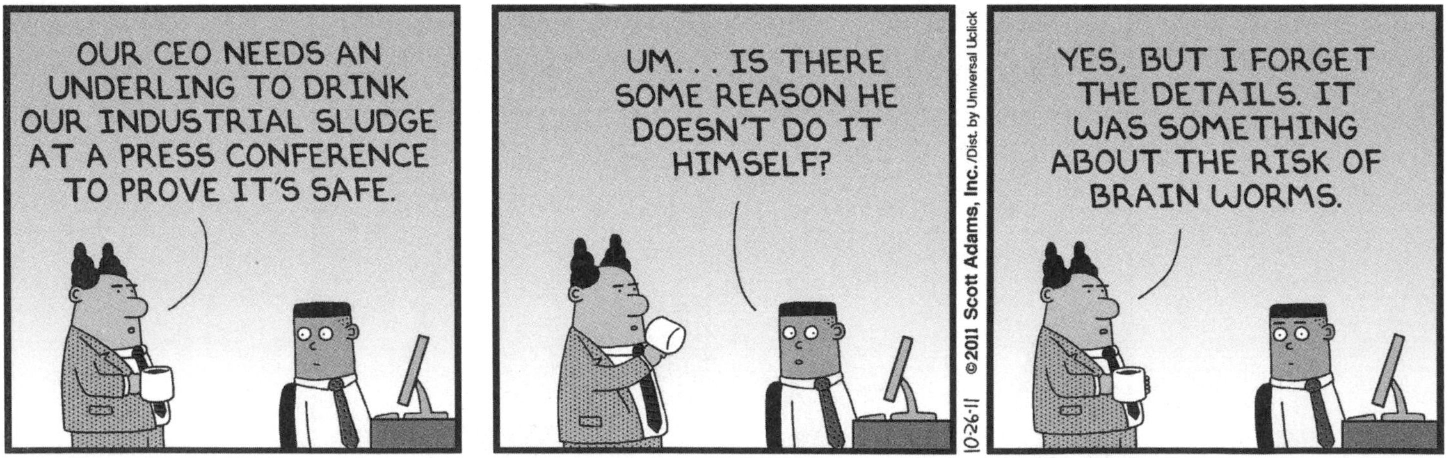
OUR CEO NEEDS AN UNDERLING TO DRINK OUR INDUSTRIAL SLUDGE AT A PRESS CONFERENCE TO PROVE IT'S SAFE.
UM. . . IS THERE SOME REASON HE DOESN'T DO IT HIMSELF?
10-26-11 ©2011 Scott Adams, Inc./Dist. by Universal Uclick
YES, BUT I FORGET THE DETAILS. IT WAS SOMETHING ABOUT THE RISK OF BRAIN WORMS.

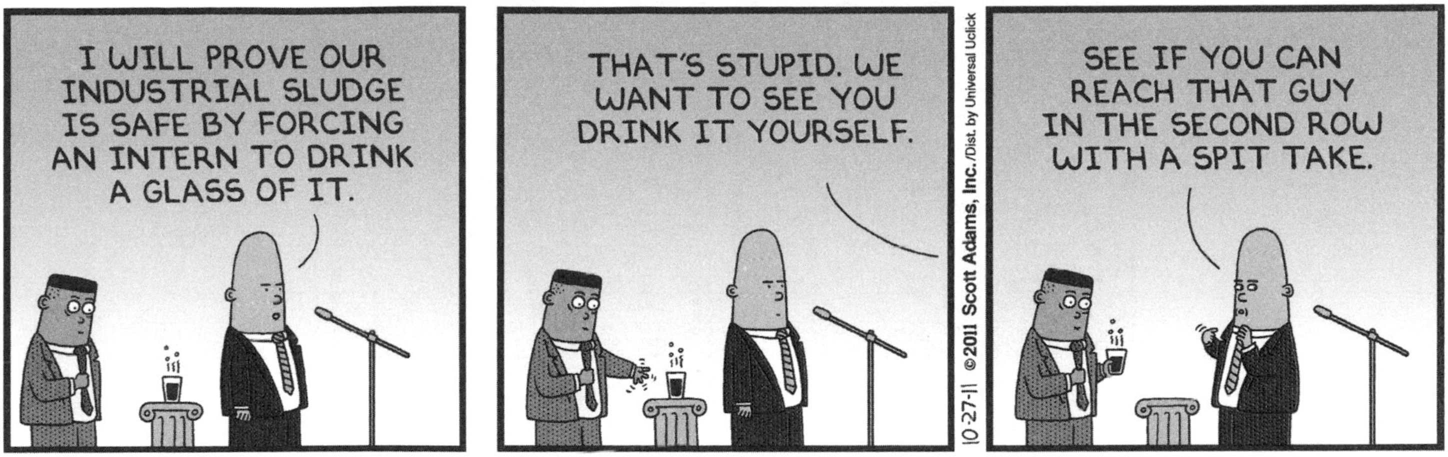
I WILL PROVE OUR INDUSTRIAL SLUDGE IS SAFE BY FORCING AN INTERN TO DRINK A GLASS OF IT.
THAT'S STUPID. WE WANT TO SEE YOU DRINK IT YOURSELF.
10-27-11 ©2011 Scott Adams, Inc./Dist. by Universal Uclick
SEE IF YOU CAN REACH THAT GUY IN THE SECOND ROW WITH A SPIT TAKE.

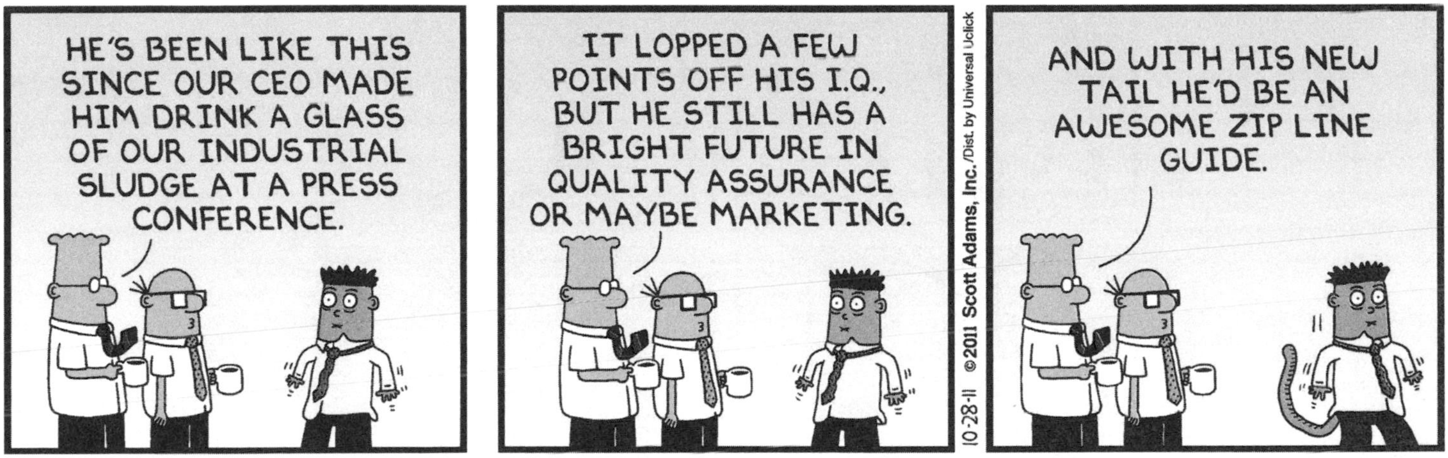
HE'S BEEN LIKE THIS SINCE OUR CEO MADE HIM DRINK A GLASS OF OUR INDUSTRIAL SLUDGE AT A PRESS CONFERENCE.
IT LOPPED A FEW POINTS OFF HIS I.Q., BUT HE STILL HAS A BRIGHT FUTURE IN QUALITY ASSURANCE OR MAYBE MARKETING.
10-28-11 ©2011 Scott Adams, Inc./Dist. by Universal Uclick
AND WITH HIS NEW TAIL HE'D BE AN AWESOME ZIP LINE GUIDE.

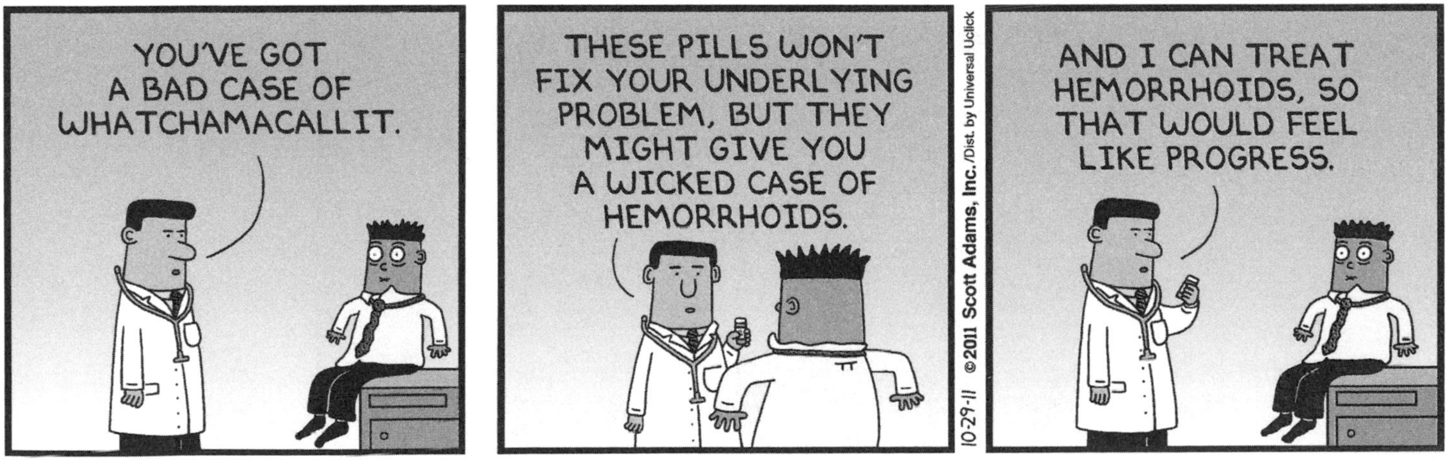
YOU'VE GOT A BAD CASE OF WHATCHAMACALLIT.
THESE PILLS WON'T FIX YOUR UNDERLYING PROBLEM, BUT THEY MIGHT GIVE YOU A WICKED CASE OF HEMORRHOIDS.
10-29-11 ©2011 Scott Adams, Inc./Dist. by Universal Uclick
AND I CAN TREAT HEMORRHOIDS, SO THAT WOULD FEEL LIKE PROGRESS.

MY ROLE IS DIGITAL MEDIA CURATION.
AM I SUPPOSED TO KNOW WHAT THAT MEANS?
HA HA! I LOOK DOWN ON YOU FOR NOT UNDERSTANDING MY TRENDY JARGON.
YOUR IGNORANCE IS ON DISPLAY FOR ALL TO SEE!
LEAVE THIS MEETING NOW! YOU ARE NOT WORTHY!
MAYBE YOU COULD JUST TELL US WHAT CURATION MEANS.
FINE. LET'S TRY THAT.
IT MEANS UM. . . UM. . .
IS IT TOO LATE FOR ME TO OVERLOOK YOUR IGNORANCE AND MOVE ON?
10-30-11

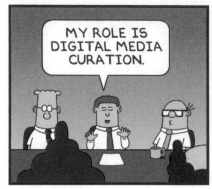

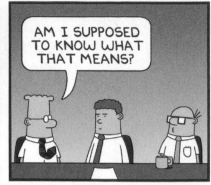

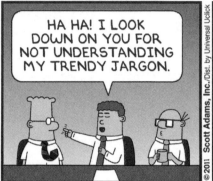

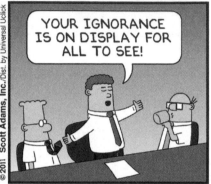

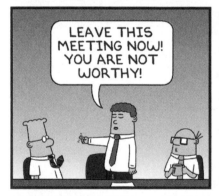

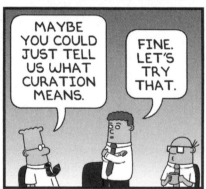

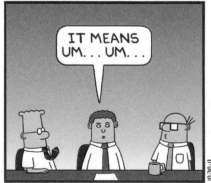

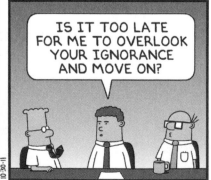

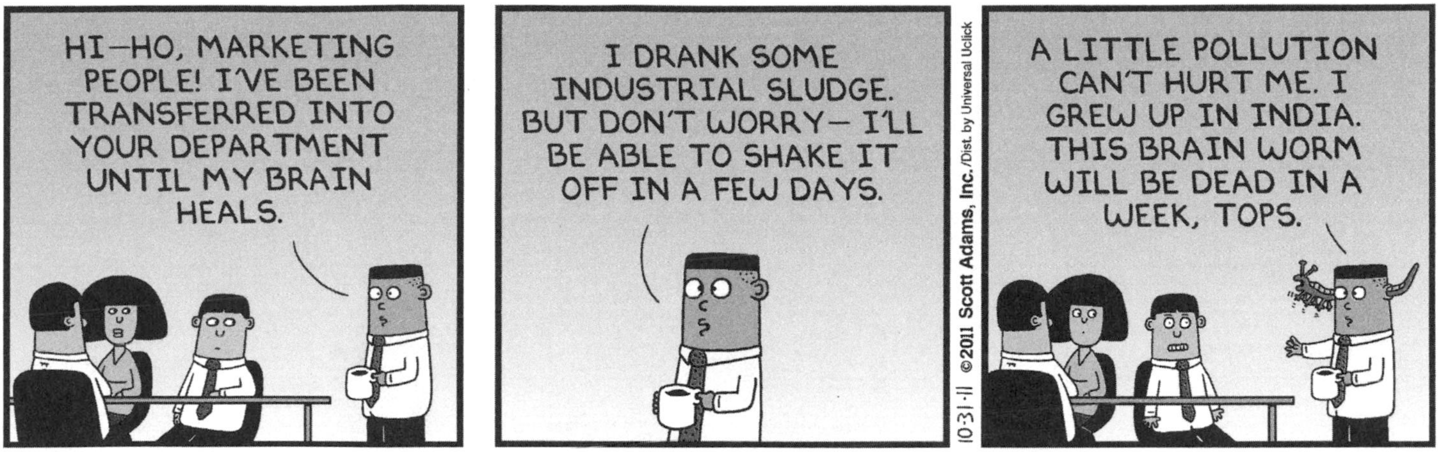
HI—HO, MARKETING PEOPLE! I'VE BEEN TRANSFERRED INTO YOUR DEPARTMENT UNTIL MY BRAIN HEALS.
I DRANK SOME INDUSTRIAL SLUDGE. BUT DON'T WORRY— I'LL BE ABLE TO SHAKE IT OFF IN A FEW DAYS.
10-31-11 ©2011 Scott Adams, Inc./Dist. by Universal Uclick
A LITTLE POLLUTION CAN'T HURT ME. I GREW UP IN INDIA. THIS BRAIN WORM WILL BE DEAD IN A WEEK, TOPS.

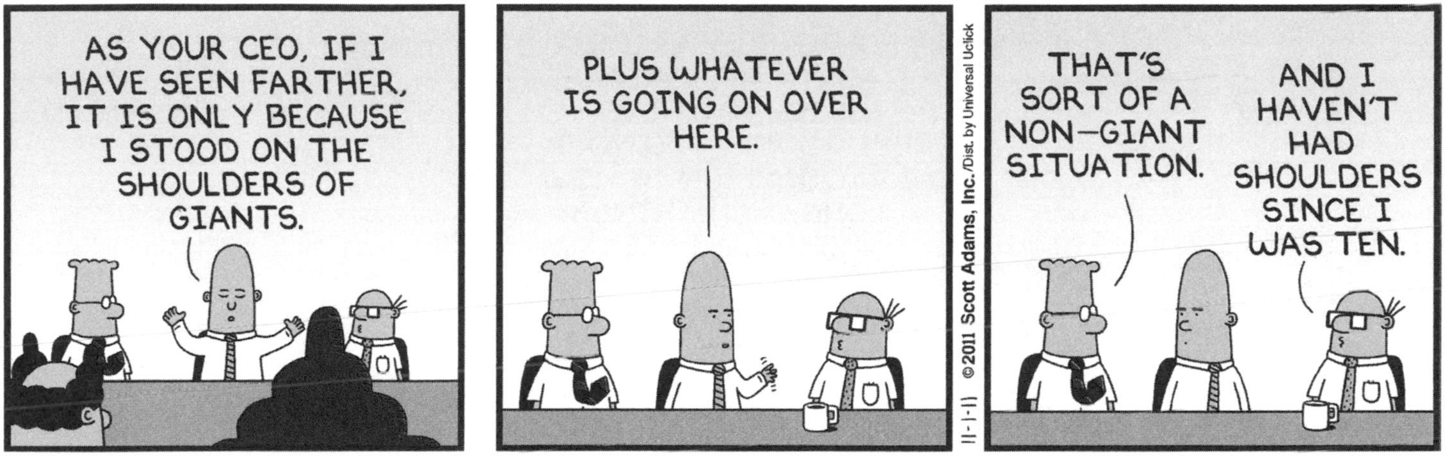
AS YOUR CEO, IF I HAVE SEEN FARTHER, IT IS ONLY BECAUSE I STOOD ON THE SHOULDERS OF GIANTS.
PLUS WHATEVER IS GOING ON OVER HERE.
11-1-11 ©2011 Scott Adams, Inc./Dist. by Universal Uclick
THAT'S SORT OF A NON—GIANT SITUATION.
AND I HAVEN'T HAD SHOULDERS SINCE I WAS TEN.

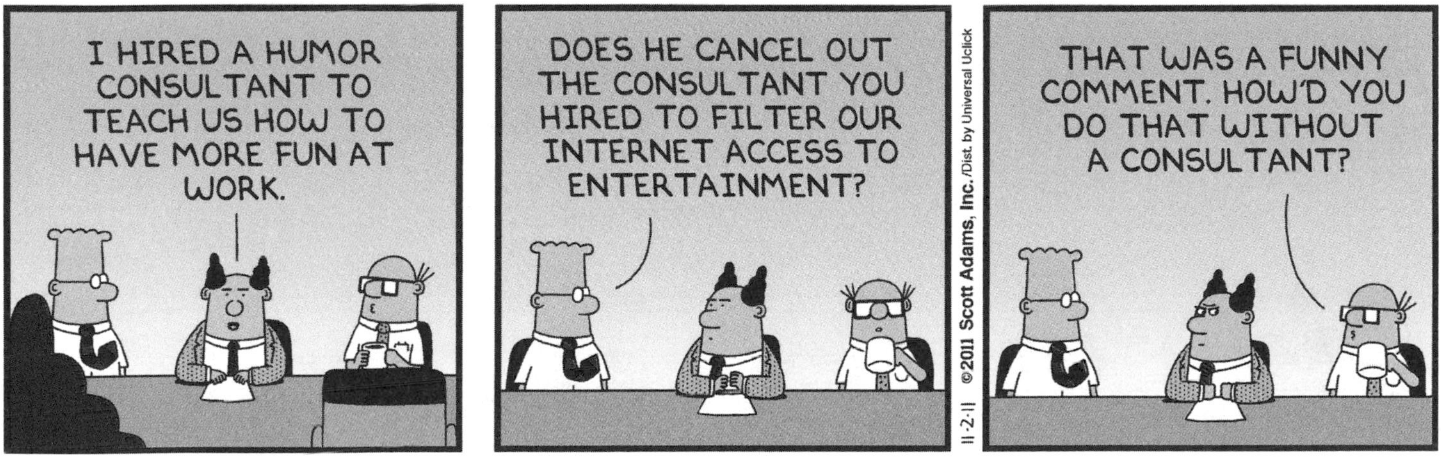
I HIRED A HUMOR CONSULTANT TO TEACH US HOW TO HAVE MORE FUN AT WORK.
DOES HE CANCEL OUT THE CONSULTANT YOU HIRED TO FILTER OUR INTERNET ACCESS TO ENTERTAINMENT?
11-2-11 ©2011 Scott Adams, Inc./Dist. by Universal Uclick
THAT WAS A FUNNY COMMENT. HOW'D YOU DO THAT WITHOUT A CONSULTANT?

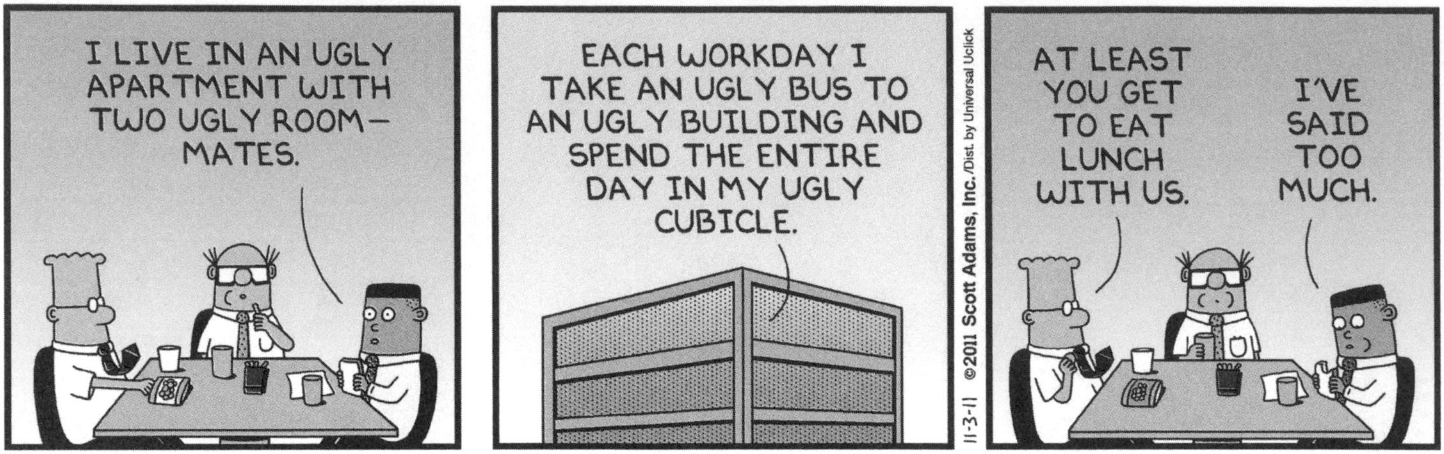
I LIVE IN AN UGLY APARTMENT WITH TWO UGLY ROOM-MATES.
EACH WORKDAY I TAKE AN UGLY BUS TO AN UGLY BUILDING AND SPEND THE ENTIRE DAY IN MY UGLY CUBICLE.
AT LEAST YOU GET TO EAT LUNCH WITH US.
I'VE SAID TOO MUCH.
11-3-11 ©2011 Scott Adams, Inc./Dist. by Universal Uclick

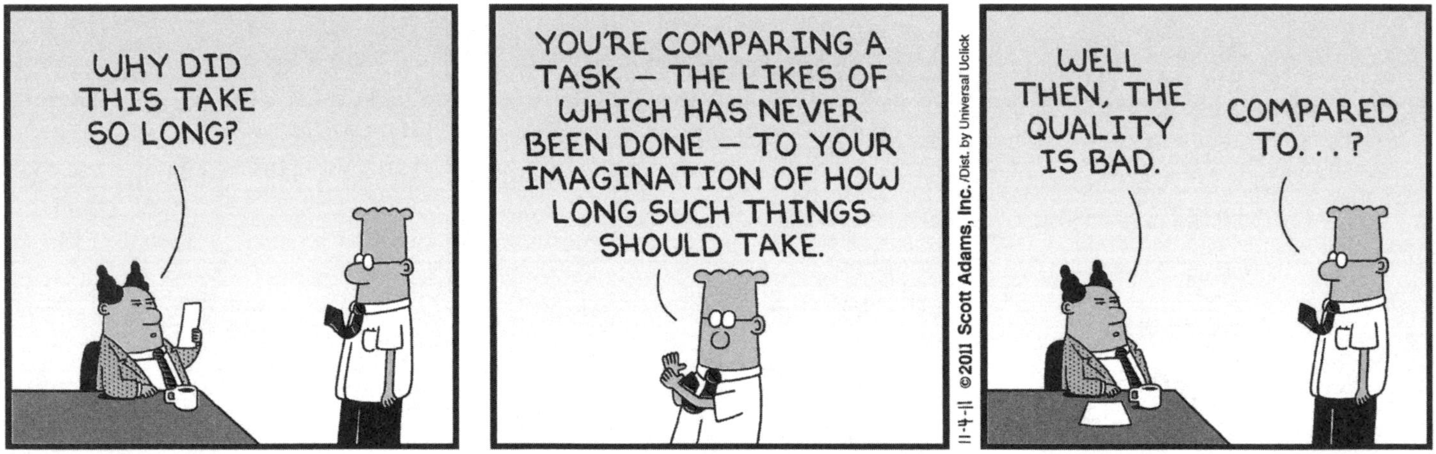
WHY DID THIS TAKE SO LONG?
YOU'RE COMPARING A TASK – THE LIKES OF WHICH HAS NEVER BEEN DONE – TO YOUR IMAGINATION OF HOW LONG SUCH THINGS SHOULD TAKE.
WELL THEN, THE QUALITY IS BAD.
COMPARED TO. . . ?
11-4-11 ©2011 Scott Adams, Inc./Dist. by Universal Uclick

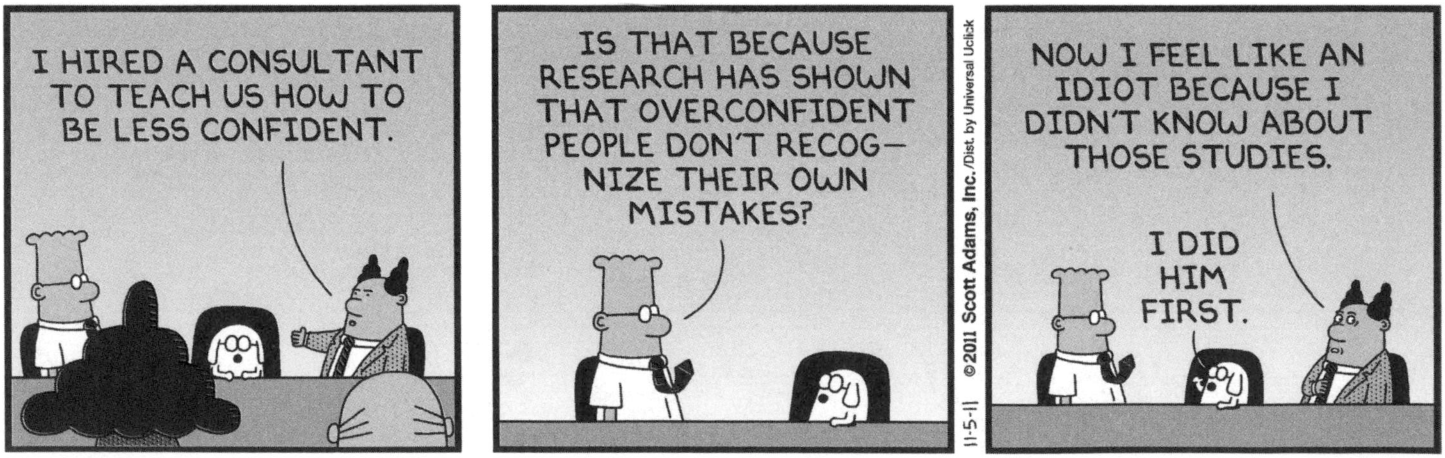
I HIRED A CONSULTANT TO TEACH US HOW TO BE LESS CONFIDENT.
IS THAT BECAUSE RESEARCH HAS SHOWN THAT OVERCONFIDENT PEOPLE DON'T RECOG-NIZE THEIR OWN MISTAKES?
NOW I FEEL LIKE AN IDIOT BECAUSE I DIDN'T KNOW ABOUT THOSE STUDIES.
I DID HIM FIRST.
11-5-11 ©2011 Scott Adams, Inc./Dist. by Universal Uclick

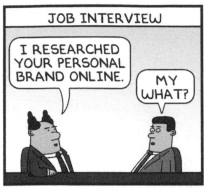

JOB INTERVIEW
I RESEARCHED YOUR PERSONAL BRAND ONLINE.
MY WHAT?
I LOOKED AT YOUR BLOG, YOUR TWEETS, AND YOUR FACEBOOK PAGE. I GOOGLED YOUR NAME AND FOLLOWED EVERY LINK.
I CHECKED YOUR CREDIT, CRIMINAL RECORD, SCHOOL TRANSCRIPTS, AND REFERENCES.
BUT THAT'S JUST THE EXTERNAL STUFF.
EXACTLY. IT'S MY ATTITUDE THAT COUNTS!
NO, I MEAN I ALSO HAVE THE RESULTS OF YOUR URINE TEST.
OH, AND APPARENTLY SOME OF YOUR SAMPLE LANDED IN A DNA TEST KIT.
AND THAT TANNING BED YOU USED LAST WEEK WAS ACTUALLY AN MRI.
HOW'S YOUR ATTITUDE NOW?
HARDER TO FAKE.
©2011 Scott Adams, Inc./Dist. by Universal Uclick
11-6-11

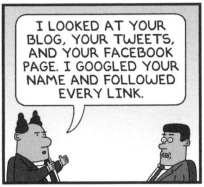

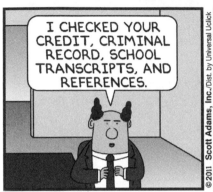

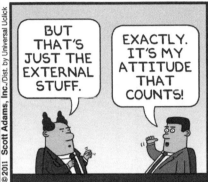

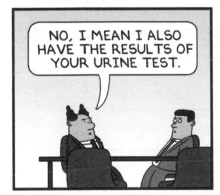

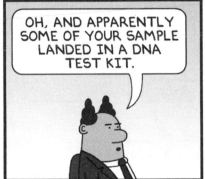

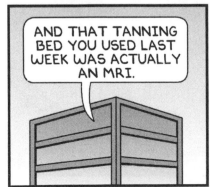

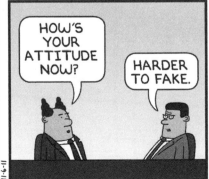

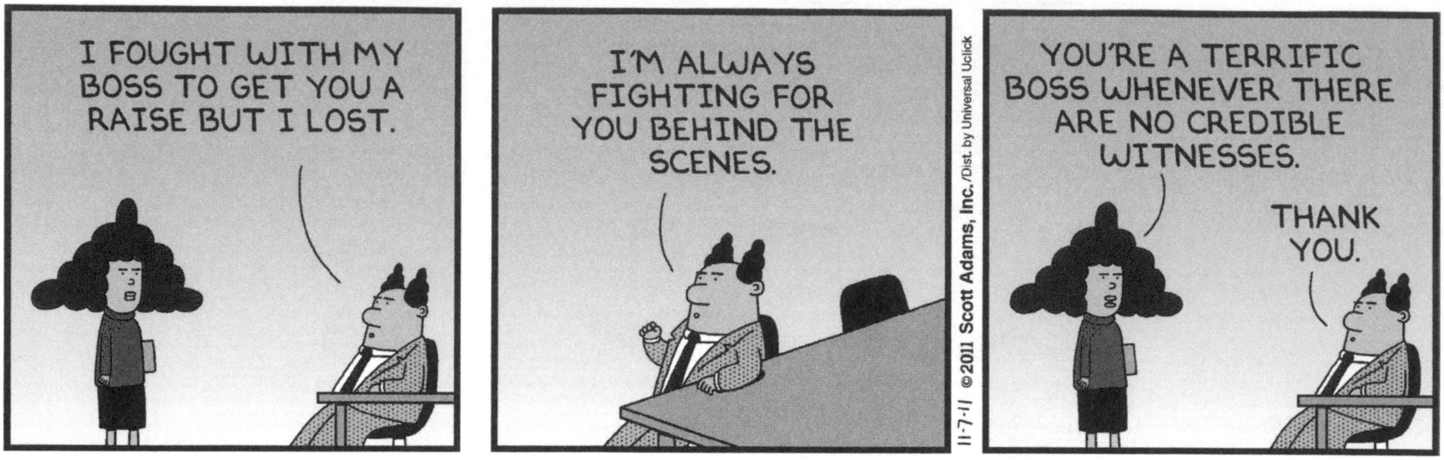
I FOUGHT WITH MY BOSS TO GET YOU A RAISE BUT I LOST.
I'M ALWAYS FIGHTING FOR YOU BEHIND THE SCENES.
11-7-11 ©2011 Scott Adams, Inc./Dist. by Universal Uclick
YOU'RE A TERRIFIC BOSS WHENEVER THERE ARE NO CREDIBLE WITNESSES.
THANK YOU.

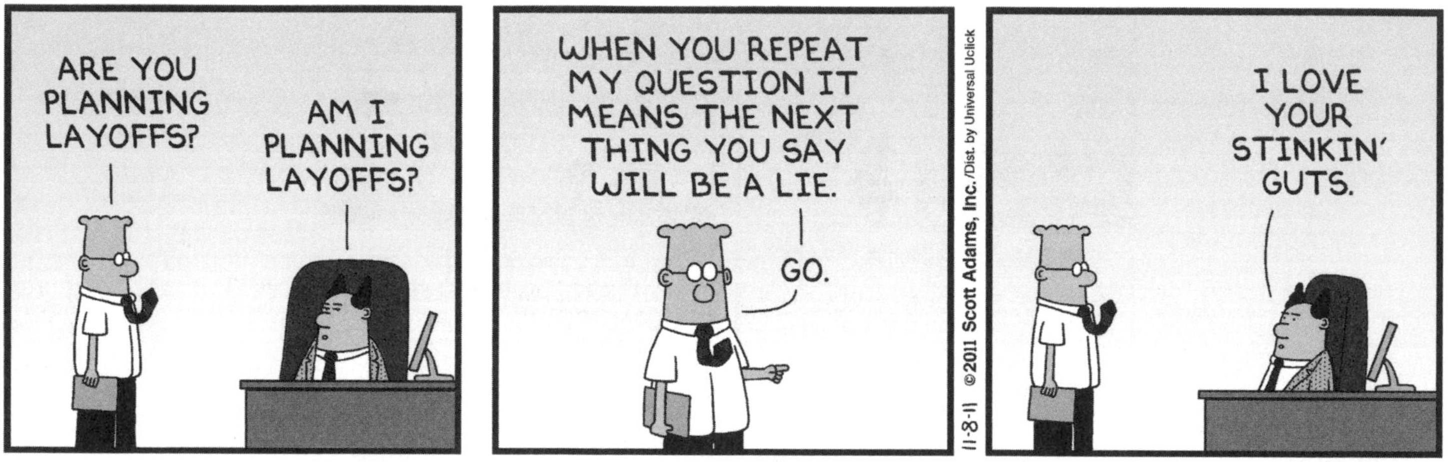
ARE YOU PLANNING LAYOFFS?
AM I PLANNING LAYOFFS?
WHEN YOU REPEAT MY QUESTION IT MEANS THE NEXT THING YOU SAY WILL BE A LIE.
GO.
11-8-11 ©2011 Scott Adams, Inc./Dist. by Universal Uclick
I LOVE YOUR STINKIN' GUTS.

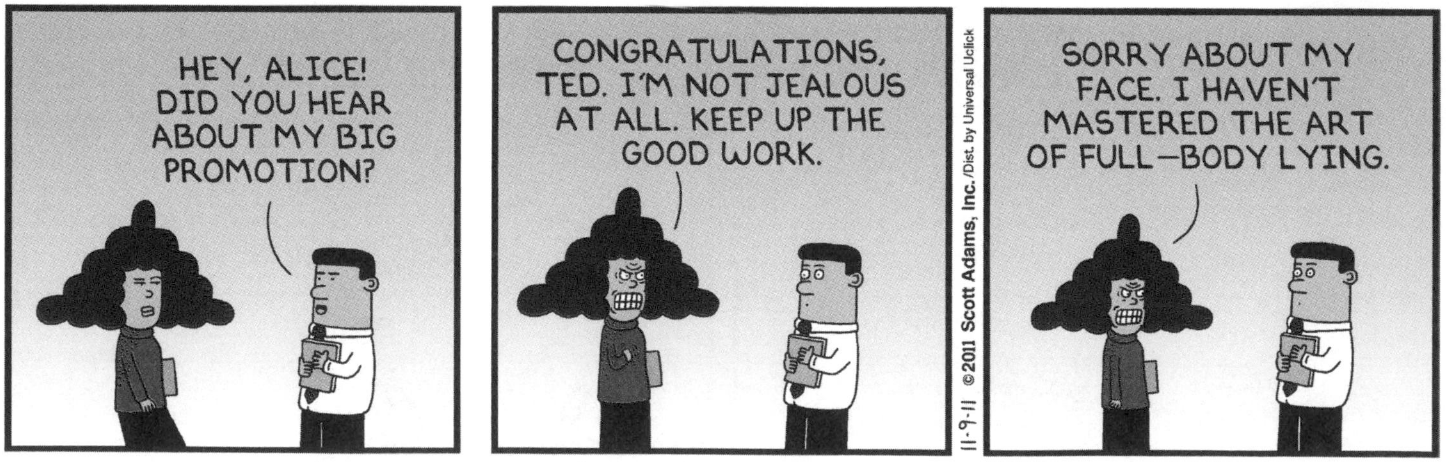
HEY, ALICE! DID YOU HEAR ABOUT MY BIG PROMOTION?
CONGRATULATIONS, TED. I'M NOT JEALOUS AT ALL. KEEP UP THE GOOD WORK.
11-9-11 ©2011 Scott Adams, Inc./Dist. by Universal Uclick
SORRY ABOUT MY FACE. I HAVEN'T MASTERED THE ART OF FULL-BODY LYING.

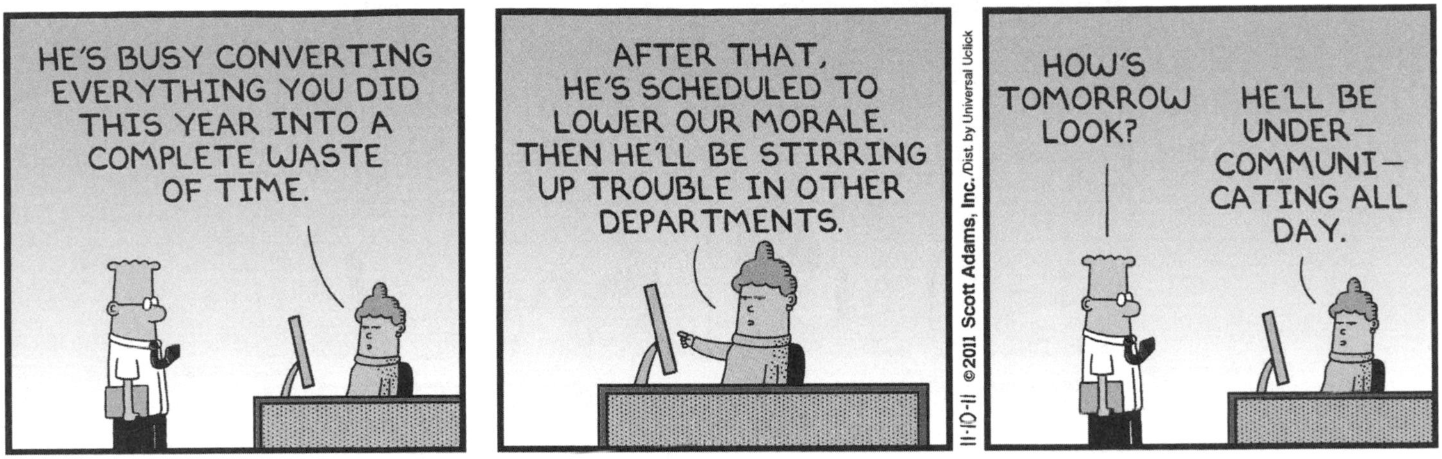
HE'S BUSY CONVERTING EVERYTHING YOU DID THIS YEAR INTO A COMPLETE WASTE OF TIME.
AFTER THAT, HE'S SCHEDULED TO LOWER OUR MORALE. THEN HE'LL BE STIRRING UP TROUBLE IN OTHER DEPARTMENTS.
11-10-11 ©2011 Scott Adams, Inc./Dist. by Universal Uclick
HOW'S TOMORROW LOOK?
HE'LL BE UNDER-COMMUNI-CATING ALL DAY.

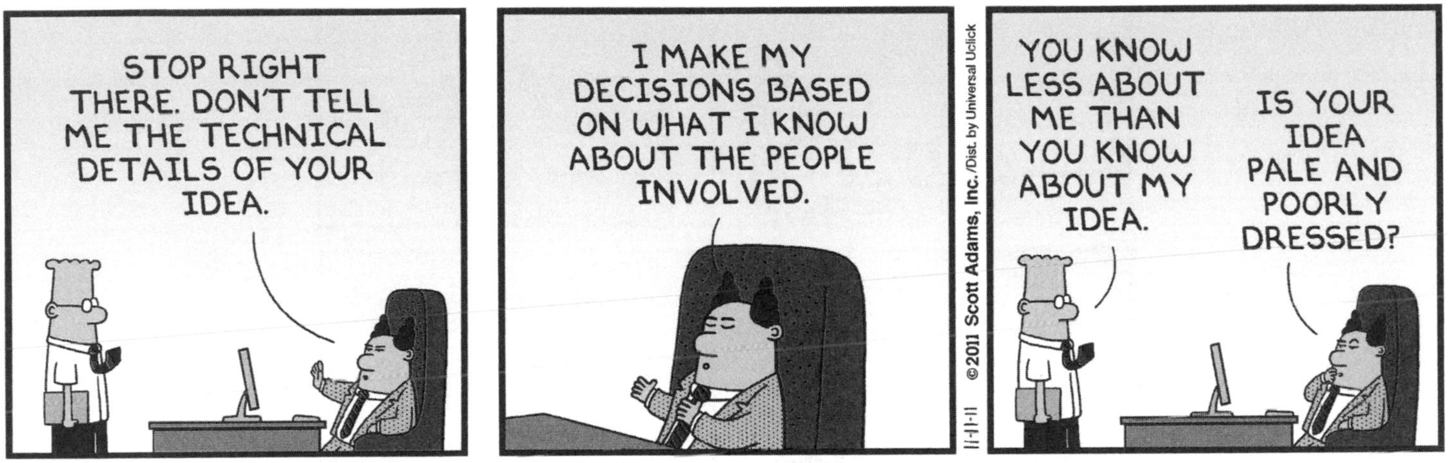
STOP RIGHT THERE. DON'T TELL ME THE TECHNICAL DETAILS OF YOUR IDEA.
I MAKE MY DECISIONS BASED ON WHAT I KNOW ABOUT THE PEOPLE INVOLVED.
11-11-11 ©2011 Scott Adams, Inc./Dist. by Universal Uclick
YOU KNOW LESS ABOUT ME THAN YOU KNOW ABOUT MY IDEA.
IS YOUR IDEA PALE AND POORLY DRESSED?

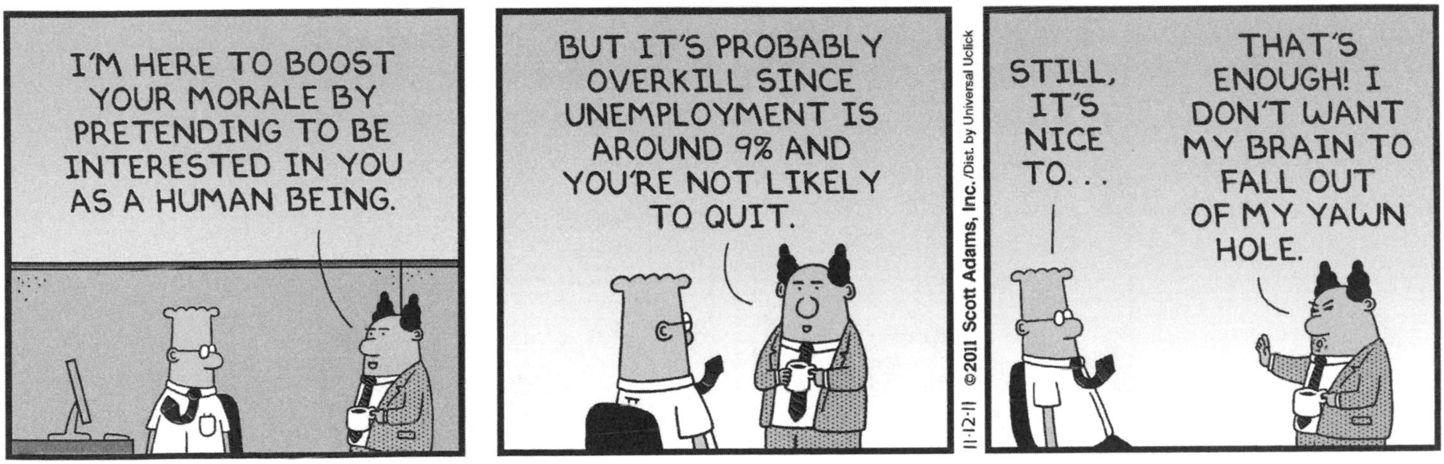
I'M HERE TO BOOST YOUR MORALE BY PRETENDING TO BE INTERESTED IN YOU AS A HUMAN BEING.
BUT IT'S PROBABLY OVERKILL SINCE UNEMPLOYMENT IS AROUND 9% AND YOU'RE NOT LIKELY TO QUIT.
11-12-11 ©2011 Scott Adams, Inc./Dist. by Universal Uclick
STILL, IT'S NICE TO. . .
THAT'S ENOUGH! I DON'T WANT MY BRAIN TO FALL OUT OF MY YAWN HOLE.

I DISCOVERED A WAY TO BEND LIGHT AROUND AN OBJECT TO FORM A CLOAK OF INVISIBILITY.
WE'LL MAKE BILLIONS SELLING IT TO THE MILITARY.
I'LL BE TESTING IT OVER THE NEXT SEVERAL MONTHS.
YOU'LL KNOW IT'S WORKING IF YOU NEVER SEE ME IN THE OFFICE.
DURING THAT TIME, DON'T SIT IN ANY EMPTY-LOOKING CHAIRS UNLESS YOU FIRST SHOUT MY NAME AND CLAP.
WHAT'S THAT OVER THERE?!
WHAT? I DON'T SEE ANYTHING.
HOW DO YOU LIKE IT SO FAR?
© 2011 Scott Adams, Inc. \Dist. by Univeral Uclick
11-13-11

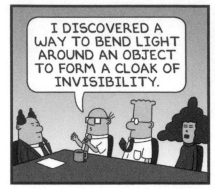

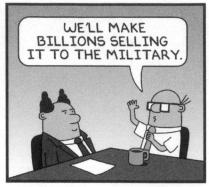

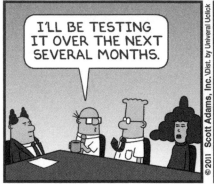

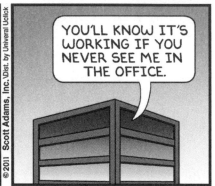

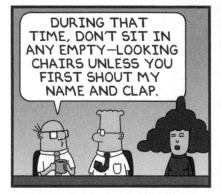

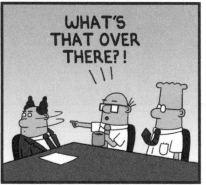

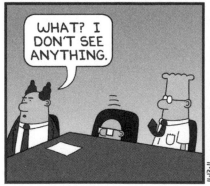

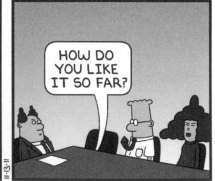

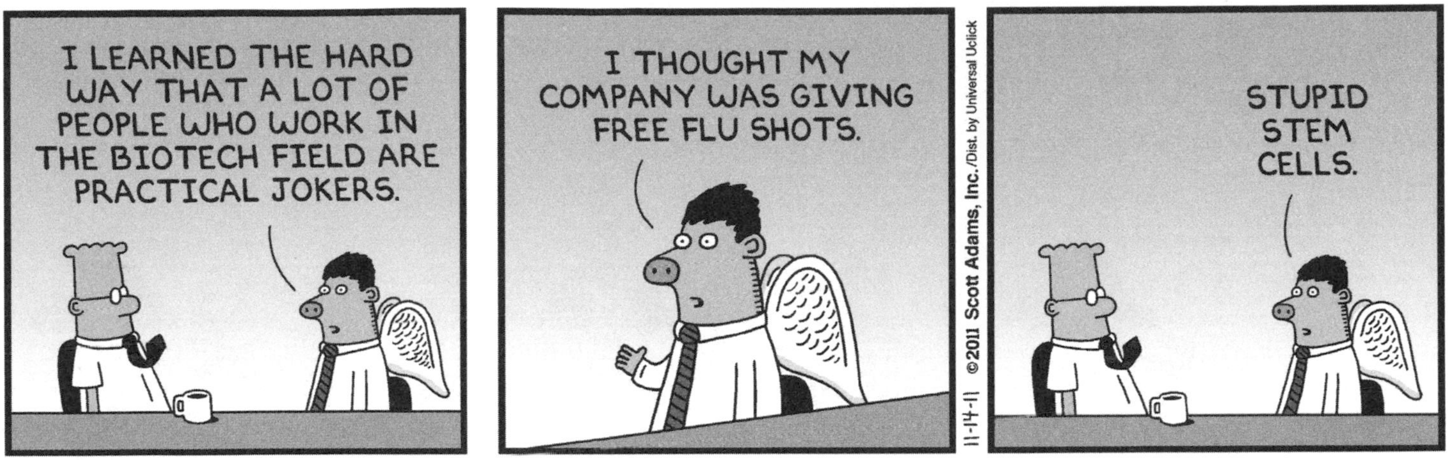
I LEARNED THE HARD WAY THAT A LOT OF PEOPLE WHO WORK IN THE BIOTECH FIELD ARE PRACTICAL JOKERS.
I THOUGHT MY COMPANY WAS GIVING FREE FLU SHOTS.
11-14-11 ©2011 Scott Adams, Inc./Dist. by Universal Uclick
STUPID STEM CELLS.

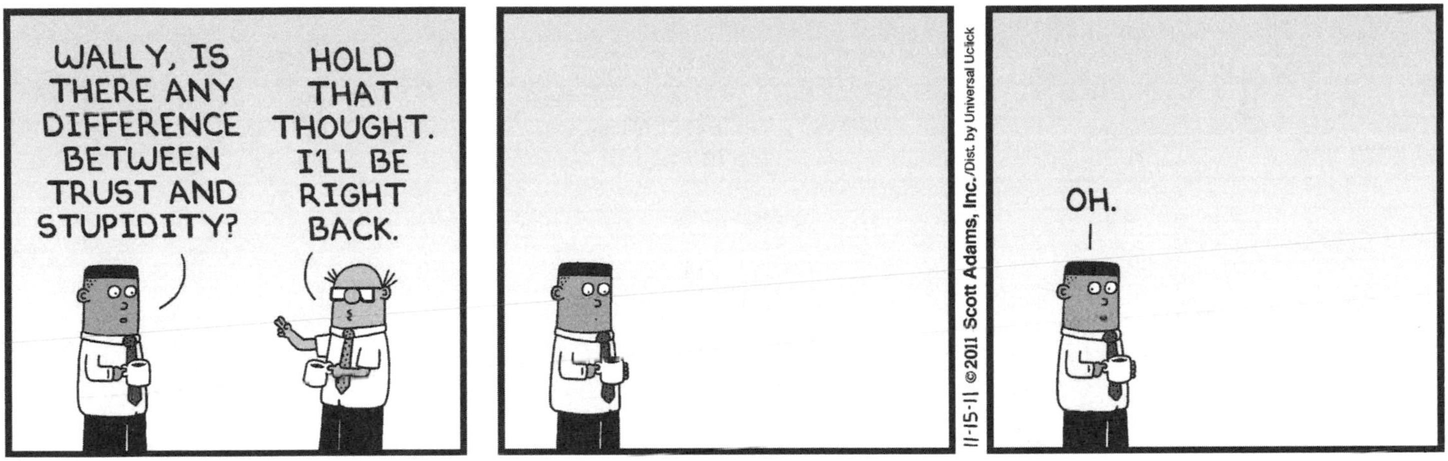
WALLY, IS THERE ANY DIFFERENCE BETWEEN TRUST AND STUPIDITY?
HOLD THAT THOUGHT. I'LL BE RIGHT BACK.
11-15-11 ©2011 Scott Adams, Inc./Dist. by Universal Uclick
OH.

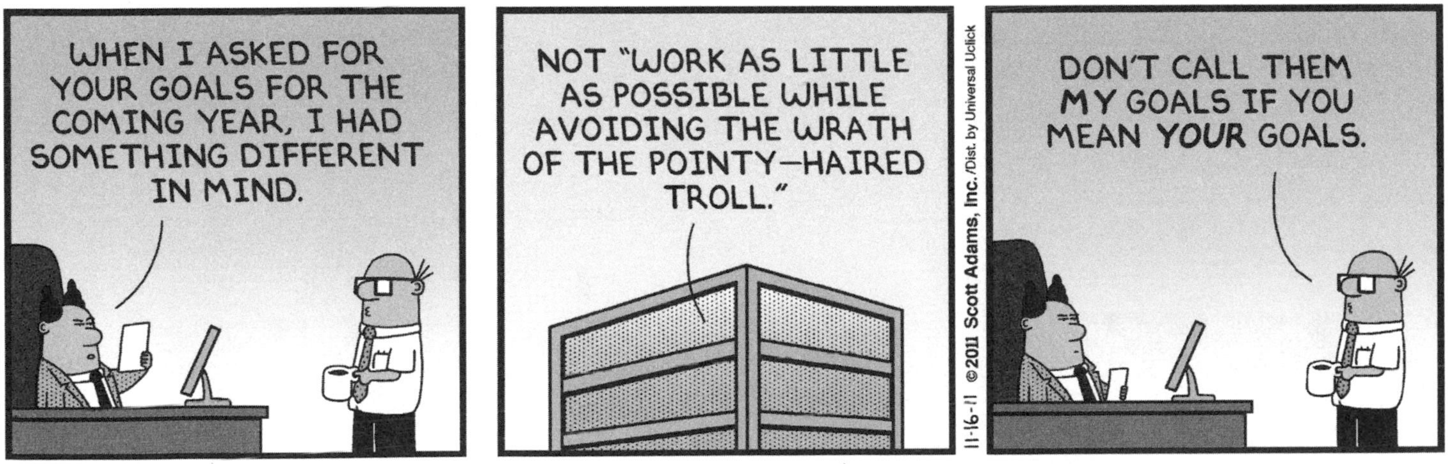
WHEN I ASKED FOR YOUR GOALS FOR THE COMING YEAR, I HAD SOMETHING DIFFERENT IN MIND.
NOT "WORK AS LITTLE AS POSSIBLE WHILE AVOIDING THE WRATH OF THE POINTY-HAIRED TROLL."
11-16-11 ©2011 Scott Adams, Inc./Dist. by Universal Uclick
DON'T CALL THEM MY GOALS IF YOU MEAN YOUR GOALS.

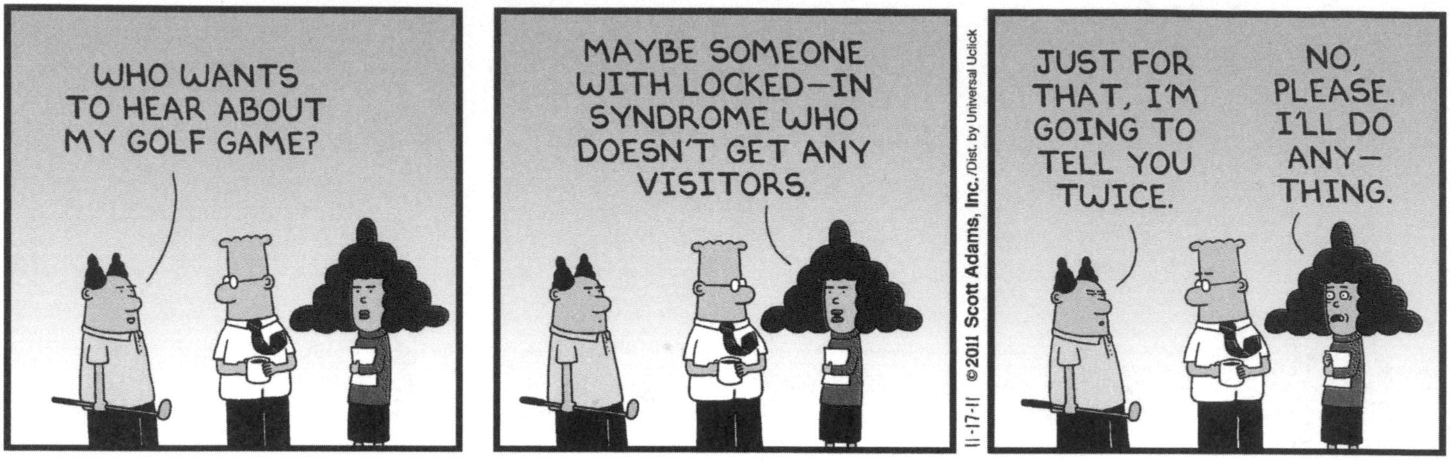
WHO WANTS TO HEAR ABOUT MY GOLF GAME?
MAYBE SOMEONE WITH LOCKED—IN SYNDROME WHO DOESN'T GET ANY VISITORS.
11-17-11 ©2011 Scott Adams, Inc./Dist. by Universal Uclick
JUST FOR THAT, I'M GOING TO TELL YOU TWICE.
NO, PLEASE. I'LL DO ANY— THING.

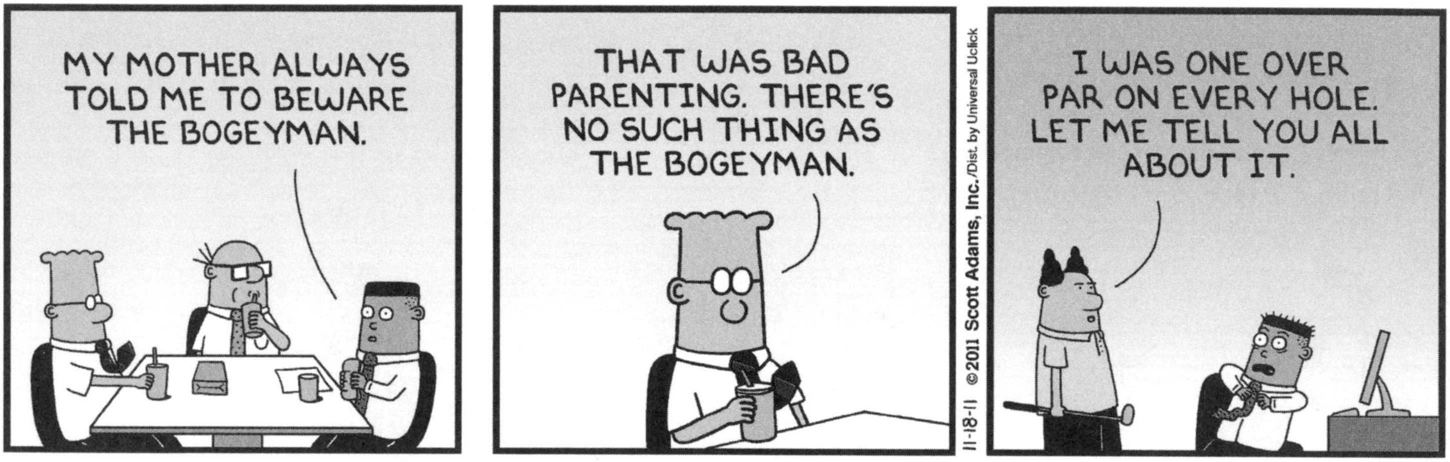
MY MOTHER ALWAYS TOLD ME TO BEWARE THE BOGEYMAN.
THAT WAS BAD PARENTING. THERE'S NO SUCH THING AS THE BOGEYMAN.
11-18-11 ©2011 Scott Adams, Inc./Dist. by Universal Uclick
I WAS ONE OVER PAR ON EVERY HOLE. LET ME TELL YOU ALL ABOUT IT.

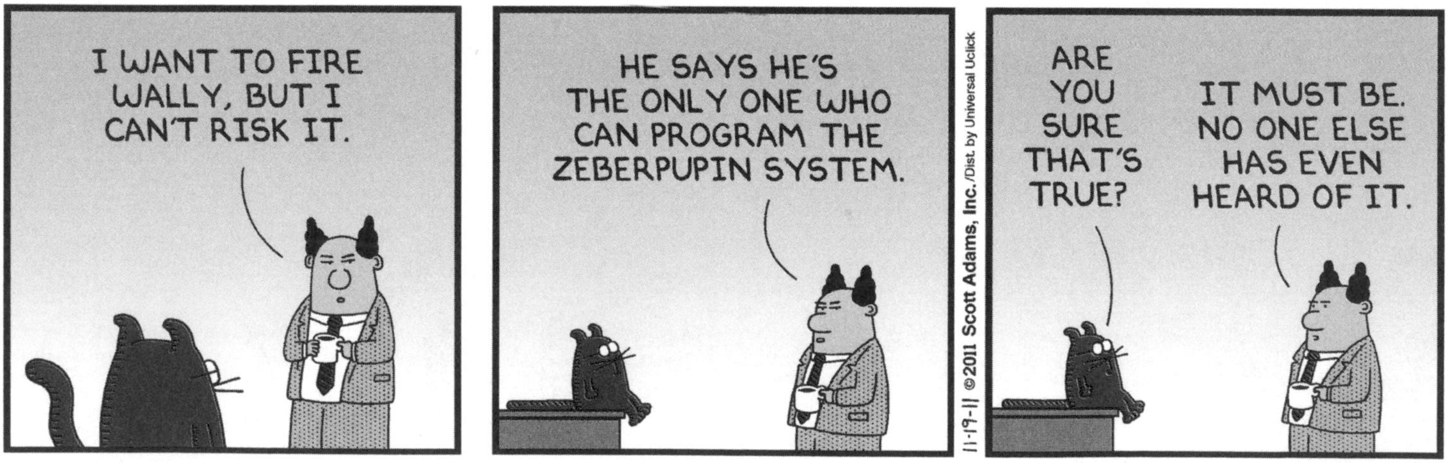
I WANT TO FIRE WALLY, BUT I CAN'T RISK IT.
HE SAYS HE'S THE ONLY ONE WHO CAN PROGRAM THE ZEBERPUPIN SYSTEM.
11-19-11 ©2011 Scott Adams, Inc./Dist. by Universal Uclick
ARE YOU SURE THAT'S TRUE?
IT MUST BE. NO ONE ELSE HAS EVEN HEARD OF IT.

I HIRED A WORLD—CLASS INVENTOR.
MEET TOBY. WHEN HE WORKED FOR OUR COMPETITOR, HE INVENTED THEIR COOLEST PRODUCT.
I WAS JUST A MEMBER OF THE TEAM.
A KEY MEMBER!
©2011 Scott Adams, Inc. \Dist. by Univeral Uclick
UNTIL THEY FIRED ME FOR STEALING.
YOU CAME TO THE RIGHT PLACE.
WE HAVE TONS OF STUFF TO STEAL AND NO ONE EVER GETS CAUGHT!
GIVE ME A HIGH FIVE WITH A BOSS HEAD IN THE MIDDLE!
SLAP!
11-20-11
THAT'S THE ONLY THING I EVER INVENTED.
HAVE YOU SEEN OUR STORAGE CLOSET?

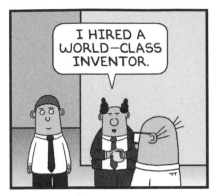

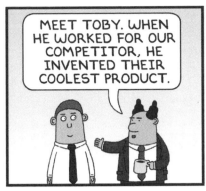

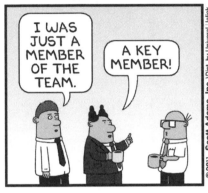

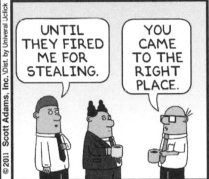

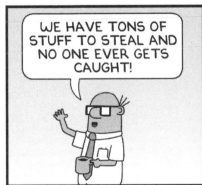

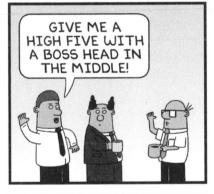

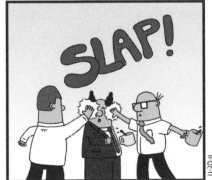